Business Ethics in Islam

Islamic business finance is based on strong ethical regulations as suggested by Islamic literature, such as the Qur'ān and the Traditions of the Prophet of Islam, and could be considered as a subclass of the wider subject of ethical standards in business. This book highlights the basic principles of Islamic business ethics and their implications in today's global business environment. It highlights the most important features of Islamic banking and finance in relation to the core principles of Sharia law. It is the most comprehensive book to date, in terms of the number of Qur'ānic verses and Traditions of the Prophet relating to this subject, which are interspersed throughout the text. It explains how ethics are defined both in general terms and within the context of an Islamic perspective. In addition, it provides a logical interpretation of Islamic principles of business ethics, while keeping in view the contemporary business practices. Topics such as digital currencies, money laundering, etc. are discussed at length. This book also discusses the new and emerging ethical issues faced by business and industry globally.

This book will be a valuable reference guide for students, teachers and researchers of Islamic banking and finance.

Hussain Mohi-ud-Din Qadri, Ph.D. is deputy chairman of the Board of Governors of Minhaj University Lahore (MUL) and associate professor at the School of Economics and Finance at MUL. He is also president of Minhaj-ul-Quran International, MQI; chairman of the Minhaj Education Society (which runs 650 schools and colleges throughout Pakistan), chairman of Aghosh Orphan Care Homes, chairman of Al-Mawakhat Islamic Microfinance and chairman of Minhaj Halal Certification Pakistan. He has also been affiliated with the University of Melbourne Australia as an honorary fellow for many years. Dr Qadri is an author of thirty books, writer of more than fifty research articles and a reputed international speaker.

Islamic Business and Finance Series

Series Editor: Ishaq Bhatti

There is an increasing need for western politicians, financiers, bankers, and indeed the western business community in general to have access to high quality and authoritative texts on Islamic financial and business practices. Drawing on expertise from across the Islamic world, this new series will provide carefully chosen and focused monographs and collections, each authored/edited by an expert in their respective field all over the world.

The series will be pitched at a level to appeal to middle and senior management in both the western and the Islamic business communities. For the manager with a western background the series will provide detailed and up-to-date briefings on important topics; for the academics, postgraduates, business communities, manager with western and an Islamic background the series will provide a guide to best practice in business in Islamic communities around the world, including Muslim minorities in the west and majorities in the rest of the world.

Islamic Social Finance
Entrepreneurship, Cooperation and the Sharing Economy
Edited by Valentino Cattelan

Rethinking Islamic Finance
Markets, Regulations and Islamic Law
Ayesha Bhatti and Saad Azmat

Social Justice and Islamic Economics
Theory, Issues and Practice
Edited by Toseef Azid and Lutfi Sunar

The Growth of Islamic Finance and Banking
Innovation, Governance and Risk Mitigation
Edited by Hussain Mohi-ud-Din Qadri and M. Ishaq Bhatti

Business Ethics in Islam
Hussain Mohi-ud-Din Qadri

For more information about this series, please visit www.routledge.com/Islamic-Business-and-Finance-Series/book-series/ISLAMICFINANCE

Business Ethics in Islam

Hussain Mohi-ud-Din Qadri

Routledge
Taylor & Francis Group
LONDON AND NEW YORK

First published 2020 by Routledge

2 Park Square, Milton Park, Abingdon, Oxon, OX14 4RN
605 Third Avenue, New York, NY 10017

Routledge is an imprint of the Taylor & Francis Group, an informa business

First issued in paperback 2020

British Library Cataloguing-in-Publication Data
A catalogue record for this book is available from the British Library

Library of Congress Cataloging-in-Publication Data
Names: Qadri, Ḥusain Mohi-ud-Din, author.
Title: Business ethics in Islam / Hussain Mohi-ud-Din Qadri.
Description: Milton Park, Abingdon, Oxon ; New York, NY : Routledge, 2020. | Series: Islamic business and finance | Includes bibliographical references and index.
Identifiers: LCCN 2019027801 | ISBN 9780367344917 (hardback) | ISBN 9780429326189 (ebook)
Subjects: LCSH: Business ethics—Islamic countries. | Business—Religious aspects—Islam. | Islamic ethics.
Classification: LCC HF5387.5.I85 Q235 2020 | DDC 297.5/644—dc23
LC record available at https://lccn.loc.gov/2019027801

ISBN: 978-0-367-34491-7 (hbk)
ISBN: 978-0-367-77679-4 (pbk)

Typeset in Times New Roman
by Apex CoVantage, LLC

Contents

Foreword

In the Name of Allah, the Most Gracious, the Most Merciful

Ethics, as conventionally understood, refers to a set of moral principles that control or influence a person's behaviour. It is also defined as a system of moral principles that deals with what is good or bad as well as what constitutes one's moral duties and obligations. If we go by the meaning of the Greek word *ēthos* or *hē ēthikē teknē*, from which the English word "ethics" is derived, then in discussing ethics or moral philosophy we are referring to nothing less than the comprehensive scope of the moral sciences in all domains of human life. Therefore, in light of its etymology, the fundamental significance of ethics as a field of study in business and economics becomes quite clear. Ethics presents itself as a very broad academic discipline due to its diverse facets. Having immense scope and complexity, ethics is very significant because of its invaluable applications, particularly in the field of business.

In the contemporary world, there has been a growing interest in business ethics. Many issues and challenges have arisen due to changes in the means of production and trade, advances in information technology, rise of globalization of consumer products, advent of internet banking, and developments in the role and impact of financial institutions and multinational corporations. The current global business environment is in dire need of finding ways to meet these challenges. Such an undertaking will require determining how to utilize ethics as well as choosing which set of ethics to use. In capitalist countries, ethics has not been prioritized in business activities for quite a long time. Further, secularist ideological orientation has pushed ethical values to a secondary place and detached economic activity from its domain. This has led to the emergence of many problems in the world. Unethical approach to business has always received criticism from the scholars of various religions, philosophers and business community around the world.

This book is precisely a treatment of business ethics in its various dimensions. It is a prominent addition in the literature on Islamic business ethics and finance, given the fact that books on the subject are relatively sparse, especially those written by Muslim scholars. Its author, Dr Hussain Mohi-ud-Din Qadri, presently the deputy chairman of the Board of Governors at Minhaj University Lahore, Pakistan and the president of Minhaj-ul-Quran International, is to be applauded for producing this substantial work on an eclectic array of issues dealing with business ethics.

He has succeeded in presenting these inherently difficult issues in a lucid way that makes them relatively easy to understand. Dr Qadri is well-qualified and capable of dealing with this subject.

He is a well-reputed author of books on Islamic economics and banking, Islamic finance, economics of natural resources, history of economic thought, political economy, and international trade. He has published dozens of volumes in English and Urdu, languages that cover a huge block of readership. I hope that this volume is his first of many more to come in the crucial area of business ethics. This volume is comprised of deeply essential topics that were published in Urdu but have now been extensively revised for this publication. Given its comprehensive handling of issues in business ethics, this volume will be of great importance to academics and scholars of various academic disciplines, particularly those in field of business ethics.

I wish Dr Qadri well at Minhaj University Lahore, Pakistan, and hope he will continue to produce impactful and scholarly works in his main academic field.

Professor M. Kabir Hassan
IDB Laureate in Islamic Banking and Finance
Designation: Professor of Finance
Address: 20 Cycas, Kenner, LA 70065, USA
Date: May 21, 2019

Author's preface

When humans look to the Lord for guidance, the Almighty Allah tells them to tread in the footsteps of His Messenger (Allah bless him and give him peace). Every aspect of the Messenger's (Allah bless him and give him peace) life and conduct is a role model for human beings.

﴿لَقَدْ كَانَ لَكُمْ فِي رَسُولِ اللَّهِ أُسْوَةٌ حَسَنَةٌ لِّمَن كَانَ يَرْجُو اللَّهَ وَالْيَوْمَ الْآخِرَ وَذَكَرَ
اللَّهَ كَثِيرًا﴾

In truth, in (the sacred person of) Allah's Messenger (Allah bless him and give him peace) there is for you a most perfect and beautiful model (of life) for every such person that expects and aspires to (meet) Allah and the Last Day and remembers Allah abundantly.

The Messenger (Allah bless him and give him peace) imparts wisdom-laden advice to humanity and guides the misguided. That is why everyone is in need of the guidance with which Allah raised him.

﴿لَقَدْ مَنَّ اللَّهُ عَلَى الْمُؤمِنِينَ إِذْ بَعَثَ فِيهِمْ رَسُولاً مِّنْ أَنفُسِهِمْ يَتْلُواْ عَلَيْهِمْ آيَاتِهِ
وَيُزَكِّيهِمْ وَيُعَلِّمُهُمُ الْكِتَابَ وَالْحِكْمَةَ وَإِن كَانُواْ مِن قَبْلُ لَفِي ضَلاَلٍ مُّبِينٍ﴾

Indeed, Allah conferred a great favour on the believers that He raised amongst them (the most eminent) Messenger (Allah bless him and give him peace) from amongst themselves, who recites to them His Revelations, purifies them, and educates them on the Book and Wisdom though, before that, they were in manifest error.

In the same way, the life of the Messenger (*Allah bless him and give him peace*) is a role model for the business community. In order to learn how he conducted himself in regard to trade and commerce, we need to make a deep study of the Qur'ānic verses and Traditions of the Prophet Muhammad (*Allah bless him and give him peace*). With the purpose of guiding sellers, manufacturers and corporations, Qur'ānic verses and Prophetic Traditions with commentary have been compiled on the following pages. Islamic business ethics not only enable a person to experience spirituality and nearness to the Lord, but they also guarantee success in this worldly life.

Introduction to ethics

Ethics, in general, denotes the moral principles or standards of human conduct and a society's perception of what is good and bad. The moral principles of a society epitomise its common values. It follows certain, but not all, core ethics that are shared by societies universally. Concerned with norms, these moral principles serve as a guide to human conduct. The ethical regulation of behaviour is indispensable for the well-being of individuals and communities.

According to the Oxford Advanced Learner's Dictionary, the term "ethics" refers to a set of "moral principles that control or influence a person's behaviour." The Merriam-Webster Dictionary defines the term as a system of moral principles that deals with what is good and bad as well as what is one's moral duty and obligation. Encyclopaedia Britannica explains, "Ethics, also called as moral philosophy, [is] the discipline concerned with what is morally good and bad, right and wrong. The term is also applied to any system or theory of moral values or principles."

An Islamic perspective

The faithful must do right, intending to merit the pleasure of Almighty Allah (The Exalted). To achieve this objective, Islam offers elements of theoretical and practical ethics. For the purpose of gaining awareness of the former, the Qur'ān and Prophetic Traditions contain sufficient material. The grand ideas of Islam were exemplified by Allah's Messenger (Allah bless him and give him peace). When asked about the character of the Prophet (Allah bless him and give him peace), 'Ā'isha (may Allah be well pleased with her) said that the character of the Prophet (Allah bless him and give him peace) was the Qur'ān. Then she recited the verse, "*And assuredly, you are placed high on the Most Glorious and Exalted (seat of) character (i.e., adorned with the Qur'ānic morality and endowed with the character traits of Allah)*" [Q.67:4] and then, "*In truth, in (the sacred person of) Allah's Messenger there is for you a most perfect and beautiful model (of life)*" [Q.33:21].[1] Whatever the Qur'ān contains of manners, directives, proscriptions, promises, warnings, the Prophet (Allah bless him and give him peace) embodied them.

As regards the theoretical basis of ethics, the Qur'ān underscores right conduct through core values which are independent of temporal and spatial boundaries. The believers are required to put them into action, emulating the normative practice of the Messenger (Allah bless him and give him peace). They include justice, integrity, truthfulness, charity, gratitude, sincerity, faithfulness, sobriety, patience, modesty, prudence and discretion. Scattered throughout the Muslim

Scripture, they direct individual and communal character and instil in us the moral rules that govern our conduct towards fellows, friends, working associates and strangers.

The faithful are under obligation to comply with Qur'ānic directives and build a righteous society where virtue is nurtured and evil is avoided. Allah says:

﴿كُنتُمْ خَيْرَ أُمَّةٍ أُخْرِجَتْ لِلنَّاسِ تَأْمُرُونَ بِالْمَعْرُوفِ وَتَنْهَوْنَ عَنِ الْمُنكَرِ وَتُؤْمِنُونَ بِاللهِ﴾

You are the best community brought forth for (the guidance of) mankind: you enjoin righteousness, forbid evil and believe in Allah.[2]

The Messenger (Allah bless him and give him peace) himself encouraged goodness and decency, more through his conduct than his discourses and orations. He described his conduct in these words:

إِنَّمَا بُعِثْتُ لِأُتَمِّمَ مَكَارِمَ الْأَخْلَاقِ.

I have been sent to perfect good character.[3]

Islamic literature enlightens us about a range of ethical values that the followers of Islam must practise. They pertain to social contracts; the institution of marriage; familial issues; equality of the sexes; and dealings with neighbours, fellows, friends and relatives. It is essential for one to deal with these categories in business transactions, in public and private life.

Notes

1 Narrated by Aḥmad b. Ḥanbal in *al-Musnad*, 6:91 §24645.

2 Qur'ān, 3:110.

3 Narrated by al-Bayhaqī in *al-Sunan al-kubrā*, 10:191 §20571.

1 Islamic economic system and its main characteristics

1.1 The importance of good intentions for traders

Purity of intention is one of the cornerstones, fundamental supports and most important integrals of religion. Islam places great stress on making Allah (The Exalted) one's sole objective in devotional acts and mutual dealings. In order to instil pure thoughts, intentions and constant Divine awareness in the faithful, Allah, the Exalted, said in the Qur'ān:

وَمَن يُهَاجِرْ فِي سَبِيلِ اللهِ يَجِدْ فِي الْأَرْضِ مُرَاغَمًا كَثِيرًا وَسَعَةً وَمَن يَخْرُجْ مِن بَيْتِهِ مُهَاجِرًا
إِلَى اللهِ وَرَسُولِهِ ثُمَّ يُدْرِكْهُ الْمَوْتُ فَقَدْ وَقَعَ أَجْرُهُ عَلَى اللهِ وَكَانَ اللهُ غَفُورًا رَّحِيمًا

And he who leaves his home, migrating towards Allah and His Messenger (Allah bless him and give him peace), and then death overtakes him (on the way), his reward with Allah is ensured and Allah is Most Forgiving, Ever-Merciful.[1]

It is essential that believers strive solely to please the Divine. However, to attain eternal salvation pure intention is a must in carrying out every matter pertaining to this world and the next.

Prophetic Traditions also give emphasis to being truthful, upright and honest in one's intention. So that believer's every deed is for the sake of Allah, the Messenger (Allah bless him and give him peace) told his community how actions are valued:

عَنْ عُمَرَ بْنِ الْخَطَّابِ أَنَّ رَسُوْلَ اللهِ قَالَ: اَلْأَعْمَالُ بِالنِّيَّةِ، وَلِكُلِّ امْرِئٍ مَا نَوَى. فَمَنْ
كَانَتْ هِجْرَتُهُ إِلَى اللهِ وَرَسُوْلِهِ فَهِجْرَتُهُ إِلَى اللهِ وَرَسُوْلِهِ، وَمَنْ كَانَتْ هِجْرَتُهُ لِدُنْيَا
يُصِيْبُهَا، أَوِ امْرَأَةٍ يَتَزَوَّجُهَا، فَهِجْرَتُهُ إِلَى مَا هَاجَرَ إِلَيْهِ.

According to 'Umar b. al-Khaṭṭāb, Allah's Messenger said: "Actions are valued according to the intention, and every man is credited with what he intended. If someone's emigration was to Allah and His Messenger, his

> emigration was therefore to Allah and His Messenger, and if someone's emigration was to acquire some worldly benefit, or to take a woman in marriage, his emigration was to that to which he emigrated."[2]

The very act of earning one's keep is an act of service to the Divine when the intention is wholesome. Ka'b b. 'Ujra (may Allah be pleased with him) narrated:

مَرَّ عَلَى النَّبِيِّ رَجُلٌ، فَرَأَى أَصْحَابُ رَسُولِ اللَّهِ مِنْ جِلْدِهِ وَنَشَاطِهِ، فَقَالُوا: يَا رَسُولَ اللَّهِ،
لَوْ كَانَ هَذَا فِيْ سَبِيْلِ اللَّهِ؟ فَقَالَ رَسُولُ اللَّهِ: إِنْ كَانَ خَرَجَ يَسْعَى عَلَى وَلَدِهِ صِغَارًا، فَهُوَ
فِيْ سَبِيْلِ اللَّهِ، وَإِنْ كَانَ خَرَجَ يَسْعَى عَلَى أَبَوَيْنِ شَيْخَيْنِ كَبِيْرَيْنِ، فَهُوَ فِيْ سَبِيْلِ اللَّهِ، وَإِنْ
كَانَ يَسْعَى عَلَى نَفْسِهِ يُعِفُّهَا، فَهُوَ فِيْ سَبِيْلِ اللَّهِ، وَإِنْ كَانَ خَرَجَ رِيَاءً وَمُفَاخَرَةً، فَهُوَ فِيْ
سَبِيْلِ الشَّيْطَانِ.

> A person passed by the Prophet (Allah bless him and give him peace), and his companions commented after seeing his body and his hard work: "Messenger of Allah, what if his work is for the sake of Allah?" Allah's Messenger replied: "If he has left (his house) for earning livelihood for his children, he is in the path of Allah, and if he has left (his house) for his old parents, it is again in the path of Allah, and if he has left his house for making his effort, he is in the path of Allah. However, if he has stepped out from his house for vanity and outward show, he is following the Devil's path."[3]

When one performs a lawful act, Allah accepts it, on condition that it is carried out for His sake.

According to Abū Hurayra'Abd al-Raḥmān b. Ṣakhr (may Allah be pleased with him):

قَالَ رَسُوْلُ اللهِ: إِنَّ اللهَ لاَ يَنْظُرُ إِلَى أَجْسَادِكُمْ وَلاَ إِلَى صُوَرِكُمْ، وَلَكِنْ يَنْظُرُ إِلَى قُلُوْبِكُمْ.
وَفِيْ رِوَايَةٍ بِلَفْظِ: إِنَّ اللهَ لاَ يَنْظُرُ إِلَى صُوَرِكُمْ وَأَمْوَالِكُمْ، وَلَكِنْ يَنْظُرُ إِلَى قُلُوْبِكُمْ وَأَعْمَالِكُمْ.

> Allah's Messenger (Allah bless him and give him peace) said: "Allah does not observe your bodies and your forms, but He does observe your hearts."
>
> In one version, the wording is: "Allah does not observe your forms and your properties, but he does observe your hearts and your deeds."[4]

Indeed, in Islam the mundane and permissible affairs of life are transformed into acts of obedience if they are accompanied by noble intentions. The act of managing even our most routine affairs of life can change into worship and devotion to Allah provided that their good intention exist. So, if someone eats nourishing food in order to can meet religious and social obligations, his or her act of consuming food will be considered worship, deserving of recompense in the world to come.

In contrast, a scripturally forbidden act remains unlawful regardless of purpose. In the light of the Qur'ān and Hadith, evil deeds cannot change into good ones under any circumstance – no matter how good the intention, how worthy the aim. The Muslim religion does not condone employing unlawful means in order to achieve "laudable" ends. It insists that not only the aim be reasonable and fair but also that the means chosen be just. Therefore, the common thesis, "the end justifies the means," is contrary to Islamic law.

Allah is so gracious that when humans intend to do good, He orders angels to record a good deed to their credit, but their transgressions are recorded against them only when they are committed.

According to Abū Hurayra (may Allah be pleased with him), Allah's Messenger (Allah bless him and give him peace) said:

يَقُوْلُ اللهُ: إِذَا أَرَادَ عَبْدِيْ أَنْ يَعْمَلَ سَيِّئَةً، فَلَا تَكْتُبُوْهَا عَلَيْهِ حَتَّى يَعْمَلَهَا، فَإِنْ عَمِلَهَا فَاكْتُبُوْهَا بِمِثْلِهَا، وَإِنْ تَرَكَهَا مِنْ أَجْلِيْ فَاكْتُبُوْهَا لَهُ حَسَنَةً. وَإِذَا أَرَادَ أَنْ يَعْمَلَ حَسَنَةً، فَلَمْ يَعْمَلْهَا، فَاكْتُبُوْهَا لَهُ حَسَنَةً. فَإِنْ عَمِلَهَا فَاكْتُبُوْهَا لَهُ بِعَشْرِ أَمْثَالِهَا إِلَى سَبْعِ مِائَةِ ضِعْفٍ.

> Allah says (to angels): "If My servant intends to commit a bad deed, you must not record it against him until he commits it. Then, if he commits it, you must record it with its equivalent (sin). If he refrains from it for My sake, you must record a good deed to his credit. If he intends to perform a good deed, but he does not perform it, you must record a good deed to his credit. If he does perform it, you must record the like of it to his credit, from ten up to seven hundred times."[5]

The following Tradition also demonstrates the vital importance of forming pious intentions even if one is unable to carry out the intended good action.

عَنْ أَنَسِ بْنِ مَالِكٍ أَنَّ رَسُولَ اللهِ رَجَعَ مِنْ غَزْوَةِ تَبُوكَ فَدَنَا مِنَ الْمَدِيْنَةِ، فَقَالَ: إِنَّ بِالْمَدِيْنَةِ أَقْوَامًا مَا سِرْتُمْ مَسِيرًا وَلَا قَطَعْتُمْ وَادِيًا، إِلَّا كَانُوْا مَعَكُمْ. قَالُوْا: يَا رَسُولَ اللهِ، وَهُمْ بِالْمَدِيْنَةِ؟ قَالَ: وَهُمْ بِالْمَدِيْنَةِ حَبَسَهُمُ الْعُذْرُ.

> According to Anas b. Mālik that Allah's Messenger returned from the Tabūk expedition and approached Medina and said: "In Medina there are people who have been with you whatever distance you have travelled and whatever valley you crossed." They said: "Messenger of Allah (g), even though they are in Medina?" He replied: "They are in Medina and a valid excuse prevented them from coming."[6]

1.2 The significance of trade and commerce in Islam

Islam is a holistic way of life for the whole of humanity as it caters to spiritual and worldly needs. Importance is attached to commerce and trade in the Divine Scripture and in the Prophetic conduct and discourses. The Qur'ān gives clear directives and regulations for running businesses. The Messenger himself (Allah bless him and give him peace) demonstrated the worth of trade by choosing it as an occupation.

Before the arrival of Islam, an Abrahamic monotheistic religion, many Arabs were traders. The Holy Book of Islam describes the trade journeys of the Arabs in various seasons as a Divine grace towards them. Social and economic prosperity of the people of Mecca depended on their trading caravans. Their two annual trade caravans, one to Yemen in the winter and the other to Syria in the summer, have been described.

لِإِيلَافِ قُرَيْشٍ○ إِيلَافِهِمْ رِحْلَةَ الشِّتَاءِ وَالصَّيْفِ○فَلْيَعْبُدُوا رَبَّ هَذَا الْبَيْتِالَّذِي
أَطْعَمَهُم مِّن جُوعٍ وَآمَنَهُم مِّنْ خَوْفٍ○

To awake drive amongst the Quraysh, they were acclimatized to the summer and the winter (commercial) trips. So they should worship the Lord of this (Sacred) House (Ka'ba, to give Him thanks), who has fed them in hunger (i.e., provided them sustenance in starving conditions) and secured them from fear (of foes i.e., blessed them with secure and peaceful life).[7]

The following ordinance urges the faithful on choosing trading as a career.

يَا أَيُّهَا الَّذِينَ آمَنُواْ لاَ تَأْكُلُواْ أَمْوَالَكُمْ بَيْنَكُمْ بِالْبَاطِلِ إِلاَّ أَن تَكُونَ تِجَارَةً عَن تَرَاضٍ مِّنكُمْ
وَلَا تَقْتُلُواْ أَنفُسَكُمْ

O believers! Do not devour one another's wealth unlawfully amongst yourselves unless it is a trade by your mutual agreement and do not kill yourselves.[8]

Another commandment charges the faithful followers of Islam to spread through the land, when the congregational prayers on Friday are, and to seek Allah's grace – that is, trade.

فَإِذَا قُضِيَتِ الصَّلَاةُ فَانتَشِرُوا فِي الْأَرْضِ وَابْتَغُوا مِن فَضْلِ اللَّهِ وَاذْكُرُوا اللَّهَ
كَثِيرًا لَّعَلَّكُمْ تُفْلِحُونَ○

Then after the Prayer is offered, disperse in the land and (then) look for Allah's bounty (i.e., sustenance). And remember Allah much so that you may attain prosperity.[9]

Even after performing pilgrimage, the faithful may engage in sale and trade so that people might reap religious and material rewards.

لَيْسَ عَلَيْكُمْ جُنَاحٌ أَن تَبْتَغُوا فَضْلًا مِّن رَّبِّكُمْ

> *And it is no sin on you if you (also) seek your Lord's bounty (through trade during the ḥajj days).*[10]

Trade is permitted in the interests of pilgrims that they may fulfil the necessaries of life. Though pilgrimage to the House of Allah is undertaken to seek Divine approval, its material benefits cannot be discounted. The yearly Muslim pilgrimage stimulates economic growth.

The Arabic word for pilgrimage is *ḥajj*. A main religious obligation, it is pilgrimage to Mecca and nearby sacred sites that all physically and financially able Muslims are required to perform at least once in their lives.[11] It is one of the five basic institutions of Islam, along with the profession of faith in Allah and Muhammad as His Messenger (Allah bless him and give him peace), prayer, obligatory alms and fasting during the holy month of Ramaḍān.

According to Ibn 'Umar (may Allah be well pleased with him and his father), Allah's Messenger (Allah bless him and give him peace) said:

> Islam has been founded on five things: (1) the testimony that there is no God but Allah and that Muhammad is Allah's Messenger, (2) performance of the ritual Prayer, (3) payment of *zakāt* (an obligatory charity), (4) the Pilgrimage, and (5) the fast of Ramaḍān.[12]

Seeing the optimum economic, strategic and diplomatic potential in the *ḥajj* season, Muslim governments should organize and manage this activity as a large-scale project. Not only does the *ḥajj* stimulate various economic sectors in Muslim lands, but the centrality of the Ka'ba contributes to anchoring the Muslim community in a world of increasing globalization and cross-border financial transactions. Moreover, the economics of the *ḥajj* may play a decisive role in strengthening relations and fostering brotherhood among the Muslim countries.

On deriving material benefit from the *ḥajj* activity, Allah says in the Qur'ān (2:198):

لَيْسَ عَلَيْكُمْ جُنَاحٌ أَن تَبْتَغُوا فَضْلًا مِّن رَّبِّكُمْ فَإِذَا أَفَضْتُم مِّنْ عَرَفَاتٍ فَاذْكُرُوا اللَّهَ عِندَ
الْمَشْعَرِ الْحَرَامِ وَاذْكُرُوهُ كَمَا هَدَاكُمْ وَإِن كُنتُم مِّن قَبْلِهِ لَمِنَ الضَّالِّينَ

> *And it is no sin on you if you (also) seek your Lord's bounty (through trade during the ḥajj days). Then when you return from 'Arafat, celebrate the remembrance of Allah near Mash'ar al-ḥarām (Muzdalifa). And remember Him as He has guided you. And you were certainly wandering disorientated before.*[13]

Ibn 'Abbās (may Allah be well pleased with him) reported:

كَانَ ذُو الْمَجَازِ وَعُكَاظٌ مَتْجَرَ النَّاسِ فِي الْجَاهِلِيَّةِ، فَلَمَّا جَاءَ الْإِسْلَامُ كَأَنَّهُمْ كَرِهُوْا ذَلِكَ، حَتَّى نَزَلَتْ: ﴿لَيْسَ عَلَيْكُمْ جُنَاحٌ أَن تَبْتَغُواْ فَضْلًا مِّن رَّبِّكُمْ﴾ فِي مَوَاسِمِ الْحَجِّ.

> Dhū al-Majāz and 'Ukāz were the markets of the people in the time of ignorance. When Islam came, people did not really like to trade in them until it was revealed: *And it is no sin on you if you (also) seek your Lord's bounty (through trade during the ḥajj days)* [Qur'ān 2:198] in the *ḥajj* festival.[14]

First and foremost, Islamic directives are meant to deliver people from penalty and attain the good pleasure of Allah in the Afterlife, yet the Divine commandments, when practised, benefit the practitioners in material terms too. The same is true of the activity of *ḥajj*. It has been observed when the Islamic *ḥajj* is celebrated, through its impact on investors' sentiments, it boosts the stock market as well.

The previous finding supports the notion that pilgrimage positively affects the Islamic investor's emotions; this principal religious obligation – drawing the believers nearer to Allah – leads to an optimistic sentiment that influences investment decisions.

Prophetic Traditions also emphasise the place of trade and merchants; some of these are cited next.

Rāfi' b. Khadīj (may Allah be well pleased with him) narrated that Allah's Messenger (Allah bless him and give him peace) was asked, "What type of earning is best?" He replied:

عَمَلُ الرَّجُلِ بِيَدِهِ، وَكُلُّ بَيْعٍ مَبْرُوْرٍ.

> A man's work with his hand and every business transaction that is approved.[15]

According to Jābir b. 'Abd Allāh (may Allah be well pleased with him), Allah's Messenger (Allah bless him and give him peace) said:

رَحِمَ اللّٰهُ عَبْدًا سَمْحًا إِذَا بَاعَ، سَمْحًا إِذَا اشْتَرَى، سَمْحًا إِذَا اقْتَضَى.

> May Allah show mercy to a man who is lenient when he sells, lenient when he buys and lenient when he asks for payment![16]

According to Sakhr al-Ghāmidī (may Allah be well pleased with him), Allah's Messenger (Allah bless him and give him peace) said:

اَللّٰهُمَّ بَارِكْ لِأُمَّتِي فِي بُكُوْرِهَا . . .

قَالَ: وَكَانَ صَخْرٌ رَجُلاً تَاجِرًا، فَكَانَ يَبْعَثُ تِجَارَتَهُ فِي أَوَّلِ النَّهَارِ فَأَثْرَى وَكَثُرَ مَالُهُ.

"Allah, bless my nation in their early morning!"

He (the narrator) said: "Sakhr was a trader, and he used to send his goods out at the beginning of the day, and his wealth grew and increased."[17]

Once Allah's Messenger (Allah bless him and give him peace) saw the people doing business so he said: "People of trade!" and they replied to him, turning their necks and their gazes towards him, and he said:

إِنَّ التُّجَّارَ يُبْعَثُونَ يَوْمَ الْقِيَامَةِ فُجَّارًا، إِلاَّ مَنِ اتَّقَى اللهَ، وَبَرَّ، وَصَدَقَ.

Indeed the merchants will be resurrected on the Day of Resurrection with the wicked, except the one who has fear of Allah, who behaves charitably and is truthful.[18]

'Umar b. al-Khaṭṭāb (may Allah be well pleased with him) narrated that the Messenger (Allah bless him and give him peace) said:

اَلْجَالِبُ مَرْزُوْقٌ، وَالْمُحْتَكِرُ مَلْعُوْنٌ.

The importer is blessed with provision and the hoarder is cursed.[19]

Ibn 'Abbās (may Allah be pleased with him) reported that Allah's Messenger (Allah bless him and give him peace) said there are twenty ways of making a livelihood. Nineteen of them are inclusively for traders and only one way is open to industrialists.[20]

1.3 The meaning of expressing gratitude to God

Gratitude (*shukr*) is a feeling of being thankful to those who do any favour to us. From the Islamic perspective, none deserves our gratitude more than Allah, from whom we received our existence and what we possess. Humans have every reason to be grateful to Allah for His loving care, mercy and favours. Everything positive – exceptional talent, good luck or fine weather – emanates from Allah. So as to inspire a feeling of thankfulness in us, the Qur'ān directs our attention to His most important handiwork:

الَّذِي خَلَقَكَ فَسَوَّاكَ فَعَدَلَكَ ۝

The One) Who created you (from a fertile ovum in the mother's womb), then, (to structure your limbs at the fetal stage,) He shaped you aright, then brought about proportionate alteration in your constitution.[21]

Since Allah has inculcated a sense of gratefulness in us, we must remain true to our primordial nature. The Prophetic Traditions enjoin us to pay thanks to the Almighty on the one hand and to be appreciative of the efforts of others for our sake, on the other hand. Ingratitude towards one's fellow beings is, in the estimation of the Messenger (Allah bless him and give him peace), in fact, lack of gratitude to the Sustainer.[22]

In many verses of the Holy Qur'ān, such as the following, Allah divides people into grateful and ungrateful classes in order to motivate us to join those who serve Him with gratitude. The faithful are required to follow in the footsteps of the Prophet Sulaymān.

قَالَ الَّذِي عِندَهُ عِلْمٌ مِّنَ الْكِتَابِ أَنَا آتِيكَ بِهِ قَبْلَ أَن يَرْتَدَّ إِلَيْكَ طَرْفُكَ فَلَمَّا رَآهُ مُسْتَقِرًّا عِندَهُ قَالَ هَذَا مِن فَضْلِ رَبِّي لِيَبْلُوَنِي أَأَشْكُرُ أَمْ أَكْفُرُ وَمَن شَكَرَ فَإِنَّمَا يَشْكُرُ لِنَفْسِهِ وَمَن كَفَرَ فَإِنَّ رَبِّي غَنِيٌّ كَرِيمٌ

Then the one who had some knowledge of the (heavenly) Book submitted: "I can bring it [the throne of the Queen] to you before your vision turns back to you (i.e., even before the twinkling of an eye)." So, when (Sulaymān [Solomon]) saw it (the throne) placed before him, he said: "This is by the Grace of my Lord so that He may put me to the test whether I thank (Him) or not. And he who thanks (Allah), his gratitude is for the good of his own self, and he who is ungrateful, then surely my Lord is Self-Sufficient, Most Generous."[23]

Although the act of displaying gratitude to the Creator for His grace is an obligation, Allah is most munificent towards those who discharge their duty. Allah says:

وَإِذْ تَأَذَّنَ رَبُّكُمْ لَئِن شَكَرْتُمْ لَأَزِيدَنَّكُمْ وَلَئِن كَفَرْتُمْ إِنَّ عَذَابِي لَشَدِيدٌ

And (recall) when your Lord proclaimed: "If you are thankful, I shall certainly increase (My blessings on) you, and if you are ungrateful, then My torment is surely severe."[24]

At another place, Allah the Exalted states how He will recompense grateful souls:

وَمَن يُرِدْ ثَوَابَ الْآخِرَةِ نُؤْتِهِ مِنْهَا وَسَنَجْزِي الشَّاكِرِينَ

And whoever desires the reward of this world, We give him of that; and whoever longs for the reward of the Hereafter, We give him of that; and soon shall We pay reward (affluently) to those who pay thanks.[25]

Allah Most High says elsewhere:

وَسَيَجْزِي اللهُ الشَّاكِرِينَ

And Allah will soon reward those who give thanks (by remaining steadfast in hardship).[26]

Also Anas b. Mālik (may Allah be pleased with him) reported that Allah's Messenger (Allah bless him and give him peace) said:

إِنَّ اللهَ لَيَرْضَى عَنِ الْعَبْدِ أَنْ يَأْكُلَ الْأَكْلَةَ فَيَحْمَدَهُ عَلَيْهَا، أَوْ يَشْرَبَ الشَّرْبَةَ فَيَحْمَدَهُ عَلَيْهَا.

Allah is pleased with a person who eats some food and then praises Him for it, or who takes a drink and then praises Him for it.[27]

It is mandatory for Muslim traders to remember Allah through contemplation and active service without fail. Even business transactions should be a means of serving the Creator. Allah says in the Holy Book:

ارْجِعْ إِلَيْهِمْ فَلَنَأْتِيَنَّهُم بِجُنُودٍ لَّا قِبَلَ لَهُم بِهَا وَلَنُخْرِجَنَّهُم مِّنْهَا أَذِلَّةً وَهُمْ
صَاغِرُونَ○قَالَ يَا أَيُّهَا الْمَلَأُ أَيُّكُمْ يَأْتِينِي بِعَرْشِهَا قَبْلَ أَن يَأْتُونِي مُسْلِمِينَ○

(Blessed with the Divine Light) are those servants (of Allah) whom neither trade nor sale diverts from the remembrance of Allah and from establishing Prayer and paying Zakāt (the Alms-due. Even whilst performing their worldly duties) they keep fearing the Day when hearts and eyes will (all) overturn (with terror), so that Allah gives them the best reward for the (good) deeds they have done, and bestows upon them (still) more out of His bounty.[28]

Nothing should divert the faithful from remembrance of Allah. They are urged to attain eternal peace through living a balanced life in the world.

يَا أَيُّهَا الَّذِينَ آمَنُوا لَا تُلْهِكُمْ أَمْوَالُكُمْ وَلَا أَوْلَادُكُمْ عَن ذِكْرِ اللَّهِ وَمَن يَفْعَلْ ذَٰلِكَ فَأُولَٰئِكَ
هُمُ الْخَاسِرُونَ○وَأَنفِقُوا مِن مَّا رَزَقْنَاكُم مِّن قَبْلِ أَن يَأْتِيَ أَحَدَكُمُ الْمَوْتُ فَيَقُولَ رَبِّ لَوْلَا
أَخَّرْتَنِي إِلَىٰ أَجَلٍ قَرِيبٍ فَأَصَّدَّقَ وَأَكُن مِّنَ الصَّالِحِينَ○وَلَن يُؤَخِّرَ اللَّهُ نَفْسًا إِذَا جَاءَ أَجَلُهَا
وَاللَّهُ خَبِيرٌ بِمَا تَعْمَلُونَ○

O believers! Let not your wealth and your children make you neglectful of the very remembrance of Allah. And whoever does so, it is they who are the losers. And spend (in the way of Allah) out of (the wealth) which We have given you before death approaches one of you, and he says: "O my Lord, why did You not give me respite for a short while so that I could donate in charity and become one of the most pious?" And Allah never grants respite to anyone when his hour of death approaches. And Allah is Well Aware of the actions that you do.[29]

True Muslims are not heedless of their obligation towards the Divine even when they are buying or selling anything in the marketplace. The Holy Prophet (Allah bless him and give him peace) said on this score:

مَنْ دَخَلَ السُّوقَ، فَقَالَ : لَا إِلَهَ إِلَّا اللهُ وَحْدَهُ لَا شَرِيْكَ لَهُ، لَهُ الْمُلْكُ، وَلَهُ الْحَمْدُ، يُحْيِيْ وَيُمِيْتُ، وَهُوَ حَيٌّ لَا يَمُوْتُ، بِيَدِهِ الْخَيْرُ، وَهُوَ عَلَى كُلِّ شَيْءٍ قَدِيْرٌ، كَتَبَ اللهُ لَهُ أَلْفَ أَلْفِ حَسَنَةٍ، وَمَحَا عَنْهُ أَلْفَ أَلْفِ سَيِّئَةٍ، وَرَفَعَ لَهُ أَلْفَ أَلْفِ دَرَجَةٍ.

Whoever enters the marketplace and says: "There is none worthy of worship except Allah, Alone, without partner, to Him belongs the dominion, and to Him is all the praise. He gives life and causes death, He is Living and does not die. In His Hand is the good, and He has power over all things," Allah shall record a million good deeds for him, wipe a million evil deeds away from him, and raise a million ranks for him.[30]

When sellers feel grateful to the Lord of Bounties within and display their thankfulness to Him through their conduct, they will certainly experience contentment and serenity. Souls fully contented with their lot may not deceive anyone, even if they suffer. The very fabric of society grows stronger through grateful people, since they are productive human beings.

1.3.1 Bounties are Divine gifts

One of the most important teachings of the Muslim religion is that the expression of thanks to Allah the Exalted is the key to attracting abundance, happiness, prosperity and inner peace. A thankful appreciation for our tangible and intangible gifts helps us focus our mind on Allah Most High, a thought we fail to care about on account of preoccupations with the materialistic world and its attractions.

Gratitude is a personality trait which corrects our perceptions by reminding us that whatever good things happen to us do not happen by coincidence, so we must not take our comforts and pleasures for granted. The bestower of grace and bounties is none other than Allah, who states in the Qur'ān:

وَمَا بِكُم مِّن نِّعْمَةٍ فَمِنَ اللهِ

And whatever blessing you have been provided with is from Allah alone.[31]

The Almighty also says,

وَوَجَدَكَ عَائِلًا فَأَغْنَىٰ ○

And He found you poor and made you rich (self-sufficient with self-contentment).[32]

The Prophet (Allah bless him and give him peace) taught his associates to express thanks to Allah, the Exalted, and entreat Him to enable them to show gratitude to Him as is due unto Him.

عَنْ مُعَاذِ بْنِ جَبَلٍ، أَنَّ رَسُوْلَ اللهِ أَخَذَ بِيَدِهِ وَقَالَ: يَا مُعَاذُ، وَاللهِ إِنِّيْ لَأُحِبُّكَ، وَاللهِ إِنِّيْ لَأُحِبُّكَ. فَقَالَ: أُوْصِيْكَ يَا مُعَاذُ، لَا تَدَعَنَّ فِيْ دُبُرِ كُلِّ صَلَاةٍ تَقُوْلُ: اللَّهُمَّ، أَعِنِّيْ عَلَى ذِكْرِكَ، وَشُكْرِكَ، وَحُسْنِ عِبَادَتِكَ.

According to Mu'ādh b. Jabal (may Allah be pleased with him), Allah's Messenger (Allah bless him and give him peace) held his hand one day, then said: "Mu'ādh, I swear by Allah I love you. I swear by Allah I love you. I advise you, Mu'ādh, that you must not fail to say at the conclusion of every ritual prayer: 'Allah, help me to remember You, to give thanks to You, and to worship You well!'"[33]

The expression of thankfulness to the Sustainer requires of us to praise the Benefactor by making mention of His benevolence and obeying Him by night and by day, in secret and in public. The tongues, the ears, the bodies and the hearts of the truly grateful servants are obedient to the Lord, so they express their gratitude by their words and deeds.

When traders really feel within their souls that their bounties are a Divine bestowal, they will share them with those who lack such bounties. They will never boast of their abundance and attribute it to their own hard work and skill like Hāmān, who said,

إِنَّمَا أُوتِيتُهُ عَلَى عِلْمٍ عِندِي

This wealth has been given to me only on the basis of (the professional) knowledge and skill I possess.[34]

1.3.2 A means of warding off punishment

The attitude of gratitude instils treasures within, and its performer is enriched by the Lord. In contrast, not feeling thankful to Allah (Most High) for all His bounties can deprive us of peace and tranquillity, even if we possess piles of wealth.

The consequence of neglecting the Almighty and His favours is too dreadful to contemplate. He says in the Qur'ān:

وَإِذْ تَأَذَّنَ رَبُّكُمْ لَئِن شَكَرْتُمْ لَأَزِيدَنَّكُمْ وَلَئِن كَفَرْتُمْ إِنَّ عَذَابِي لَشَدِيدٌ

And (recall) when your Lord proclaimed: "If you are thankful, I shall certainly increase (My blessings on) you, and if you are ungrateful, then My torment is surely severe."[35]

Making one ungrateful is the Devil's primary mission. After refusing to bow down to the Prophet Adam (peace be upon him), Satan the Archdeceiver said:

ثُمَّ لَآتِيَنَّهُم مِّن بَيْنِ أَيْدِيهِمْ وَمِنْ خَلْفِهِمْ وَعَنْ أَيْمَانِهِمْ وَعَن شَمَائِلِهِمْ وَلَا تَجِدُ أَكْثَرَهُمْ شَاكِرِينَ

I will assuredly approach them from their front, from their rear, from their right and from their left, and (consequently) You will not find most of them grateful.[36]

Faith in Allah implies gratefulness, while ingratitude implies disbelief in the eyes of the Lord of all:

فَاذْكُرُونِي أَذْكُرْكُمْ وَاشْكُرُوا لِي وَلَا تَكْفُرُونِ

So remember Me, I shall remember you. And always be thankful to Me and never be ungrateful to Me.[37]

However, Allah, Most Kind to His creatures, provides us a way to escape that punishment by rendering thanks to Him. He says:

مَّا يَفْعَلُ اللَّهُ بِعَذَابِكُمْ إِن شَكَرْتُمْ وَآمَنتُمْ وَكَانَ اللَّهُ شَاكِرًا عَلِيمًا ○

Why should Allah torment you if you become grateful and believe? And Allah is Most Appreciative (of every truth), Well Aware (of every act).[38]

Gratitude is an obligation, not an option; therefore, we should thank Allah, the Exalted, for everything that He has provided us.

1.3.3 Focusing on the positive

An attitude of gratitude fosters positivity in believers, which always results in a win–win situation. Incorporating gratitude into one's life leaves a beneficial effect on one's personality, so that one develops an optimistic outlook and is appreciative of commonplace blessings. Instead of dwelling on problems, difficulties and sufferings, grateful souls focus on possibilities and solutions. This behaviour increases their level of happiness and satisfaction. The following Prophetic Tradition teaches us a sanguine attitude in good and hard times alike.

According to Ṣuhayb (may Allah be pleased with him), Allah's Messenger (Allah bless him and give him peace) said:

عَجَبًا لِأَمْرِ الْمُؤْمِنِ، إِنَّ أَمْرَهُ كُلَّهُ لَهُ خَيْرٌ، وَلَيْسَ ذَلِكَ لِأَحَدٍ إِلَّا لِلْمُؤْمِنِ؛ إِنْ أَصَابَتْهُ سَرَّاءُ، شَكَرَ، فَكَانَ خَيْرًا لَهُ. وَإِنْ أَصَابَتْهُ ضَرَّاءُ، صَبَرَ، فَكَانَ خَيْرًا لَهُ.

> How wonderful is the case of the believer, for all his affairs are good. This does not apply to anyone but the believer. If something good happens to him, he is thankful for it and that is good for him; if something bad happens to him, he bears it with patience, and that is good for him.[39]

Good times are opportunities for demonstrating gratitude, whilst moments of trial are occasions for holding oneself in patience. The people who are patient in tribulation, adversity and distress may not get ruffled, since Allah is with them and loves them.

إِنَّ اللَّهَ مَعَ الصَّابِرِينَ

> *Allah is (always) with those who observe patience.*[40]

1.3.4 Recognizing the favour of others

Feeling and expressing gratitude is a great virtue and the most exquisite form of courtesy which we must practise. We must cultivate the habit of being grateful to our fellows for all the things they do for our sake. According to the Prophet (Allah bless him and give him peace), genuine gratitude to Allah implies giving thanks to the doers of good.

According to Abū Sa'īd (may Allah be pleased with him), Allah's Messenger (Allah bless him and give him peace) said:

مَنْ لَمْ يَشْكُرِ النَّاسَ، لَمْ يَشْكُرِ اللَّهَ.

> Whoever is not grateful to the people is not grateful to Allah.[41]

The preceding Tradition demonstrates that anyone who does not feel grateful to his or her fellow beings, then how can that ungrateful be grateful to the Cherisher and Sustainer of the worlds?

'Abd Allāh b. 'Umar (may Allah be well pleased with him and his father) reported that Allah's Messenger (Allah bless him and give him peace) said:

مَنِ اسْتَعَاذَ بِاللهِ فَأَعِيْذُوْهُ، وَمَنْ سَأَلَ بِاللهِ فَأَعْطُوْهُ، وَمَنْ دَعَاكُمْ فَأَجِيبُوْهُ، وَمَنْ صَنَعَ إِلَيْكُمْ
مَعْرُوْفًا فَكَافِئُوْهُ، فَإِنْ لَمْ تَجِدُوْا مَا تُكَافِئُوْنَهُ فَادْعُوْا لَهُ حَتَّى تَرَوْا أَنَّكُمْ قَدْ كَافَأْتُمُوْهُ.

> Whoever seeks protection for the sake of Allah, grant him protection, and whoever asks for the sake of Allah, give him. Whoever invites you, respond to him. Whoever does some good to you, reciprocate to him, but if you do not have the means to do so, then supplicate for him until you feel that you have reciprocated.[42]

Exchanging a gift was the Prophet's normative practice, and believers, emulating the Prophet (Allah bless him and give him peace), ought to repay the favours that are done to them. If they are unable to reciprocate gifts, then they should acknowledge the goodness of the giver. Otherwise the recipients of favours will be classed as ungrateful people. This theme emanates from the following Tradition.

Jābir b. 'Abd Allāh (may Allah be well pleased with him and his father) reported that Allah's Messenger (Allah bless him and give him peace) said:

مَنْ أُعْطِيَ عَطَاءً فَوَجَدَ فَلْيَجْزِ بِهِ، وَمَنْ لَمْ يَجِدْ فَلْيُثْنِ، فَإِنَّ مَنْ أَثْنَى فَقَدْ شَكَرَ،
وَمَنْ كَتَمَ فَقَدْ كَفَرَ.

> Whoever is given something and can afford it, let him give something in return, and if he cannot afford it, let him express his appreciation for him, for if he expresses his appreciation for him, he is grateful to him, but whoever conceals it, he has shown ingratitude.[43]

Expressing feelings of love and appreciation must be a selfless act. Through genuine courtesy, respect and appreciation for other fellows' considerate behaviour, we ought to acknowledge their goodness, not expect some sort of return. That is not to say that reciting expressions of gratitude and praise should not be contagious.

Getting into the habit of thanking other members of society for their kindheartedness and thoughtfulness implies that one has eyes for seeing and appreciating good and virtue. In addition, in many a Tradition, the Messenger (Allah bless him and give him peace) prohibited us from dwelling on the undesirable traits of people so that our minds may be free from sinful emotions such as hatred, envy, malice, malignity and revenge. Nor are the believers licensed to jeer at one another, speak ill in the absence of their fellows, use offensive nicknames and allow themselves to harbour suspicions.[44]

1.3.5 Choosing a positive attitude

The act of thanking Allah and one's fellows has a positive psychological effect on one's mind; one does not but the blame on others for all the pains and sufferings of life. These people, when afflicted with a calamity, turn their gaze heavenwards and, committing their affair to Allah, submit:

إِنَّا لِلَّهِ وَإِنَّا إِلَيْهِ رَاجِعُونَ

Indeed, to Allah we belong and to Him we shall return.[45]

Grateful people look at the bright side of the picture. Therefore, their mood is not unsettled over petty issues, dark moments and disappointing results. A positive mental attitude, in fact, enables us to put up with hardships of life without sullenness, bitterness, acrimony and animosity towards anyone. To sum up, grateful people are less neurotic and they do not become caught up in narcissism.

1.3.6 Gratitude through actions

Generally, we associate gratitude with verbal expression. However, gratefulness is feeling thankful, and it is a positive emotion which should be evident from our conduct. The life of Allah's Messenger (Allah bless him and give him peace) is a perfect example to illustrate the point. It is related that al-Mughīra was heard saying:

قَامَ النَّبِيُّ حَتَّى تَوَرَّمَتْ قَدَمَاهُ، فَقِيلَ لَهُ: غَفَرَ اللَّهُ لَكَ مَا تَقَدَّمَ مِنْ ذَنْبِكَ وَمَا تَأَخَّرَ؟ قَالَ: أَفَلَا أَكُونُ عَبْدًا شَكُورًا؟

The Prophet (Allah bless him and give him peace) stood in prayer until his feet became swollen. It was said to him, "Allah has forgiven you your past and future wrong actions." He replied, "Should I not be a grateful slave?"[46]

1.3.7 Multiplication of blessings

Allah adds more favours to people who express their gratitude to Him. Allah says:

وَإِذْ تَأَذَّنَ رَبُّكُمْ لَئِن شَكَرْتُمْ لَأَزِيدَنَّكُمْ وَلَئِن كَفَرْتُمْ إِنَّ عَذَابِي لَشَدِيدٌ

And (recall) when your Lord proclaimed: "If you are thankful, I shall certainly increase (My blessings on) you, and if you are ungrateful, then My torment is surely severe."[47]

As Muslims, we need to recognize all goodness in our lives and then turn our attention to its source. As a result, our heads will bow down before the Bestower by way of gratitude. It will lead us to fulfil our obligation of thanking Allah for His beneficence in every circumstance. Thus, we will have more Divine blessings in our lives and increase our level of satisfaction.

1.3.8 A prerequisite for eternal success

It is essential that individuals practise gratitude as part of their daily life since it will deliver them in this world and the next.

Ibn 'Abbās (may Allah be pleased with him) reported that Allah's Messenger (Allah bless him and give him peace) said:

أَرْبَعٌ مَنْ أُعْطِيَهُنَّ أُعْطِيَ خَيْرَ الدُّنْيَا وَالْآخِرَةِ: قَلْبًا شَاكِرًا، وَلِسَانًا ذَاكِرًا، وَبَدَنًا عَلَى الْبَلَاءِ
صَابِرًا، وَزَوْجَةً لا تَبْغِيهِ خَوْناً فِي نَفْسِهَا وَلاَ مَالِهِ.

> Whoever has been granted four qualities has been blessed with the best of this world and the Hereafter: a grateful heart, a tongue that remembers Allah, a body which is patient during suffering, and a wife who is not unfaithful to her husband and is not dishonest with regard to his property.[48]

1.4 Islamic guidance in wealth acquisition

Many businesspeople and employees complain of a paucity of resources and excessive expenditure, and find it difficult to live within their means. There are business, property and media tycoons who live in comfortable circumstances, yet they feel discontented with their fortune. In contrast, there are a few individuals who have enough resources to meet their needs, yet they live on low incomes.

If wealth is earned with purity of intention and employed for good purposes, then work rises to an act of worship in the sight of Allah. Rules pertaining to the acquisition of wealth in the Muslim religion demonstrate its importance. Material goods are vital for fulfilling one's responsibilities, supporting dependents and reducing destitution in society.

The Muslim religion urges us to working to earn, and regards work as significant, a sacred struggle for justice and an act of worship. Allah most high says:

وَابْتَغِ فِيمَا آتَاكَ اللَّه الدَّارَ الأَخِرَةَ وَلاَ تَنسَ نَصِيبَكَ مِنَ الدُّنْيَا

> *And seek the home of the Hereafter with what (wealth) Allah has given you, and (also) do not forget your share of the world.*[49]

Seeking good things in the life of this world in addition to the life after death is endorsed in the Qur'ān:

وِمِنْهُم مَّن يَقُولُ رَبَّنَا آتِنَا فِي الدُّنْيَا حَسَنَةً وَفِي الآخِرَةِ حَسَنَةً وَقِنَا عَذَابَ النَّارِ

And there are others of them who submit: "O our Lord, grant us excellence in this world, and excellence in the Hereafter (as well), and save us from the torment of Hell."[50]

The next verse reveals that how Allah Almighty rewards those who are vigilant about the affairs of both worlds.

أُولَئِكَ لَهُمْ نَصِيبٌ مِّمَّا كَسَبُواْ وَاللّهُ سَرِيعُ الْحِسَابِ

It is they for whom there is a share of their (virtuous) earning, and Allah is Swift at reckoning.[51]

It is the Divine intention that humans should look for means of sustenance on land and sea. The Sustainer subjected canals, seas, rivers and oceans to them. The treasures of the deep waters as well as the marine creatures are there for human benefit. Furthermore, we may get numerous other benefits from the great body of water that covers a large portion of Earth. Regarding the beneficial nature of natural streams of water, Allah says:

اللهُ الَّذِي خَلَقَ السَّمَاوَاتِ وَالأَرْضَ وَأَنزَلَ مِنَ السَّمَاءِ مَاءً فَأَخْرَجَ بِهِ مِنَ الثَّمَرَاتِ رِزْقًا لَّكُمْ
وَسَخَّرَ لَكُمُ الْفُلْكَ لِتَجْرِيَ فِي الْبَحْرِ بِأَمْرِهِ وَسَخَّرَ لَكُمُ الأَنْهَارَ

Allah is He Who created the heavens and the earth and poured down water from the sky and then by means of this water produced fruits for you as provision. And He has made vessels subservient to you so that they may sail in the sea by Allah's command, and He has (also) put rivers under your control.[52]

The following Hadith highlights the significance of earning one's keep:

> According to Abu Hurayra (may Allah be pleased with him), Allah's Messenger (Allah bless him and give him peace) said that there are some sins which are not blotted out by means of ritual prayer, fasting, major and minor pilgrimage. The Companions asked what wipes them out. The Prophet (Allah bless him and give him peace) answered that (they are pardoned by) one's distress, grief and sorrow.[53]

In another Hadith, the Prophet (Allah bless him and give him peace) said if someone enters morning tired as a result of working (diligently) with his hands, his sins are pardoned.[54]

Islam spread by the grace of the Lord. A careful study of the dissemination of faith shows that many times, Allah – though having power over everything – spread His religion by means of wealth and affluence. This fact justifies the acquisition of wealth. The following narratives are cases in point.

1 According to 'Umar (may Allah be pleased with him), Allah's Messenger (Allah bless him and give him peace) commanded the Companions to donate to charity. Coincidently, he had wealth for donation with him on that occasion. Therefore, he thought: "I shall surpass Abū Bakr the veracious today, if I surpass him any day!" He, therefore, brought half of his property, so Allah's Messenger (Allah bless him and give him peace) asked: "What have you kept for your family?" He said: "The same amount." Meanwhile, Abū Bakr (may Allah be pleased with him) brought the entire property of his house, whereupon the Messenger (Allah bless him and give him peace) said: "Abū Bakr, what have you kept for your family?" He said: "I have kept for them Allah and His Messenger!" 'Umar (may Allah be pleased with him) said to himself: "By Allah! I will never beat him (where the performance of good deeds is concerned)!"[55]
2 After the migration to Medina, one of the most pressing problems the associates of the Prophet (Allah bless him and give him peace) and the general public faced in the city was the shortage of water. So scarce was water that it could be obtained only at the well of Rūma. The owner of the well sold water. The Prophet (Allah bless him and give him peace) drew the believers' attention to its purchasing. 'Uthmān (may Allah be pleased with him) paid money for the well and devoted it to the good of the faithful. However, the owner sold just half of the well on condition that he would draw water from it on alternate days. When it was 'Uthmān's turn the believers freely drew and preserved water for a couple of days. Not able to make a fortune, the owner had no choice but to sell the rest of the well, which 'Uthmān (may Allah be pleased with him) bought for eight thousand dirhams. He devoted it to the service of the whole population.[56]

The rest of this section illustrates some points of the Islamic way of life which ensure financial prosperity and stability. If they are practised, they are sure to do good to one not only economically, but also socially and religiously.

1.4.1 Self-sufficiency

The foremost aspect of seeking self-sufficiency is depending on Allah alone for the fulfilment of all needs. The reward of refraining from asking from others for financial support is growing independent of creatures.

Allah's Messenger (Allah bless him and give him peace) said:

مَنِ اسْتَعَفَّ، أَعَفَّهُ اللّٰه. وَمَنِ اسْتَغْنَى، أَغْنَاهُ اللّٰه.

If someone seeks charity (by not begging), Allah will keep him chaste, and if someone seeks independence, Allah will grant him independence.[57]

The following narrative illustrates the point of turning to the Almighty for the satisfaction of one's needs. 'Abd al-Raḥmān b. 'Awf (may Allah be well pleased with him) neither begged nor accepted the offer of financial support; thus Allah enriched him instantly. Anas (may Allah be well pleased with him) reported the incident:

قَدِمَ عَبْدُ الرَّحْمَنِ بْنُ عَوْفٍ الْمَدِيْنَةَ فَآخَى النَّبِيُّ بَيْنَهُ وَبَيْنَ سَعْدِ بْنِ الرَّبِيعِ الْأَنْصَارِيِّ، فَعَرَضَ عَلَيْهِ أَنْ يُنَاصِفَهُ أَهْلَهُ وَمَالَهُ. فَقَالَ عَبْدُ الرَّحْمَنِ: بَارَكَ اللهُ لَكَ فِي أَهْلِكَ وَمَالِكَ! دُلَّنِي عَلَى السُّوْقِ. فَرَبِحَ شَيْئًا مِنْ أَقِطٍ وَسَمْنٍ، فَرَآهُ النَّبِيُّ a بَعْدَ أَيَّامٍ وَعَلَيْهِ وَضَرٌ مِنْ صُفْرَةٍ، فَقَالَ النَّبِيُّ a : مَهْيَمْ يَا عَبْدَ الرَّحْمَنِ= قَالَ: يَا رَسُوْلَ اللهِ، تَزَوَّجْتُ امْرَأَةً مِنَ الْأَنْصَارِ، قَالَ: فَمَا سُقْتَ فِيْهَا؟ فَقَالَ: وَزْنَ نَوَاةٍ مِنْ ذَهَبٍ، فَقَالَ النَّبِيُّ: أَوْلِمْ وَلَوْ بِشَاةٍ.

> When 'Abd al-Raḥmān b. 'Awf (may Allah be well pleased with him) arrived in Medina, the prophet (Allah bless him and give him peace) established brotherhood between him and Sa'd b. al-Rabī' al-Anṣārī (may Allah be well pleased with him). He offered to divide his wives and property in half with him, but 'Abd al-Raḥmān (may Allah be well pleased with him) said: "May Allah bless you in your family and property! Direct me to the market." He made a small profit in dried yoghurt and ghee. Some days later the Prophet (Allah bless him and give him peace) saw him with traces of yellow scent on him. The Prophet (Allah bless him and give him peace) said: "What is this, 'Abd al-Raḥmān?" He said: "I have married a woman of the Anṣār." He said: "How much did you give her?" He said: "A date-stone of gold." The Prophet (Allah bless him and give him peace) said to him: "Hold a wedding-feast, even if only with a sheep."[58]

If anyone treads the golden rule of self-sufficiency, they will be satisfied with their lot. Reliance on one's resources alone signifies that one meets the needs of life. Those who go on chasing material gains of life, no matter how affluent they are, will always feel they do not have enough – which is the very essence of privation and indigence. Blessed are the individuals who are satisfied with the way things are.

According to 'Abd Allāh b. 'Umar (may Allah be pleased with him and his father), Allah's Messenger (Allah bless him and give him peace) said:

قَدْ أَفْلَحَ مَنْ أَسْلَمَ، وَرُزِقَ كَفَافًا، وَقَنَّعَهُ اللهُ بِمَا آتَاهُ.

> He is successful who has embraced Islam, has been provided with sufficient sustenance and made contended by Allah with what He bestows upon him.[59]

A great many people inflict poverty, unhappiness and hardship on themselves when they may live with peace and tranquillity. When they take the abundance of others into consideration, they needlessly and incessantly suffer. The Messenger (Allah bless him and give him peace) enjoined his followers to compare themselves with socially inferior people. With this mindset, everyone will render thanks to the Lord for His bounties.

Abū Hurayra (may Allah be pleased with him) reported that Allah's Messenger (Allah bless him and give him peace) said:

أُنْظُرُوْا إِلَى مَنْ هُوَ أَسْفَلَ مِنْكُمْ، وَلَا تَنْظُرُوْا إِلَى مَنْ هُوَ فَوْقَكُمْ، فَإِنَّهُ أَجْدَرُ أَنْ لَا تَزْدَرُوْا نِعْمَةَ اللهِ عَلَيْكُمْ.

Look at those who are beneath you and do not look at those who are above you, for it is more suitable that you should not consider as less the blessing of Allah.[60]

The truly prosperous person is one who finds internal satisfaction in whatever Allah has granted him or her. Such an individual is free from envy, greed and other sources of inner anguish. On this score Abu Hurayra (may Allah be pleased with him) related that Allah's Messenger (Allah bless him and give him peace) said:

لَيْسَ الْغِنَى عَنْ كَثْرَةِ الْعَرَضِ، وَلَكِنَّ الْغِنَى غِنَى النَّفْسِ.

Richness is not an abundance of worldly goods, rather richness is contentment with one's lot.[61]

People who do not practise self-sufficiency and who surrender to overriding, compulsive greed for more and more are deprived of satisfaction even if they acquire huge amounts of wealth.

Ibn al-Zubayr (may Allah be pleased with him) said while delivering a sermon on the pulpit in Mecca.

يَا أَيُّهَا النَّاسُ، إِنَّ النَّبِيَّ a كَانَ يَقُوْلُ: لَوْ أَنَّ ابْنَ آدَمَ أُعْطِيَ وَادِيًا مَلْئًا مِنْ ذَهَبٍ، أَحَبَّ إِلَيْهِ ثَانِيًا، وَلَوْ أُعْطِيَ ثَانِيًا، أَحَبَّ إِلَيْهِ ثَالِثًا، وَلَا يَسُدُّ جَوْفَ ابْنِ آدَمَ إِلَّا التُّرَابُ، وَيَتُوْبُ اللهُ عَلَى مَنْ تَابَ.

People, the Prophet (Allah bless him and give him peace) used to say: "If the son of Adam possessed a valley filled with gold, he would want a second. If he were to be given a second, he would want a third. The belly of the son of Adam will only be filled by earth. Allah turns to whoever turns in repentance to Him."[62]

The Companions of Allah's Messenger (Allah bless him and give him peace) learned the path of self-reliance from their Master and internalized it. Taking the words of the Prophet (Allah bless him and give him peace) to heart, a number of Companions never asked anybody for anything. The Prophet (Allah bless him and give him peace) said:[63]

وَلَا تَسْأَلُوا النَّاسَ شَيْئًا.

And do not ask the people for anything.

'Awf b. Mālik al-Ashja'ī relates how a good number of the companions of the Messenger (Allah bless him and give him peace) conducted themselves after listening to this counsel.

فَلَقَدْ رَأَيْتُ بَعْضَ أُوْلَئِكَ النَّفَرِ، يَسْقُطُ سَوْطُ أَحَدِهِمْ، فَمَا يَسْأَلُ أَحَدًا يُنَاوِلُهُ إِيَّاهُ.

I saw that some of those people, if they dropped a whip, they would not ask anyone to hand it to them.[64]

1.4.2 Moderation in spending and upholding table manners

The solution to economic ills is economising, not rushing headlong into cutthroat competition for amassing more and more wealth. Holding a just balance between extremes while spending is needed in the life of a Muslim, as the Messenger (Allah bless him and give him peace) said:

اَلِاقْتِصَادُ فِي النَّفَقَةِ نِصْفُ الْمَعِيْشَةِ.

Moderation in spending is a half of economy.[65]

Those who practise moderation in spending their resources are not financially ruined. The key to economic prosperity, therefore, is living within one's means.

According to 'Abd Allāh (may Allah be pleased with him), the Prophet (Allah bless him and give him peace) said:

مَا عَالَ مَنِ اقْتَصَدَ.

If someone maintains a balance, he will not suffer poverty.[66]

According to Abū al-Dardā' (may Allah be pleased with him), the Prophet (Allah bless him and give him peace) said part of a man's wisdom lies in his moderation in economic affairs.[67]

Moderation in expenditure does not signify going miserly or wearing shabby clothes. The Messenger (R.A) enjoined his followers to remember the Almighty all the time. Islam does not frown on being well dressed or consuming good food, providing that one can afford that through his or her Halal earnings.

ثُمَّ أَفَاضَ الْقَوْمُ فِيْ ذِكْرِ الْغِنَى، فَقَالَ: لَا بَأْسَ بِالْغِنَى لِمَنِ اتَّقَى، وَالصِّحَّةُ لِمَنِ اتَّقَى خَيْرٌ مِنَ الْغِنَى، وَطِيْبُ النَّفْسِ مِنَ النَّعِيْمِ.

> Then he (the Messenger) spoke to the people about being rich. He said: "There is nothing wrong with being rich for one who has piety, but good health, for one who has piety, is better than riches, and being of good cheer is a blessing."[68]

People who wash their hands prior to having a meal will find an increase in their resources. Anas b. Mālik (may Allah be pleased with him) reported that Allah's Messenger (Allah bless him and give him peace) said:

مَنْ أَحَبَّ أَنْ يُكْثِرَ اللهُ خَيْرَ بَيْتِهِ، فَلْيَتَوَضَّأْ إِذَا حَضَرَ غَدَاؤُهُ وَإِذَا رُفِعَ.

> Whoever would like Allah to increase the goodness of his house should perform ablutions (wash hands) when his breakfast is brought to him and when it is taken away.[69]

The practitioners of Islam extensively recite the *basmala*, or *bismillāh*, in everyday life. They pronounce it at the opening of each pious action in order to receive a blessing from the Almighty. They must utter *bismillāh* before eating as Allah's Name blesses the food in a way that a little quantity of food becomes sufficient for many people. The term *bismillāh* signifies the Islamic phrase *bismillāhi r-raḥmani r-raḥīm* (in the name of Allah, the Lord of Mercy, the Giver of Mercy). On this score, 'Ā'isha (may Allah be well pleased with her) narrated:

كَانَ رَسُوْلُ اللهِ يَأْكُلُ طَعَامًا فِيْ سِتَّةٍ نَفَرٍ مِنْ أَصْحَابِهِ، فَجَاءَ أَعْرَابِيٌّ فَأَكَلَهُ بِلُقْمَتَيْنِ، فَقَالَ رَسُوْلُ اللهِ: أَمَا أَنَّهُ لَوْ كَانَ قَالَ: بِسْمِ اللهِ لَكَفَاكُمْ، فَإِذَا أَكَلَ أَحَدُكُمْ طَعَامًا فَلْيَقُلْ: بِسْمِ اللهِ، فَإِنْ نَسِيَ أَنْ يَقُوْلَ: بِسْمِ اللهِ فِيْ أَوَّلِهِ، فَلْيَقُلْ: بِسْمِ اللهِ فِيْ أَوَّلِهِ وَآخِرِهِ.

> Allah's Messenger (Allah bless him and give him peace) was eating food with six of his Companions when a Bedouin came and ate it all in two bites. Allah's Messenger (Allah bless him and give him peace) said: "Had he said *bismillāh*, it would have sufficed you (all). When any one of you eats food, let him say *bismillāh*, and if he forgets to say *bismillāh* at the beginning, let him say *bismillāhifīawwali-hīwaakhiri-hī* (in the Name of Allah at the beginning and at the end)."[70]

1.4.3 Seeking forgiveness

Feeling regret about sins and vile actions, and forming the intention to change one's ways and habits, are guarantors of improving one's life. Allah says in the Qur'ān:

وَأَنِ اسْتَغْفِرُواْ رَبَّكُمْ ثُمَّ تُوبُواْ إِلَيْهِ يُمَتِّعْكُم مَّتَاعًا حَسَنًا إِلَى أَجَلٍ مُّسَمًّى

And that you should seek forgiveness from your Lord, then repent before Him (with true hearts). He will keep you glad and gratified with an excellent provision till an appointed term.[71]

The Prophet Nūḥ (e) told his people how they might increase their worldly blessings:

فَقُلْتُ اسْتَغْفِرُوا رَبَّكُمْ إِنَّهُ كَانَ غَفَّارًا○يُرْسِلِ السَّمَاءَ عَلَيْكُم مِّدْرَارًا○وَيُمْدِدْكُمْ
بِأَمْوَالٍ وَبَنِينَ وَيَجْعَل لَّكُمْ جَنَّاتٍ وَيَجْعَل لَّكُمْ أَنْهَارًا○

Seek forgiveness from your Lord. Surely, He is Most Forgiving. He will send down on you torrents of rain, and will help you with wealth and sons and will grow for you gardens and will make streams flow for you.[72]

By making sincere repentance and resolving within to mend their ways, believers may enjoy ample provision, as the Prophet Muhammad (Allah bless him and give him peace) said:

مَنْ لَزِمَ الْاسْتِغْفَارَ جَعَلَ اللهُ لَهُ مِنْ كُلِّ هَمٍّ فَرَجًا، وَمِنْ كُلِّ ضِيقٍ مَخْرَجًا،
وَرَزَقَهُ مِنْ حَيْثُ لاَ يَحْتَسِبُ.

Whoever persists in asking for forgiveness, Allah will grant him relief from every worry, and a way out from every hardship, and will grant him provision from (sources) he could never imagine.[73]

1.4.4 Putting trust in Allah Almighty

If the faithful ardently believe that the source of their sustenance is none but Allah, then the Lord of Mercy grants them sustenance the way that He provides for birds.

'Umar (may Allah be pleased with him) narrated that he heard Allah's Messenger (Allah bless him and give him peace) say:

لَوْ أَنَّكُمْ تَوَكَّلْتُمْ عَلَى اللهِ حَقَّ تَوَكُّلِهِ، لَرَزَقَكُمْ كَمَا يَرْزُقُ الطَّيْرَ، تَغْدُو خِمَاصًا وَتَرُوحُ بِطَانًا.

If you were to rely upon Allah with the reliance He is due, you would be like the birds: they go out hungry in the morning and come back with full bellies in the evening.[74]

Reliance upon the Sustainer does not suggest that one should give up seeking the lawful means of earning a livelihood. Birds are not granted food in their nests; rather they are given seeds and grains when they go out and strive.

Those who commit their affairs to Allah are granted with wealth through such source they are unaware of.

According to ʻImrān b. Ḥuṣayn (may Allah be pleased with him), Allah's Messenger (Allah bless him and give him peace) said:

مَنِ انْقَطَعَ إِلَى اللهِ، كَفَاهُ اللهُ كُلَّ مَؤُوْنَةٍ وَرَزَقَهُ مِنْ حَيْثُ لَا يَحْتَسِبُ. وَمَنِ انْقَطَعَ
إِلَى الدُّنْيَا وَكَّلَهُ اللهُ إِلَيْهَا.

If someone, abstaining (from the world) is devoted to Allah, Allah will suffice him in all the ordeals and will provide for him whence he cannot imagine. If someone (abstaining from Allah) is devoted to this world, Allah will entrust him to it.[75]

That Allah sustains creatures and humans implies that people should rely on Him for material benefits.

وَكَأَيِّن مِن دَابَّةٍ لاَ تَحْمِلُ رِزْقَهَا اللَّه يَرْزُقُهَا وَإِيَّاكُمْ وَهُوَ السَّمِيعُ الْعَلِيمُ

And many an animal there is that does not carry its sustenance (with it)! Allah provides for them and for you too. And He is All-Hearing, All-Knowing.[76]

The sole Sustainer is Allah. This theme occurs in the following verse as well.

وَمَا خَلَقْتُ الْجِنَّ وَالْإِنسَ إِلَّا لِيَعْبُدُونِ○مَا أُرِيدُ مِنْهُم مِّن رِّزْقٍ وَمَا أُرِيدُ أَن يُطْعِمُونِ○
إِنَّ اللَّهَ هُوَ الرَّزَّاقُ ذُو الْقُوَّةِ الْمَتِينُ○

And I created the jinn and human beings solely to adopt My servitude. I do not ask for any sustenance (i.e., earning) from them, nor do I require that they should feed Me. Truly, Allah alone is the Sustainer of everyone, the Lord of Great Might, the Strongest.[77]

Abū al-Dardāʻ (may Allah be pleased with him) reported that Allah's Messenger (Allah bless him and give him peace) said:

إِنَّ اللهَ فَرَغَ إِلَى كُلِّ عَبْدٍ مِنْ خَلْقِهِ مِنْ خَمْسٍ: مِنْ أَجَلِهِ، وَعَمَلِهِ، وَمَضْجِعِهِ، وَأَثَرِهِ، وَرِزْقِهِ.

> Allah has predetermined five things for every man He has created: his period of life, his action, his lying down, his moving about and his provision.[78]

Seeing that the Sustainer has decreed their provision, people put their trust in Allah that He would not let them starve. This does not imply that they neglect work, relying on the Lord. The Tradition in the next section also carries this meaning.

1.4.5 Worship

According to Abū Hurayra (may Allah be pleased with him), Allah's Messenger (Allah bless him and give him peace) said:

إِنَّ اللَّهَ تَعَالَى يَقُولُ: يَا ابْنَ آدَمَ، تَفَرَّغْ لِعِبَادَتِي أَمْلَأْ صَدْرَكَ غِنًى، وَأَسُدَّ فَقْرَكَ.
وَإِلاَّ تَفْعَلْ مَلأَتُ يَدَيْكَ شُغْلاً، وَلَمْ أَسُدَّ فَقْرَكَ.

> Allah Most High says: "Son of Adam! Devote yourself to My worship, for I shall fill your breast with sufficiency and allay your poverty, but if you do not do so, I shall fill your hands with labour, and I shall not allay your poverty!"[79]

Economic or commercial activities do not stop a true believer from remembering Allah and following the ethical path prescribed by the prophet of Islam. Allah's promise about the day of judgement keep reminding the believer that he or she will be rewarded or punished for every act they commit in this world.

رِجَالٌ لَّا تُلْهِيهِمْ تِجَارَةٌ وَلَا بَيْعٌ عَن ذِكْرِ اللَّهِ وَإِقَامِ الصَّلَاةِ وَإِيتَاءِ الزَّكَاةِ يَخَافُونَ يَوْمًا تَتَقَلَّبُ
فِيهِ الْقُلُوبُ وَالْأَبْصَارُ

> *(Blessed with the Divine Light) are those servants (of Allah) whom neither trade nor sale diverts from the remembrance of Allah and from establishing Prayer and paying zakāt (the Alms-due). Even whilst performing their worldly duties) they keep fearing the Day when hearts and eyes will (all) overturn (with terror).*[80]

The faithful are urged not to fall asleep after praying the morning prayer as sleep this time deprives one of earning. The Messenger (Allah bless him and give him peace) said:

> When you have offered the morning prayer (*al-fajr*), do not go to sleep becoming neglectful of seeking your livelihood, since it prevents (the acquisition of) sustenance.[81]

1.4.6 Fear of Allah the Exalted

The Arabic word for God-fearing is *taqwā,* which signifies living by Divine commandments, shunning His prohibitions and dreading His displeasure.

When a believer fears Allah – that is, keeps from evil and guards against wickedness – Allah opens out to him or her all kinds of blessings from the earth and the sky. On the contrary, people are punished for violating His ordinances.

وَلَوْ أَنَّ أَهْلَ الْقُرَى آمَنُواْ وَاتَّقَواْ لَفَتَحْنَا عَلَيْهِم بَرَكَاتٍ مِّنَ السَّمَاءِ وَالأَرْضِ وَلَكِن كَذَّبُواْ
فَأَخَذْنَاهُم بِمَا كَانُواْ يَكْسِبُونَ

But if the inhabitants of (these) towns had embraced faith and adopted God wariness, We would have opened to them blessings from the heaven and the earth. But they rejected (the truth). So We seized them with (torment) for (the impious acts) they used to perpetrate.[82]

1.4.7 Obedience to Divine commandments

Standing fast by the Divine teachings results in nourishment from above and from beneath one's feet. The theme of receiving satisfaction and happiness as a result of laying down one's head to the Lord's directives runs in the following verse.

وَلَوْ أَنَّهُمْ أَقَامُواْ التَّوْرَاةَ وَالإِنجِيلَ وَمَا أُنزِلَ إِلَيهِم مِّن رَّبِّهِمْ لأَكَلُواْ مِن فَوْقِهِمْ وَمِن تَحْتِ أَرْجُلِهِم

And had they established (their systems by enforcing) the Torah and the Injīl (the Gospel), and whatever (more) was sent down to them from their Lord, they would have (been provided with the material resources so abundantly that they would have) received sustenance from above and from beneath their feet (as well, but the sustenance would never have exhausted).[83]

1.4.8 Joining ties of kinship

Maintaining ties of kinship is an obligation and severing them is a prohibition. Furthermore, the Most Merciful Lord rewards individuals who take care of their relatives in the life of this world by expanding their means of livelihood.

Anas b. Mālik (may Allah be pleased with him) reported that he heard Allah's Messenger (Allah bless him and give him peace) say:

مَنْ سَرَّهُ أَنْ يُبْسَطَ لَهُ فِي رِزْقِهِ أَوْ يُنْسَأَ لَهُ فِي أَثَرِهِ، فَلْيَصِلْ رَحِمَهُ.

Anyone who would be delighted to have his provision increased or his life lengthened should maintain ties of kinship.[84]

Thawbān (may Allah be pleased with him) related that Allah's Messenger (Allah bless him and give him peace) said:

لَا يَزِيدُ فِيْ الْعُمْرِ إِلَّا الْبِرُّ، وَلَا يَرُدُّ الْقَدَرَ إِلَّا الدُّعَاءُ، وَإِنَّ الرَّجُلَ لَيُحْرَمُ الرِّزْقَ
بِالذَّنْبِ يُصِيبُهُ.

> Nothing increases one's lifespan except righteousness and nothing repels the Divine decree except supplication, and a man may be deprived of provision by a sin that he commits.[85]

1.4.9 *Being grateful to God*

Adopting an attitude of gratitude towards Allah Most High for His bounties opens up the portals of Divine mercy and bestowal. The attitude of gratitude instils riches within, and its performer is enriched by the Lord.

وَإِذْ تَأَذَّنَ رَبُّكُمْ لَئِن شَكَرْتُمْ لَأَزِيدَنَّكُمْ وَلَئِن كَفَرْتُمْ إِنَّ عَذَابِي لَشَدِيدٌ

> *And (recall) when your Lord proclaimed: "If you are thankful, I shall certainly increase (My blessings on) you, and if you are ungrateful, then My torment is surely severe."*[86]

If one falls on hard times, instead of moaning about destitution before all, one must still turn to the Lord of the universe and entreat Him for relief. Allah then remedies the supplicant's poverty.

'Abd Allāh b. Mas'ūd (may Allah be pleased with him) related that Allah's Messenger (Allah bless him and give him peace) said:

مَنْ نَزَلَتْ بِهِ فَاقَةٌ فَأَنْزَلَهَا بِالنَّاسِ، لَمْ تُسَدَّ فَاقَتُهُ. وَمَنْ نَزَلَتْ بِهِ فَاقَةٌ فَأَنْزَلَهَا بِاللَّهِ،
فَيُوْشِكُ اللَّهُ لَهُ بِرِزْقٍ عَاجِلٍ أَوْ آجِلٍ.

> Whoever suffers from destitution and he beseeches the people for it, his destitution will not end. And whoever suffers from destitution and he beseeches Allah for it, Allah will send provisions to him, sooner or later.[87]

1.4.10 *Almsgiving*

Spending your wealth in obedience to Allah to help out the less fortunate is a virtuous act. According to Qur'ān, an act of charity attracts the Mercy of Allah and increases the wealth of a doer because of the blessings, that mercy adds into the wealth.

قُلْ إِنَّ رَبِّي يَبْسُطُ الرِّزْقَ لِمَن يَشَاءُ مِنْ عِبَادِهِ وَيَقْدِرُ لَهُ وَمَا أَنفَقْتُم مِّن شَيْءٍ فَهُوَ يُخْلِفُهُ
وَهُوَ خَيْرُ الرَّازِقِينَ

Say: "Surely, my Lord releases sustenance in abundance for whom He wills and restrains for whom (He likes). And whatever you spend (in the way of Allah), He will increase it with more in recompense. And He is the Best Sustainer."[88]

That generous souls are repaid for their magnanimity is established by the following Tradition.

According to Abū Hurayra (may Allah be pleased with him):

قَالَ رَسُولُ اللهِ إِنَّ اللهَ قَالَ لِيْ: أَنْفِقْ أُنْفِقْ عَلَيْكَ، وَقَالَ رَسُولُ اللهِ: يَمِيْنُ اللهِ مَلْأَى لَا يَغِيْضُهَا
سَحَّاءُ اللَّيْلَ وَالنَّهَارَ، أَرَأَيْتُمْ مَا أَنْفَقَ مُذْ خَلَقَ السَّمَاءَ وَالْأَرْضَ؟ فَإِنَّهُ لَمْ يَغِضْ مَا فِيْ يَمِيْنِهِ.

Allah's Messenger (Allah bless him and give him peace) said: "Allah said to me, 'Spend and I will spend on you.'" Then Allah's Messenger (Allah bless him and give him peace) said, "The right hand of Allah is full, not diminished by any expenditure, bountiful by night and by day. Do you not see what Allah has spent since He created the heaven and the earth, for what His right hand holds has not reduced?"[89]

Giving to charity is reciprocated by Allah's generosity, whilst hoarding results in the restriction of provisions. The Messenger (Allah bless him and give him peace) said:

لَا تُوْعِيْ فَيُوْعِيَ اللهُ عَلَيْكِ، ارْضَخِيْ مَا اسْتَطَعْتِ.

Do not hoard and so have Allah hoarding from you, but give such small amounts as you can.[90]

Giving charity to those in difficulty is a means of growth, and clinging to wealth in a miserly fashion wards off Divine bestowal and abundance. The Prophet (Allah bless him and give him peace), urging on the merit of charity, said that angels invoke blessings on the people who are generous with their resources.

مَا مِنْ يَوْمٍ يُصْبِحُ الْعِبَادُ فِيْهِ إِلَّا مَلَكَانِ يَنْزِلَانِ، فَيَقُوْلُ أَحَدُهُمَا: اللَّهُمَّ، أَعْطِ مُنْفِقًا
خَلَفًا. وَيَقُوْلُ الْآخَرُ: اللَّهُمَّ، أَعْطِ مُمْسِكًا تَلَفًا.

Every day when the morning dawns on the slaves of Allah, two angels descend. One of them prays, "Allah, reward thc one who spends," while the other one prays, "Allah, ruin the one who withholds."[91]

The following narrative highlights the virtue of spending on the indigent. Abu Hurayra (may Allah be pleased with him) reported that the Prophet (Allah bless him and give him peace) said:

بَيْنَا رَجُلٌ بِفَلَاةٍ مِنَ الْأَرْضِ فَسَمِعَ صَوْتًا فِيْ سَحَابَةٍ: اسْقِ حَدِيقَةَ فُلَانٍ، فَتَنَحَّى ذَلِكَ السَّحَابُ فَأَفْرَغَ مَاءَهُ فِيْ حَرَّةٍ، فَإِذَا شَرْجَةٌ مِنْ تِلْكَ الشِّرَاجِ قَدْ اسْتَوْعَبَتْ ذَلِكَ الْمَاءَ كُلَّهُ، فَتَتَبَّعَ الْمَاءَ فَإِذَا رَجُلٌ قَائِمٌ فِيْ حَدِيقَتِهِ يُحَوِّلُ الْمَاءَ بِمِسْحَاتِهِ: فَقَالَ لَهُ: يَا عَبْدَ اللهِ، مَا اسْمُكَ؟ قَالَ: فُلَانٌ، لِلْاِسْمِ الَّذِيْ سَمِعَ فِيْ السَّحَابَةِ. فَقَالَ لَهُ: يَا عَبْدَ اللهِ، لِمَ تَسْأَلُنِيْ عَنِ اسْمِيْ؟ فَقَالَ: إِنِّيْ سَمِعْتُ صَوْتًا فِيْ السَّحَابِ الَّذِيْ هَذَا مَاؤُهُ، يَقُولُ: اسْقِ حَدِيقَةَ فُلَانٍ لِاسْمِكَ، فَمَا تَصْنَعُ فِيْهَا؟ قَالَ: أَمَّا إِذْ قُلْتَ هَذَا، فَإِنِّيْ أَنْظُرُ إِلَى مَا يَخْرُجُ مِنْهَا، فَأَتَصَدَّقُ بِثُلُثِهِ، وَآكُلُ أَنَا وَعِيَالِيْ ثُلُثًا، وَأَرُدُّ فِيْهَا ثُلُثَهُ.

> While a man was in the wilderness, he heard a voice in a cloud: "Irrigate the garden of so-and-so." The cloud moved and sent its water onto stony ground, where there was one of these channels that absorbed all of that water. He followed the water, and found a man standing in his garden, and diverting that water with his shovel. He said to him: "Slave of Allah, what is your name?" He said: "So-and-so" – the same name that he had heard from the cloud. He said to him: "Slave of Allah, why did you ask me about my name?" He said: "I heard a voice in the cloud from which this water came, saying: 'Irrigate the garden of so-and-so,' and it was your name. What do you do with it?" so he said: "As you have said this, I look at what it produces, and I give one-third in charity, my family and I eat one-third, and I use one-third as seeds for the next crop."[92]

Charitable spending does not signify expending one's material goods on the destitute and the needy alone. If a believer provides for his or her dependents in order to seek Divine approbation, then even meeting familial needs will be recorded as work of piousness to his or her credit in the sight of Allah, the Exalted.

Abū Mas'ūd (may Allah be pleased with him) narrated that the Prophet (Allah bless him and give him peace) said:

إِذَا أَنْفَقَ الرَّجُلُ عَلَى أَهْلِهِ يَحْتَسِبُهَا، فَهُوَ لَهُ صَدَقَةٌ.

> When a man spends on his family with the intention of seeking reward, (whatever he spends) is credited to his account as a charitable donation.[93]

From the Islamic perspective, there are various categories of charity-related spendings. One's foremost obligation is towards one's immediate family.

Ḥakīm b. Ḥizām (may Allah be pleased with him) narrated that the Prophet (Allah bless him and give him peace) said:

«اَلْيَدُ الْعُلْيَا خَيْرٌ مِنَ الْيَدِ السُّفْلَى، وَابْدَأْ بِمَنْ تَعُوْلُ. وَخَيْرُ الصَّدَقَةِ عَنْ ظَهْرِ غِنًى وَمَنْ يَسْتَعْفِفْ يُعِفَّهُ اللّٰه، وَمَنْ يَسْتَغْنِ يُغْنِهِ اللّٰه.

The upper hand is better than the lower (i.e., receiving) hand, and begin (charity) with your dependents. The best charitable donation is the disposal of superfluous wealth. If someone abstains from seeking (fulfilment of needs), Allah saves him from seeking (i.e., begging), and if someone adopts needlessness (affluence), Allah will grant him richness.[94]

The following Hadith signifies that taking care of the financial needs of one's parents is an obligation. Furthermore, it licenses one's father to meet his needs from the earnings of his progeny.

عَنْ عَمْرِو بْنِ شُعَيْبٍ عَنْ أَبِيْهِ عَنْ جَدِّهِ، أَنَّ رَجُلًا أَتَى النَّبِيَّ فَقَالَ: يَا رَسُوْلَ اللّٰهِ، إِنَّ لِيْ مَالًا وَوَلَدًا وَإِنَّ وَالِدِيْ يَحْتَاجُ مَالِيْ. قَالَ: أَنْتَ وَمَالُكَ لِوَالِدِكَ، إِنَّ أَوْلَادَكُمْ مِنْ أَطْيَبِ كَسْبِكُمْ، فَكُلُوْا مِنْ كَسْبِ أَوْلَادِكُمْ.

According to 'Amr b. Shu'āyb, on the authority of his father, his grandfather said that a man came to the Prophet (Allah bless him and give him peace) and said: "Messenger of Allah, I have wealth and children, and my father is in need of my wealth." The Messenger (Allah bless him and give him peace) said: "You and your wealth belong to your father. Your children are among the purest of your earnings, so you may take from your children's earnings."[95]

In the Muslim religion, the scope of charity is very comprehensive. Meeting the needs of those near to one, apart from one's immediate family, is an act of merit and depriving them of their necessaries is an act of disobedience.

Thawbān (may Allah be pleased with him) reported that Allah's Messenger (Allah bless him and give him peace) said:

The best dinar that a man spends is a dinar he spends on his dependents, and a dinar that a man spends on his riding animal in the cause of Allah, and a dinar that he spends on his associates in the cause of Allah.[96]

Indeed, practising charity is a deed of colossal merit in the sight of Allah. Purifying one's self and wealth, this virtue instils peace and tranquillity in one's mind. Yet some people, despite dispensing their wealth, fail to experience inner contentment because they make the mistake of reminding people of their generosity. Thus, they reduce their alms to false charity. The Qur'ān warns people against making charity vain by inflicting reproach and insult on the poor.

يَا أَيُّهَا الَّذِينَ آمَنُواْ لاَ تُبْطِلُواْ صَدَقَاتِكُم بِالْمَنِّ وَالْأَذَى كَالَّذِي يُنفِقُ مَالَهُ رِئَاءَ النَّاسِ وَلاَ يُؤْمِنُ بِاللهِ وَالْيَوْمِ الآخِرِ فَمَثَلُهُ كَمَثَلِ صَفْوَانٍ عَلَيْهِ تُرَابٌ فَأَصَابَهُ وَابِلٌ فَتَرَكَهُ صَلْدًا لاَّ يَقْدِرُونَ عَلَى شَيْءٍ مِّمَّا كَسَبُواْ وَاللهُ لاَ يَهْدِي الْقَوْمَ الْكَافِرِينَ

O believers! Do not ruin your charity donations (later) by taunts of doing favour and hurting feelings like the one who gives charity to show off his wealth to the people and believes in neither Allah nor the Last Day. His case is like a smooth rock covered with a thin coat of soil. Then heavy rain falls on it, washes it clean and leaves it (the same) bare and hard (rock). So these (pretentious people) shall get nothing out of their earning. And Allah does not guide the disbelievers.[97]

1.4.11 Kindness towards the indigent

People who take care of the needs of the indigent are granted help as well as sustenance. On this score, the following Prophetic Traditions are noteworthy.

عَنْ مُصْعَبِ بْنِ سَعْدٍ، قَالَ: رَأَى سَعْدٌ أَنَّ لَهُ فَضْلًا عَلَى مَنْ دُوْنَهُ، فَقَالَ النَّبِيُّ a : هَلْ تُنْصَرُوْنَ وَتُرْزَقُوْنَ إِلاَّ بِضُعَفَائِكُمْ.

According to Muṣ'ab b. Sa'd (may Allah be pleased with him), once it occurred to Sa'd (may Allah be pleased with him) that he was superior to those below him and those financially weaker. So the Prophet (Allah bless him and give him peace) said: "(Never forget that) you are granted support and sustenance only by means of your weaklings and destitute."[98]

Another Tradition reinforces the theme of receiving material help from the Divine as a result of helping out the disenfranchised sections of society.

According to Abū al-Dardā' (may Allah be pleased with him), he heard the Prophet (Allah bless him and give him peace) say:

أَبْغُوْنِي الضُّعَفَاءَ، فَإِنَّمَا تُرْزَقُوْنَ وَتُنْصَرُوْنَ بِضُعَفَائِكُمْ.

Seek me among your weak ones, for you are only provided with sustenance and granted assistance through your weak.[99]

1.4.12 Trade and commerce

Ibn 'Abbās (may Allah be pleased with him) reported that Allah's Messenger (Allah bless him and give him peace) said there are 20 ways of making a livelihood: 19 of them are inclusively for traders and just one way is open to industrialists.[100]

1.4.13 Working for the Hereafter

Doing good deeds for the benefit in the life after death has a positive effect on one's mind. One feels inner peace and satisfaction, and becomes oriented. Allah puts wealth and self-sufficiency within.

The Messenger (Allah bless him and give him peace) said:

مَنْ كَانَتِ الدُّنْيَا هَمَّهُ، فَرَّقَ اللَّهُ عَلَيْهِ أَمْرَهُ، وَجَعَلَ فَقْرَهُ بَيْنَ عَيْنَيْهِ، وَلَمْ يَأْتِهِ مِنَ الدُّنْيَا إِلَّا
مَا كُتِبَ لَهُ. وَمَنْ كَانَتِ الْآخِرَةُ نِيَّتَهُ، جَمَعَ اللَّهُ لَهُ أَمْرَهُ، وَجَعَلَ غِنَاهُ فِي
قَلْبِهِ، وَأَتَتْهُ الدُّنْيَا وَهِيَ رَاغِمَةٌ.

Whoever is focused only on this world, Allah confounds his affairs and makes him fear poverty constantly, and he will not get anything of this world except that which has been decreed for him. Whoever is focused on the Hereafter, Allah will settle his affairs for him and make him feel content with his lot, and his provision and worldly gains will undoubtedly come to him.[101]

'Abd Allāh (may Allah be pleased with him) reported that he heard the Prophet (Allah bless him and give him peace) say:

مَنْ جَعَلَ الْهُمُومَ هَمًّا وَاحِدًا، هَمَّ الْمَعَادِ، كَفَاهُ اللَّهُ هَمَّ دُنْيَاهُ. وَمَنْ تَشَعَّبَتْ بِهِ
الْهُمُوْمُ فِيْ أَحْوَالِ الدُّنْيَا، لَمْ يُبَالِ اللَّهُ فِيْ أَيِّ أَوْدِيَتِهِ هَلَكَ.

Whoever focuses all his concerns on one thing, the Hereafter, Allah will relieve him of worldly concerns, but whoever has disparate concerns scattered among a number of worldly issues, Allah will not care in which of its valleys he died.[102]

1.5 The means of sustenance in life

Allah, the Exalted, never penalises people when they do not deserve chastisement. When they conceive, concoct and execute iniquity, they are seized by the Almighty. Due to disobedience, the wicked suffer as the Qur'ān testifies:

وَمَا أَصَابَكُم مِّن مُّصِيبَةٍ فَبِمَا كَسَبَتْ أَيْدِيكُمْ وَيَعْفُواْ عَن كَثِيرٍ

And whatever misfortune befalls you (comes upon you) as a result of that (evil work) which your own hands have done whilst He forgives most of your (misdeeds).[103]

Similarly, the resources of people are restricted when they turn away from the Divine guidance. The following verses and Tradition illustrate the point:

1 When people flout Divine ordinances, the Almighty punishes them by restricting their means of livelihood. They become miserable as they never realise the cause of their inconvenience.

Thawbān (may Allah be pleased with him) related that Allah's Messenger (Allah bless him and give him peace) said:

لَا يَزِيْدُ فِيْ الْعُمْرِ إِلَّا الْبِرُّ، وَلَا يَرُدُّ الْقَدَرَ إِلَّا الدُّعَاءُ، وَإِنَّ الرَّجُلَ لَيُحْرَمُ الرِّزْق
بِالذَّنْبِ يُصِيْبُهُ.

> Nothing increases one's life span except righteousness and nothing repels the Divine decree except supplication, and a man may be deprived of provision by a sin that he commits.[104]

2 Sincere acts of worship enlarge one's sustenance. Conversely, disregarding the Divine recollection results in poverty and destitution, to which the Qur'ān (20:124) testifies.

﴿وَمَنْ أَعْرَضَ عَن ذِكْرِي فَإِنَّ لَهُ مَعِيشَةً ضَنكًا وَنَحْشُرُهُ يَوْمَ الْقِيَامَةِ أَعْمَى﴾

> *And whoever turns away from My direction and guidance (i.e., remembrance and advice), his worldly sustenance will be narrowed, and We shall raise him blind on the Day of Resurrection (as well).*

3 Because of non-payment of the mandated charity, Allah deprives people of rain, upon which individuals, the community and national prosperity depends.

'Abd Allah b. 'Umar (may Allah be well pleased with him and his father) reported that Allah's Messenger (Allah bless him and give him peace) said:

وَلَمْ يَمْنَعُوا زَكَاةَ أَمْوَالِهِمْ إِلاَّ مُنِعُوا الْقَطْرَ مِنَ السَّمَاءِ وَلَوْلَا الْبَهَائِمُ لَمْ يُمْطَرُوا

> They do not withhold the obligatory charity of their wealth, but rain will be withheld from the sky, and were it not for the animals, no rain would fall on them.[105]

4 Reluctance to dedicate oneself to worship of the Lord results in destitution.

إِنَّ اللَّهَ تَعَالَى يَقُولُ يَا ابْنَ آدَمَ تَفَرَّغْ لِعِبَادَتِي أَمْلأْ صَدْرَكَ غِنًى وَأَسُدَّ فَقْرَكَ وَإِلاَّ تَفْعَلْ
مَلأْتُ يَدَيْكَ شُغْلًا وَلَمْ أَسُدَّ فَقْرَكَ

> Allah Most High says: "Son of Adam! Devote yourself to My worship, for I shall fill your breast with sufficiency and allay your

poverty, but if you do not do so, I shall fill your hands with labour, and I shall never allay your poverty!"[106]

All people crave blessings from the Almighty so that they might live with ease and peace of mind. To have our desires fulfilled, we must turn to the Divine, since it is Allah who

للّه يَبْسُطُ الرِّزْقَ لِمَنْ يَشَاءُ وَيَقْدِر

"releases the provision abundantly for whom He pleases and restrains (for whom He wills).[107]

5 Allah has forewarned of usurious transactions. Dealers in interest will always live in want of one thing or another, never feeling satisfaction, and their gains will be deprived of blessings.

يَمْحَقُ اللّهُ الْرِّبَا وَيُرْبِي الصَّدَقَاتِ وَاللّهُ لاَ يُحِبُّ كُلَّ كَفَّارٍ أَثِيمٍ

Allah eliminates usury (i.e., deprives usurious profits of prosperous growth) and multiplies alms gifts (i.e., increases blessings of clean wealth manifold through charity donations).[108]

6 When earners diminish the rights of their customers or employers, they ward off good fortune. Cheats contribute to their destruction with their own hands. The following Tradition affirms this thesis.

'Abd Allah b. 'Umar (may Allah be well pleased with him and his father) related that the Messenger (Allah bless him and give him peace) said:

وَلَمْ يَنْقُصُوا الْمِكْيَالَ وَالْمِيزَانَ إِلاَّ أُخِذُوا بِالسِّنِينَ وَشِدَّةِ الْمَؤُنَةِ وَجَوْرِ السُّلْطَانِ عَلَيْهِمْ

They do not cheat in weights and measures but they will be stricken with famine, severe calamity and the oppression of their rulers.[109]

7 Breadwinners have the right to eat and drink what they desire within the confines of Sharia. What they are not licensed to do is squander resources. If people of means do not use their fortune and provisions wisely, properly, fully and to good effect, then their abundance might turn into nothing.

عَنْ عَائِشَةَ قَالَتْ: دَخَلَ النَّبِيُّ الْبَيْتَ فَرَأَى كِسْرَةً مُلْقَاةً، فَأَخَذَهَا فَمَسَحَهَا ثُمَّ
أَكَلَهَا، وَقَالَ: يَا عَائِشَةُ، أَكْرِمِيْ كَرِيمًا، فَإِنَّهَا مَا نَفَرَتْ عَنْ قَوْمٍ قَطُّ فَعَادَتْ إِلَيْهِمْ.

'Ā'isha (may Allah be well pleased with her), the Mother of the Faithful, related that Allah's Messenger (Allah bless him and give him peace) entered the house and saw a piece of bread that had been thrown (on the floor). He picked it up, wiped it and ate it, and said: "'Ā'isha, show honour to the precious (that is, food), for if the blessing of food departs from people, it never comes back."[110]

The theme of eating one's meal and not wasting anything, even if it falls on the ground, is reinforced in another Tradition:

عَنْ أَنَسٍ أَنَّ رَسُوْلَ اللهِ كَانَ إِذَا أَكَلَ طَعَامًا لَعِقَ أَصَابِعَهُ الثَّلَاثَ، قَالَ: وَقَالَ: إِذَا سَقَطَتْ لُقْمَةُ أَحَدِكُمْ، فَلْيُمِطْ عَنْهَا الْأَذَى، وَلْيَأْكُلْهَا، وَلَا يَدَعْهَا لِلشَّيْطَانِ. وَأَمَرَنَا أَنْ نَسْلُتَ الْقَصْعَةَ، قَالَ: فَإِنَّكُمْ لَا تَدْرُوْنَ فِيْ أَيِّ طَعَامِكُمُ الْبَرَكَةُ.

According to Anas (may Allah be pleased with him) that when Allah's Messenger (R.A) ate food, he would lick his three fingers, and he said: "If one of you drops a morsel, let him remove the dirt from it and eat it, and not leave it for the Devil." And he commanded us to wipe the platter and he said: "You do not know in which part of your food the blessing is."[111]

1.6 Turning to Divine guidance

Whose words can be truer than Allah's and His Messenger's? What they promise is truthful, so humans should follow all the sacred guidance found in the Holy Qur'ān and the Prophetic Traditions. These principles are the surest and quickest ways of making money, given that their source is Divine.

فِيهِ وَمَنْ أَصْدَقُ مِنَ اللهِ حَدِيثًا

And who is more truthful in word than Allah?[112]

In the same chapter, the theme of Allah's truthfulness is reiterated.

وَالَّذِينَ آمَنُواْ وَعَمِلُواْ الصَّالِحَاتِ سَنُدْخِلُهُمْ جَنَّاتٍ تَجْرِي مِن تَحْتِهَا الْأَنْهَارُ خَالِدِينَ فِيهَا أَبَدًا وَعْدَ اللهِ حَقًّا وَمَنْ أَصْدَقُ مِنَ اللهِ قِيلًا

But those who have believed and persistently did pious acts, We shall soon admit them to Gardens with rivers flowing beneath. They will reside in them for ever. This is Allah's true promise, and who can be more truthful in Word than Allah?[113]

Elsewhere Allah Himself stresses the truthfulness of His words:

وَفِي السَّمَاءِ رِزْقُكُمْ وَمَا تُوعَدُونَ○فَوَرَبِّ السَّمَاءِ وَالْأَرْضِ إِنَّهُ لَحَقٌّ مِّثْلَ مَا أَنَّكُمْ تَنطِقُونَ○

And (also) there is sustenance for you in the heaven and (all that too) which you are promised. So, by the Lord of heavens and the earth, this (promise of Ours) is true just as is your speech.[114]

1.7 A caution on earning money

A word of caution seems pertinent here. Of course, people are under obligation to win bread for themselves and their dependents. But they must not rush headlong into earning in such a way as to sow the seeds of their destruction. The Prophet (Allah bless him and give him peace) forbade people from falling in love with wealth.

According to 'Uqba b. 'Āmir (may Allah be pleased with him), Allah's Messenger (Allah bless him and give him peace) said:

إِنِّي لَسْتُ أَخْشَى عَلَيْكُمْ أَنْ تُشْرِكُوْا بَعْدِي، وَلَكِنِّي أَخْشَى عَلَيْكُمُ الدُّنْيَا أَنْ تَنَافَسُوْا فِيْهَا، وَتَقْتَتِلُوْا فَتَهْلِكُوْا كَمَا هَلَكَ مَنْ كَانَ قَبْلَكُمْ.

I do not fear that you might fall into polytheists after I am gone, but I am afraid that you might be captivated by the love of the world and that you might combat one another and perish as perished those who were before you.[115]

While earning our upkeep, we must not cast Divine ordinances into oblivion; riches must not distract us from the remembrance of the Lord. Allah says:

يَا أَيُّهَا الَّذِينَ آمَنُوا لَا تُلْهِكُمْ أَمْوَالُكُمْ وَلَا أَوْلَادُكُمْ عَن ذِكْرِ اللهِ وَمَن يَفْعَلْ ذَلِكَ فَأُولَئِكَ هُمُ الْخَاسِرُونَ○

O believers! Let not your wealth and your children make you neglectful of the very remembrance of Allah. And whoever does so, it is they who are the losers.[116]

Notes

1 Qur'ān 4:100.
2 Narrated by al-Bukhārī in *al-Ṣaḥīḥ*: *al-Īmān* [Faith], Ch.: What has come to inform us that actions are judged according to one's intention and sincerity, and every man is credited with what he intended, 1:30 §54.
3 Narrated by al-Ṭabarānī in *al-Mu'jam al-kabīr*, 19:129 §282.
4 Narrated by Imam Muslim in *al-Ṣaḥīḥ*: *al-Birr wa al-Ṣilawa al-Ādāb* [Piety, Affinity and Good Manners], Ch.: The prohibition of wronging the Muslim, deserting him, scorning him, shedding his blood, and assaulting his honour and his property, 4:1986 §2564; al-Daylamī in *al-Firdaws bi-Ma'thūr al-Khiṭāb*, 1:166 §614; and Ibn al-Mubārak in *Kitāb al-Zuhd*, 1:540 §1544.
5 Narrated by al-Bukhārī in *al-Ṣaḥīḥ*: *al-Tawḥīd* [The Affirmation of Oneness], Ch.: Allah's saying: "They wish to change the verdict of Allah *[yurīdūna an yubaddilūKalāmAllāh]*" [Q.48:15], 6:2724 §7062; and Abū Nu'aym in *al-Musnad al-Mustakhraj*, 1:27 §335.

6 Narrated by al-Bukhārī in *al-Ṣaḥīḥ*: *al-Maghāzī* [Military Expeditions], Ch.: The Prophet (Allah bless him and give him peace) alighting at *al-ḥijr*, 4:1610 §4161.
7 Qur'ān 106:1–4.
8 Ibid., 4:29.
9 Ibid., 62:10.
10 Ibid., 2:198.
11 Ibid., 3:97.
12 Narrated by al-Bukhārī in *al-Ṣaḥīḥ*: *al-Īmān*, [Ch.: The Prophet's (Allah bless him and give him peace) saying: "Islam is based on five things," 1:21 §8; and Muslim in *al-Ṣaḥīḥ*: *al-Īmān*, Ch.: Explanation of the pillars of Islam and its powerful supports, 1:45 §16].
13 Qur'ān 2:198.
14 Narrated by al-Bukhārī in *al-Ṣaḥīḥ*: Bk.:*Ṣadaqa al-fiṭr*, Ch.: Trading during the days of the Festival and selling in the markets of the time of ignorance, 2:628 §1681.
15 Narrated by Aḥmad b. Ḥanbal in *al-Musnad*, 4:141 §17265; al-Hindī in *Kanz al-'Ummāl*, 4:124 §9861; and al-Khaṭīb al-Tabrīzī in *Mishkāt al-Maṣābīḥ*, 2:133 §2783.
16 Narrated by Ibn Mājah in *al-Sunan*: *al-Tijārāt* [Trade], Ch.: Being lenient during transactions, 2:742 §2203.
17 Narrated by Ibn Mājah in *al-Sunan*: *al-Tijārāt* [Trade], Ch.: The blessing that is hoped for when starting one's day early, 2:752 §2236.
18 Narrated by al-Tirmidhī in *al-Sunan*: *al-Buyū'* [Sales], Ch.: What has been related about those who deal in trade and what the Prophet (Allah bless him and give him peace) called them, 3:515 §1210; 'Abd b. Ḥumayd in *al-Musnad*, 1:299 §966; and al-Mundhirī in *al-Targhībwa al-Tarhīb*, 2:365 §2745.
19 Narrated by Ibn Mājah in *al-Sunan*: *al-Tijārāt* [Trade], Ch.: Hoarding and importing, 2:728 §2153; al-Dārimī in *al-Sunan*, 2:324 §2544; and al-Bayhaqī in *al-Sunan al-Kubrā*, 6:30 §10934.
20 Narrated by al-Hindī in *Kanz al-'Ummāl*, 4:16 §9874.
21 Qur'ān 82:7.
22 Narrated by al-Ṭabarānī in *al-Mu'jam al-awsaṭ*, 4:51 §3582.
23 Qur'ān 27:40.
24 Ibid., 14:7.
25 Ibid., 3:145.
26 Ibid., 3:144.
27 Narrated by Imam Muslim in *al-Ṣaḥīḥ*: Remembrance [dhikr], supplication [du'ā'], repentance [tawba] and seeking forgiveness [istighfār], Ch.: It is recommend to praise Allah after eating and drinking, 4:2095 §2734.
28 Qur'ān 24:37–38.
29 Ibid., 63:9–11.
30 Narrated by al-Tirmidhī in *al-Sunan*, *al-Da'awāt* [Supplications], Ch.: What one says when entering the marketplace, 5:491 §3428.
31 Qur'ān 16:53.
32 Ibid., 93:8.
33 Narrated by Abū Dāwūd in *al-Sunan*: *al-Ṣalāt* [The ritual prayer], Ch.: Seeking forgiveness [*al-istighfār*], 2:86 §1522; al-Nasā'ī in *al-Sunan al-Kubrā*: Ch.: What is recommended with regard to supplication in the wake of the prescribed ritual prayers, 6:32 §9937; Ibn Ḥibbān in *al-Ṣaḥīḥ*, 5:365 §2021; al-Bayhaqī in *al-Sunan al-Ṣughrā*, 1:27 §17; al-Nasā'ī in *'Amal al-Yawmwa al-Layla*, 1:187 §109; and Ibn al-Sunnī in *'Amal al-Yawmwa al-Laila*, 1:45 §119.
34 Qur'ān 28:78.
35 Ibid., 14:7.
36 Ibid., 7:17.
37 Ibid., 2:152.
38 Ibid., 4:147.

39 Narrated by Imam Muslim in *al-Ṣaḥīḥ*: *al-Zuhdwa al-Raqā'iq* [Abstinence and the softening of hearts], Ch.: The believer's affair is all good, 4:2295 §2999.
40 Qur'ān 2:153.
41 Narrated by al-Tirmidhī in *al-Sunan*: *al-Zakāt* [The Alms-due], Ch.: What has been related about being grateful to the one who was kind to you, 4:339 §1955.
42 Narrated by Abū Dāwūd in *al-Sunan*: *al-Zakāt* [The Alms-due], Ch.: Giving someone who asks for the sake of Allah, 2:128 §1672.
43 Narrated by Ibn Mājah in *al-Sunan*: *al-Adab* [Good Manners], Ch.: Regarding gratitude for acts of kindness, 4:255 §4813.
44 Qur'ān 49:11–12.
45 Ibid., 2:156.
46 Narrated by al-Bukhārī in *al-Ṣaḥīḥ*: *al-Tafsīr* [Interpretation], Ch.: Allah's words, "*So that Allah forgives, for your sake, all the earlier and later sins (of all those people) of your Umma ([Community] who struggled, fought and sacrificed by your command), and (this way) may complete His blessing on you (outwardly and inwardly) in the form of Islam's victory and forgiveness for your Umma (Community), and may keep (your Umma) firm-footed on the straight path (through your mediation)*," 4:1830 §4556.
47 Qur'ān 14:7.
48 Narrated by al-Ṭabarānī in *al-Mu'jam al-Kabīr*, 11:134 §11275.
49 Qur'ān 28:77.
50 Ibid., 2:201.
51 Ibid., 2: 202.
52 Ibid., 14:32.
53 Narrated by al-Ṭabarānī in *al-Mu'jam al-awsaṭ*, 1:38 §102; al-Haythamī in *Majma' al-Zawā'id*, 4:64; and al-Sarkhasī in *al-Mabsūṭ*, 30:258.
54 Narrated by al-Ṭabarānī in *al-Mu'jam al-awsaṭ*, 7:289 §7520; and Ibn Qudāma in *al-Mughnī*, 1:437 §1660.
55 Narrated by al-Tirmidhī in *al-Sunan*, The virtues according to Allah's Messenger (Allah bless him and give him peace), Ch.: The virtues of Abū Bakr and 'Umar (may Allah be well pleased with them), 6:52 §3675; and Ibn AbūḍT'Āṣim in *Kitāb al-Sunna*, 2:579 §1240.
56 Narrated by al-Tirmidhī in *al-Sunan*: *al-Manāqib* [Virtues], Ch.: The virtues of 'Uthman b. Affan(may Allah be pleased with him), 5:627 §3703; and al-Nasā'ī in *al-Sunan*, *al-Aḥbās* [The Sacred Struggle], Ch.: An endowment for the mosques, 6:235 §3608.
57 Narrated by Aḥmad b. Ḥanbal in *al-Musnad*, 3:3 §11002.
58 Narrated by al-Bukhārī in *al-Ṣaḥīḥ*: *Faḍā'il al-Ṣaḥāba* [The Excellent Merits of the Companions], Ch.: How the Prophet (R.A) established brotherhood between his Companions, 3:1432 §3722.
59 Narrated by Imam Muslim in *al-Ṣaḥīḥ*: *al-Zakāt* [The Alms-due], Ch.: Sufficiency and contentment, 2:730 §1054; 'Abd b. Ḥumayd in *al-Musnad*, 1:136 §341; Ibn Dirham in *Kitāb al-Zuhd wa Ṣifat al-Zāhidīn*, 1:56 §93; and Ibn Abī'Āṣim in *Kitāb al-Zuhd*, 1:8.
60 Narrated by Ibn Mājah in *al-Sunan*: *al-Zuhd* [Abstinence], Ch.: Contentment, 2:1387 §4142; and al-Suyūṭī in *al-Jāmi' al-Ṣaghīr*, 1:381 §559.
61 Ibid., 2:1386 §4137.
62 Narrated by al-Bukhārī in *al-Ṣaḥīḥ*: *al-Riqāq* [The softening of hearts], Ch.: The affliction of wealth about which one should be careful, 5:2364 §6074.
63 Narrated by Sunan Abi Dawud Hadith Number 9:1642
64 Narrated by Imam Muslim in *al-Ṣaḥīḥ*: *al-Zakāt* [The Alms-due], Ch.: It is disliked to beg from people, 2:721 §1043; and al-Nawawī in *Riyāḍ al-Ṣāliḥīn*, 1:119 §529.
65 Narrated by al-Ṭabarānī in *al-Mu'jam al-Awsaṭ*, 7:25 §6744; and al-Bayhaqī in *Shu'ab al-Īmān*, 5:254 §6567.
66 Narrated by al-Ṭabarānī in *al-Mu'jam al-Kabīr*, 10:108 §10118; and al-Haythamī in *Majma' al-Zawā'id*, 10:252.

67 Narrated by Aḥmad b. Ḥanbal in *al-Musnad*, 5:194 §21742; Ibn Abī Shayba in *al-Muṣannaf*, 7:124 §34688; al-Ṭabarānī in *Musnad al-Shāmiyyīn*, 2:352 §1482; al-Daylamī in *al-Firdaws bi-Ma'thūr al-Khiṭāb*, 4:6 §6010; and al-Haythamī in *Majma' al-Zawā'id*, 4:74.
68 Narrated by Ibn Mājah in *al-Sunan*: *al-Tijārāt* [Trade], Ch.: Eating good, wearing good, 2:724 §2141; al-Ḥusaynī in *al-Bayān wa al-Ta'rīf*, 2:271 §1701; and al-Ḥakīm al-Tirmidhī in *Nawādir al-Uṣūl*, 1/212.
69 Ibn Mājah in *al-Sunan*, *al-Aṭ'ima* [Foodstuffs], Ch.: Ablution (washing hands) when eating, 3:1085 §3260.
70 Narrated by Ibn Mājah in *al-Sunan*, *al-Aṭ'ima* [Foodstuffs], Ch.: Saying *bismillah* when eating, 2:1086 §3264.
71 Qur'ān 11:3.
72 Ibid., 71:10–12.
73 Narrated by Ibn Mājah in *al-Sunan*: *al-Adab* [Proper conduct], Ch.: Seeking forgiveness, 2:1254 §3819; and al-Mundharī in *al-Targhībwa al-Tarhīb*, 2:309 §2502.
74 Narrated by Ibn Mājah in *al-Sunan*: *al-Zuhd* [Abstinence], Ch.: Reliance and certain faith, 2:1394 §4164.
75 Narrated by al-Mundhirī in *al-Targhībwa al-Tarhīb*, 2:341 §2642; and al-Qurṭubī in *Jāmi' Aḥkām al-Qur'ān*, 18:161.
76 Qur'ān 29:60.
77 Ibid., 51:56–58.
78 Narrated by al-Tirmidhī in *al-Sunan*: *Ṣifat al-Qiyāmawa al-Raqā'iqwa al-Wara'* [The Attributes of Resurrection, the Softening of Hearts and God wariness], Ch.: (30), 4:642 §3466; and Ibn Ḥibbān in *al-Ṣaḥīḥ*, 2:119 §393.
79 Ibid.
80 Qur'ān 24:37.
81 Narrated by al-Hindī in *Kanz al-'Ummāl*, 4:21 §9299; and al-Sha'rānī in *Kashf al-gumma 'an jamī' al-umma*, 2:3.
82 Qur'ān 7:96.
83 Ibid., 5:66.
84 Narrated by al-Bukhārī in *al-Ṣaḥīḥ*: *al-Buyū'* [Sales], Ch.: Someone who wants to increase his provision, 2:728 §1961.
85 Narrated by Ibn Mājah in *al-Sunan*: *al-Fitan* [Troubles], Ch.: Punishments, 2:1334 §4022.
86 Qur'ān 14:7.
87 Narrated by al-Tirmidhī in *al-Sunan*: *al-Zuhd* [Abstinence], Ch.: What has been related about anxiety over the world and love for it, 4:563 §2326.
88 Qur'ān 34:39.
89 Narrated by Imam Muslim in *al-Ṣaḥīḥ*: *al-Zakāt* [The Alms-due], Ch.: Encouragement to spend and glad tidings of compensation for the one who spends on good deeds, 2:691 §993; and al-Bukhārī in *al-Ṣaḥīḥ*: *al-Tafsīr*[Interpretation of the Qur'ān], Ch.: His words, "When His Throne was on the water," 4:1724 §4407.
90 Narrated by al-Bukhārī in *al-Ṣaḥīḥ*: *al-Zakāt* [The Alms-due], Ch.: Giving as much charity as possible, 2:520 §1367; and Aḥmad b. Ḥanbal in *al-Musnad*, 6:139 §25125.
91 Narrated by al-Bukhārī in *al-Ṣaḥīḥ*: *al-Zakāt* [The Alms-due], Ch.: The words of Allah Almighty: *"So he who gives away (his wealth in the way of Allah) and commits himself to piousness, and affirms the good (the Dīn [Religion] of truth and life after death through charity and God wariness)* (92:5–6)," 2:522 §1374; and al-Nasā'ī in *al-Sunan al-Kubrā*, 5:375 §9178.
92 Narrated by Imam Muslim in *al-Ṣaḥīḥ*: *al-Zuhdwa al-Raqā'iq* [Abstinence and the softening of hearts], Ch.: The virtue of spending on the poor and wayfarers, 4:2288 §2984.
93 Narrated by al-Bukhārī in *al-Ṣaḥīḥ*: *al-Īmān* [Faith], Ch.: What has come to inform us that actions are judged in accordance with the intention and the sincerity, and every

man is entitled to what he intended, 1:30 §55; and Muslim in *al-Ṣaḥīḥ*: *al-Zakāt* [The Alms-due], Ch.: The excellent merit of expenditure and charity bestowed upon the close relatives, the spouse, the children and the parents, even if they were polytheists, 2:695 §1002.

94 Narrated by al-Bukhārī in *al-Ṣaḥīḥ*: *al-Zakāt* [The Alms-due], Ch.: There is no charity without wealth, 2:518 §1361; Muslim in *al-Ṣaḥīḥ*: *al-Zakāt* [The Alms-due], Ch.: Explaining that the upper hand is better than the lower hand, that the upper hand is the spender, and that the lower is the taker, 2:717 §1034; and al-Dārimī in *al-Sunan*, 1:476 §1652.

95 Narrated by Abū Dāwūd in *al-Sunan*: *al-Ijāra* [Employment], Ch.: A man taking from his son's wealth, 3:289 §3530; Abū Nu'aym in *ḥilya al-Awliyā'*, 9:241; and al-KhaṭībBaghdādī in *TārīkhBaghdād*, 12:48 §6425.

96 Narrated by Imam Muslim in *al-Ṣaḥīḥ*: *al-Zakāt* [The Alms-due], Ch.: The virtue of spending on one's family and slaves, and the sin of the one who neglects them or withholds maintenance from them, 2:691 §994; Ibn Mājah in *al-Sunan*: *al-Jihād* [The Sacred Struggle], Ch.: The excellent merit of expenditure in the cause of Allah, 2:922 §2760; and al-Bukhārī in *al-Adab al-Mufrad*, 1:262 §748.

97 Qur'ān 2:264.

98 Narrated by al-Bukhārī in *al-Ṣaḥīḥ*: *al-Jihād* [The Sacred Struggle], Ch.: Someone who seeks the assistance of the weak and the righteous in warfare, 3:1061 §2739; and Ibn Ḥibbān in *al-Ṣaḥīḥ*, 11:85 §4767.

99 Narrated byAbū Dāwūd in *al-Sunan*: *al-Jihād* [The Sacred Struggle], Ch.: Seeking the assistance of the wretched horses and the weaklings, 3:32 §2594; and al-Bayhaqī in *al-Sunan al-Kubrā*, 3:345 §6181.

100 Narrated by al-Hindī in *Kanz al-'Ummāl*, 4:16 §9874.

101 Narrated by Ibn Mājah in *al-Sunan*: *al-Zuhd* [Abstinence], Ch.: Being concerned with this world, 2:1375 §4105.

102 Ibid., 2:1375 §4106.

103 Qur'ān 42:30.

104 Narrated by Ibn Mājah in *al-Sunan*: *al-Fitan* [Troubles], Ch.: Punishments, 2:1334 §4022.

105 Narrated by Ibn Mājah in *al-Sunan*, *al-Fitan* [The troubles], Ch.: Punishments, 2:1332 §4019.

106 Narrated by al-Tirmidhī in *al-Sunan*: *Ṣifat al-Qiyāmawa al-Raqā'iqwa al-Wara'* [The Attributes of Resurrection, the Softening of Hearts and God wariness], Ch.: (30), 4:642 §3466.

107 Qur'ān 13:26.

108 Ibid., 2:276.

109 Narrated by Ibn Mājah in *al-Sunan*, *al-Fitan*[The troubles], Ch.: Punishments, 2:1332 §4019.

110 Narrated by Ibn Mājah in *al-Sunan*: *al-Aṭ'ima* [Foodstuffs], Ch.: The prohibition of throwing food, 2:1112 §3353; and al-'Ajlūnī in *Kashf al-Khafā'*, 1:194.

111 Narrated by Imam Muslim in *al-Ṣaḥīḥ*: *al-Ashriba* [Beverages], Ch.: The normative practice of the Messenger (Allah bless him and give him peace) is to eat with three fingers, 3:1607 §2034; Ibn Ḥibbān in *Ṭabaqāt al-Muḥaddithīn bi-Iṣbahān*, 3:88; and Ibn ḥazm in *al-Muḥlī*, 7:435.

112 Qur'ān 4:87.

113 Ibid., 4:122.

114 Ibid., 51:22–23.

115 Narrated by Imam Muslim in *al-Ṣaḥīḥ*: *al-Faḍā'il* [Excellent Merits], Ch.: Establishment of the Basin [*ḥawḍ*] of our Prophet (Allah bless him and give him peace) and its qualities, 4:1796 §2296; and al-Shaybānī in *al-Āḥādwa al-Mathānī*, 5:45 §2583.

116 Qur'ān 63:9.

Bibliography

The Holy Qur'ān

'Abd b. Ḥumayd, Abū Muhammad b. Naṣr al-Kasī (d. 249/863). *Al-Musnad.* Cairo, Egypt: Maktaba al-Sunna, 1408/1988.
Abū Dāwūd, Sulaymān b. Ash'ath b. Isḥāq b. Bashīr al-Sijistānī (202–275/817–889). *Al-Sunan.* Beirut, Lebanon: Dār al-Fikr, 1414/1994.
Abū Nu'aym, Aḥmad b. 'Abd Allāh b. Aḥmad b. Isḥāq b. Mūsā b. Mihrān al-Aṣbahānī (336–430/948–1038). *al-Musnad al-Mustakhraj'alāṢaḥīḥ al-Imām Muslim.* Beirut, Lebanon: Dār al-Ilm, 1421/2001.
Abū Nu'aym, Aḥmad b. 'Abd Allāh b. Aḥmad b. Isḥāq b. Mūsā b. Mihrān al-Aṣbahānī (336–430/948–1038). *ḥilya al-Awliyā'wa Ṭabaqāt al-Aṣfiyā'.* Beirut, Lebanon: Dār al-Kitāb al-'Arabī, 1400/1980.
'Ajlūnī, Ismā'īl b. 'Umar al-. *Kashf al-khafā'wamuzīl al-ilbās'ammaashtaḥarāmin al-aḥādīth'alāalsinat al-nās.* Beirut, Lebanon: Mu'assasa al-Risāla, 1985.
Baghdādī, Khaṭīb al-. *Tārīkh Baghdād.* Beirut, Lebanon: Dar al-Kotob al-Ilmiyah, n.d.
Bayhaqī, Aḥmad b. al-Ḥusayn al-. *Al-Sunan al-kubrā.* Mecca, Saudi Arabia: Maktaba Dār al-Bāz, 1994.
———. *Shu'ab al-Īmān.* Beirut, Lebanon: Dar al-Kotob al-Ilmiyah, 1990.
Bukhārī, Abū'Abd Allāh Muhammad b. Ismā'īl b. Ibrahīm b. Mughīra al-. (194–256/810–870). *Al-Ṣaḥīḥ.* Beirut, Lebanon, Damascus, Syria: Dār al-Qalam, 1401/1981.
Dāraquṭnī, 'Alī b. 'Umar al-. *Al-Sunan.* Beirut, Lebanon: Dār al-Ma'rifa, 1966.
Dārimī, 'Abd Allāh al-. *Al-Sunan.* Beirut, Lebanon: Dār al-Kitāb al-'Arabī, 1407.
Daylamī, Abū Shujā'Shīrawayh. *Al-Firdaws bi ma'thūr al-khiṭāb.* Mecca, Saudi Arabia: Dar al-Kotob al-Ilmiyah, 1986.
Ḥakīm al-Tirmidhī, Abū 'Abd Allāh Muhammad b. 'Alī b al-Ḥasan b. Bashir al-. *Nawādir al-UṣūlfīAadīth al-Rasūl.* Beirut, Lebanon: Dār al-Jīl, 1992.
Ḥanbal, Aḥmad b. *Al-Musnad.* Beirut, Lebanon: Dar al-Kotob al-Ilmiyah, 1986.
Haythamī, Nūr al-Dīn Abū al-Ḥasan'Alī al-. *Majma' al-zawā'idwamanba' al-fawā'id.* Cairo: Dār al-Rayān li al-Turāth, 1987.
Hindī, Ḥusām al-Dīn'Alā' al-Dīn'Alī al-Muttaqī al-. *Kanz al-'ummāl.* Beirut, Lebanon: Mu'assasa al-Risāla, 1979.
Ibn Abī'āṣim, 'Amr. *Al-Sunna.* Beirut, Lebanon: Al-Maktab al-Islāmī, 1400AH.
Ibn al-Mubārak, Abū'Abd al-Raḥmān 'Abd Allāh b. Wāḍiḥ al-Marwazī (118–181/736–798). *Kitābal-Zuhd.* Beirut, Lebanon: Dār al-Kutub al-'Ilmiyya, 1426/2005.
Ibn al-Sunnī, Aḥmad b. Muhammad al-Daynūrī (284–364AH). *'Amal al-Yawm wa al-Layla.* Beirut, Lebanon: Dār Ibn ḥazm, 1425/2004.
Ibn Dirham, Abū Sa'īd Aḥmad b. Muhammad b. Ziyād b. Bishr b. Dirham. *Al-Zuhdwa Ṣifat al-Zāhidīn.* Ṭanṭā: Dār al-Ṣaḥāba li-Tutrāth, 1408AH.
Ibn Ḥibbān, Abūḥātim Muhammad. *Al-Ṣaḥīḥ.* Beirut, Lebanon: Mu'assasa al-Risāla, 1993.
Ibn Mājah, Abū 'Abd Allāh Muhammad b. Yazīd al-Qazwīnī (209–273/824–887). *Al-Sunan.* Beirut, Lebanon: Dār al-Kutub, 2001.
Ibn Qudāma al-Maqdisī. *Al-Mughnī fī fiqh al-Imām Aḥmad b. Ḥanbal al-Shaybānī.* Beirut, Lebanon: Dar al-Fikr, 1405AH.
Khaṭīb al-Tabrīzī, Walī al-Dīn Abū 'Abd Allāh Muhammad b. 'Abd Allāh al-(d. 741AH). *Mishkāt al-Maṣābīḥ.* Beirut, Lebanon: Dār al-Kutub al-'Ilmiyya, 1424/2003.
Mundhirī, 'Abd al-'Aẓīm al-. *Al-Targhībwa al-tarhīb.* Beirut, Lebanon: Dar al-Kotob al-Ilmiyah, 1417AH.

Muslim, Ibn al-Ḥajjāj Abū al-Ḥasan al-Qushayrī al-Naysābūrī (206–261/821–875). *Al-Mu'jam al-kabīr*. Mosul: Maktaba al-'Ulūmwa al-ḥikam, 1997.

Nasā'ī, Aḥmad b. Shu'ayb Abū 'Abd al-Raḥmān al- (215–303/830–915). *al-Sunan*. Beirut, Lebanon: Dār al-Kutub al-'Ilmiyya, 1416/1995.

———. *al-Sunan al-Kubrā*. Beirut, Lebanon: Dār al-Kutub al-'Ilmiyya, 1411/1991.

———. *'Amal al-Yawmwa al-Layla*. Beirut, Lebanon: Mu'assisa al-Risāla, 1407/1987.

Nawawī, Abū Zakariyyā Yaḥyā b. Sharaf b. Murrī b. al-Ḥasan b. al-Ḥusayn b. Muhammad b. Jumu'a b. Ḥizām al- (631–677/1233–1278). *Riyāḍ al-Ṣāliḥīn min Kalām Sayyid al-Mursalīn*. Beirut, Lebanon: Dār al-Khayr, 1412/1991.

Qurṭubī, Abū' Abd Allāh Muhammad b. Aḥmad al-. *Al-Jāmi' li aḥkām al-Qur'ān*. Cairo: Dār al-Sha'b, 1372AH.

Sarakhsī, Shams al-Dīn al-. *Al-Mabsūṭ*. Beirut, Lebanon: Dār al-Ma'rifa, 1978.

Sha'rānī al-. *Kashf al-gumma 'an jamī' al-umma*. Beirut, Lebanon: Dār Iḥyā' al-Turāth al-'Arabī, 2002.

Ṭabarānī, Sulaymān b. Aḥmad al-. *Al-Mu'jam al-awsaṭ*. Cairo: Dār al-Ḥaramayn, 1415AH.

———. *Al-Mu'jam al-kabīr*. Mosul: Maktaba al-'Ulūmwa al-ḥikam, 1983.

———. *Al-Mu'jam al-ṣaghīr*. Beirut, Lebanon: al-Maktab al-Islāmī, 1985.

———. *Musnad al-Shāmiyyīn*. Beirut, Lebanon: Mu'assasa al-Risāla, 1985.

Ṭabarī, AbūJa'far Muhammad b. Jarīr al-. *Tārīkh al-umamwa al-mulūk*. Beirut, Lebanon: Dar al-Kotob al-Ilmiyah, 1407AH.

Tirmidhī, Abū 'Īsā Muhammad b. 'Īsā al-. *Al-Sunan*. Beirut, Lebanon: Dār Iḥyā' al-Turāth al-'Arabī, n.d.

2 The key features of the Islamic economic system

The features of the economic system that the Almighty Allah and His Messenger (Allah bless him and give him peace) gave to humanity are notable. It is older than any other economic system (such as socialism, communism and capitalism) that is practiced in non-Muslim lands. It has survived centuries, and, instead of exhibiting signs of outdatedness, has proved its worth.

Whosoever takes Prophet Muhammad as his role model, he may observe truthfulness, honesty, and business acumen as traits of personality in his life, even before his proclamation of prophethood. Description of such traits in a beautiful narration given below is much enlightening for the business community.

عَنْ عَطَاءِ بْنِ يَسَارٍ قَالَ: لَقِيْتُ عَبْدَ اللهِ بْنَ عَمْرِو بْنِ الْعَاصِ ، قُلْتُ: أَخْبِرْنِيْ عَنْ صِفَةِ
رَسُوْلِ اللهِ فِيْ التَّوْرَاةِ، قَالَ: أَجَلْ، وَاللهِ إِنَّهُ لَمَوْصُوْفٌ فِيْ التَّوْرَاةِ بِبَعْضِ صِفَتِهِ فِيْ الْقُرْآنِ:
﴿يَا أَيُّهَا النَّبِيُّ إِنَّا أَرْسَلْنَاكَ شَاهِدًا وَمُبَشِّرًا وَنَذِيرًا﴾، وَحِرْزًا لِلْأُمِّيِّيْنَ أَنْتَ عَبْدِيْ وَرَسُوْلِيْ،
سَمَّيْتُكَ الْمُتَوَكِّلَ، لَيْسَ بِفَظٍّ وَلَا غَلِيْظٍ وَلَا سَخَّابٍ فِيْ الْأَسْوَاقِ، وَلَا يَدْفَعُ بِالسَّيِّئَةِ
السَّيِّئَةَ، وَلَكِنْ يَعْفُوْ وَيَغْفِرُ.

> 'Aṭā' b. Yasār narrated: "I met 'Abd Allāh b. 'Amr b. al-'āṣ and I said: 'Tell me the way Allah's Messenger (Allah bless him and give him peace) is described in the Torah.' He said: 'Indeed, by Allah, some of the characteristics by which he is described in the Qur'ān can also be found in the Torah: "Prophet, We have sent you as a witness, a bringer of good news and a warner and a refuge for the unlettered. You are My slave and My Messenger. I have called you the one in whom people put their trust, one who is neither coarse nor vulgar and who neither shouts in the markets nor repays evil with evil, but rather pardons and forgives."[1]

This chapter discusses some key features of the Islamic economic system.

2.1 Positive aspects of sale and trade

This section explains important commandments for Muslims.

2.1.1 Earning a living

Nowhere does the Almighty Allah's law require humans to deprive themselves of the Divine blessings that are necessary for their well-being and development. Rather, the faithful are under obligation to work. The very act of making a living is service to the Almighty. Making physical and mental efforts at work is a must. Allah says:

وَجَعَلْنَا اللَّيْلَ وَالنَّهَارَ آيَتَيْنِ فَمَحَوْنَا آيَةَ اللَّيْلِ وَجَعَلْنَا آيَةَ النَّهَارِ مُبْصِرَةً لِّتَبْتَغُواْ فَضْلاً مِّن رَّبِّكُمْ

And We have made the night and the day two signs (of Our might). Then We made the Sign of the night dark and We made the sign of the day bright so that you might look for your Lord's bounty (provision).[2]

Even Friday is not a day for relaxing, as is generally understood by the masses. The Qur'ān enjoins the faithful to disperse in the land when the congregational worship is ended.

فَإِذَا قُضِيَتِ الصَّلَاةُ فَانتَشِرُوا فِي الْأَرْضِ وَابْتَغُوا مِن فَضْلِ اللَّهِ

Then after the Prayer is offered, disperse in the land and (then) look for Allah's bounty (i.e., sustenance).[3]

There is a deep relation between input and output at work. This universal law is stated in the Most Sacred Book of Islam:

وَأَن لَّيْسَ لِلْإِنسَانِ إِلَّا مَا سَعَى

"*And that man (according to justice) will get only that for which he strives.*"[4]

Several statements of the Prophet (Allah bless him and give him peace) from the Hadith literature highlight the significance of earning one's keep.

There is nothing wrong with doing manual labour in order to earn a living. Al-Miqdām (may Allah be well pleased with him) reported Allah's Messenger (Allah bless him and give him peace) said:

مَا أَكَلَ أَحَدٌ طَعَامًا قَطُّ خَيْرًا مِنْ أَنْ يَأْكُلَ مِنْ عَمَلِ يَدِهِ، وَإِنَّ نَبِيَّ اللهِ دَاوُدَ e كَانَ يَأْكُلُ مِنْ عَمَلِ يَدِهِ.

No one eats any better food than someone who eats from what he earns by the work of his own hands. Allah's Prophet, Dāwūd (Allah bless him and give him peace), used to eat from what he earned by the work of his own hands.[5]

According to 'Ā'isha (may Allah be well pleased with her), the mother of the faithful, the associates of the Prophet (Allah bless him and give him peace) won their bread with the sweat of their brow:

كَانَ أَصْحَابُ رَسُوْلِ اللّٰه a عُمَّالَ أَنْفُسِهِمْ.

> The Companions of Allah's Messenger (Allah bless him and give him peace) used to work doing manual labour.[6]

In the Muslim religion, making efforts to gain a lawful living is an act of worship.

According to Ab'd Allah (may Allah be pleased with him), the Prophet (Allah bless him and give him peace) said:

طَلَبُ الحَلَالِ فَرِيْضَةٌ بَعْدَ الْفَرِيْضَةِ.

> Trying to gain a lawful livelihood is (the most important) obligation after obligatory worship.[7]

Blessed are the labourers who work diligently and sincerely: Allah's Messenger (Allah bless him and give him peace) labelled them the best of breadwinners.

On the authority of Abū Hurayra (may Allah be pleased with him), the Prophet (Allah bless him and give him peace) said:

خَيْرُ الْكَسْبِ كَسْبُ الْعَامِلِ إِذَا نَصَحَ.

> A labourer's wage is best of all wages provided that he works sincerely.[8]

The Prophet (Allah bless him and give him peace) gave glad tidings to those who engage in doing manual labour until they tire themselves out:

مَنْ أَمْسَى كَالاً مِنْ عَمَلِ يَدَيْهِ أَمْسَى مَغْفُوْرًا لَهُ.

> If someone got tired working manually until evening, he entered evening forgiven and pardoned.[9]

'Umar (may Allah be pleased with him), advising those who are ruled to work diligently to earn a living, said:

> None of you must lag behind in the matter of seeking livelihood and (just) pray: "Allah, grant me with provisions," and he should know that the sky rains neither gold nor silver.[10]

It goes without saying that earning one's keep obligates one to shun begging. Breadwinners are productive members of the community, but beggars are burdens on their working fellow beings.

According to Abū Hurayra (may Allah be pleased with him), Allah's Messenger (Allah bless him and give him peace) said:

لَأَنْ يَحْتَطِبَ أَحَدُكُمْ حُزْمَةً عَلَى ظَهْرِهِ، خَيْرٌ لَهُ مِنْ أَنْ يَسْأَلَ أَحَدًا فَيُعْطِيَهُ أَوْ يَمْنَعَهُ.

> It is better for you to carry a bundle of firewood on your back than to go and beg from someone who might then give to you or refuse to give you anything.[11]

Al-Zubayr b. al-'Awwām (may Allah be pleased with him) related that the Prophet (Allah bless him and give him peace) said:

لَأَنْ يَأْخُذَ أَحَدُكُمْ أَحْبُلَهُ خَيْرٌ لَهُ مِنْ أَنْ يَسْأَلَ النَّاسَ.

> It is better for you to take a rope (to tie up a bundle of firewood) than to beg from people.[12]

Abū Hurayra (may Allah be pleased with him) reported that Allah's Messenger (Allah bless him and give him peace) said:

مَنْ سَأَلَ النَّاسَ أَمْوَالَهُمْ تَكَثُّرًا، فَإِنَّمَا يَسْأَلُ جَمْرًا، فَلْيَسْتَقِلَّ أَوْ لِيَسْتَكْثِرْ.

> Whoever begs from the people in order to amass wealth, it is as if he is asking for a live coal, so let him ask for a little or a lot.[13]

Begging is illegal from the Islamic perspective. However, it is permissible to ask for charity in three situations – although even then a believer is not allowed to practise the profession of beggary and carry around a begging bowl.

Abū Hurayra (may Allah be pleased with him) narrated that Allah's Messenger (Allah bless him and give him peace) said asking for help is not lawful except for in one of three cases:

1 A man who has incurred a debt (in order to reconcile between two parties), for whom it is permissible to ask for help until he has paid it off, then he should refrain;
2 A man who has been stricken by a calamity that has destroyed all his wealth, for whom it is permissible to ask for help until he gets enough to get by – or he may have said – he gets enough to meet his basic needs;
3 A man who is stricken by poverty and three men of wisdom among his people acknowledge that So-and-so has been stricken by poverty, and he is not

habitual of begging then it becomes permissible for him to ask for help until he gets enough to get by – or he may have said – to meet his basic needs.

Apart from these situations, begging on the streets as habit for a source of earning is prohibited in Islam.[14]

2.1.2 Moderation in earning

Seeking a livelihood is essential for the faithful, as the Prophetic Tradition affirms, "Trying to gain a lawful livelihood is (the most important) obligation after obligatory worship."[15] This does not entail, however, that work should occupy all of one's waking hours. By maintaining a balance in life, the faithful may fulfil their duties towards the Lord and His creatures.

On moderation in seeking a living, according to Jābir b. 'Abd Allāh (may Allah be well pleased with him and his father), Allah's Messenger (Allah bless him and give him peace) said:

أَيُّهَا النَّاسُ، اتَّقُوا اللَّهَ، وَأَجْمِلُوْا فِيْ الطَّلَبِ، فَإِنَّ نَفْسًا لَنْ تَمُوْتَ حَتَّى تَسْتَوْفِيَ رِزْقَهَا، وَإِنْ أَبْطَأَ عَنْهَا فَاتَّقُوا اللَّهَ، وَأَجْمِلُوْا فِيْ الطَّلَبِ، خُذُوْا مَا حَلَّ وَدَعُوْا مَا حَرُمَ.

> People, fear Allah and be moderate in seeking a living, for no soul will die until it has received all its provision even if it is slow in coming. So fear Allah and be moderate in seeking provision; take what is permissible and leave what is prohibited.[16]

The faithful are enjoined not to forget the Hereafter when accumulating resources for here and now.

أَعْظَمُ النَّاسِ هَمًّا الْمُؤْمِنُ الَّذِيْ يَهُمُّ بِأَمْرِ دُنْيَاهُ وَأَمْرِ آخِرَتِهِ.

> According to the one who has the most concerns is the believer who is concerned about both his worldly affairs and his Hereafter.[17]

Businesspeople, shopkeepers, vendors, employees, manual workers and others will not be able to provide for their families if they shun the duties of their job. Imam al-Rāzī holds that the faithful must not exhaust themselves entirely with no time for themselves or their parents, dependents, and kith and kin: the Sustainer has guaranteed everyone sustenance with His words in the Glorious Qur'ān[18]

فَكُلُوا مِمَّا رَزَقَكُمُ اللَّهُ حَلَالًا طَيِّبًا

> *"So always eat of that clean and lawful sustenance which Allah has given you."*[19]

If anyone keeps their duty to Allah by working, the Qur'ān states that the Almighty will provide for them from where they even do not expect.

وَمَن يَتَّقِ اللَّهَ يَجْعَل لَّهُ مَخْرَجًا ○ وَيَرْزُقْهُ مِنْ حَيْثُ لاَ يَحْتَسِبُ وَمَن يَتَوَكَّلْ عَلَى اللَّهِ فَهُوَ حَسْبُهُ

And whoever fears Allah, He makes a way out for him (from pain and grief of this world and the Hereafter), and He gives him sustenance from a source which he can never think of. And whoever puts his trust in Allah, then He (Allah) is Sufficient for him.[20]

2.1.3 Freedom to work

Everyone has the right to seek employment, to take a job, or to pursue a profession of his or her choice such as agriculture, business and farming. None may be denied this inalienable right on the grounds of colour, caste, ethnicity or religious orientation. Allah says:

وَأَحَلَّ اللَّهُ الْبَيْعَ وَحَرَّمَ الرِّبَا

Whereas Allah has declared trade (i.e., buying and selling) lawful and usury unlawful.[21]

2.1.4 Acquisition of wealth

Humans need a means of sustenance in order to survive, hence the obligation of earning and amassing wealth. Allah says:

رَّبُّكُمُ الَّذِي يُزْجِي لَكُمُ الْفُلْكَ فِي الْبَحْرِ لِتَبْتَغُواْ مِن فَضْلِهِ إِنَّهُ كَانَ بِكُمْ رَحِيمًا

Your Lord is He Who makes (the ships and) vessels sail in the sea (and rivers) for you so that you may look for His bounty (i.e., sustenance through internal and external trade). Indeed, He is Ever-Merciful towards you.[22]

فَإِذَا قُضِيَتِ الصَّلَاةُ فَانتَشِرُوا فِي الْأَرْضِ وَابْتَغُوا مِن فَضْلِ اللَّهِ

Then after the Prayer is offered, disperse in the land and (then) look for Allah's bounty (i.e., sustenance).[23]

2.1.5 Sharing personal resources

The Messenger of Islam (Allah bless him and give him peace) built a social fabric in which individuals considered themselves trustees of their personal possessions. The Messenger (Allah bless him and give him peace) urged charitable donations to the poor and needy, so that they might benefit from the sustenance of the people of substance. According to Abū Hurayra (may Allah be pleased with him), Allah's Messenger (Allah bless him and give him peace) said:

طَعَامُ الْوَاحِدِ يَكْفِي الِاثْنَيْنِ، وَطَعَامُ الِاثْنَيْنِ يَكْفِي الْأَرْبَعَةَ، وَطَعَامُ الْأَرْبَعَةِ يَكْفِي الثَّمَانِيَةَ.

The food of one is sufficient for two, the food of two is sufficient for four, and the food of four is sufficient for eight.[24]

According to Abū Sa'īd al-Khudrī (may Allah be pleased with him), Allah's Messenger (Allah bless him and give him peace) said to his associates:

مَنْ كَانَ مَعَهُ فَضْلُ ظَهْرٍ فَلْيَعُدْ بِهِ عَلَى مَنْ لَا ظَهْرَ لَهُ، وَمَنْ كَانَ لَهُ فَضْلٌ مِنْ زَادٍ فَلْيَعُدْ بِهِ عَلَى مَنْ لَا زَادَ لَهُ. قَالَ: فَذَكَرَ مِنْ أَصْنَافِ الْمَالِ مَا ذَكَرَ حَتَّى رَأَيْنَا أَنَّهُ لَا حَقَّ لِأَحَدٍ مِنَّا فِي فَضْلٍ.

"Whoever has a surplus travelling animal should return it to one who does not possess any and whoever possesses surplus baggage should return it to one who does not have any." Then he mentioned various kinds of wealth and we started feeling as if we did not have any right to what is surplus to us.[25]

2.1.6 Consumption of Halal

Far from eating what is illicit and impure, believers earn and consume wholesome food. Whatever foods and beverages Allah has prohibited are injurious to one's health. Allah says:

وَكُلُوا۟ مِمَّا رَزَقَكُمُ ٱللَّهُ حَلَـٰلًا طَيِّبًا وَٱتَّقُوا۟ ٱللَّهَ ٱلَّذِيٓ أَنتُم بِهِۦ مُؤْمِنُونَ

And eat of the pure and lawful things Allah has provided for you and always fear Allah in Whom you believe.[26]

يَا أَيُّهَا النَّاسُ كُلُوا۟ مِمَّا فِي الْأَرْضِ حَلَالًا طَيِّباً

O mankind! Eat of that which is lawful and pure in the earth.[27]

وَيُحِلُّ لَهُمُ الطَّيِّبَاتِ وَيُحَرِّمُ عَلَيْهِمُ الْخَبَآئِثَ

(The Prophet) declares wholesome things lawful and impure ones unlawful for them.[28]

However, one may eat unlawful food if one's life is threatened, with the proviso there are no *halal* food and beverages within access. The Qur'ān supports this thesis.

فَمَنِ اضْطُرَّ فِي مَخْمَصَةٍ غَيْرَ مُتَجَانِفٍ لِّإِثْمٍ فَإِنَّ اللَّهَ غَفُورٌ رَّحِيمٌ

> *Then if someone gets into a survival situation (and is forced by) ravenous hunger (and intense thirst i.e., driven by dire necessity, provided) he is not prone to sinning (i.e., eats what is forbidden without being wilfully inclined to sin), then Allah is indeed Most Forgiving, Ever-Merciful.*[29]

The consumption of wholesome food requires one not to eat anything that is unlawfully acquired. One form of illicit earning is taking bribes.

'Abd Allah b. 'Amr (may Allah be well pleased with him) reported:

لَعَنَ رَسُوْلُ اللهِ الرَّاشِيَ وَالْمُرْتَشِيَ.

> Allah's Messenger (Allah bless him and give him peace) cursed the one who gives a bribe and the one who takes it.[30]

A worker should do his or her best when working. Any kind of stealing will incur Divine displeasure and penalty in the Hereafter.

'Adiyy b. 'Umayra al-Kindī narrated that Allah's Messenger (Allah bless him and give him peace) said:

يَا أَيُّهَا النَّاسُ، مَنْ عُمِّلَ مِنْكُمْ لَنَا عَلَى عَمَلٍ، فَكَتَمَنَا مِنْهُ مِخْيَطًا فَمَا فَوْقَهُ، فَهُوَ غُلٌّ يَأْتِيْ بِهِ يَوْمَ الْقِيَامَةِ. فَقَامَ رَجُلٌ مِنَ الْأَنْصَارِ أَسْوَدُ، كَأَنِّيْ أَنْظُرُ إِلَيْهِ، فَقَالَ: يَا رَسُوْلَ اللّهِ، اقْبَلْ عَنِّي عَمَلَكَ، قَالَ: وَمَا ذَاكَ؟ قَالَ: سَمِعْتُكَ تَقُوْلُ كَذَا وَكَذَا، قَالَ: وَأَنَا أَقُولُ ذَلِكَ: مَنِ اسْتَعْمَلْنَاهُ عَلَى عَمَلٍ، فَلْيَأْتِ بِقَلِيْلِهِ وَكَثِيرِهِ، فَمَا أُوْتِيَ مِنْهُ أَخَذَهُ، وَمَا نُهِيَ عَنْهُ انْتَهَى.

> "People, whoever among you is appointed by us to do some work, and he conceals a needle or less from us, it will be a yoke of iron on his neck that he will bring on the Day of Rising." An Anṣārī man who was black – it is as if I can see him now – stood up and said: "Allah's Messenger, dismiss me from working for you." He said: "Why is that?" He said: "I heard you say such and such." He said: "I do say that. Whoever we appoint to do some work, let him bring everything, whether it is a little or a lot. Whatever he is given, he may take, and whatever he is forbidden, let him refrain from it."[31]

2.1.7 Balanced approach

Believers keep to a just balance in all matters, including spending. Sticking to the essence of the Divine inspiration cited next, they eschew the twin extremes of wastefulness and stinginess:

وَالَّذِينَ إِذَا أَنفَقُوا لَمْ يُسْرِفُوا وَلَمْ يَقْتُرُوا وَكَانَ بَيْنَ ذَلِكَ قَوَامًا○

And (these) are the people who are neither extravagant nor miserly when they spend. And their spending is (based on) a balance between the two extremes (of extravagance and miserliness).[32]

The following Traditions also urge economising, which is a solution to economic ills.

Ibn 'Umar (may Allah be well pleased with him and his father) related that Allah's Messenger (Allah bless him and give him peace) said:

اَلْاِقْتِصَادُ فِيْ النَّفَقَةِ نِصْفُ الْمَعِيْشَةِ.

Moderation in spending is a half of economy.[33]

'Abd Allāh b. Mas'ūd (may Allah be well pleased with him) reported that Allah's Messenger (Allah bless him and give him peace) said:

مَا عَالَ مَنِ اقْتَصَدَ.

If someone maintains a balance, he will not suffer poverty.[34]

However, moderation in using one's resources does not mean stinginess, shabbiness and avoidance of Divine bounties, as the following Traditions establish. The faithful ought to wear good clothes and consume quality food, if they can afford to, and give thanks to Allah, the Exalted.

'Umar b. al-Khaṭṭāb (may Allah be pleased with him) narrated that he heard Allah's Messenger (Allah bless him and give him peace) say:

مَنْ لَبِسَ ثَوْبًا جَدِيْدًا فَقَالَ: الْحَمْدُ لِلّٰهِ الَّذِيْ كَسَانِيْ مَا أُوَارِيْ بِهِ عَوْرَتِيْ وَأَتَجَمَّلُ بِهِ فِيْ حَيَاتِيْ، ثُمَّ عَمَدَ إِلَى الثَّوْبِ الَّذِيْ أَخْلَقَ فَتَصَدَّقَ بِهِ، كَانَ فِيْ كَنَفِ اللهِ، وَفِيْ حِفْظِ اللهِ وَفِيْ سَتْرِ اللهِ، حَيًّا وَمَيِّتًا.

Whoever wears a new garment and then says: "All praise is due to Allah who clothed me with what I may cover my nakedness, and what I may beautify myself with in my life, and then he takes the garment that has worn out and gives it in charity, he shall be under Allah's guard, Allah's protection, and Allah's covering, alive and dead."[35]

According to Sālim:

عَنِ ابْنِ عُمَرَ أَنَّ رَسُوْلَ اللهِ a رَأَى عَلَى عُمَرَ قَمِيْصًا أَبْيَضَ، فَقَالَ: ثَوْبُكَ هَذَا غَسِيْلٌ أَمْ جَدِيْدٌ؟ قَالَ: لَا بَلْ غَسِيْلٌ، قَالَ: الْبَسْ جَدِيْدًا وَعِشْ حَمِيْدًا وَمُتْ شَهِيْدًا.

> Ibn 'Umar (may Allah be well pleased with him and his father) reported that Allah's Messenger (Allah bless him and give him peace) saw 'Umar wearing a white shirt and said: "Is this garment of yours washed or a new one?" 'Umar said: "Rather it has been washed." Allah's Messenger (Allah bless him and give him peace) said: "Wear new clothes, live a good life and die as martyr."[36]

2.1.8 *Timely payment of wages*

Employees must be paid for their work as soon as they complete it. Withholding wages or employing delaying tactics are irksome to a worker, and Islam treats this as a form of oppression. Entrepreneurs must not delay paying workers' wages.

'Abd Allāh b. 'Umar (may Allah be pleased with him and his father) related that Allah's Messenger (Allah bless him and give him peace) said:

أَعْطُوا الْأَجِيرَ أَجْرَهُ قَبْلَ أَنْ يَجِفَّ عَرَقُهُ.

> Give the worker his wages before his sweat dries.[37]

The command in the Hadith to pay the worker before his or her perspiration dries means that payment should be made immediately after the completion of the assignment, even if the worker does not sweat.[38]

If the people of means do not pay hired workers or employees promptly, then they are oppressors in the sight of the Prophet (Allah bless him and give him peace). He said:

مَطْلُ الْغَنِيِّ ظُلْمٌ.

> Delay in payment on the part of a rich man is injustice.[39]

In the following Tradition, the Prophet (Allah bless him and give him peace) warned against the exploitation of workers.

قَالَ اللّٰهُ تَعَالَى: ثَلَاثَةٌ أَنَا خَصْمُهُمْ يَوْمَ الْقِيَامَةِ، رَجُلٌ أَعْطَى بِي ثُمَّ غَدَرَ، وَرَجُلٌ
بَاعَ حُرًّا فَأَكَلَ ثَمَنَهُ، وَرَجُلٌ اسْتَأْجَرَ أَجِيرًا فَاسْتَوْفَى مِنْهُ وَلَمْ يُعْطِهِ أَجْرَهُ.

> The Almighty Allah says: I will be an adversary against three people on the Day of Rising: (one of them will be) a man who hires an employee and gets full work from him and then does not pay him his wages.[40]

Rendering one's services to someone against an agreed payment is a contract. Muslim law enjoins both employers and employees to fulfil their mutual duties. Allah pithily charges the faithful,

يَا أَيُّهَا الَّذِينَ آمَنُوا أَوْفُوا بِالْعُقُود

"O believers! Fulfil (your) promises."[41]

Elsewhere Allah depicts the character of the ardent faithful,

وَالْمُوفُونَ بِعَهْدِهِمْ إِذَا عَاهَدُوا

"And when they make a promise, they fulfil it."[42]

2.1.9 Paying zakāt

Prescribed charity, or *zakāt*, is distributed among the have-nots and the needy as per the tenet of the Qur'ān verse given next. It forges a bond between the haves and the have-nots in society. The compulsory payment of charity is an effective way to redistribute the wealth.

لاَ يَكُونَ دُولَةً بَيْنَ الْأَغْنِيَاءِ مِنكُمْ

(This distribution system is to ensure) that (the whole wealth) may not circulate (only) amongst the rich of you (but should circulate amongst all the classes of society).[43]

Two further forms of financial help for the poor come from *kharāj* (land tax) and *'ushr* (one tenth of the produce of land).

2.1.10 Charitable donations

Ardent believers care about the needy, the poor, the disabled and the impecunious in order to seek the pleasure of the Almighty. Economic ills may be minimised through the distribution of wealth. The following revelations clearly bid the followers of Islam to share their resources.

Almsgiving offered by a believing Muslim is multiplied in its recompense. Allah says in the Qur'ān (2:261):

مَّثَلُ الَّذِينَ يُنفِقُونَ أَمْوَالَهُمْ فِي سَبِيلِ اللهِ كَمَثَلِ حَبَّةٍ أَنبَتَتْ سَبْعَ سَنَابِلَ فِي كُلِّ سُنبُلَةٍ مِّئَةُ حَبَّةٍ وَاللهُ يُضَاعِفُ لِمَن يَشَاءُ وَاللهُ وَاسِعٌ عَلِيمٌ

The example of those who spend their wealth in the way of Allah is like (that) grain out of which seven ears shoot forth. (And then) each ear bears a hundred grains (i.e., they are rewarded seven hundred times). And Allah multiplies (still more) for whom He likes. And Allah is Infinite, All-Knowing.

A balanced spending in the sight of Allah Almighty is between the two extremes of extravagance and miserliness.

وَالَّذِينَ إِذَا أَنفَقُوا لَمْ يُسْرِفُوا وَلَمْ يَقْتُرُوا وَكَانَ بَيْنَ ذَٰلِكَ قَوَامًا○

And (these) are the people who are neither extravagant nor miserly when they spend. And their spending is (based on) a balance between the two extremes (of extravagance and miserliness).[44]

In the following verses, Allah highlights the excellent merit of practising charity.

يَا أَيُّهَا الَّذِينَ آمَنُواْ أَنفِقُواْ مِمَّا رَزَقْنَاكُم

Believers! Spend (in the cause of Allah) out of whatever We have provided for you.[45]

وَيُطْعِمُونَ الطَّعَامَ عَلَى حُبِّهِ مِسْكِينًا وَيَتِيمًا وَأَسِيرًا○

And they give (their own) food, in deep love of Allah, to the needy, orphan and prisoner (out of sacrifice, despite their own desire and need for it).[46]

لَّيْسَ الْبِرَّ أَن تُوَلُّواْ وُجُوهَكُمْ قِبَلَ الْمَشْرِقِ وَالْمَغْرِبِ وَلَكِنَّ الْبِرَّ مَنْ آمَنَ بِاللهِ وَالْيَوْمِ الْآخِرِ وَالْمَلآئِكَةِ وَالْكِتَابِ وَالنَّبِيِّينَ وَآتَى الْمَالَ عَلَى حُبِّهِ ذَوِي الْقُرْبَى وَالْيَتَامَى وَالْمَسَاكِينَ وَابْنَ السَّبِيلِ وَالسَّآئِلِينَ وَفِي الرِّقَابِ وَأَقَامَ الصَّلاَةَ وَآتَى الزَّكَاةَ

Righteousness is not merely that you turn your faces to the east or the west. But true righteousness is that a person believes in Allah, the Last Day, the angels, the Book (revealed by Allah) and the Messengers. Driven by love for Allah, he spends (his) wealth on the kindred, the orphans, the needy, the wayfarers and those who ask and in (liberating slaves') necks, and establishes Prayer and pays zakāt (the Alms-due).[47]

Giving to charity is vital, but if one does not have the means to dispense wealth, then lesser forms of assistance also suffice.

According to Abū Mūsā al-Ash'arī (Allah be pleased with him), on the authority of his father, his grandfather reported:

قَالَ النَّبِيُّ: عَلَى كُلِّ مُسْلِمٍ صَدَقَةٌ، قَالُوْا: فَإِنْ لَمْ يَجِدْ؟ قَالَ: فَيَعْمَلُ بِيَدَيْهِ فَيَنْفَعُ نَفْسَهُ وَيَتَصَدَّقُ، قَالُوْا: فَإِنْ لَمْ يَسْتَطِعْ أَوْ لَمْ يَفْعَلْ؟ قَالَ: فَيُعِيْنُ ذَا الْحَاجَةِ الْمَلْهُوْفَ، قَالُوْا: فَإِنْ لَمْ يَفْعَلْ؟ قَالَ: فَيَأْمُرُ بِالْخَيْرِ، أَوْ قَالَ: بِالْمَعْرُوْفِ، قَالَ: فَإِنْ لَمْ يَفْعَلْ؟ قَالَ فَيُمْسِكُ عَنِ الشَّرِّ فَإِنَّهُ لَهُ صَدَقَةٌ.

> The Prophet (Allah bless him and give him peace) said: "Every Muslim must give charity?' The Companions asked: "And if he does not have anything?' He said: "Then he should work with his hands and help himself and give charity." The Companions asked: "And if he cannot work or does not work?" He said: "Then he should help the needy oppressed person who seeks help." The Companions asked: "And if he does not do it?" He said: "He should command the good," or he said: "Command the correct." He said: "And if he does not do that?" He said: "Then he should refrain from the evil. That is charity for him."[48]

On the Day of Resurrection, the Divine Essence will safeguard souls that spent their personal belongings secretly. Abū Hurayra (may Allah be pleased with him) narrated that the Prophet (Allah bless him and give him peace) said:

> سَبْعَةٌ يُظِلُّهُمُ اللَّهُ فِيْ ظِلِّهِ يَوْمَ لَا ظِلَّ إِلَّا ظِلُّهُ، اَلْإِمَامُ الْعَادِلُ، وَشَابٌّ نَشَأَ فِيْ عِبَادَةِ رَبِّهِ، وَرَجُلٌ قَلْبُهُ مُعَلَّقٌ فِيْ الْمَسَاجِدِ، وَرَجُلَانِ تَحَابَّا فِي اللَّهِ اجْتَمَعَا عَلَيْهِ وَتَفَرَّقَا عَلَيْهِ، وَرَجُلٌ طَلَبَتْهُ امْرَأَةٌ ذَاتُ مَنْصِبٍ وَجَمَالٍ فَقَالَ: إِنِّيْ أَخَافُ اللَّهَ، وَرَجُلٌ تَصَدَّقَ أَخْفَى حَتَّى لَا تَعْلَمَ شِمَالُهُ مَا تُنْفِقُ يَمِيْنُهُ، وَرَجُلٌ ذَكَرَ اللَّهَ خَالِيًا فَفَاضَتْ عَيْنَاهُ.

> There are seven whom Allah will shade with His shade on the day when there is no shade but His shade: a just Imam, a youth who grows up worshipping Allah, a man whose heart is attached to the mosques, two men who love each other for the sake of Allah alone, meeting for that reason and parting for that reason, a man who refuses the advances of a noble and beautiful woman, saying: "I fear Allāh," a man who gives charity and conceals it so that his left hand does not know what his right hand gives, and a man who remembers Allah when he is alone and his eyes overflow with tears.[49]

The Prophet (Allah bless him and give him peace) commanded his followers to take responsibility for helping those around them and others in need.

According to Abū Hurayra (may Allah be pleased with him), Allah's Messenger (Allah bless him and give him peace) said:

> إِنَّ اللَّهَ قَالَ لِيْ: أَنْفِقْ، أُنْفِقْ عَلَيْكَ، وَقَالَ رَسُولُ اللَّهِ: يَمِيْنُ اللَّهِ مَلْأَى لَا يَغِيْضُهَا سَحَّاءُ اللَّيْلَ وَالنَّهَارَ، أَرَأَيْتُمْ مَا أَنْفَقَ مُذْ خَلَقَ السَّمَاءَ وَالْأَرْضَ؟ فَإِنَّهُ لَمْ يَغِضْ مَا فِيْ يَمِيْنِه.

> Allah said to me, "Spend and I will spend on you." Then Allah's Messenger (Allah bless him and give him peace) said, "The right hand of Allah is full, not diminished by any expenditure bountiful by night and by day. Do you not see what Allah has spent since He created the heaven and the earth, for what His right-hand holds has not reduced?"[50]

Abū Hurayra (may Allah be pleased with him) narrated the Messenger (Allah bless him and give him peace) said:

مَنْ أَنْفَقَ زَوْجَيْنِ فِيْ سَبِيْلِ اللّٰهِ نُوْدِيَ مِنْ أَبْوَابِ الْجَنَّةِ: يَا عَبْدَ اللّٰهِ، هَذَا خَيْرٌ.

> If anyone has spent his effort in two kinds of actions in the cause of Allah, he will be summoned from the gates of the Garden of Paradise, "Servant of Allah, this door is better."[51]

On the authority of Abū Hurayra (may Allah be pleased with him), the Prophet (Allah bless him and give him peace) said:

مَا مِنْ يَوْمٍ يُصْبِحُ الْعِبَادُ فِيْهِ إِلَّا مَلَكَانِ يَنْزِلَانِ، فَيَقُوْلُ أَحَدُهُمَا: اللَّهُمَّ، أَعْطِ مُنْفِقًا خَلَفًا. وَيَقُوْلُ الْآخَرُ: اللَّهُمَّ، أَعْطِ مُمْسِكًا تَلَفًا.

> Every day when the morning dawns on the slaves of Allah, two angels descend. One of them prays, "Allah, reward the one who spends," while the other one prays, "Allah, ruin the one who withholds."[52]

On the one hand, the Almighty, Allah, highlights the excellent merit of spending in His way, and on the other hand He warns against being miserly.

وَلَا يَحْسَبَنَّ الَّذِينَ يَبْخَلُونَ بِمَا آتَاهُمُ اللّٰهُ مِن فَضْلِهِ هُوَ خَيْرًا لَّهُمْ بَلْ هُوَ شَرٌّ لَّهُمْ

> *And those who are niggardly in giving away (from the wealth) which Allah has bestowed upon them out of His bounty must never consider this miserliness of any benefit to themselves; it is rather injurious to them.*[53]

إِنَّ اللّٰهَ لَا يُحِبُّ مَن كَانَ مُخْتَالًا فَخُورًا○الَّذِينَ يَبْخَلُونَ وَيَأْمُرُونَ النَّاسَ بِالْبُخْلِ وَيَكْتُمُونَ مَا آتَاهُمُ اللّٰهُ مِن فَضْلِهِ

> *Surely, Allah does not like the one who is arrogant (i.e., self-conceited) and boastful (i.e., egoist), those who are miserly and bid others (also) to be miserly and hide that (blessing) which Allah has granted them of His bounty.*[54]

2.1.11 Social welfare

People who are able are under obligation to support the less privileged, so that none goes without the necessities of life. For this purpose, they pay *zakāt* on their capital. But this is not enough. Allah Almighty has made due upon all the wealthy people to support the destitutes of their society in their difficulties, which is extra to what they pay as *zakat*. As Quran says:

وَفِي أَمْوَالِهِمْ حَقٌّ لِّلسَّائِلِ وَالْمَحْرُومِ○

And in their wealth was appointed a due share for the beggars and the destitute (i.e., all the needy).[55]

وَالَّذِينَ فِي أَمْوَالِهِمْ حَقٌّ مَّعْلُومٌ○لِّلسَّائِلِ وَالْمَحْرُومِ○

And those (who are committed to sacrifice and) in whose wealth there is a fixed share, of one who begs and of one who is needy but does not beg.[56]

Prophetic Traditions also reinforce this theme of meeting the needs of the downtrodden, so that they may live with dignity and honour.

According to Fatima Bint e Qais (may Allah be pleased with her), when asked about *zakāt*, the Prophet (Allah bless him and give him peace) said:

إِنَّ فِيْ الْمَالِ لَحَقًّا سِوَى الزَّكَاةِ.

Indeed, there is a duty on wealth aside from *zakāt* (the Alms-due).[57]

When Allah, the Exalted, granted the Prophet (Allah bless him and give him peace) victories, According to Abū Hurayra (may Allah be pleased with him), Allah's Messenger (Allah bless him and give him peace) said:

أَأَنَا أَوْلَى بِالْمُؤْمِنِيْنَ مِنْ أَنْفُسِهِمْ، فَمَنْ تُوُفِّيَ مِنَ الْمُؤْمِنِيْنَ فَتَرَكَ دَيْنًا، فَعَلَيَّ قَضَاؤُهُ، وَمَنْ تَرَكَ مَالاً فَلِوَرَثَتِهِ.

I have more right to be the protector of the believers than themselves. If any believer dies leaving a debt, I will pay it. If anyone leaves property, it goes to his heirs.[58]

The caliph 'Alī (may Allah be pleased with him) stressed the obligatory nature of alms. Allah has prescribed for affluent Muslims to spend money (by way of charity) as to eliminate the poverty of the destitute.[59]

2.1.12 Obligation of the state

Individuals must earn their own keep and not rely on anyone else for the satisfaction of their needs. If, however, some individuals living within an Islamic state are unable to exert themselves due to some sort of disability or circumstance, then the state must step forward and address their fundamental needs. The basic needs of the populace which a government must meet are indicated in the following Tradition:

According to 'Uthmān (may Allah be pleased with him), Allah's Messenger (Allah bless him and give him peace) said:

لَيْسَ لِابْنِ آدَمَ حَقٌّ فِيْ سِوَى هَذِهِ الْخِصَالِ: بَيْتٌ يَسْكُنُهُ، وَثَوْبٌ يُوَارِي عَوْرَتَهُ، وَجِلْفُ الْخُبْزِ وَالْمَاءِ.

> There is no right for the son of Adam in other than these things: a house which he lives in, a garment which covers his nakedness, and *jilf* (a piece of bread) and water."[60]

An Islamic state is supposed to settle the debt of the deceased if his or her heirs are not able to do so. When the Messenger (Allah bless him and give him peace) was granted victories, he proclaimed the state policy:

أَنَا أَوْلَى بِالْمُؤْمِنِيْنَ مِنْ أَنْفُسِهِمْ، فَمَنْ تُوُفِّيَ مِنَ الْمُؤْمِنِيْنَ فَتَرَكَ دَيْنًا، فَعَلَيَّ قَضَاؤُهُ، وَمَنْ تَرَكَ مَالاً فَلِوَرَثَتِهِ.

> I have more right to be the protector of the believers than themselves. If any believer dies leaving a debt, I will pay it. If anyone leaves property, it goes to his heirs.[61]

Additionally, the government restricts all economy-related activities that run contrary to Islamic teachings, for instance, gambling, smuggling, bribery, extortion, illegal trade, black markets, money laundering and all financial crimes.

The following incidence, which transpired during the epoch of the second caliph of Islam, spells out what a Muslim state is supposed to do if its citizens are unable to meet their basics of life. Many people and animals died in 18 AH because of a long drought.[62] This famine reduced the earth to ashes. Because of the severity of weather, the period was named the Year of Drought. 'Umar (May Allah be well pleased with him), the caliph, did his best to help the affected population with camels, wheat and oil. Rising to his feet, 'Umar (May Allah be well pleased with him) supplicated: "Allah! Provide them (people requesting for rain) at the tops of the mountains!" Allah answered the supplication and abundant rain fell. At this, the caliph first extolled the Divine for relieving them. His next words indicate the course of action that he intended to take if rain had not fallen:

> By Allah, had Allah not given us relief, I would not have left the people of any Muslim's house with wealth without putting a like number of

impoverished people with him. Two will not perish with food that supports one person.[63]

2.1.13 *Property rights*

Allah, the Exalted, is the real owner of the heavens, the earth and the entire universe. As vicegerents of the Almighty, humans are allowed to acquire property,

لِّلرِّجَالِ نَصِيبٌ مِّمَّا اكْتَسَبُواْ وَلِلنِّسَاء نَصِيبٌ مِّمَّا اكْتَسَبْنَ

"*Men will have a share of what they earn, and women will have a share of what they earn.*"[64] However, they are not absolute owners. Rather they are His deputies on earth, so they hold capital, wealth and resources as trustees. One's right to property is approved when one fulfils the condition attached to it, which is charitable spending.

يَا أَيُّهَا الَّذِينَ آمَنُواْ أَنفِقُواْ مِمَّا رَزَقْنَاكُم مِّن قَبْلِ أَن يَأْتِيَ يَوْمٌ لاَّ بَيْعٌ فِيهِ

O believers! Spend (in the cause of Allah) out of whatever We have provided for you, before the Day comes when there will be no trading.[65]

Elsewhere Allah explicitly states that humans are merely His deputies and custodians and, doing the bidding of their Master, they ought to be generous with their resources:

آمِنُوا بِاللَّهِ وَرَسُولِهِ وَأَنفِقُوا مِمَّا جَعَلَكُم مُّسْتَخْلَفِينَ فِيهِ

Believe in Allah and His Messenger (Allah bless him and give him peace) and spend (in His cause) out of that (wealth) in which He has made you His vicegerents (and trustees).[66]

The key doctrine of Islamic economic thought is the ownership of resources; it is understood to be a trust and its disposal is a test of faith.

The Muslim Scripture tells the faithful that if they dispense wealth, they pass the test.

وَهُوَ الَّذِي جَعَلَكُمْ خَلاَئِفَ الأَرْضِ وَرَفَعَ بَعْضَكُمْ فَوْقَ بَعْضٍ دَرَجَاتٍ لِّيَبْلُوَكُمْ فِي مَا آتَاكُمْ

And He is the One Who has made you vicegerents in the earth, and exalted some of you over others in ranks, so that He may test you by means of (things) which He has bestowed upon you (as a trust).[67]

These verses indicate that wealth involves responsibilities. The recipients of material resources must strive towards philanthropy and piousness.

2.1.14 *The institution of inheritance*

So that wealth may flow from the affluent to the destitute in society, Quran provides us with a comprehensive law of inheritance. If personal possessions and property are justly distributed following an owner's demise, the circulation of wealth will help alleviate grinding poverty and promote a humanitarian-based society. The Scriptural verses on the ordinance of dividing inheritance are cited next.

لِّلرِّجَالِ نَصِيبٌ مِّمَّا تَرَكَ الْوَالِدَانِ وَالْأَقْرَبُونَ وَلِلنِّسَاءِ نَصِيبٌ مِّمَّا تَرَكَ الْوَالِدَانِ وَالْأَقْرَبُونَ مِمَّا
قَلَّ مِنْهُ أَوْ كَثُرَ نَصِيبًا مَّفْرُوضًا

Men have a share in (the assets) that their parents and nearest kin leave behind, and women (also) have a share in the inheritance of their parents and the nearest kin. Be it small or large, the share has been fixed (by Allah).[68]

يُوصِيكُمُ اللَّهُ فِي أَوْلَادِكُمْ لِلذَّكَرِ مِثْلُ حَظِّ الْأُنثَيَيْنِ فَإِن كُنَّ نِسَاءً فَوْقَ اثْنَتَيْنِ فَلَهُنَّ ثُلُثَا مَا
تَرَكَ وَإِن كَانَتْ وَاحِدَةً فَلَهَا النِّصْفُ وَلِأَبَوَيْهِ لِكُلِّ وَاحِدٍ مِّنْهُمَا السُّدُسُ مِمَّا تَرَكَ إِن كَانَ لَهُ
وَلَدٌ فَإِن لَّمْ يَكُن لَّهُ وَلَدٌ وَوَرِثَهُ أَبَوَاهُ فَلِأُمِّهِ الثُّلُثُ فَإِن كَانَ لَهُ إِخْوَةٌ فَلِأُمِّهِ السُّدُسُ

Allah commands you concerning (the inheritance of) your children: The share of a son is equal to that of two daughters; then if there are only daughters (two or) more, they are entitled to two-thirds of the inheritance; if there is only one daughter, her share will be one half; the mother and the father of the deceased will get one-sixth of the inheritance each if the deceased leaves children behind; but in case the deceased has no children and the heirs are only his mother and his father, the mother's share is one-third (and the rest is the father's); then, if he has brothers and sisters, the mother will have a sixth portion.[69]

2.1.15 *A general misconception about Islamic law of inheritance*

One may misunderstand this Quranic verse providing the law of inheritance by considering it against the principle of equality as different ratios of the share of inheritance among males and females are described in this verse. Prior to the discussion of the Islamic law of inheritance, it is necessary to understand the difference between the principle of equality and the principle of justice. We will understand the difference between these two, by giving an example from a daily life, below.

If a cake is to be distributed among four people, any one way out of two could be adopted to do so. One approach is to divide the cake into four equal portions; this option is called principle of equality. The other approach is to divide the same cake between four people according to their need and hunger; in result of this approach, one may get less and other may get more share of the cake but at the end all four people are happy and satisfied as each one got the share of the cake according to his need and hunger. This approach is called the principle of justice. Islam advocates the principle of justice while providing the law of inheritance and not the principle of equality only. It is the principle of justice which differentiates Islamic economic system from other capitalistic or socialistic economic systems.

According to the Sharia Law "rights comes along with duties", which means a person with more rights will have more obligations on him and a person with less rights will have less obligations on him. If we look at the household formation of a Muslim family, we will observe that the male member of the household is considered responsible for taking care of the financial needs of the family and the female members of the family are relieved of such burden. However, in the contemporary world, female members of any household are earning their living through jobs and businesses equally like men, but it is not made obligatory on women to fulfil the financial need of a household. They may like to support their partner in running the household financially or they decide not to do so; no religious law binds them in this area. Whereas if a male member of the family does not fulfil the responsibility of providing the basic necessities of life to his family and he is healthy and capable enough to do so as well, he is liable in the sight of Sharia Law and will be considered sinful in case of non-compliance.

In light of Muslim family structure, it becomes easy to understand why a female child gets half of what a male child gets from inheritance. Because the male member is supposed to provide house and all other necessities of living to the women who becomes his wife, whereas the women getting married and moving in her husband's house with no further financial obligations makes the male child to deserve more from the inheritance.

One may come up with an argument that in some households female member of the family is the only bread earner. How will this law accommodate such case? Answer to this assumption is that it is a universally known effect that laws are made while keeping the majority and not the exceptions. However, there are other laws in Shariah which can accommodate such exceptions in the contemporary world.

وَلَكُمْ نِصْفُ مَا تَرَكَ أَزْوَاجُكُمْ إِن لَّمْ يَكُن لَّهُنَّ وَلَدٌ فَإِن كَانَ لَهُنَّ وَلَدٌ فَلَكُمُ الرُّبُعُ مِمَّا تَرَكْنَ
مِن بَعْدِ وَصِيَّةٍ يُوصِينَ بِهَا أَوْ دَيْنٍ وَلَهُنَّ الرُّبُعُ مِمَّا تَرَكْتُمْ إِن لَّمْ يَكُن لَّكُمْ وَلَدٌ فَإِن كَانَ لَكُمْ
وَلَدٌ فَلَهُنَّ الثُّمُنُ مِمَّا تَرَكْتُم مِّن بَعْدِ وَصِيَّةٍ تُوصُونَ بِهَا أَوْ دَيْنٍ وَإِن كَانَ رَجُلٌ يُورَثُ كَلَالَةً
أَوِ امْرَأَةٌ وَلَهُ أَخٌ أَوْ أُخْتٌ فَلِكُلِّ وَاحِدٍ مِّنْهُمَا السُّدُسُ فَإِن كَانُوا أَكْثَرَ مِن ذَٰلِكَ فَهُمْ
شُرَكَاءُ فِي الثُّلُثِ

And for you, the share in the property your wives leave is one half, provided they have no children. In case they have offspring, then there is one-fourth of inheritance for you, (that too) after (the fulfilment of) the will that may have been made or after the (payment of) debt. And the share of your wives in the assets you leave is one-fourth, provided you have no children. But if you have children, then their share in your inheritance is one-eighth, after (the fulfilment of) the will made pertaining to (the inheritance) or the payment of (your) debt. In the case of a man or a woman who leaves neither parents nor children, but who has a brother or a sister (on the mother's side i.e., a uterine brother or a sister), there is a one-sixth share for each of the two. But if they are more than that, they all will be sharers in one-third.[70]

يَسْتَفْتُونَكَ قُلِ اللّٰهُ يُفْتِيكُمْ فِي الْكَلَالَةِ إِنِ امْرُؤٌ هَلَكَ لَيْسَ لَهُ وَلَدٌ وَلَهُ أُخْتٌ فَلَهَا نِصْفُ مَا تَرَكَ وَهُوَ يَرِثُهَا إِن لَّمْ يَكُن لَّهَا وَلَدٌ فَإِن كَانَتَا اثْنَتَيْنِ فَلَهُمَا الثُّلُثَانِ مِمَّا تَرَكَ وَإِن كَانُوا إِخْوَةً رِّجَالًا وَنِسَاءً فَلِلذَّكَرِ مِثْلُ حَظِّ الْأُنثَيَيْنِ

They seek edict (i.e., judgment under Islamic law) from you. Say: "Allah ordains pertaining to (the inheritance of) kalāla (the deceased leaving neither children nor parents behind): If a man dies childless but has one sister, she shall have (as her share) half (the property) that he leaves. (If, on the contrary, a sister is kalāla, then in the case of her death) the brother will be (the sole) heir (to his sister), if she has no children. Then, if (after a kalāla brother's death) two (sisters) are (the heirs), they are entitled to share two-thirds of (the property) he leaves. And if (in the case of the deceased who is kalāla) he has some brothers and sisters, male (as well as) female heirs, then the share of each male shall be as much as the (portion of) two females."[71]

One's heirs to a fortune have a legal right over it. If, however, heirs divide an inheritance in the presence of orphans and the needy, the Qur'ān bids them to bestow something on them:

وَإِذَا حَضَرَ الْقِسْمَةَ أُوْلُواْ الْقُرْبَىٰ وَالْيَتَامَىٰ وَالْمَسَاكِينُ فَارْزُقُوهُم مِّنْهُ وَقُولُواْ لَهُمْ قَوْلًا مَّعْرُوفًا

If the relatives (other than heirs) and the orphans and the indigent are present on the occasion of the division (of inheritance), give them also something out of it and say to them good and nice words.[72]

On the importance of practising the injunctions pertaining to inheritance, a Tradition is cited next.

According to Ibn 'Abbās (may Allah be pleased with him), the Prophet (Allah bless him and give him peace) said:

أَقْسِمُوا الْمَالَ بَيْنَ أَهْلِ الْفَرَائِضِ عَلَى كِتَابِ اللّٰهِ.

Divide the wealth among those who are entitled to a share of inheritance according to the Book of Allah[73]

Many people in the Muslim world tend to practically disinherit women. They should mull over the following Prophetic Tradition and the care the Messenger (Allah bless him and give him peace) gave to women. 'Amir b. Sa'd b. Abī Waqqāṣ reported that his father said:

مَرِضْتُ بِمَكَّةَ مَرَضًا فَأَشْفَيْتُ مِنْهُ عَلَى الْمَوْتِ، فَأَتَانِي النَّبِيُّ يَعُوْدُنِي، فَقُلْتُ: يَا رَسُوْلَ اللهِ، إِنَّ لِيْ مَالًا كَثِيْرًا وَلَيْسَ يَرِثُنِي إِلَّا ابْنَتِيْ، أَفَأَتَصَدَّقُ بِثُلُثَيْ مَالِيْ؟ قَالَ: لَا، قَالَ: قُلْتُ: فَالشَّطْرُ؟ قَالَ: لَا، قُلْتُ: الثُّلُثُ؟ قَالَ: الثُّلُثُ كَبِيرٌ إِنَّكَ إِنْ تَرَكْتَ وَلَدَكَ أَغْنِيَاءَ خَيْرٌ مِنْ أَنْ تَتْرُكَهُمْ عَالَةً يَتَكَفَّفُونَ النَّاسَ، وَإِنَّكَ لَنْ تُنْفِقَ نَفَقَةً إِلَّا أُجِرْتَ عَلَيْهَا حَتَّى اللُّقْمَةَ تَرْفَعُهَا إِلَى فِي امْرَأَتِكَ.

I became very ill in Mecca and thought I was going to breathe my last. The Prophet (Allah bless him and give him peace) came to visit me and I submitted: "Messenger of Allah, I have a lot of property and my only heir is one daughter. Should I will away two-thirds of my property and leave a third?" "No," the Prophet (Allah bless him and give him peace) answered. I said: "A half?" "No," the Prophet (Allah bless him and give him peace) answered. I said: "A third?" The Prophet (Allah bless him and give him peace) said: "A third is a lot. It is better to leave your heirs wealthy than to make them beg from people with their hands. Whatever you spend on maintenance is charity, even the morsel you put in your wife's mouth."[74]

2.1.16 *Justice and benevolence*

According to Imam al-Rāghib al-Aṣfahānī, '*adl* (justice) denotes that whatever is obligatory for individuals to give must be given, and whatever they have the right to take should take.

The Qur'ān emphasizes justice and fairness when dealing in trade. Heeding this Scriptural directive, the believers engaged in business must not cheat when selling a commodity. Allah says:

لَا تَظْلِمُونَ وَلَا تُظْلَمُونَ

Deal not unjustly, and you shall not be dealt with unjustly.[75]

يَا أَيُّهَا الَّذِينَ آمَنُواْ لَا تَأْكُلُواْ أَمْوَالَكُمْ بَيْنَكُمْ بِالْبَاطِلِ إِلاَّ أَن تَكُونَ تِجَارَةً عَن تَرَاضٍ مِّنكُمْ

O believers! Do not devour one another's wealth unlawfully amongst yourselves unless it is a trade by your mutual agreement.[76]

The faithful are enjoined to give people their due without diminishing their rights. The Prophet Shu'ayb (peace be upon him) commanded his people:

وَيَا قَوْمِ أَوْفُواْ الْمِكْيَالَ وَالْمِيزَانَ بِالْقِسْطِ وَلَا تَبْخَسُواْ النَّاسَ أَشْيَاءَهُمْ

And, O my people, give full measure and full weight with justice, and do not give people their things less than their due.[77]

Another Qur'ānic injunction, *iḥsān* (meaning beauty, balance, betterment, benevolence, piety and goodness) takes believers towards a higher moral plane. It points to beauty in utterance, performance and general behaviour. It requires the faithful to interact with others cordially and sincerely, with benign well-wishing and kind words. Allah commands believers to adopt a benevolent attitude towards their parents.

وَوَصَّيْنَا الْإِنسَانَ بِوَالِدَيْهِ حُسْنًا

And We have enjoined man to behave benevolently towards his parents.[78]

The following verses emphasize the importance of benevolence while dealing with others:

هَلْ جَزَاءُ الْإِحْسَانِ إِلَّا الْإِحْسَانُ○

And is the reward of good anything but good?[79]

and,

لِّلَّذِينَ أَحْسَنُواْ الْحُسْنَىٰ وَزِيَادَةٌ

For those who do pious works there is good recompense and more (added to it).[80]

The Almighty Allah loves benevolent actions and the people who internalize benevolence:

إِنَّ اللهَ لَمَعَ الْمُحْسِنِيْنَ

Verily Allah blesses the men of spiritual excellence with His companionship.[81]

إِنَّ اللهَ يُحِبُّ الْمُحْسِنِيْنَ

Certainly, Allah loves the doers of good.[82]

The Almighty Allah also says:

وَأَنفِقُواْ فِي سَبِيلِ اللهِ وَلَا تُلْقُواْ بِأَيْدِيكُمْ إِلَى التَّهْلُكَةِ وَأَحْسِنُوٓاْ إِنَّ اللهَ يُحِبُّ الْمُحْسِنِينَ

And spend in the cause of Allah and do not cast yourselves into destruction with your own hands – and adopt spiritual excellence. Verily, Allah loves the spiritually excellent.[83]

Ardent believers in Islam are those who selflessly interact with all. Abū Dharr (may Allah be pleased with him) narrated that Allah's Messenger (Allah bless him and give him peace) said:

اِتَّقِ اللهِ حَيْثُمَا كُنْتَ، وَأَتْبِعِ السَّيِّئَةَ الْحَسَنَةَ تَمْحُهَا، وَخَالِقِ النَّاسَ بِخُلُقٍ حَسَنٍ.

Fear Allah wherever you may be, follow up a bad deed with a good deed and it will efface it, and deal with people with good character.[84]

Allah enjoins justice and benevolence:

إِنَّ اللهَ يَأْمُرُ بِالْعَدْلِ وَالْإِحْسَانِ وَإِيتَاءِ ذِي الْقُرْبَى وَيَنْهَى عَنِ الْفَحْشَاءِ وَالْمُنكَرِ وَالْبَغْيِ
يَعِظُكُمْ لَعَلَّكُمْ تَذَكَّرُونَ

Indeed, Allah enjoins justice and benevolence (towards everyone), and giving away to the kindred, and forbids indecency, evil deeds, defiance and disobedience. He admonishes you so that you may remember with concern.[85]

The preceding Scriptural verse shows concern for justness and fair play in the sphere of social domain and ethical matters. In the true sense of the word, justice requires that everything takes its own proper place. Therefore, all deviation, excess, defect, extremism and violation of other people's rights run contrary to the fundamental principle of justice.

Justice is workable in normal circumstances; hence it was prescribed first.

2.2 Prohibitive aspects of sale and trade

2.2.1 Oaths

So that they may do a roaring trade, sellers should not make a habit of swearing oaths by Almighty Allah. Giving one's word excessively is as good as swindling. The Prophet (Allah bless him and give him peace) warned against swearing oaths while selling.

According to Abū Hurayra (may Allah be pleased with him), Allah's Messenger (Allah bless him and give him peace) said:

اَلْحَلِفُ مَنْفَقَةٌ لِلسِّلْعَةِ مُمْحَقَةٌ لِلرِّبْحِ.

Beware of swearing a great deal when selling, for it brings about a (ready) sale, then erases (the blessing).[86]

On another occasion the Prophet (Allah bless him and give him peace) said:

اَلْحَلِفُ مُنَفِّقَةٌ لِلسِّلْعَةِ مُمْحِقَةٌ لِلْبَرَكَةِ.

Taking oaths hastens the sale of goods but eradicates the blessings.[87]

2.2.2 Hoarding

The act of collecting and keeping large amounts of wealth secretly so that other people will go without is disobedience. Individuals who hoard resources will perish, as the following verse testifies:

الَّذِي جَمَعَ مَالًا وَعَدَّدَهُ○يَحْسَبُ أَنَّ مَالَهُ أَخْلَدَهُ○كَلَّا لَيُنبَذَنَّ فِي الْحُطَمَةِ○وَمَا أَدْرَاكَ مَا الْحُطَمَةُ○نَارُ اللَّهِ الْمُوقَدَةُ○الَّتِي تَطَّلِعُ عَلَى الْأَفْئِدَةِ○إِنَّهَا عَلَيْهِم مُّؤْصَدَةٌ○فِي عَمَدٍ مُّمَدَّدَةٍ○

(Woe to him) who accumulates wealth and keeps counting it! He thinks that his riches will keep him alive forever. By no means! He will certainly be cast into al-ḥuṭama *(the fire). And what will make you understand what* al-ḥuṭama *(the fire) is? (It) is a fire kindled by Allah. That will rise over the hearts (with its torture). Indeed, that (fire) will be closed upon them all around, in towering columns (of fierce flames and they will not find any way to escape).*[88]

In order to deter the faithful from hoarding necessary commodities for living such as food, fuel and electricity, the Messenger (Allah bless him and give him peace) said:

مَنِ احْتَكَرَ فَهُوَ خَاطِئٌ.

Whoever hoards is a sinner.[89]

مَنِ احْتَكَرَ طَعَامًا أَرْبَعِينَ لَيْلَةً، فَقَدْ بَرِئَ مِنَ اللهِ تَعَالَى، وَبَرِئَ اللهُ تَعَالَى مِنْهُ.

> If anyone withholds grain for forty nights (out of the desire for a high price), he is free from Allah's obligation and Allah will renounce him.[90]

2.2.3 *Ambiguities in a contract*

Sales that carry an element of uncertainty, deception and exploitation are unlawful. Islamic economic thought builds a just society where customers may purchase articles while putting blind faith in the integrity of vendors. This is possible only when sellers do not engage in hypocritical conduct. The Prophet (Allah bless him and give him peace) prohibited such business deals.

عَنْ أَبِي هُرَيْرَةَ قَالَ: نَهَى رَسُولُ اللَّهِ عَنْ بَيْعِ الْغَرَرِ، وَبَيْعِ الْحَصَاةِ.

> Abū Hurayra (may Allah be pleased with him) narrated: "Allah's Messenger (Allah bless him and give him peace) prohibited the *al-gharar* (a business contract which entails an element of uncertainty or hazard) sale and the *al-ḥasāt* (transaction conducted by throwing stones) sale."[91]

2.2.4 *Usury*

Charging interest, an illegal way of amassing wealth, is strictly prohibited. What the Almighty disapproves may never carry any good.

الَّذِينَ يَأْكُلُونَ الرِّبَا لاَ يَقُومُونَ إِلاَّ كَمَا يَقُومُ الَّذِي يَتَخَبَّطُهُ الشَّيْطَانُ مِنَ الْمَسِّ ذَلِكَ
بِأَنَّهُمْ قَالُواْ إِنَّمَا الْبَيْعُ مِثْلُ الرِّبَا وَأَحَلَّ اللّهُ الْبَيْعَ وَحَرَّمَ الرِّبَا

> *Those who live on usury will not be able to stand (on the Day of Judgment), but like the one whom Satan has made insane with his touch (i.e., damnation). This is because they used to say that trade (i.e., buying and selling) is similar to usury, whereas Allah has declared trade (i.e., buying and selling) lawful and usury unlawful.*[92]

يَمْحَقُ اللّهُ الْرِّبَا وَيُرْبِي الصَّدَقَاتِ

> *Allah eliminates usury (i.e., deprives usurious profits of prosperous growth) and multiplies alms gifts (i.e., increases blessings of clean wealth manifold through charitable donations).*[93]

يَا أَيُّهَا الَّذِينَ آمَنُواْ لاَ تَأْكُلُواْ الرِّبَا أَضْعَافًا مُّضَاعَفَةً وَاتَّقُواْ اللّهَ لَعَلَّكُمْ تُفْلِحُونَ

> *O believers! Do not live on usury doubled and redoubled, and keep fearing Allah so that you may prosper.*[94]

فَإِن لَّمْ تَفْعَلُوا۟ فَأْذَنُوا۟ بِحَرْبٍ مِّنَ ٱللَّهِ وَرَسُولِهِۦ

But if you do not do so, then be warned of the declaration of war from Allah and His Holy Messenger (Allah bless him and give him peace).[95]

The Messenger (Allah bless him and give him peace) also disapproved usury and illustrated its evil nature in various Traditions which are discussed in the detail in Chapter 4 under the heading of "Prohibition of *ribā* in Hadith".

2.2.5 Dealing in prohibited things

The Qur'ān forbids the consumption of prohibited things; their sale and trade is also illegal. Carrion, blood, swine, the animals over which Allah's name is not pronounced at the time of slaughtering are all prohibited, as well as the meat of animals that have been dedicated to idols. Allah says:

إِنَّمَا حَرَّمَ عَلَيْكُمُ ٱلْمَيْتَةَ وَٱلدَّمَ وَلَحْمَ ٱلْخِنزِيرِ وَمَآ أُهِلَّ بِهِۦ لِغَيْرِ ٱللَّهِ

He has made unlawful for you only the dead animals and blood and the flesh of swine and the animal over which, whilst sacrificing, the name of someone other than Allah has been invoked.[96]

If something is scripturally prohibited, the faithful are not allowed to consume it. Nor may they trade it, as is evidenced from the following narrative.

عَنْ عَبْدِ الرَّحْمَنِ بْنِ وَعْلَةَ السَّبَإِيِّ مِنْ أَهْلِ مِصْرَ، أَنَّهُ سَأَلَ عَبْدَ اللهِ بْنَ عَبَّاسٍ عَمَّا يُعْصَرُ مِنَ الْعِنَبِ. فَقَالَ ابْنُ عَبَّاسٍ: إِنَّ رَجُلًا أَهْدَى لِرَسُوْلِ اللهِ رَاوِيَةَ خَمْرٍ، فَقَالَ لَهُ رَسُوْلُ اللهِ: هَلْ عَلِمْتَ أَنَّ اللهَ قَدْ حَرَّمَهَا؟ قَالَ: لَا، فَسَارَّ إِنْسَانًا، فَقَالَ لَهُ رَسُوْلُ اللهِ: بِمَ سَارَرْتَهُ؟ فَقَالَ: أَمَرْتُهُ بِبَيْعِهَا، فَقَالَ: إِنَّ الَّذِي حَرَّمَ شُرْبَهَا حَرَّمَ بَيْعَهَا، قَالَ: فَفَتَحَ الْمَزَادَةَ حَتَّى ذَهَبَ مَا فِيْهَا.

'Abd al-Raḥmān b. Wa'la al-Sabā'ī, who was from Egypt, reported that he asked 'Abd Allah b. 'Abbās (may Allah be well pleased with him) about what is extracted from grapes. Ibn 'Abbās (may Allah be well pleased with him) said that a man gave Allah's Messenger (Allah bless him and give him peace) a small water-skin full of wine, and Allah's Messenger (Allah bless him and give him peace) asked him: "Do you know that the Almighty Allah, has forbidden it?" He said: "No," then he whispered to another man. Allah's Messenger (Allah bless him and give him peace) said: "What have you whispered about?" He said: "I told him to sell it." The Messenger (peace be upon him) said: "The One Who has forbidden drinking it has also forbidden selling it." So he opened the skin until its contents drained away.[97]

2.2.6 *Determination of price*

Islamic economic theory holds that the market is to be free and to respond to the natural laws of supply and demand. In other words, prices are controlled by factors beyond human control. As a general principle, individuals are not to interfere in the free market by fixing prices and setting profit margins. Nor can prices be fixed by government fiat. To dispense justice in society, Islamic law introduced ethics to both sellers and purchasers. However, if the need arises, the state may interfere.

Islam is in favour of free markets where buyers and sellers may make a deal and agree on any price without taking undue advantage of any party's ignorance. This doctrine is illustrated by the following Hadith narrative.

عَنْ عُرْوَةَ يَعْنِي ابْنَ أَبِي الْجَعْدِ الْبَارِقِيَّ، قَالَ: أَعْطَاهُ النَّبِيُّ a دِينَارًا يَشْتَرِيْ بِهِ أُضْحِيَّةً أَوْ
شَاةً، فَاشْتَرَى شَاتَيْنِ، فَبَاعَ إِحْدَاهُمَا بِدِيْنَارٍ فَأَتَاهُ بِشَاةٍ وَدِيْنَارٍ، فَدَعَا لَهُ
بِالْبَرَكَةِ فِيْ بَيْعِهِ، كَانَ لَوِ اشْتَرَى تُرَاباً لَرَبِحَ فِيْهِ.

'Urwa – Ibn al-Ja'd al-Bāriqī (may Allah be pleased with him) – narrated that the Prophet (Allah bless him and give him peace) gave him a *dinar* to buy a sacrificial animal, or a sheep for him. So he bought two sheep and sold one for a dinar, and he came back with a sheep and a dinar. He (the Prophet) prayed for blessing for him in his business dealings, and (after that) if he had bought dust he would have made a profit.[98]

However, if purchasers realise later on that they have been charged exorbitantly, they are entitled to nullify the contract within a reasonable period of time and take back their money. In such an event, the seller will be bound to cooperate.

Islam is a religion of justice. It does not limit profits, nor does it approve of exploitation in any way. The Prophet (Allah bless him and give him peace) expressed condemnation of artificially inflating prices.

According to Ma'qal b. Yasār (may Allah be well pleased with him), a Companion of the Prophet (Allah bless him and give him peace).

The Umayyad governor, 'Ubayd Allāh b. Ziyād, came to visit him when he was bedridden due to an illness. After inquiring after him, the visitor said if he knew he had wrongfully shed blood. Ma'qal b. Yasār answered in the negative. Then 'Ubayd Allāh b. Ziyād said if he knew of any instance in which he had interfered with the prices of the Muslims' goods. Again Ma'qal replied that he did not know. Then Ma'qal asked the people to help him sit up. The people complied. Then he said, "Listen, 'Ubayd Allāh, and I will tell you something which I heard from Allah's Messenger (Allah bless him and give him peace). I heard Allah's Messenger (Allah bless him and give him peace) say, 'Whoever interferes with the prices of the Muslims' goods in order to raise them deserves that Allah should make him sit in the Fire on the Day of Resurrection." When asked if he had heard this from Allah's Messenger (Allah bless him and give him peace), the ailing Companion replied, "Yes, more than once or twice."[99]

Indeed, in general circumstances people may store commodities for future use. Some store wheat or rice for a year, for example, and this action is not in contravention of Sharia. However, on the basis of previously mentioned Prophetic Traditions on hoarding, scholars have deduced that hoarding is unlawful under two conditions. First, hoarding is injurious to the people of a country. Second, the hoarder forces price up in order to make a healthy profit.[100]

The Islamic rationale for not fixing prices or profit margins for traders is logical and this doctrine is practised intentionally. If prices rise in the market due to the shortage of certain commodities, it will be in accordance with the law of supply and demand. To force a shopkeeper to sell articles at a low fixed rate would be injustice. The conduct of the Messenger (Allah bless him and give him peace) in the following Tradition reinforces this point.

According to Anas b. Mālik (may Allah be pleased with him):

غَلَا السِّعْرُ بِالْمَدِيْنَةِ عَلَى عَهْدِ رَسُوْلِ اللهِ ، فَقَالَ النَّاسُ: يَا رَسُوْلَ اللهِ، غَلَا السِّعْرُ فَسَعِّرْ لَنَا، فَقَالَ: إِنَّ اللهَ هُوَ الْمُسَعِّرُ الْقَابِضُ الْبَاسِطُ الرَّازِقُ، إِنِّيْ لَأَرْجُوْ أَنْ أَلْقَى رَبِّيْ وَلَيْسَ أَحَدٌ يَطْلُبُنِيْ بِمَظْلَمَةٍ فِيْ دَمٍ وَلَا مَالٍ.

> When prices rose during the time of Allah's Messenger (Allah bless him and give him peace) in Medina, the people said: "Messenger of Allah, prices have risen, so fix the prices for us." He said: "Indeed, Allah is the One who fixes prices, who withholds, gives lavishly and provides, (and) I hope that when I meet my Lord none will have any claim on me for an injustice regarding blood or property."[101]

The Islamic Fiqh Council of the Organization of Islamic Countries, OIC, in its fifth session, gave the following useful findings on fixing the prices of commodities and setting profit margins:

1 There is no restriction on the percentage of profit a trader may make in his or her transactions. It is generally left to the merchants themselves, the business environment, and the nature of the merchant and of the goods. Regard should be given, however, to the ethics recommended by the Sharia, such as moderation, contention, leniency and indulgence.
2 *Haria* texts have spelt out the necessity to keep transactions free of illicit acts like fraud, cheating, deceit, forgery, concealment of actual benefits and monopoly, which are detrimental to society and individuals.
3 Governments should not be involved in fixing prices except when obvious problems are noticed within the market and the price, due to artificial

factors. In this case, governments should intervene by applying adequate means to mitigate these factors, the causes of defects, excessive price increases and fraud.

An important key feature of Islamic economic thought and the Islamic economic system is freedom for businesspeople and natural competition in the marketplace. Though the interference of the state in the economic affairs is not encouraged, certain circumstances may require it. If artificial forces, like hoarding or manipulation of prices by opportunists, get in the way of the free market, then the obvious solution lies in controlling prices and profit ratio. Public interest demands that the masses should not be left at the mercy of exploitative forces.

2.2.7 *Miserliness*

The Almighty Allah does not love people of means who refrain from sharing their resources with the financially distressed and the needy. If anyone is afflicted with niggardliness and selfishness, they are the bane of their own life, inflict penury on their family and do not offer hospitality to their guests.

إِنَّ اللهَ لَا يُحِبُّ مَن كَانَ مُخْتَالًا فَخُورًا○الَّذِينَ يَبْخَلُونَ وَيَأْمُرُونَ النَّاسَ بِالْبُخْلِ
وَيَكْتُمُونَ مَا آتَاهُمُ اللهُ مِن فَضْلِهِ وَأَعْتَدْنَا لِلْكَافِرِينَ عَذَابًا مُّهِينًا○

Surely, Allah does not like the one who is arrogant (i.e., self-conceited) and boastful (i.e., egoist) those who are miserly and bid others (also) to be miserly and hide that (blessing) which Allah has granted them of His bounty. And We have prepared a disgraceful torment for the disbelievers.[102]

Blessed souls are endowed with generosity and do not possess avarice, as Allah Almighty states:

وَمَن يُوقَ شُحَّ نَفْسِهِ فَأُوْلَئِكَ هُمُ الْمُفْلِحُونَ○

And he who is saved from the miserliness of his (ill-commanding) self, it is they who are successful and victorious.[103]

The generous tread the road to the Garden of Paradise, whereas the stingy turn their faces in the direction of the fire of Hell. Abū Hurayra (may Allah be pleased with him) reported that the Prophet (Allah bless him and give him peace) said:

اَلسَّخِيُّ: قَرِيْبٌ مِنَ اللّٰهِ، قَرِيْبٌ مِنَ الْجَنَّةِ، قَرِيْبٌ مِنَ النَّاسِ، بَعِيْدٌ مِنَ النَّارِ. وَالْبَخِيْلُ: بَعِيْدٌ
مِنَ اللّٰهِ، بَعِيْدٌ مِنَ الْجَنَّةِ، بَعِيْدٌ مِنَ النَّاسِ، قَرِيْبٌ مِنَ النَّارِ. وَلَجَاهِلٌ
سَخِيٌّ أَحَبُّ إِلَى اللّٰهِ عَزَّ وَجَلَّ مِنْ عَالِمٍ بَخِيْلٍ.

> The generous person is close to Allah, close to Paradise, close to the people and far from the Fire. The miserly person is far from Allah, far from Paradise, far from the people and close to the Fire. The ignorant generous person is more beloved to Allah than the worshipping stingy person.[104]

Traders must inculcate the habit of generosity which is dear to the Divine. Should they take the opposite path, then it is little wonder if they wreck their lives. The Messenger (Allah bless him and give him peace) cautioned the followers of Islam against the habit of stinginess.

وَاتَّقُوا الشُّحَّ، فَإِنَّ الشُّحَّ أَهْلَكَ مَنْ كَانَ قَبْلَكُمْ، حَمَلَهُمْ عَلَى أَنْ سَفَكُوْا دِمَاءَهُمْ وَاسْتَحَلُّوْا مَحَارِمَهُمْ.

> Beware of stinginess, for stinginess destroyed those who came before you and caused them to shed their blood and regard as permissible what had been forbidden to them.[105]

One of the portents of the Final Hour is stinginess, as the Messenger (Allah bless him and give him peace) said that time would seem to get shorter, knowledge would diminish and miserliness would surface.[106]

Notes

1 Narrated by al-Bukhārī in *al-Ṣaḥīḥ*: *al-Buyū'* [Sales], Ch.: Shouting in the marketplace is disliked, 2:747 §2018.
2 Quran, 17:12.
3 Ibid., 62:10.
4 Ibid., 53:39.
5 Narrated by al-Bukhārī in *al-Ṣaḥīḥ*: *al-Buyū'* [Sales], Ch.: A man's earning and his working with his own hands, 2:730 §1966; al-Ṭabarānī in *al-Mu'jam al-Kabīr*, 20:267 §631; and al-Bayhaqī in *al-Sunan al-Kubrā*, 6:127 §11471.
6 Narrated by al-Bukhārī in *al-Ṣaḥīḥ*: *al-Buyū'* [Sales], Ch.: A man's earning and his working with his own hands, 2:730 §1965.
7 Narrated by al-Ṭabarānī in *al-Mu'jam al-Kabīr*, 10:74 §9993.
8 Narrated by al-Daylamī in *al-Firdaws bi-Ma'thūr al-Khiṭāb*, 2:180 §2910; al-Mundhirī in *al-Targhībwa al-Tarhīb*, 1:315 §1161; and al-Haythamī in *Majma' al-Zawā'id*, 4:61 §6213.
9 Narrated by al-Ṭabarānī in *al-Mu'jam al-Awsaṭ*, 7:289 §7520; and al-Haythamī in *Majma' al-Zawā'id*, 4:63 §6238.
10 Narrated by al-Kittānī in *al-Tartīb al-idāriyya*, 2:23.
11 Narrated by al-Bukhārī in *al-Ṣaḥīḥ*: *al-Buyū'* [Sales], Ch.: A man's earning and his working with his own hands, 2:730 §1968.
12 Ibid., 2:730 §1969.
13 Narrated by Imam Muslim in *al-Ṣaḥīḥ*: *al-Zakāt* [The Alms-due], Ch.: The one for whom it is permissible to ask for help, 2:720 §1041.
14 Ibid., 2:722 §1044; and Ibn 'Abd al-Barr in *al-Tamhīd*, 5:100–101.
15 Narrated by al-Bayhaqī in *al-Sunan al-kubrā*, 6:128 §11695; al-Quḍā'ī in *Musnad al-Shihāb*, 1:104 §121; al-Daylamī in *al-Firdaws bi-Ma'thūr al-Khiṭāb*, 2:441 §3918; and Abū Nu'aym in *ḥilya al-Awliyā'*, 7:126.

16 Narrated by Ibn Mājah in *al-Sunan*: *al-Tijārāt* [Trade], Ch.: Moderation in seeking to earn a living, 2:725 §2144; Ibn al-Jārūd in *al-Muntaqā*, 1:144 §556; and al-Qaysarānī in *Tadhkirat al-ḥuffāẓ*, 3:1083.
17 Narrated by Ibn Mājah in *al-Sunan*: *al-Tijārāt* [Trade], Ch.: Moderation in seeking to earn a living, 2:725 §2143; and al-Kinānī in *Miṣbāḥ al-Zujāja*, 4:169 §1395.
18 Qur'ān 16:114.
19 Al-Rāzī, *al-Tafsīr al-Kabīr*, 12:61.
20 Qur'ān 65:2–3.
21 Ibid., 2:275.
22 Ibid., 17:66.
23 Ibid., 62:10.
24 Narrated by Imam Muslim in *al-Ṣaḥīḥ*: *al-Ashriba* [Beverages], Ch.: The virtue of sharing a small amount of food, and the food of two is sufficient or three, and so on, 3:1630 §2059.
25 Narrated by Imam Muslim in *al-Ṣaḥīḥ*: *al-Luqaṭa* [Stray Thing Found by Anyone], Ch.: It is meritorious to spend the surplus wealth, 3:1354 §1728; Abū Dāwūd in *al-Sunan*: *al-Zakāt* [The Alms-Due], Ch.: The rights relating to property, 2:125 §1663.
26 Qur'ān 5:88.
27 Ibid., 2:168.
28 Ibid., 7:157.
29 Ibid., 5:3.
30 Narrated by Abū Dāwūd in *al-Sunan*, *al-Qaḍā'* [Judgements], Ch.: Regarding bribery being disliked, 3:300 §3580; Ibn al-Ja'd in *al-Musnad*, 1:406 §2767; and al-Qazwīnī in *al-Tadwīn*, 2:496.
31 Narrated by Abū Dāwūd in *al-Sunan*, *al-Qaḍā'* [Judgements], Ch.: Regarding gifts for workers, 3:300 §3581.
32 Qur'ān 25:67.
33 Narrated by al-Ṭabarānī in *al-Mu'jam al-Awsaṭ*, 7:25 §6744; and al-Bayhaqī in *Shu'ab al-Īmān*, 5:254 §6567.
34 Narrated by al-Ṭabarānī in *al-Mu'jam al-Kabīr*, 10:108 §10118; and al-Haythamī in *Majma' al-Zawā'id*, 10:252.
35 Narrated by al-Tirmidhī in *al-Sunan*: *al-Jumu'a* [The Friday Congregational Prayer], Ch.: (8), 5:558 §3560.
36 Narrated by Ibn Mājah in *al-Sunan*: *al-Libās* [Clothing], Ch.: What a man should say when he puts on a new garment, 2:1178 §3558.
37 Narrated by Ibn Mājah in *al-Sunan*: *al-Ruhun*[Pawning], Ch.: Wages of workers, 2:817 §2443; and al-Bayhaqī in *al-Sunan al-kubrā*, 6:120 §11434.
38 Al-Manāwī, *al-Taysīr bi-sharḥ al-Jāmi' al-ṣaghīr*, 1:171.
39 Narrated by al-Bukhārī in *al-Ṣaḥīḥ*: *al-Istiqrāḍwaadā' al-duyūn* [Asking for Loans and Paying Debts], Ch.: Any delay in payment on the part of a rich person is injustice, 2:845 §2270; al-Tirmidhī in *al-Sunan*: *al-Buyū'* [Sales], Ch.: What has been related about the rich person's procrastination in paying debt is oppression, 3:600 §1308; and Ibn Ḥajar al-'Asqalānī in *al-DirāyafīTakhrījAḥādīth al-Hidāya*, 2:164 §812.
40 Narrated by al-Bukhārī in *al-Ṣaḥīḥ*: *al-Ijāra* [Hiring], Ch.: The sin of someone who withholds the wages of an employee, 2:792 §2150; Ibn Mājah in *al-Sunan*: *al-Ruhun*[Pawning], Ch.: Wages of workers, 2:816 §2442; and al-Kāsānī in *Badā'i' al-ṣanā'i'*, 4:174.
41 Qur'ān: 5:1.
42 Ibid., 2:177.
43 Ibid., 59:7.
44 Ibid., 25:67.
45 Ibid., 2:254.
46 Ibid., 76:8.
47 Ibid., 2:177.

48 Narrated by al-Bukhārī in *al-Ṣaḥīḥ*: *al-Adab* [Proper conduct], Ch.: Every right thing is charity, 5:2241 §5676; and Abū al-Maḥāsin in *Mu'taṣar al-Mukhtaṣar*, 2:23.
49 Narrated by al-Bukhārī in *al-Ṣaḥīḥ*: *al-Jamā'awa al-Imāma* [The Ritual Prayer Congregation and Prayer-Leadership], Ch.: Someone who sits in the mosque waiting for the prayer and the excellence of mosques, 1:234 §629; and Ibn al-Mubārak in *Kitāb al-Zuhd*, 1:473 §1342.
50 Narrated by Imam Muslim in *al-Ṣaḥīḥ*: *al-Zakāt* [The Alms-due], Ch.: Encouragement to spend and glad tidings of compensation for the one who spends on good deeds, 2:691 §993; and al-Bukhārī in *al-Ṣaḥīḥ*: *al-Tafsīr*[Interpretation of the Qur'ān], Ch.: His words, "When His Throne was on the water," 4:1724 §4407.
51 Narrated by al-Bukhārī in *al-Ṣaḥīḥ*: *al-Ṣawm* [Fasting], Ch.: *Al-Rayyān* (a gate in the Garden) is for the fasters, 2:671 §1798.
52 Narrated by al-Bukhārī in *al-Ṣaḥīḥ*: *al-Zakāt* [The Alms-due], Ch.: The words of Allah Almighty*: "So he who gives away (his wealth in the way of Allah) and commits himself to piousness, and affirms the good (the Dīn [Religion] of truth and life after death through charity and God wariness)* (92:5–6)," 2:522 §1374; Muslim in *al-Ṣaḥīḥ*: *al-Zakāt* [The Alms-Due], Ch.: Concerning someone who speds and someone who withholds, 2:700 §1010; and al-Nasā'ī in *al-Sunan al-Kubrā*, 5:375 §9178.
53 Qur'ān 3:180.
54 Ibid., 4:36–37.
55 Ibid., 51:19.
56 Ibid., 70:24–25.
57 Narrated by al-Tirmidhī in *al-Sunan*: *al-Zakāt* [The Alms-due], Ch.: What has come to us about there is a duty on wealth besides from the Alms-due, 3:48 §660; al-Dāraquṭnī in *al-Sunan*, 2:125; and Sā'īd b. Manṣūr in *al-Sunan*, 5:100 §926.
58 Narrated by al-Bukhārī in *al-Ṣaḥīḥ*: Bk: *al-Kafāla* [Sureties], Ch.: Debts, 2:805 §2176; Muslim in *al-Ṣaḥīḥ*: *al-Farā'iḍ* [Shares of Inheritance], Ch.: If someone leaves some wealth, let it be inherited by his relatives, 3:1237 §1619; and al-Bayhaqī in *al-Sunan al-Kubrā*, 7:53 §13123.
59 Narrated by Sā'īd b. Manṣūr in *al-Sunan*, 5:109 §3578; al-Haythamī in *Majma' al-zawā'id*, 3:62 §4324; and Ibn ḥazm in *al-Muḥallā*, 6:158.
60 Narrated by al-Tirmidhī in *al-Sunan*: *al-Zuhd* [Abstinence], Ch.: (30) 4:571 §2341; al-Ḥākim in *al-Mustadrak*, 4:347 §7867; and al-Maqdisī in *al-Aḥādīthal-Mukhtāra*, 1:455 §329.
61 Narrated by al-Bukhārī in *al-Ṣaḥīḥ*: Bk: *al-Kafāla* [Sureties], Ch.: Debts, 2:805 §2176; Muslim in *al-Ṣaḥīḥ*: *al-Farā'iḍ* [Shares of Inheritance], Ch.: If someone leaves some wealth, let it be inherited by his relatives, 3:1237 §1619; Aḥmad b. Ḥanbal in *al-Musnad*, 2:453 §9847; and al-Bayhaqī in *al-Sunan al-Kubrā*, 7:53 §13123.
62 Cited by al-Ṭabarī in *Tārīkh al-Umamwa al-Mulūk*, 2:507.
63 Narrated by al-Bukhārī in *al-Adab al-mufrad*, 198 §562.
64 Qur'ān 4:32.
65 Ibid., 2:254.
66 Ibid., 57:7.
67 Ibid., 6:165.
68 Ibid., 4:7.
69 Ibid., 4:11.
70 Ibid., 4:12.
71 Ibid., 4:176.
72 Ibid., 4:8.
73 Narrated by Imam Muslim in *al-Ṣaḥīḥ*: *al-Farā'iḍ* [Shares of Inheritance], Ch.: Give the shares of inheritance to those who are entitled to them, and whatever is left goes to the closest male relative, 3:1234 §1615; and 'Abd al-Razzāq in *al-Muṣannaf*, 10:249 §19004.

74 Narrated by al-Bukhārī in *al-Ṣaḥīḥ*: *a-Farāi'ḍ* [Shares of Inheritance], Ch.: Inheritance by daughters, 6:2476 §6352.
75 Qur'ān 2:279.
76 Ibid., 4:29.
77 Ibid., 11:85.
78 Ibid., 29:8.
79 Ibid., 55:60.
80 Ibid., 10:26.
81 Ibid., 29:69.
82 Ibid., 2:195.
83 Ibid., 2:195.
84 Narrated by al-Tirmidhī in *al-Sunan*: *al-Birr wa al-ṣila*[Piety and Filial Duty], Ch.: What has come to us about social interaction, 4:355 §1987; al-Dārimī in *al-Sunan*, 2:415 §2791; Ibn Abī Shayba in *al-Muṣannaf*, 5:211 §25324; and al-Bazzār in *al-Musnad*, 9:416 §4022.
85 Qur'ān 16:90.
86 Narrated by Imam Muslim in *al-Ṣaḥīḥ*: *al-Musāqāt* [Sharecropping], Ch.: The prohibition of swearing oaths when selling, 3:1228 §1607; and al-Nasā'ī in *al-Sunan*: *al-Buyū'* [Sales], Ch.: The one who sells his product by means of false oaths, 7:246 §4460.
87 Narrated by al-Bukhārī in *al-Ṣaḥīḥ*: *al-Buyū'* [Sales], Ch.: What is disliked regarding swearing when buying and selling, 2:735 §1981; and Muslim in *al-Ṣaḥīḥ*: *al-Buyū'* [Sales], Ch.: The prohibition of swearing oaths when buying and selling, 3:1228 §1606.
88 Qur'ān 104:2–9.
89 Narrated by Imam Muslim in *al-Ṣaḥīḥ*: *al-Musāqāt* [Sharecropping], Ch.: The prohibition of hoarding staple foods, 3:1227 §1605; and al-Bayhaqī in *al-Sunan al-Kubrā*, 6:29 §10930.
90 Narrated by Aḥmad b. Ḥanbal in *al-Musnad*, 2:33 §4880.
91 Narrated by al-Tirmidhī in *al-Sunan*: *al-Buyū'* [Sales], Ch.: What has been related about sales of *al-gharar* (a sale involving uncertainty or deceit) are disliked, 3:532 §1230.
92 Qurān 2:275.
93 Ibid., 2:276.
94 Ibid., 3:130.
95 Ibid., 2:279.
96 Qur'ān 2:173.
97 Narrated by Imam Muslim in *al-Ṣaḥīḥ*: *al-Musāqāt* [Sharecropping], Ch.: The prohibition of selling wine, 3:1206 §1579.
98 Narrated by Abū Dāwūd in *al-Sunan*: *al-Buyū'* [Sales], Ch.: Regarding an agent doing something other than what he was instructed to do, 3:256 §3384; and al-Zayla'ī in *Naṣb al-Rāya*, 4:90.
99 Narrated by Aḥmad b. Ḥanbal in *al-Musnad*, 5:27 §20328.
100 Yusuf Al Qardawi, The Lawful and Prohibited in Islam, www.islamicstudies.info/literature/*halal*-ḥarām.htm
101 Narrated by Ibn Mājah in *al-Sunan*: *al-Tijārāt* [Trade], Ch.: Whoever does not like to fix prices, 2:741 §2200.
102 Qur'ān 4:36–37.
103 Ibid., 59:9.
104 Narrated by al-Tirmidhī in *al-Sunan*: *Kitāb al-birr wa al-ṣila*[The Book of Piety and Filial Duty], Ch.: What has been related about generosity, 4:342 §1961.
105 Muslim in *al-Ṣaḥīḥ*: *al-Birr wa al-Ṣilawa al-Ādāb* [Piety, Affinity and Good Manners], Ch.: The prohibition of oppression, 4:1996 §2578; and al-Bayhaqī in *al-Sunan al-Kubrā*, 10:134 §20237.

106 Narrated by al-Bukhārī in *al-Ṣaḥīḥ*: *al-Fitan* [Tribulations], Ch.: The emergence of tribulations, 6:2590 §6652; and Muslim in *al-Ṣaḥīḥ*: Bk: *al-Fitanwaashrāṭ al-sā'a* [Tribulations and the Portents of the Final Hour], Ch.: When two Muslims confront each other with their swords, 4:2215.

Bibliography

The Holy Qur'ān

'Abd al-Razzāq, Abū Bakr b. Hammām b. Nāfi' al-Ṣan'ānī (126–211/744–826). *Al-Muṣannaf*. Beirut, Lebanon: al-Maktab al-Islāmī, 1403AH.

Abū al-Mahāsin, Yūsuf b. Mūsā al-Ḥanafī. *al-Mu'taṣarmin al-MukhtasarminMashkal al-āthār*. Beirut, Lebanon: 'ālim al-Kutub, 1418/1998.

Abū Dāwūd, Sulaymān b. Ash'ath b. Isḥāq b. Bashīr al-Sijistānī (202–275/817–889). *Al-Sunan*. Beirut, Lebanon: Dār al-Fikr, 1414/1994.

Abū Nu'aym, Aḥmad b. 'Abd Allāh b. Aḥmad b. Isḥāq b. Mūsā b. Mihrān al-Aṣbahānī (336–430/948–1038). *Ḥilya al-Awliyā'wa Ṭabaqāt al-Aṣfiyā'*. Beirut, Lebanon: Dār al-Kitāb al-'Arabī, 1400/1980.

Al Qardawi, Yusuf, *The Lawful and Prohibited in Islam*, www.islamicstudies.info/literature/halal-ḥarām.htm

'Asqalānī, Ibn Ḥajar Aḥmad b. 'Alī al-. *Al-Dirāyafītakhrījaḥādīth al-Hidāya*. Beirut, Lebanon: Dār al-Ma'rifa, n.d.

Bayhaqī, Aḥmad b. al-Ḥusayn al-. *Al-Sunan al-kubrā*. Mecca, Saudi Arabia: Maktaba Dār al-Bāz, 1994.

———. *Shu'ab al-Īmān*. Beirut, Lebanon: Dar al-Kotob al-Ilmiyah, 1990.

Bazzār, Aḥmad b. 'Amr al-. *Al-Musnad* (*al-Baḥr al-zakhār*). Beirut, Lebanon: Mu'assasa'Ulūm al-Qur'ān, 1409AH.

Bukhārī, Abū'Abd Allāh Muhammad b. Ismā'īl b. Ibrahīm b. Mughīra al-. (194–256/810–870). *Al-ṢaḥĪḥ*. Beirut, Lebanon, Damascus, Syria: Dār al-Qalam, 1401/1981.

Dāraquṭnī, 'Alī b. 'Umar al-. *Al-Sunan*. Beirut, Lebanon: Dār al-Ma'rifa, 1966.

Dārimī, 'Abd Allāh al-. *Al-Sunan*. Beirut, Lebanon: Dār al-Kitāb al-'Arabī, 1407.

Daylamī, Abū Shujā 'Shīrawayh al-. *Al-Firdaws bi ma'thūr al-khiṭāb*. Mecca, Saudi Arabia: Dar al-Kotob al-Ilmiyah, 1986.

Ḥanbal, Aḥmad b. *Al-Musnad*. Beirut, Lebanon: Dar al-Kotob al-Ilmiyah, 1986.

Haythamī, Nūr al-Dīn Abū al-Ḥasan'Alī al-. *Majma' al-zawā'idwamanba' al-fawā'id*. Cairo: Dār al-Rayān li al-Turāth, 1987.

Ibn Abī Shayba, 'Abd Allāh b. Muhammad. *Al-Muṣannaf*. Riyadh: Maktaba al-Rushd, 1409AH.

Ibn al-Ja'd, Abū al-Ḥasan'Alī b. Ja'd b. 'Ubayd Hāshimī (133–230/750–845). *Al-Musnad*. Beirut, Lebanon: Mu'assisa Nādir, 1410/1990.

Ibn al-Jārūd, Abū Muhammad 'Abd Allāh b. 'Alī (d. 307/919). *Al-Muntaqā min al-Sunan al-Musnadā*. Beirut, Lebanon: Mu'assisa al-Kitāb al-Thaqāfiyya, 1418/1988.

Ibn al-Mubārak, Abū 'Abd al-RaḥMān 'Abd Allāh b. WāḍiḤ al-Marwazī (118–181/736–798). *Kitābal-Zuhd*. Beirut, Lebanon: Dār al-Kutub al-'Ilmiyya, 1411/1991.

Ibn al-Qaysarānī, Abū al-Faḍl Muhammad b. Ṭāhir b. 'Alī b. AḥMad al-Maqdasī (448–507/1056–1113). *Tadhkira al-ḥuffāẓ*. Riyadh, Saudi Arabia: Dār al-Sami'ī, 1415AH.

Ibn Ḥazm, 'AlīAḥmad b. Sa'īd. *Al-Muḥallā*. Beirut, Lebanon: Dār al-āfāq al-Jadīda, n.d.

Ibn Mājah, Abū 'Abd Allāh Muhammad b. Yazīd al-Qazwīnī (209–273/824–887). *Al-Sunan*. Beirut, Lebanon: Dār al-Kutub al-'Ilmiyya, 1419/1998.

Kāsānī, 'Alā' al-Dīn al-. *Badā'i'al-sanā'i'*. Beirut, Lebanon: Dār al-Kitāb al-'Arabī, 1982.

Kinānī, Aḥmad b. Abī Bakr b. Ismā'īl al- (762–840AH). *Miṣbāḥ al-Zujāja fī Zawa'īd b. Mājah.* Beirut, Lebanon: Dār al-'Arabiyya, 1403AH.

Kittānī, Muhammad 'Abd al-ḥayy b. 'Abd al-Kabīr b. Muhammad al-Ḥasanī al-Idrīsī al- (1305–1382/1888–1962). *Al-Tartīb al-idāriyya.* Beirut, Lebanon: Dar al-Kotob al-Ilmiyah, 1422/2001.

Munāwī, 'Abd al-Ra'ūf b. Tāj al-Dīn al-. *al-Taysīr bi-sharḥ al-Jāmi' al-ṣaghīr.* Saudi Arabia, Riyadh: Maktaba al-Imām al-Shāfi'ī, 1408/1988 AD.

Mundhirī, 'Abd al-'Aẓīm al-. *Al-Targhībwa al-tarhīb.* Beirut, Lebanon: Dar al-Kotob al-Ilmiyah, 1417AH.

Muslim, Ibn al-*Ḥajjāj* Abū al-Ḥasan al-Qushayrī al-Naysābūrī (206–261/821–875). *Al-Mu'jam al-kabīr.* Mosul: Maktaba al-'Ulūmwa al-ḥikam, 1983.

Nasā'ī, Aḥmad b. Shu'ayb Abū 'Abd al-Raḥmān al- (215–303/830–915). *al-Sunan.* Beirut, Lebanon: Dār al-Kutub al-'Ilmiyya, 1416/1995.

———. *al-Sunan al-Kubrā.* Beirut, Lebanon: Dār al-Kutub al-'Ilmiyya, 1411/1991.

———. *'Amal al-Yawmwa al-Layla.* Beirut, Lebanon: Mu'assisa al-Risāla, 1407/1987.

Qazwīnī, 'Abd al-Karīm b. Muhammad Rāfi'ī al-. *Al-Tadwīn fī Akhbār Qazwīn.* Beirut, Lebanon: Dār al-Kutub al-'Ilmiyya, 1987.

Qudā'ī, Abū 'Abd Allāh Muhammad b. Salama b. Ja'far b. 'Alī al- (d. 454/1062). *Musnad al-Shihāb.* Beirut, Lebanon: Mu'assisa al-Risāla, 1407AH.

Rāzī, Fakhr al-Dīn Muhammad b. 'Umar al-. *Al-Tafsīr al-kabīr.* Beirut, Lebanon: Dar al-Kotob al-Ilmiyah, 1421AH.

Sa'īd b. Manṣūr, Abū'Uthmān al-Khurāsānī (d. 227 AH). *Al-Sunan.* Riyadh, Saudi Arabia: Dār al-Aṣma'ī, 1414AH.

Ṭabarānī, Sulaymān b. Aḥmad al-. *Al-Mu'jam al-awsaṭ.* Cairo: Dār al-Ḥaramayn, 1415AH.

———. *Al-Mu'jam al-kabīr.* Mosul: Maktaba al-'Ulūmwa al-ḥikam, 1983.

Ṭabarī, Abū Ja'far Muhammad b. Jarīr al-. *Ṭārīkh al-umamwa al-mulūk.* Beirut, Lebanon: Dar al-Kotob al-Ilmiyah, 1407AH.

Tirmidhī, Abū 'Īsā Muhammad b. 'Īsā al-. *Al-Sunan.* Beirut, Lebanon: Dār Iḥyā' al-Turāth al-'Arabī, n.d.

Zayla'ī, Abū Muhammad 'Abd Allāh b. Yūsuf al-Ḥanafī al- (d. 762/1360). *Naṣb al-Rāya li-Aḥadīth al-Hidāya.* Egypt: Dār al-Ḥadīth, 1357/1938.

3 Reflections on licit and illicit transactions

Al-ḥalāl (the lawful) means permitted by Allah Almighty and with respect to which no restriction exists. *Al-ḥarām* (the unlawful) means absolutely prohibited by the Allah Almighty; anyone who engages in it is liable to incur the punishment of Allah Almighty in the Hereafter, as well as legal punishment in this world.

The followers of Islam are obligated to understand the principles of Islamic economic system, including and what is permissible and prohibited under Sharia. The caliph ʻUmar (may Allah be pleased with him) said:

لاَ يَبِيْعُ فِيْ سُوْقِنَا إِلاَّ مَنْ يَفْقَهُ.

> The only people who sell (in the marketplaces of the Muslims) must understand (the dos and don'ts of Islamic economics).[1]

The Qur'ān enjoins the faithful to consume what is lawful and prohibits them from consuming what is illicit, impure and forbidden. Allah says:

﴿يَا أَيُّهَا النَّاسُ كُلُواْ مِمَّا فِي الأَرْضِ حَلاَلاً طَيِّباً وَلاَ تَتَّبِعُواْ خُطُوَاتِ الشَّيْطَانِ إِنَّهُ لَكُمْ عَدُوٌّ مُّبِينٌ﴾

> *O mankind! Eat of that which is lawful and pure in the earth. And do not follow in the footsteps of Satan. Verily, he is your declared enemy.*[2]

The requirement to partake in the good things that Allah Almighty has provided as sustenance is reiterated at another point:

﴿وَكُلُواْ مِمَّا رَزَقَكُمُ اللّهُ حَلاَلاً طَيِّبًا وَاتَّقُواْ اللّهَ الَّذِيَ أَنتُم بِهِ مُؤْمِنُونَ﴾

> *And eat of the pure and lawful things Allah has provided for you and always fear Allah in Whom you believe.*[3]

In the following verse, one of the functions of Allah's Messenger (Allah bless him and give him peace) is explained.

﴿يَأْمُرُهُم بِالْمَعْرُوفِ وَيَنْهَاهُمْ عَنِ الْمُنكَرِ وَيُحِلُّ لَهُمُ الطَّيِّبَاتِ وَيُحَرِّمُ عَلَيْهِمُ الْخَبَآئِثَ﴾

Who enjoins on them virtues and forbids them vices, declares wholesome things lawful and impure ones unlawful for them.[4]

It is essential for the faithful to follow the directives of the Holy Prophet (Allah bless him and give him peace) and to seek what is permitted. He (Allah bless him and give him peace) said:

طَلَبُ كَسْبِ الْحَلَالِ فَرِيْضَةٌ بَعْدَ الْفَرِيْضَةِ.

Trying to gain a lawful livelihood is (the most important) obligation after obligatory worship.[5]

Similarly, the Prophet (Allah bless him and give him peace) said, on the authority of Jābir (may Allah be pleased with him), at another place:

لَا تَسْتَبْطِئُوْا الرِّزْقَ فَإِنَّهُ لَمْ يَكُنْ عَبْدٌ لِيَمُوْتَ حَتَّى يَبْلُغَهُ آخِرُ رِزْقٍ هُوَ لَهُ، فَأَجْمِلُوْا فِي الطَّلَبِ، أَخْذِ الْحَلَالِ وَتَرْكِ الْحَرَامِ.

Do not be lazy in earning your livelihood and no one will die before attaining last share of his pre-destined livelihood. Seek well your bread, accept the lawful bread and reject the unlawful one.[6]

Consuming *halal* food and beverages must be the concern of everyone, Muslim or non-Muslim, as they are nourishing and good for the body. To the consumers of lawful sustenance from the Islamic perspective is granted God wariness, generosity of heart and chastity.

Abū Bakr the veracious (may Allah be pleased with him) reported that the Holy Prophet (Allah bless him and give him peace) said:

مَنْ نَبَتَ لَحْمُهُ مِنَ السُّحْتِ، فَالنَّارُ أَوْلَى بِهِ.

Hell is more fitting for him whose flesh is nourished by what is unlawful.[7]

According to al-Nu'mān b. Bashīr (may Allah be pleased with him), he heard Allah's Messenger (Allah bless him and give him peace) say:

اَلْحَلَالُ بَيِّنٌ، وَالْحَرَامُ بَيِّنٌ، وَبَيْنَهُمَا مُشَبَّهَاتٌ لَا يَعْلَمُهَا كَثِيْرٌ مِنَ النَّاسِ، فَمَنِ اتَّقَى الْمُشَبَّهَاتِ اسْتَبْرَأَ لِدِيْنِهِ وَعِرْضِهِ، وَمَنْ وَقَعَ فِي الشُّبُهَاتِ كَرَاعٍ يَرْعَى حَوْلَ الْحِمَى يُوشِكُ

أَنْ يُوَاقِعَهُ. أَلَا، وَإِنَّ لِكُلِّ مَلِكٍ حِمًى. أَلَا، إِنَّ حِمَى اللهِ فِيْ أَرْضِهِ مَحَارِمُهُ. أَلَا، وَإِنَّ فِي الْجَسَدِ مُضْغَةً، إِذَا صَلَحَتْ صَلَحَ الْجَسَدُ كُلُّهُ، وَإِذَا فَسَدَتْ فَسَدَ الْجَسَدُ كُلُّهُ. أَلَا، وَهِيَ الْقَلْبُ.

> The lawful is clear and the unlawful is clear. But there are doubtful things between the two about which most people have no knowledge. Whoever shows caution with regard to what is doubtful exercises prudence in respect of his religion and his honour. Whoever gets involved in the doubtful things is like a herdsman who grazes his animals near a private preserve. He is bound to enter it. Because every king has a private preserve and the private preserves of Allah on His earth are the things that He has made forbidden. Because there is a piece of flesh in the body, the nature of which is that when it is sound, the entire body is sound, and when it is corrupt, the entire body is corrupt: because it is the heart.[8]

Abū Hurayra (may Allah be pleased with him) reported that Allah's Messenger (Allah bless him and give him peace) said:

أَيُّهَا النَّاسُ، إِنَّ اللهَ طَيِّبٌ لَا يَقْبَلُ إِلَّا طَيِّبًا، وَإِنَّ اللهَ أَمَرَ الْمُؤْمِنِيْنَ بِمَا أَمَرَ بِهِ الْمُرْسَلِيْنَ فَقَالَ: ﴿يَا أَيُّهَا الرُّسُلُ كُلُوا مِنَ الطَّيِّبَاتِ وَاعْمَلُوا صَالِحًا إِنِّي بِمَا تَعْمَلُونَ عَلِيمٌ﴾. وَقَالَ: ﴿يَا أَيُّهَا الَّذِينَ آمَنُوا كُلُوا مِن طَيِّبَاتِ مَا رَزَقْنَاكُمْ﴾. ثُمَّ ذَكَرَ الرَّجُلَ يُطِيْلُ السَّفَرَ أَشْعَثَ أَغْبَرَ يَمُدُّ يَدَيْهِ إِلَى السَّمَاءِ، يَا رَبِّ، يَا رَبِّ، وَمَطْعَمُهُ حَرَامٌ، وَمَشْرَبُهُ حَرَامٌ، وَمَلْبَسُهُ حَرَامٌ، وَغُذِيَ بِالْحَرَامِ، فَأَنَّىٰ يُسْتَجَابُ لِذَٰلِكَ؟

> People, Allah is good and does not accept anything but that which is good. Allah has enjoined the believers that which He has enjoined the Messengers. He says: "*O (My Esteemed) Messengers! Eat of the pure things (as your practice is) and do good deeds with persistence. Surely, I am Well Aware of whatever (deed) you do*" [Qur'ān 23:51]. Also, He says: "*O believers! Eat of those pure and clean things which We have provided for you*" [Qur'ān 2:172]. Then he mentioned a man who has undertaken a lengthy journey and is dishevelled and dusty, raising his hands towards heaven and saying: "Lord, Lord!" But his food is unlawful, his drink is unlawful, his clothing is unlawful, and he is nourished with what is unlawful, so how can he receive a response?[9]

To sum up, what Islam recommends is beneficial to the human condition of body and mind, and what it outlaws is injurious to health – whether or not we are aware of that.

3.1 The basic principles for *halal* and *ḥarām*

Living a life that brings one closer to Allah Almighty and His Messenger (Allah bless him and give him peace) is inconceivable without knowing what pleases and displeases them. The Holy Qur'ān and the conduct of the Prophet (Allah bless him and give him peace), enshrined in the compendiums of Traditions, illustrate what is permissible and impermissible. The following are the main points of the righteous code of conduct.

1 To make lawful and to prohibit is the prerogative of the Almighty Allah alone.
2 The basic *aṣl* (origin) refers to the permissibility of things.
3 What is *ḥalāl* (lawful) is sufficient, while what is *ḥarām* (unlawful) is superfluous.
4 Prohibiting the lawful, and authorizing the unlawful, is akin to falling into polytheism.
5 Whatever is conducive to the unlawful is in itself unlawful.
6 The prohibition of things is due to their inherent impurity and harmfulness.
7 When it is forbidden to perform an act, it is also forbidden to request its performance.
8 Good intentions do not transform the unlawful into lawful.
9 When prohibition and exigency conflict, preference is given to prohibition. Consequently, a person may not sell to another person a thing which he or she has given to his or her creditor as security for debt.
10 Treating the unlawful as lawful is prohibited.
11 An accessory attached to an object in fact is also attached to it in law; it cannot be dealt with separately. For example, when a pregnant animal is sold, the young in its womb is sold with it.
12 The unlawful is prohibited to everyone alike.
13 Doubtful things (which are not clear whether they are halal or haram) are to be avoided.
14 Necessity dictates exceptions.
15 Necessity renders proscribed things permissible.[10]

3.2 Islamic guidelines on the slaughtering of animals

The Muslim religion seeks good treatment of animals when they are alive and has prescribed rules of slaughter (*ḍabīḥa*) which aim for a quick and relatively painless death. The modern practices that run contrary to *halal* slaughter bring about great suffering to animals. Some of the Islamic rules on sacrificing an animal are given in the Traditions that follow.

According to Shaddād b. Aws (may Allah be well pleased with him), Allah's Messenger (Allah bless him and give him peace) said:

إِنَّ اللهَ كَتَبَ الْإِحْسَانَ عَلَى كُلِّ شَيْءٍ، فَإِذَا قَتَلْتُمْ فَأَحْسِنُوا الْقِتْلَةَ، وَإِذَا ذَبَحْتُمْ
فَأَحْسِنُوا الذَّبْحَ، وَلْيُحِدَّ أَحَدُكُمْ شَفْرَتَهُ، فَلْيُرِحْ ذَبِيحَتَهُ.

> Allah has prescribed spiritual excellence in the treatment of everything. If you sacrifice an animal, you must perform the slaughter most caringly, and let one of you sharpen the blade, in order to set the sacrificial animal at rest (causing it least discomfort)![11]

If the slaughtering tool, such as a blade, causes blood to flow, and Allah's Name is mentioned, then one may eat of the slaughtered animal. In contrast, slaughtering an animal using a nail, a tooth or a bone is prohibited. In a rigorously authenticated Tradition, the Holy Prophet (Allah bless him and give him peace) said:

أَرِنْ أَوْ أَعْجِلْ، مَا أَنْهَرَ الدَّمَ وَذُكِرَ اسْمُ اللهِ عَلَيْهِ فَكُلُوْا مَا لَمْ يَكُنْ سِنًّا أَوْ ظُفْرًا.

> Make the slaughtering quick, (using) whatever makes the blood flow, and (when) Allah's Name has been mentioned, then eat from it, except (from those animals who are being slaughtered) by the tooth and nail.[12]

In another Tradition, the Messenger (Allah bless him and give him peace) prohibited eating the meat of an animal that is shot at and killed before getting slaughtered:

عَنِ ابْنِ عَبَّاسٍ أَنَّ النَّبِيَّ نَهَى عَنِ الْمُجَثَّمَةِ.

> Ibn 'Abbās (may Allah be well pleased with him) narrated that the Prophet (Allah bless him and give him peace) prohibited *al-mujaththama* (an animal shot at and killed before getting slaughtered).[13]

If meat is imported from foreign countries where the animal is not slaughtered according to the tenets of Sharia – for example, the animal is killed with an electric current or with a bullet – it will not be lawful to consume it. In addition, it is illegal to benefit from its sale or purchase.

Muslims are permitted to consume only meat that has been prepared according to Islamic religious law. So, if an animal is killed in a way that is not permitted by the primary sources of Islam, its consumption is prohibited, as the following verse shows:

﴿حُرِّمَتْ عَلَيْكُمُ الْمَيْتَةُ وَالْدَّمُ وَلَحْمُ الْخِنْزِيرِ وَمَا أُهِلَّ لِغَيْرِ اللهِ بِهِ وَالْمُنْخَنِقَةُ وَالْمَوْقُوذَةُ
وَالْمُتَرَدِّيَةُ وَالنَّطِيحَةُ وَمَا أَكَلَ السَّبُعُ إِلاَّ مَا ذَكَّيْتُمْ وَمَا ذُبِحَ عَلَى النُّصُبِ﴾

> *Forbidden to you is carrion (the animal that dies and is not slaughtered according to Islamic law) and (the discharged) blood and pork and that (animal) on which the name of someone other than Allah has been invoked whilst slaughtering and (the animal) that dies by strangling or by a violent blow (not by any sharp instrument) or by falling from a height or the one that has been gored to death or which has been ripped apart and gnawed by a wild beast, save the one which you slaughter (before it dies), and (that animal too is forbidden) which has been slaughtered on idolatrous altars (dedicated to false gods).*[14]

The meat on which the name of Allah is not mentioned prior to slaughtering the animal.

﴿وَلَا تَأْكُلُوا مِمَّا لَمْ يُذْكَرِ اسْمُ اللهِ عَلَيْهِ وَإِنَّهُ لَفِسْقٌ﴾

> *And do not eat of (the meat of the animal) over which the Name of Allah has not been pronounced (at the time of slaughter). Verily, it is a sin (to eat that meat).*[15]

Another condition for eating the meat of an animal is that the slaughter must be performed by either a Muslim or one of the People of the Book (Jews and Christians):

﴿الْيَوْمَ أُحِلَّ لَكُمُ الطَّيِّبَاتُ وَطَعَامُ الَّذِينَ أُوتُوا الْكِتَابَ حِلٌّ لَّكُمْ وَطَعَامُكُمْ حِلٌّ لَّهُمْ﴾

> *This day, good and pure things have been made lawful for you. And the sacrificed animal of those given the (Revealed) Book is (also) lawful for you, whilst your sacrificed animal is lawful for them.*[16]

The method of slaughter that Muslims employ is generally challenged by animal rights activists as causing unnecessary suffering to the animal. Muslims disagree, holding that the Islamic method of killing animals is a humane and less painful way of slaughter.

The following rules pertaining to Islamic slaughter must be observed:[17]

1. The slaughtering must be performed by either a Muslim or one of the people of the Book.
2. The slaughterer must invoke the name of Allah before making the cut.[18]
3. The animal must be killed by cutting the throat with one continuous motion of a sharp knife.
4. The cut must sever at least three of the following: the trachea, oesophagus and the two blood vessels on either side of the throat.
5. The spinal cord must not be cut.
6. Animals must be treated well before being killed.
7. Animals must not see other animals being killed.
8. The knife must not be sharpened in the animal's presence.
9. The knife blade must be free of blemishes that might tear the wound.
10. The animal must not be in an uncomfortable position.
11. The animal must be allowed to bleed out and be completely dead before further processing.

Animals killed in this way do not suffer terribly since the cut is made quickly and cleanly; they lose consciousness before the brain can perceive severe pain.

The whole life of an ardent believer and his or her activities are dedicated to Divine service. The Islamic religious law requires that, before setting up a trade, taking a job, or investing in a business, the faithful must evaluate whether his or her primary revenues will be legal or illegal. It goes without saying that they, the righteous, must follow what the Allah Almighty charges them to do and shun what he does not approve.

3.3 Licit businesses

The faithful dedicate their life to Allah, the Exalted, and endeavour to live by His directives. As members of society, however, they are under obligation to earn money in order to survive. Before applying for a job or investing in a business, one must consider whether the activity is endorsed by Sharia. Determining whether a source of earning is unlawful is not an exacting task. If a form of trade does not run contrary to ordinances issued by Allah Almighty and the Prophet (Allah bless him and give him peace), then it is approved. As a general principle, the primary sources of Islam enumerate prohibitions in a certain domain, and what is left out is acceptable. This juristic maxim is supported by the following verse:

﴿أُحِلَّتْ لَكُم بَهِيمَةُ الْأَنْعَامِ إِلَّا مَا يُتْلَى عَلَيْكُمْ﴾

The quadrupeds (i.e., cattle) have been made lawful for you except those (animals) that will be announced to you afterwards.[19]

3.3.1 The selling of copies of the Qur'ān

Scholars proficient in Islamic law hold divergent views regarding selling and buying a *muṣḥaf* – an Arabic term used from the divinely revealed Books like Qur'ān. There are three opinions upon this matter.

First, Ḥanbalī scholars hold that the trade of *muṣḥaf* is not permitted in Muslim religious law, and such transactions are regarded as unlawful. Ibn 'Umar (Allah be well pleased with him and his father) said:

وَدِدْتُ أَنِّي قَدْ رَأَيْتُ الْأَيْدِي تُقْطَعُ فِي بَيْعِ الْمَصَاحِفِ.

I wish to witness the mutilation of hands due to (their) trading of *muṣḥafs*.[20]

Ibn 'Umar's wish, as cited, indicated that selling and buying a *muṣḥaf* was impermissible.

Second, according to Shafi'ī scholars – and also reportedly an opinion of Aḥmad b. Ḥanbal – it is legal to sell and purchase a *muṣḥaf*, even though the transaction itself is regarded with aversion. On the authority of Ibn 'Abbās (may Allah be well pleased with him):

كُنَّا لَا نَرَى بَأْسًا أَنْ يَبِيعَ الْمُصْحَفَ وَيَشْتَرِي بِثَمَنِهِ مُصْحَفًا هُوَ أَفْضَلُ مِنْهُ، وَلَا بَأْسَ أَنْ يُبَادَلَ الْمُصْحَفُ بِالْمُصْحَفِ، فَرَخَّصَ فِي شِرَاءِ الْمُصْحَفِ.

"We considered no harm in selling a *muṣḥaf* and the profit was used to buy a better one. It is fine to exchange a *muṣḥaf* with another *muṣḥaf*." So Ibn 'Abbās allowed the sale and the purchase (of a *muṣḥaf*).[21]

The previous report is weak due to its narrator, Layth.

عَنْ زِيَادٍ مَوْلَى لِسَعْدٍ أَنَّهُ سَأَلَ عَبْدَ اللهِ بْنَ عَبَّاسٍ وَمَرْوَانَ بْنَ الْحَكَمِ عَنْ بَيْعِ الْمَصَاحِفِ لِتِجَارَةٍ فِيْهَا فَقَالاَ: لاَ نَرَى أَنْ نَجْعَلَهُ مَتجَرًا، وَلَكِنْ مَا عَمِلْتَ بِيَدَيْكَ فَلاَ بَأْسَ بِهِ.

Ziyād, a servant of Sa'd, reported that once he asked Ibn 'Abbās (may Allah be well pleased with him) and Marwān b. al-ḥakam about the trading of a *muṣḥaf* by way of business. Both of them answered, "We do not allow a *muṣḥaf* as commodity for trading, but the one made by your own hand is permitted for you to sell."[22]

Ibn 'Abbās (may Allah be well pleased with him) approved the sale of a *muṣḥaf* on condition that it is not reduced to a trade commodity. This conclusion demonstrates selling and buying a *muṣḥaf* is sanctioned, but it is better to avoid such a trade.

Third, according to Mālikī scholars, several Shāfi'ī scholars and one opinion of Aḥmad b. Ḥanbal, the trade of the *muṣḥaf* is legal and not disapproved.

The third stance is the most flexible, and also the opinion most suitable to the Muslim community. The sale of a *muṣḥaf* is legal as there are no precise decrees on the prohibition of selling a *muṣḥaf*. Both narrations recorded from Ibn 'Umar (may Allah be well pleased with him and his father) and Ibn 'Abbās (may Allah be pleased with him) mentioned earlier are weak in rank, due to certain narrators in the chain of transmission, hence the ruling contained in them is not binding.

The sale of the Qur'ān may not be banned on account of the following verse:

﴿فَوَيْلٌ لِّلَّذِينَ يَكْتُبُونَ الْكِتَابَ بِأَيْدِيهِمْ ثُمَّ يَقُولُونَ هَذَا مِنْ عِندِ اللهِ لِيَشْتَرُوا بِهِ ثَمَنًا قَلِيلًا فَوَيْلٌ لَّهُم مِّمَّا كَتَبَتْ أَيْدِيهِمْ وَوَيْلٌ لَّهُم مِّمَّا يَكْسِبُونَ﴾

So a serious disaster awaits those who write the Book with their own hands, then say: "This is from Allah," just to earn a paltry price for that. So they will face destruction (owing to the Book) that their hands have written and (for the compensation) that they are earning.[23]

In the verse, prohibition is regarding tampering with the words of revelation; its injunction cannot be extended to trading a copy of the Holy Qur'ān.

Thus, it is lawful to buy and sell a *muṣḥaf* because the faithful have continually done so to date, and Muslim scholars have not taken objection to this practice. If it were illegal to buy and sell *muṣḥafs*, then this would prevent people from acquiring and benefiting from the Holy Qur'ān.

3.3.2 Purchase and sale of clothing

Islam instructs men and women to dress in a modest way. Men and women have separate dress codes. Allah characterizes the type of garments that Muslims may wear in the following verse:

﴿يَا بَنِي آدَمَ قَدْ أَنزَلْنَا عَلَيْكُمْ لِبَاسًا يُوَارِي سَوْءَاتِكُمْ وَرِيشًا وَلِبَاسُ التَّقْوَى ذَلِكَ خَيْرٌ ذَلِكَ مِنْ آيَاتِ اللهِ لَعَلَّهُمْ يَذَّكَّرُونَ﴾

O mankind! Surely, We have sent down for you (such) clothing that hides your private parts and adds (to your) aesthetic value. And (in addition to your outward clothes, We have also provided you an inward dress as well, and that is) the dress of God wariness (which) is the best. All of this (inner and outer attires) are the signs of Allah so that they may take advice.[24]

The clothes the faithful wear should meet these fundamental requirements, which are based on the previously cited verse: they must protect the chastity of the wearers, so wearing scanty clothes that fail to guard one's chastity is not lawful; and wearers should look presentable. Wearing shabby clothes, for people of substance who are able to buy good clothes, is a deviant behaviour. Clothes should fulfil another very significant human need: they should be suitable for the season. Any clothes that fulfil these requirements are lawful, and may be purchased and sold.

In order to promote modesty among men, Islam prohibits them from wearing silk clothes. The prohibition is based on the following Prophetic Tradition:

عَنْ أَبِي مُوسَى أَنَّ رَسُولَ اللهِ قَالَ: أُحِلَّ الذَّهَبُ وَالْحَرِيرُ لِإِنَاثِ أُمَّتِي، وَحُرِّمَ عَلَى ذُكُورِهَا.

According to Abū Musa (may Allah be pleased with him), Allah's Messenger (Allah bless him and give him peace) said: "Gold and silk are permitted to the females among my people but prohibited to the males."[25]

The Messenger (Allah bless him and give him peace) gave a list of permissible and impermissible actions to his community. Accordingly it is impermissible for men to wear silk.

عَنِ الْبَرَاءِ بْنِ عَازِبٍ قَالَ: أَمَرَنَا النَّبِيُّ بِسَبْعٍ وَنَهَانَا عَنْ سَبْعٍ، أَمَرَنَا بِاتِّبَاعِ الْجَنَائِزِ، وَعِيَادَةِ الْمَرِيْضِ، وَإِجَابَةِ الدَّاعِيْ، وَنَصْرِ الْمَظْلُوْمِ، وَإِبْرَارِ الْقَسَمِ، وَرَدِّ السَّلَامِ، وَتَشْمِيْتِ الْعَاطِسِ، وَنَهَانَا عَنْ آنِيَةِ الْفِضَّةِ، وَخَاتَمِ الذَّهَبِ، وَالْحَرِيْرِ وَالدِّيْبَاجِ، وَالْقَسِّيِّ وَالْإِسْتَبْرَقِ.

It is related that al-Barā'b. Azib (may Allah be well pleased with him) said: "The Prophet (Allah bless him and give him peace) instructed us to do seven things and forbade us seven. He instructed us to join funeral processions, to visit the sick, to accept invitations, to help the wronged, to fulfil the oaths, to return the greeting and to bless people who sneeze. He forbade us silver vessels, gold rings, silk, fine silk, *qassī* and *istibraq* (other kinds of silk and brocade)."[26]

Another prohibition pertaining to clothes is found in the Tradition of the Prophet (Allah bless him and give him peace) whose mercy and intercession everyone will crave on the Day of Judgment. As narrated by 'Alī (may Allah be well pleased with him), the Prophet (Allah bless him and give him peace) said to him:

لَا تُبْرِزْ فَخِذَكَ وَلَا تَنْظُرْ إِلَى فَخِذِ حَيٍّ وَلَا مَيِّتٍ.

Do not show your thigh, and do not look at the thigh of anyone, living or dead.[27]

3.3.3 Options in a sale contract

When a sale is effected, the option rests with the seller and the buyer to nullify the sale before they part company, or both the parties waive the right to nullify.

According to Ibn 'Umar (Allah be well pleased with him and his father), the Prophet (Allah bless him and give him peace) said:

إِذَا تَبَايَعَ الرَّجُلَانِ فَكُلُّ وَاحِدٍ مِنْهُمَا بِالْخِيَارِ مَا لَمْ يَتَفَرَّقَا وَكَانَا جَمِيعًا، أَوْ يُخَيِّرُ أَحَدُهُمَا الْآخَرَ فَتَبَايَعَا عَلَى ذَلِكَ، فَقَدْ وَجَبَ الْبَيْعُ، وَإِنْ تَفَرَّقَا بَعْدَ أَنْ يَتَبَايَعَا وَلَمْ يَتْرُكْ وَاحِدٌ مِنْهُمَا الْبَيْعَ، فَقَدْ وَجَبَ الْبَيْعُ.

When two men enter into a transaction, each one of them has the option (of revoking) so long as they have not parted and are still together. But if one of them gives the other the choice to decide and they agree on a deal, then it becomes binding. If they part after that and neither of them cancelled it, then the transaction becomes binding.[28]

Ḥakīm b. Ḥizām (may Allah be pleased with him) reported that the Prophet (Allah bless him and give him peace) said:

اَلْبَيِّعَانِ بِالْخِيَارِ مَا لَمْ يَتَفَرَّقَا، أَوْ قَالَ: حَتَّى يَتَفَرَّقَا، فَإِنْ صَدَقَا وَبَيَّنَا بُورِكَ لَهُمَا فِي بَيْعِهِمَا، وَإِنْ كَتَمَا وَكَذَبَا مُحِقَتْ بَرَكَةُ بَيْعِهِمَا.

The seller and the buyer have the option (to revoke the sale) as long as they have not separated (or he said: "until they separate"). If they speak

> the truth and make things clear, they will be blessed in their sale. If they conceal and lie, the blessing of their transaction will be obliterated.[29]

Both the buyer and the seller have the right to insist on an "option to cancel" period, an interval during which either party may revoke the contract. The "option to cancel" period, however, is not valid if the two parties insist on an imprecise period. For instance, Zayd accepts an offer to purchase a motorcycle from Bakr, and Zayd stipulates an option that he has a period of three days to return the motorcycle if he wishes. If Bakr agrees, this becomes a valid condition of the sale.

3.3.4 Paying an amount in instalments

Buying a product on instalment means that one pays a sum of money in small parts over a fixed period of time. Many shopkeepers and companies sell their commodities to customers in this fashion. Even numerous banks purchase products from the market and sell them to customers on instalment.[30]

The two parties must agree to the mode of payment before the confirmation of the contract, whether it is on instalment or in cash. The Prophet (Allah bless him and give him peace) permitted that a sum of money be paid under a deferred payment arrangement. The Prophet (Allah bless him and give him peace) also acted in like manner when he bought eatables from a Jew and left his sword with him as security.

عَنْ عَائِشَةَ أَنَّ النَّبِيَّ اشْتَرَى طَعَامًا مِنْ يَهُودِيٍّ إِلَى أَجَلٍ، وَرَهَنَهُ دِرْعًا مِنْ حَدِيْدٍ.

> According to 'Ā'isha (may Allah be well pleased with her) that the Prophet (Allah bless him and give him peace) bought some food from a Jew to be paid at a later fixed date, and left his iron armour with him as a security.[31]

Payment in instalments is lawful because there is no difference between paying an amount of money on the spot, or at intervals – provided that both parties are in accord. This agreement is legal as it was established by precedent Barīra (may Allah be well pleased with her) freed herself from slavery with nine *awqiya* (a unit of currency) over a period of nine years. When the Messenger (Allah bless him and give him peace) was told about her intention, he did not take exception to it.

عَنْ عَائِشَةَ j قَالَتْ: جَاءَتْنِي بَرِيْرَةُ فَقَالَتْ: كَاتَبْتُ أَهْلِيْ عَلَى تِسْعِ أَوَاقٍ.

> It is related that 'Ā'isha (may Allah be well pleased with her) said: "Barīra came to me and said: 'My people have given me a freedom-contract for nine *awqiyas*, one *awqiya* per year.'"[32]

The preceding Hadith establishes the legality of making payments at intervals by instalments.

If a customer is willing to pay a higher amount of money as compensation for delaying payment, then the deal is permissible. The Hadith given next establishes this point:

عَنِ ابْنِ عَبَّاسٍ قَالَ قَدِمَ رَسُولُ اللهِ الْمَدِينَةَ وَالنَّاسُ يُسْلِفُونَ فِي الثَّمَرِ الْعَامَ وَالْعَامَيْنِ، أَوْ قَالَ: عَامَيْنِ أَوْ ثَلَاثَةً، شَكَّ إِسْمَاعِيلُ، فَقَالَ: مَنْ سَلَّفَ فِي تَمْرٍ فَلْيُسْلِفْ فِي كَيْلٍ مَعْلُومٍ وَوَزْنٍ مَعْلُومٍ.

Ibn ʻAbbās (may Allah be pleased with him) narrated: "When Allah's Messenger (Allah bless him and give him peace) came to Medina, people used to pay for fruit one or two years in advance (or he said: "two or three years." Ismā'īl was unsure). He said: 'Whoever pays for dates in advance should only do so for a specified measure and specified weight.'"[33]

This Hadith has also addressed the question in regards to the payments by instalments, as it is evident from this Hadith that the customer could be charged more while paying in the form of instalments.

Scholars differ concerning the ruling on this issue. A few consider it to be a form of interest and regard it unlawful. In contrast, the majority have legalised it.

3.3.5 Donation of organs from human bodies

Organ transplantation is a surgical procedure in which an organ is transferred from one body to another. Successfully transplanted organs include hearts, brains, kidneys, lungs, livers, pancreases and intestines. Organ transplantation is widely practised the world over. Through the tremendous advancement of science in recent times, organ transplantation has saved many lives and alleviated the pain of innumerable patients.

Islamic scholars differ in their perspectives about this issue, and there are different stances on it. The critics hold that the sale and purchase of human organs is prohibited. They make a case that since organs are a gift from Allah, they are not the property of human beings. The sale and purchase of things that one does not own is not lawful, as per the decree of the Messenger (Allah bless him and give him peace).

لَا تَبِعْ مَا لَيْسَ عِنْدَكَ.

Do not sell that which you do not possess.[34]

Human beings are honourable and the noblest of creation. That is why donating or selling organs of human bodies negates the nobility Allah has conferred on them.

﴿وَلَقَدْ كَرَّمْنَا بَنِي آدَمَ وَحَمَلْنَاهُمْ فِي الْبَرِّ وَالْبَحْرِ وَرَزَقْنَاهُم مِّنَ الطَّيِّبَاتِ وَفَضَّلْنَاهُمْ عَلَىٰ كَثِيرٍ مِّمَّنْ خَلَقْنَا تَفْضِيلًا﴾

And We have indeed honoured the children of Adam and provided them with (means of transport) over the land and in the sea (i.e., in the cities, deserts, rivers and oceans) and bestowed upon them sustenance out of clean and pure things. And We have exalted them above most of Our creation by conferring on them superiority.[35]

However, the majority of scholars hold organ transplantation to be lawful on the basis of the argument that the needs of the living carry greater significance than those of the dead. The importance of rescuing a human being can be determined from the Qur'ānic verse that states,

وَمَنْ أَحْيَاهَا فَكَأَنَّمَا أَحْيَا النَّاسَ جَمِيعًا

"And whoever (saved him from unjust murder and) made him survive, it would be as if he saved the lives of all the people (of society, i.e., he rescued the collective system of human life)."[36] Due to the importance placed on the sanctity of human life, most Muslim jurists validate organ donation. This stance has gained precedence in Muslim lands.

In cases of starvation which threatens human life, the consumption of what is unlawful becomes lawful:

The following verse of Qur'ān provides the law of exemption in the cases where human life is threatening. Same verse provides support to the argument of Muslim jurists favouring organ transplantation.

﴿فَمَنِ اضْطُرَّ فِي مَخْمَصَةٍ غَيْرَ مُتَجَانِفٍ لِّإِثْمٍ فَإِنَّ اللَّهَ غَفُورٌ رَّحِيمٌ﴾

Then if someone gets into a survival situation (and is forced by) ravenous hunger (and intense thirst i.e., driven by dire necessity, provided) he is not prone to sinning (i.e., eats what is forbidden without being wilfully inclined to sin), then Allah is indeed Most Forgiving, Ever-Merciful.[37]

Out of necessity, organ transplantation is permissible so that patients might not suffer unnecessarily and their lives might be rescued. Furthermore, a cardinal principle of Islamic jurisprudence pertaining to this issue is that necessity overrides prohibition.

3.4 Classification of prohibited business transactions

Since Islam is a complete way of life, it covers every aspect of religious, spiritual, social, political, economic and ethical life. Islam has proscribed all business transactions that result in fraud, injustice and exploitation involving any of the contracting parties. The Muslim religion necessitates basing all financial and business transactions on transparency, accuracy and fairness. It requires the disclosure of all defects of saleable products, so that a seller might not take undue advantage of the other party. This section discusses some transactions which Islam has prohibited, so that none may incur the wrath of Allah, the Exalted, and operate at a loss. The prohibited transactions have been categorised under seven headings:

1 Prohibition on certain foods and drinks;
2 Illicit earning of wealth;
3 Sale or purchase of gambling products;
4 Defect in a commodity when entrusted to merchant;
5 Unsaleable things;
6 Sale of what is in your possession;
7 Transaction of interest-based commodities;
8 Sale is permissible on profit-giving commodities.

3.4.1 Prohibition on certain foods and drinks

It is an Islamic principle that if Allah prohibits the consumption of any commodity – for instance, intoxicants, corpses, swine, dogs, idols and other similar items – its manufacturing and trade is not permitted as well. A general principle on this score is given here. The Messenger (Allah bless him and give him peace) said:

إِذَا حَرَّمَ شَيْئًا حَرَّمَ ثَمَنَهُ.

> When Allah prohibits something, He prohibits its sale too.[38]

Then the Prophet (Allah bless him and give him peace), to illustrate the point, gave some examples:

إِنَّ اللّٰهَ وَرَسُوْلَهُ حَرَّمَ بَيْعَ الخَمْرِ، وَالْمَيْتَةِ، وَالخِنْزِيْرِ، وَالأَصْنَامِ.

> Allah and His Messenger (Allah bless him and give him peace) have made the sale of wine, carrion, pigs and idols unlawful.[39]

The faithful are prohibited from eating or drinking the previously mentioned harmful items. Drinking alcohol is injurious to one's health, and its harmful effects appear on the body, hence its unlawfulness. The flesh of an animal which dies before being slaughtered or hunted is also prohibited. The Qur'ān refers to swine as *khinzīr* – a derogatory term. The consumption of pork may result in fatal diseases which are more common in Europe and the United States than other parts of the world.

3.4.2 Illicit earning of wealth

The Qur'ān in many verses commands the faithful to internalise religious instructions in words and deeds (2:208; 24:51; 30:30; 33:70; 41:30; 61:2–3). This Divine decree has led to the creation of a number of rules and regulations to determine and judge the relationship between intentions and deeds, claims and acts.

Any raw material which is produced or supplied intentionally to manufacture commodity, which is illegal in Islam is not licit too, for instance, the sale of weapons during days of sedition, civil strife and bloodshed. Likewise, producing grapes for those people who make intoxicants out of them, and precisely selling silken dresses for male customers is not permitted by Muslim law.

If an individual who has accumulated massive wealth through usury, forgery, gambling, prohibited games, or any other unlawful means constructs a mosque, or establishes a charitable foundation, or performs some other good work, his or her wrongdoing will not be righted. In Islam, noble aims and intentions do not turn vices into virtues. This message is carried in the following verse:

﴿إِلَيْهِ يَصْعَدُ الْكَلِمُ الطَّيِّبُ وَالْعَمَلُ الصَّالِحُ يَرْفَعُهُ﴾

The pure words ascend to Him alone, and He is the One Who elevates (the grades of) a pious deed.[40]

Bringing home to his followers the importance of forming right intention, the Prophet (Allah bless him and give him peace) educated his companions on this subject.

According to 'Umar b. al-Khaṭṭāb (may Allah be pleased with him), Allah's Messenger (Allah bless him and give him peace) said:

اَلْأَعْمَالُ بِالنِّيَّةِ، وَلِكُلِّ امْرِئٍ مَا نَوَى. فَمَنْ كَانَتْ هِجْرَتُهُ إِلَى اللهِ وَرَسُوْلِهِ فَهِجْرَتُهُ إِلَى اللهِ وَرَسُوْلِهِ، وَمَنْ كَانَتْ هِجْرَتُهُ لِدُنْيَا يُصِيبُهَا، أَوِ امْرَأَةٍ يَتَزَوَّجُهَا، فَهِجْرَتُهُ إِلَى مَا هَاجَرَ إِلَيْهِ.

Actions are valued according to the intention, and every man is credited with what he intended. If someone's emigration was to Allah and His Messenger (Allah bless him and give him peace), his emigration was therefore to Allah and His Messenger (Allah bless him and give him peace), and if someone's emigration was to acquire some worldly benefit, or to take a woman in marriage, his emigration was to that to which he emigrated.[41]

3.4.3 Sale or purchase of gambling products

The sale or purchase of the product that is the underlying cause of gambling is forbidden. However, it is permissible to play with a piece of equipment used for leisure without gambling, provided that it does not awaken the desire for it within. It is the same whether or not the tool was manufactured for gambling. Nonetheless, it is appropriate to avoid playing with or using things that were manufactured for gambling, which is a forbidden practice and a cardinal sin.

Modern insurance companies and their practices are objectionable from a religious perspective.

3.4.4 *Defect in a commodity*

Sometimes a commodity is destroyed in the process of its manufacturing and becomes useless for the customer. For example, a tailor, while cutting cloth for making a suit, may, by mistake, reduce the size.

Should a commodity suffer damage in the possession of an employee, and his or her negligence or incompetence is not proven, no compensation is due from the worker. For example, if an ailing person dies in the course of treatment for reasons unrelated to the cure, or a vehicle catches fire outside a mechanic's garage and not through any failure to protect it, then the worker will not be held liable. But if the worker is careless and ruins the asset, he or she will have to make good on the damages. However, if he or she is experienced, alert and works to the best of his or her capacity, then no compensation may be claimed for the damage.[42]

3.4.5 *Unsaleable things*

An unsaleable item is such that its utilisation is inescapable and that there is legally no remuneration on it, for instance, water, pairing of animals like camels, dogs, cats and so on.

3.4.6 *Sale of what is in one's possession*

A fundamental stipulation for a valid sale is that the commodity must be in one's possession. If the commodity that is sold cannot be delivered, the transaction is incomplete and hence invalid. One may not sale anything that one has yet to receive. The sale of a fish in a pond or fruit on a tree is not legally valid.

The following Traditions establish the point that it is unlawful to sell commodities before taking possession of them. The Messenger (Allah bless him and give him peace) said:

لاَ تَبِعْ مَا لَيْسَ عِنْدَكَ.

Do not sell that which you do not possess.[43]

Ibn 'Umar (Allah be well pleased with him and his father) said:

اِبْتَعْتُ زَيْتًا فِيْ السُّوْقِ، فَلَمَّا اسْتَوْجَبْتُهُ لِنَفْسِيْ لَقِيَنِيْ رَجُلٌ فَأَعْطَانِيْ بِهِ رِبْحًا حَسَنًا،
فَأَرَدْتُ أَنْ أَضْرِبَ عَلَى يَدِهِ، فَأَخَذَ رَجُلٌ مِنْ خَلْفِيْ بِذِرَاعِيْ، فَالْتَفَتُّ فَإِذَا زَيْدُ بْنُ

ثَابِتٍ، فَقَالَ: لَا تَبِعْهُ حَيْثُ ابْتَعْتَهُ حَتَّى تَحُوْزَهُ إِلَى رَحْلِكَ، فَإِنَّ رَسُولَ اللهِ نَهَى أَنْ تُبَاعَ السِّلَعُ حَيْثُ تُبْتَاعُ حَتَّى يَحُوْزَهَا التُّجَّارُ إِلَى رِحَالِهِمْ.

I bought some olive oil in the marketplace, and when it came into my possession I was met by a man who offered me a good profit for it, and I wanted to make a deal with him, but a man behind me took hold of my arm. I turned around and saw that it was Zayd b. Thābit (may Allah be pleased with him). He said: "Do not sell it where you bought it until you take it to your place, for Allah's Messenger (Allah bless him and give him peace) forbade selling merchandise where it was bought, before the merchants moved them to their places."[44]

Ḥakīm b. Ḥizām (may Allah be pleased with him) narrated:

أَتَيْتُ رَسُولَ اللهِ فَقُلْتُ: يَأْتِينِي الرَّجُلُ يَسْأَلُنِي مِنَ الْبَيْعِ مَا لَيْسَ عِنْدِيْ، أَبْتَاعُ لَهُ مِنَ السُّوقِ ثُمَّ أَبِيعُهُ، قَالَ: لَا تَبِعْ مَا لَيْسَ عِنْدَكَ.

I came to Allah's Messenger (Allah bless him and give him peace) and said: "A man came to me asking to buy something that I did not have. Can I buy it from the market for him and then give it to him?" The Messenger (Allah bless him and give him peace) said: "Do not sell what is not with you."[45]

3.4.7 Transaction of interest-based commodities

The transaction of an interest-based commodity is not lawful. However, if the price of a commodity is determined at the time of sale, then sale on credit is permissible. On the purchase of an item with payment to be made at a future date, the words of the Almighty read:

﴿يَا أَيُّهَا الَّذِينَ آمَنُوا إِذَا تَدَايَنتُم بِدَيْنٍ إِلَىٰ أَجَلٍ مُّسَمًّى فَاكْتُبُوهُ﴾

O you who believe! When you deal with each other, in transactions involving future obligations in a fixed period of time, reduce them to writing.[46]

The legality of buying things on credit is proved from the normative practice of Allah's Messenger (Allah bless him and give him peace).

عَنْ عَائِشَةَ أَنَّ النَّبِيَّ اشْتَرَى طَعَامًا مِنْ يَهُوْدِيٍّ إِلَى أَجَلٍ وَرَهَنَهُ دِرْعًا مِنْ حَدِيْدٍ.

According to 'Ā'isha (may Allah be well pleased with her) that the Prophet (Allah bless him and give him peace) bought some food from a Jew to be paid at a later fixed date, and left his iron armour with him as a security.[47]

3.4.8 Sale is permissible on profit-giving commodities

If a saleable commodity is not useful and profit-giving, its transaction is not valid: for example, a transaction involving a single grain of rice or vermin.

3.5 Unlawful things that are prohibited for everyone

Islamic law pertaining to lawful and unlawful things are universal in nature. Islamic religious regulations in the form of permissible and impermissible things are equally applicable to every believer, whether white or black, an Arab or a non-Arab, poor or rich. The Muslim religion demonstrates that there are no privileged groups or persons when it comes to conforming to Islamic law.

The act of stealing is forbidden for every practitioner of Islam and its punishment is the same no matter who commits the crime. To illustrate this point, a famous Hadith is quoted here.

عَنْ عَائِشَةَ زَوْجِ النَّبِيِّ أَنَّ قُرَيْشًا أَهَمَّهُمْ شَأْنُ الْمَرْأَةِ الَّتِي سَرَقَتْ فِيْ عَهْدِ النَّبِيِّ فِيْ غَزْوَةِ الْفَتْحِ. فَقَالُوْا: مَنْ يُكَلِّمُ فِيْهَا رَسُوْلَ اللهِ؟ فَقَالُوْا: وَمَنْ يَجْتَرِئُ عَلَيْهِ إِلَّا أُسَامَةُ بْنُ زَيْدٍ حِبُّ رَسُوْلِ اللهِ ، فَأُتِيَ بِهَا رَسُوْلُ اللهِ فَكَلَّمَهُ فِيْهَا أُسَامَةُ بْنُ زَيْدٍ، فَتَلَوَّنَ وَجْهُ رَسُوْلِ اللهِ، فَقَالَ: أَتَشْفَعُ فِيْ حَدٍّ مِنْ حُدُوْدِ اللهِ؟ فَقَالَ لَهُ أُسَامَةُ: اسْتَغْفِرْ لِيْ يَا رَسُوْلَ اللهِ، فَلَمَّا كَانَ الْعَشِيُّ قَامَ رَسُوْلُ اللهِ فَاخْتَطَبَ، فَأَثْنَى عَلَى اللهِ بِمَا هُوَ أَهْلُهُ ثُمَّ قَالَ: أَمَّا بَعْدُ، فَإِنَّمَا أَهْلَكَ الَّذِيْنَ مِنْ قَبْلِكُمْ أَنَّهُمْ كَانُوا إِذَا سَرَقَ فِيْهِمُ الشَّرِيْفُ تَرَكُوْهُ، وَإِذَا سَرَقَ فِيْهِمُ الضَّعِيْفُ أَقَامُوْا عَلَيْهِ الْحَدَّ، وَإِنِّيْ وَالَّذِيْ نَفْسِيْ بِيَدِهِ لَوْ أَنَّ فَاطِمَةَ بِنْتَ مُحَمَّدٍ سَرَقَتْ، لَقَطَعْتُ يَدَهَا، ثُمَّ أَمَرَ بِتِلْكَ الْمَرْأَةِ الَّتِيْ سَرَقَتْ، فَقُطِعَتْ يَدُهَا.

The wife of the Prophet (Allah bless him and give him peace), ‘Ā’isha (may Allah be well pleased with her), narrates: “The Quraysh were concerned about the case of the woman who had stolen, at the time of Allah’s Messenger (Allah bless him and give him peace), on the occasion of the conquest of Mecca. They said, ‘Who will speak to Allah’s Messenger (Allah bless him and give him peace) concerning her?’ Then they said: ‘No one but Usāma b. Zayd, the beloved of Allah’s Messenger (Allah bless him and give him peace), would dare to do that.’ She was brought to Allah’s Messenger (Allah bless him and give him peace), and Usāma b. Zayd spoke concerning her. The colour of the face of Allah’s Messenger (Allah bless him and give him peace) changed, and he said, ‘Are you interceding concerning one of the prescribed punishments of Allah?’ Usāma said to him, ‘Pray for forgiveness for me, Messenger of Allah!’ When evening came, Allah’s Messenger (Allah bless him and give him peace) stood up and delivered a sermon. He praised Allah as He deserves to be praised, then said: ‘Furthermore, those who went before you were doomed because, if a nobleman among them stole, they would let him off, but if a lowly person stole, they would carry

> out the prescribed punishment on him. By the One in Whose Hand is my soul, if Fāṭima the daughter of Muhammad were to steal, I would cut off her hand.' Then he ordered that the hand of the woman who had stolen be cut off."[48]

If a Muslim steals from a disbeliever, the prescribed punishment can be enforced against him or her. Ibn Rushd reports that there is a consensus among the Muslims on this point.[49]

A crime of stealing was brought before the Messenger (Allah bless him and give him peace), involving Ṭa'īma b. al-Ubayriq, nominally a Muslim but really a hypocrite, and a Jew. Ṭa'īma stole a set of armour and, fearful of being caught, planted it in the house of a Jew. On account of his outward profession of faith, the Muslim community sided with Ṭa'īma. But the Messenger (Allah bless him and give him peace) exonerated the Jew from the charge and established justice following the revelation of the following verses:

﴿إِنَّا أَنزَلْنَا إِلَيْكَ الْكِتَابَ بِالْحَقِّ لِتَحْكُمَ بَيْنَ النَّاسِ بِمَا أَرَاكَ اللهُ وَلاَ تَكُن لِّلْخَآئِنِينَ
خَصِيمًاوَاسْتَغْفِرِ اللهِ إِنَّ اللهَ كَانَ غَفُورًا رَّحِيمًاوَلاَ تُجَادِلْ عَنِ الَّذِينَ يَخْتَانُونَ أَنفُسَهُمْ إِنَّ
اللهَ لاَ يُحِبُّ مَن كَانَ خَوَّانًا أَثِيمًايَسْتَخْفُونَ مِنَ النَّاسِ وَلاَ يَسْتَخْفُونَ مِنَ اللهِ وَهُوَ مَعَهُمْ إِذْ
يُبَيِّتُونَ مَا لاَ يَرْضَى مِنَ الْقَوْلِ وَكَانَ اللهُ بِمَا يَعْمَلُونَ مُحِيطًاهَاأَنتُمْ هَؤُلاَءِ جَادَلْتُمْ عَنْهُمْ فِي
الْحَيَاةِ الدُّنْيَا فَمَن يُجَادِلُ اللهَ عَنْهُمْ يَوْمَ الْقِيَامَةِ أَم مَّن يَكُونُ عَلَيْهِمْ وَكِيلًا﴾

> *(O Glorious Messenger!) Surely, We have revealed to you the Book based on Truth so that you may judge between the people in accordance with (the Truth) which Allah has shown to you. And (never) become a contender on behalf of the treacherous ones. And implore Allah's forgiveness. Allah is indeed Most Forgiving, Ever-Merciful. And do not plead (in defence of) those who are deceiving their own souls. Surely, Allah does not like anyone who is a committed betrayer and sinner. They hide (their deceitfulness) from people (feeling ashamed), but feel no shame before Allah, whilst He is with them when they hold consultations (secretly) at night about that matter which Allah disapproves. And Allah has encompassed whatever they do. Beware! You are those who pleaded on their behalf in the life of this world, but who will contend with Allah on their behalf (even) on the Day of Resurrection, or who will be their advocate (on that Day too)?*[50]

Islam does not favour selective application of Divine laws. The Qur'ān lays this bare as criminal:

﴿وَمِنْ أَهْلِ الْكِتَابِ مَنْ إِن تَأْمَنْهُ بِقِنطَارٍ يُؤَدِّهِ إِلَيْكَ وَمِنْهُم مَّنْ إِن تَأْمَنْهُ بِدِينَارٍ لاَّ يُؤَدِّهِ
إِلَيْكَ إِلاَّ مَا دُمْتَ عَلَيْهِ قَآئِمًا ذَلِكَ بِأَنَّهُمْ قَالُواْ لَيْسَ عَلَيْنَا فِي الأُمِّيِّينَ سَبِيلٌ وَيَقُولُونَ عَلَى
اللهِ الْكَذِبَ وَهُمْ يَعْلَمُونَ﴾

And amongst the People of the Book there is a type that if you trust him with a heap of wealth, he will return it to you. And some amongst them are such that if you trust him with one dīnār *(a gold coin), he will not return it to you unless you keep standing over him. That is because they say: "There is no blame on us in the matter of the illiterate." And they fabricate a lie against Allah and they know it themselves (as well).*[51]

Another Tradition on practising equality and justice shows that the Prophet of Islam (Allah bless him and give him peace) was truly a man of exemplary character, since he did not seek exemption in the application of the universal law of Islam to even his own person.

عَنْ عَبْدِ الرَّحْمَنِ بْنِ أَبِيْ لَيْلَى عَنْ أُسَيْدِ بْنِ حُضَيْرٍ رَجُلٍ مِنْ الْأَنْصَارِ، قَالَ: بَيْنَمَا هُوَ
يُحَدِّثُ الْقَوْمَ وَكَانَ فِيْهِ مِزَاحٌ بَيْنَا يُضْحِكُهُمْ، فَطَعَنَهُ النَّبِيُّ فِيْ خَاصِرَتِهِ بِعُوْدٍ فَقَالَ: أَصْبِرْنِيْ.
فَقَالَ: اصْطَبِرْ. قَالَ: إِنَّ عَلَيْكَ قَمِيْصًا وَلَيْسَ عَلَيَّ قَمِيْصٌ. فَرَفَعَ النَّبِيُّ عَنْ قَمِيْصِهِ
فَاحْتَضَنَهُ وَجَعَلَ يُقَبِّلُ كَشْحَهُ. قَالَ: إِنَّمَا أَرَدْتُ هَذَا يَا رَسُوْلَ اللهِ.

According to 'Abd al- Raḥman b. Abī Layla, while Usayd b. Ḥuḍayr, one of the Ansars, was talking to the people and joking to make them laugh, the Prophet (Allah bless him and give him peace) poked him in the ribs with a stick. He said: "Let me retaliate." The Prophet (Allah bless him and give him peace) said: "Retaliate." He said: "You are wearing a shirt but I am not wearing a shirt." The Prophet (Allah bless him and give him peace) lifted his shirt and he embraced him and kissed his side. He said: "This is all I wanted, Allah's Messenger (Allah bless him and give him peace)."[52]

3.6 Illicit businesses

Unlawful business activities generate profits in a way that transgresses the limits of Allah, the Exalted, and causes one to fall into sin. Some instances of prohibited business activities include the manufacturing and marketing of intoxicants, marketing of pork and unlawfully killed animals. On the following pages are some unlawful forms of business that the Messenger (Allah bless him and give him peace) forbade because a purchaser is unable to weigh, count or measure the goods for sale.

3.6.1 Ambiguities in a contract (bay' al-gharar)

The foundation of prohibited sales is *bay' al-gharar* – a risky transaction that contains elements of uncertainty or speculation. *Bay' al-gharar* is not permissible as in this possibility of deception. It may cause undue loss to one party and unfair enrichment to the other. To understand this type of sale, some definitions of *al-gharar* are given next:

Al-Sarkhasī writes:

Al-gharar is a thing whose outcome is hidden.[53]

'Alī b. Muhammad al-Jurjānī defines the term:

> *Al-gharar* is a commodity whose outcome cannot be perceived; (neither the buyer nor the seller) is in the knowledge of the sold product whether it is sound or not.[54]

Bay' al-gharar is the transaction of a commodity which is inaccessible at the time of a business deal. The buyer, therefore, cannot determine whether or not it fits the description. Examples of this include the sale of fruits on trees before they ripen, and the sale of fish in water before they are caught. Purchasing and selling unborn animals are further examples of uncertain transactions, hence their prohibition. *Bay' al-gharar* is not lawful because the purchaser is not sure of the kind, make and quality of a particular commodity.

The Holy Prophet (Allah bless him and give him peace) forbade effecting a sale of contract whose acquisition was absolutely impossible. '

Abd Allāh b. 'Umar (may Allah be pleased with him and his father) reported:

أَنَّ رَسُوْلَ اللّٰهِ نَهَى عَنْ بَيْعِ الثِّمَارِ حَتَّىٰ يَبْدُوَ صَلاَحُهَا، نَهَى الْبَائِعَ وَالْمُبْتَاعَ.

> Allah's Messenger (Allah bless him and give him peace) forbade selling dates until it was clear that they were sound. He forbade both the buyer and the seller.[55]

3.6.2 Selling fetuses or animals still unborn (bay'ḥabal al-ḥabāla)

The sale of *ḥabal al-ḥabāla* (unborn animals) was a normal practice in the Time of Ignorance; the Arabs used to sell the fetus of a camel still in the womb of a she-camel. This is prohibited in the Muslim religion seeing that it is the sale of an unidentified, non-existent and non-deliverable entity.[56]

عَنْ عَبْدِ اللّٰهِ عَنْ رَسُوْلِ اللّٰهِ a أَنَّهُ نَهَى عَنْ بَيْعِ حَبَلِ الْحَبَلَةِ.

> According to 'Abd Allāh (may Allah be pleased with him) that Allah's Messenger (Allah bless him and give him peace) forbade selling *ḥabal al-ḥabāla* (selling the unborn offspring of a female animal).[57]

The second reason for the prohibition of this sale is the fact that the seller does not possess the entity. This economic code of Islam is supported by the Prophetic prohibition:

عَنِ بْنِ عَبَّاسٍ أَنَّ رَسُوْلَ اللّٰهِ a نَهَى عَنْ بَيْعِ الْمَضَامِيْنِ، وَالْمَلاَقِيْحِ، وَحَبَلِ الْحَبَلَةِ.

> According to Ibn 'Abbās (may Allah be pleased with him), Allah's Messenger (Allah bless him and give him peace) prohibited selling a

commodity still in hand (undelivered) or unripened dates and animals not born yet.[58]

Different forms of sale mentioned in the following Tradition are prohibited as they carry elements of uncertainty.

It was narrated that Abū Sa'īd al-Khudrī (may Allah be pleased with him) said:

نَهى رَسُوْلُ اللهِ عَنْ شِرَاءِ مَا فِيْ بُطُوْنِ الْأَنْعَامِ حَتَّى تَضَعَ، وَعَمَّا فِيْ ضُرُوْعِهَا إِلَّا بِكَيْلٍ،
وَعَنْ شِرَاءِ الْعَبْدِ وَهُوَ آبِقٌ، وَعَنْ شِرَاءِ الْمَغَانِمِ حَتَّى تُقْسَمَ، وَعَنْ شِرَاءِ الصَّدَقَاتِ حَتَّى
تُقْبَضَ، وَعَنْ ضَرْبَةِ الْغَائِصِ.

Allah's Messenger (Allah bless him and give him peace) forbade selling what is in the wombs of cattle until they give birth, and selling what is in their udders unless it is measured out, and selling a slave who has fled, and selling gains of war until they have been distributed, and selling charity until it has been received, and (selling) what a diver is going to bring up.[59]

3.6.3 Transaction of stones (bay' al-ḥasāt)

Bay' al-ḥasāt is a business deal concluded by means of pebbles. When the purchaser throws a stone at the seller's commodity, the contract of sale is concluded. Alternatively, the seller may tell the buyer that on whatever article a stone thrown by him falls will be sold to him. In contemporary world sale of commodity through ballot, where the buyer is not certain exactly of which item he will have to buy in the result of ballot, is comparable to *bay' al-ḥasāt*. For example, some of the housing societies sell their plots through ballot system after receiving the price of plot from the buyer, whereas the buyer is uncertain about the shape and location of the plot which he or she may get and is forced to buy after the balloting.

The Prophet (Allah bless him and give him peace) prohibited such a business deal.

عَنْ أَبِيْ هُرَيْرَةَ قَالَ: نَهَى رَسُوْلُ اللهِ عَنْ بَيْعِ الْغَرَرِ وَبَيْعِ الْحَصَاةِ.

According to Abū Hurayra (may Allah be pleased with him): "Allah's Messenger (Allah bless him and give him peace) prohibited the *al-gharar* (a business contract which entails an element of uncertainty or hazard) sale and the *al-ḥasāt* (transaction conducted by throwing stones) sale."[60]

قَالَ الشَّافِعِيُّ وَمَعْنَى بَيْعِ الْحَصَاةِ أَنْ يَقُولَ الْبَائِعُ لِلْمُشْتَرِي إِذَا نَبَذْتُ إِلَيْكَ بِالْحَصَاةِ فَقَدْ
وَجَبَ الْبَيْعُ فِيمَا بَيْنِي وَبَيْنَكَ . وَهَذَا شَبِيهٌ بِبَيْعِ الْمُنَابَذَةِ وَكَانَ هَذَا مِنْ بُيُوعِ أَهْلِ الْجَاهِلِيَّة

> Imam al-Shāfi'ī said: "And the meaning of *al-ḥasāt* sale is when the seller says to the buyer: 'When I toss the pebble at you, then the sale between you and I is final.' This resembles the sale of *munābadha* and this was one of the selling practices of the people of ignorance."[61]

Nowadays some plots are sold by drawing lots. Sellers sometimes advertise a number of specific pieces of land so that would-be purchasers know which one they might acquire. This form of sale is allowed under Muslim law. But if the advertisement does not specify what piece of ground the purchaser will get after casting lots, then this method of selling is akin to a business deal concluded by means of pebbles, and it is unlawful as per the prohibition of the Prophet (Allah bless him and give him peace).

Since a contract of sale is a serious matter, it must not be concluded in such an unreliable manner as throwing stones at saleable products. Closing a sale in this arbitrary fashion may lead to injustice to either party. To pre-empt this problem, this type of sale is prohibited.

3.6.4 *Sale of goods without inspection* (bay' al-munābadha)

Bay' al-munābadha refers to a deal in which one individual says to another: "Give me what you have at hand in return for what I have at hand." Neither party had knowledge of what the other had close at hand, so it is akin to gambling. This business deal, which was prevalent in pre-Islamic times, was closed by throwing a garment from one party to another without making any inspection by either party. The Messenger (Allah bless him and give him peace) prohibited a business transaction where both parties agree to barter one commodity for another without examining the goods.

عَنْ أَبِي هُرَيْرَةَ أَنَّ رَسُوْلَ اللّٰه نَهَى عَنْ الْمُلاَمَسَةِ وَالْمُنَابَذَةِ.

> According to Abū Hurayra (may Allah be pleased with him), Allah's Messenger (Allah bless him and give him peace) forbade the *al-mulāmasa* sale and the *al-munābadha* sale.[62]

According to Imam al-Tirmidhī *al-munābadha means*:

إِذَا نَبَذْتُ إِلَيْكَ بِالْحَصَاةِ فَقَدْ وَجَبَ الْبَيْعُ فِيمَا بَيْنِي وَبَيْنَكَ

"When I throw something to you, the sale between you and I is concluded."[63]

3.6.5 *Sale of goods by touching* (bay' al-mulāmasa)

Bay' al-mulāmasa was popular in the pre-Islamic time. This deal was closed when a person touched a garment – but he was not allowed to unfold it or examine what was in it. This also describes a deal in which the purchase was made by night and the purchaser did not know what was included it.[64]

The following Tradition is related from Abū Sa'īd (may Allah be pleased with him) on the prohibition of such a sale:

أَنَّ رَسُوْلَ اللهِ نَهَى عَنِ الْمُنَابَذَةِ وَهِيَ: طَرْحُ الرَّجُلِ ثَوْبَهُ بِالْبَيْعِ إِلَى الرَّجُلِ قَبْلَ أَنْ يُقَلِّبَهُ أَوْ
يَنْظُرَ إِلَيْهِ، وَنَهَى عَنِ الْمُلاَمَسَةِ، وَالْمُلاَمَسَةُ: لَمْسُ الثَّوْبِ لاَ يَنْظُرُ إِلَيْهِ.

Allah's Messenger (Allah bless him and give him peace) forbade the *al-munābadha* sale – which is a sale in which a man throws his garment to another man without him turning it over or examining it. He also forbade the *al-mulāmasa* sale – which is to buy a garment by touching it without examining it.[65]

3.6.6 Sale for years in advance (bay' al-sinīn)

Bay' al-sinīn is a type of sale in which the object is agricultural produce – for example, fruits or dates – which is sold for years in advance. A seller and a purchaser make a deal whereby the latter purchases from the former the produce of land for years ahead. Uncertainty is involved here as the purchaser may get nothing due to damage to fruit. That is why the Muslim religion prohibits this form of transaction.

عَنْ جَابِرِ بْنِ عَبْدِ اللهِ أَنَّ النَّبِيَّ نَهَى عَنْ بَيْعِ السِّنِيْنَ وَوَضَعَ الْجَوَائِحَ.

According to Jābir b. 'Abd Allāh (may Allah be well pleased with him and his father), the Prophet (Allah bless him and give him peace) forbade selling crops for years in advance, and (he recommended) that the seller waive the payment in the event of the crop being damaged by blight (after it has ripened and been sold).[66]

3.6.7 Trading grains in ears for dry grains (bay' al-muḥāqala)

Bay' al-muḥāqala is a type of sale in which grains in ears are traded for dry grains. It may also refer to a business transaction in which a landlord lets a piece of land on lease to an individual who pays rent in the form of its grain production.

The definitions of *bay' al-muḥāqala* offered by Imam Muslim are as follows.

الْمُحَاقَلَةُ بَيْعُ الزَّرْعِ الْقَائِمِ بِالْحَبِّ كَيْلًا

Al-muḥāqala means selling standing crops for grains by measure.[67]

الْمُحَاقَلَةُ أَنْ يُبَاعَ الْحَقْلُ بِكَيْلٍ مِنَ الطَّعَامِ مَعْلُومٍ

Al-muḥāqala refers to selling the field for a known measure of food.[68]

In both sale and lease, *bay' al-muḥāqala* is prohibited; the elements of interest and ignorance creep into this deal.

The Prophet (Allah bless him and give him peace) forbade *bay' al-muḥāqala*.

Rāfi' b. Khadīj (may Allah be pleased with him) reported:

،نَهَى رَسُوْلُ اللَّهِ عَنِ الْمُحَاقَلَةِ وَالْمُزَابَنَةِ، وَقَالَ: إِنَّمَا يَزْرَعُ ثَلَاثَةٌ: رَجُلٌ لَهُ أَرْضٌ فَهُوَ يَزْرَعُهَا
وَرَجُلٌ مُنِحَ أَرْضًا فَهُوَ يَزْرَعُ مَا مُنِحَ، وَرَجُلٌ اسْتَكْرَى أَرْضًا بِذَهَبٍ أَوْ فِضَّةٍ.

Allah's Messenger (Allah bless him and give him peace) forbade *al-muḥāqala* (crops in the field are sold for dry wheat, or land is leased out for wheat) and *al-muzābana* and said: "Only three should cultivate: A man who has land and cultivates it (himself), a man who has been given some land so he cultivates what has been given to him, and a man who rents out land for gold and silver."[69]

عَنْ سَعِيْدِ بْنِ الْمُسَيَّبِ أَنَّ رَسُوْلَ اللَّهِ نَهَى عَنْ بَيْعِ الْمُزَابَنَةِ وَالْمُحَاقَلَةِ، وَالْمُزَابَنَةُ: أَنْ يُبَاعَ
ثَمَرُ النَّخْلِ بِالتَّمْرِ. وَالْمُحَاقَلَةُ: أَنْ يُبَاعَ الزَّرْعُ بِالْقَمْحِ، وَاسْتِكْرَاءُ الْأَرْضِ بِالْقَمْحِ.

According to Sa'īd b. al-Musayyab that Allah's Messenger (Allah bless him and give him peace) forbade *al-muzābana* and *al-muhāqala* transactions. *Al-muzābana* is when dates on the tree are sold for dry dates, and *al-muhāqala* is when crops in the field are sold for dry wheat, or land is leased out for wheat.[70]

3.6.8 Sale with exception (bay' al-thunyā)

Bay' al-thunyā means to make an exception for one item among those purchased, without revealing to the purchaser what item was excluded. If a seller says: "I sold these cows to you excepting some of them," so that the cows he or she did not propose to sell were left ambiguous, hence the illegality of the deal.

عَنْ جَابِرٍ، أَنَّ رَسُوْلَ اللَّهِ نَهَى عَنِ الْمُحَاقَلَةِ وَالْمُزَابَنَةِ وَالْمُخَابَرَةِ وَالثُّنْيَا إِلاَّ أَنْ تُعْلَمَ.

According to Jābir (may Allah be well pleased with him) narrated: "Allah's Messenger (Allah bless him and give him peace) prohibited *al-muḥāqala*(selling un-harvested grain in the field in exchange for harvested grain), *al-muzābana* (selling an estimated amount of fresh dates on the tree for dried dates that are measured, or the same for grapes), *al-mukhābara* (renting land in exchange for a portion of its produce), and making an exception (in a sale) unless it is made known."[71]

However, if the seller makes an exception, mentioning it, then this business transaction is legal. In this case, the would-be buyer will not be left in the dark. In confirmation of this principle, a Hadith is cited next:

عَنْ جَابِرٍ ، قَالَ: اشْتَرَى مِنِّي رَسُوْلُ اللهِ بَعِيْرًا وَاسْتَثْنَى ظَهْرَهُ إِلَى الْمَدِيْنَةِ.

Jābir (may Allah be well pleased with him) reported: "Allah's Messenger (Allah bless him and give him peace) bought a camel from me and got its back exempted until (reaching) Medina."[72]

3.6.9 Selling produce before its goodness appears

Fruit should be sold only when it ripens. The faithful are forbidden to purchase fruit before its goodness appears.

This is related from Ibn 'Umar (may Allah be well pleased with him and his father):

نَهَى النَّبِيُّ عَنْ بَيْعِ الثَّمَرَةِ حَتَّى يَبْدُوَ صَلَاحُهَا، وَكَانَ إِذَا سُئِلَ عَنْ صَلَاحِهَا قَالَ: حَتَّى
تَذْهَبَ عَاهَتُهُ.

The Prophet (Allah bless him and give him peace) forbade selling dates until it was clear that they were good. When he was asked about when this was, he said: "When the danger of blight has passed."[73]

عَنِ ابْنِ عُمَرَ أَنَّ رَسُوْلَ اللهِ نَهَى عَنْ بَيْعِ النَّخْلِ حَتَّى يَزْهُوَ، وَعَنْ السُّنْبُلِ حَتَّى يَبْيَضَّ
وَيَأْمَنَ الْعَاهَةَ، نَهَى الْبَائِعَ وَالْمُشْتَرِي.

Ibn 'Umar (may Allah be well pleased with him and his father) narrated that Allah's Messenger (Allah bless him and give him peace) forbade selling the fruit of date palms until it began to develop colour (turn yellow or red) and ears (of grain) until they turned white (having developed) and were free of blight. He forbade that to the seller and the buyer.[74]

عَنْ أَنَسٍ أَنْ رَسُوْلَ اللهِ نَهَى عَنْ بَيْعِ الْحَبِّ حَتَّى يَشْتَدَّ، وَعَنْ بَيْعِ الْعِنَبِ حَتَّى يَسْوَدَّ،
وَعَنْ بَيْعِ التَّمْرِ حَتَّى يَحْمَرَّ وَيَصْفَرَّ.

Anas (may Allah be well pleased with him) narrates that the Messenger of Allah (Allah bless him and give him ease) forbade the sale of grain until it is strong and the sale of grapes until they become black, and the sale of dates until they turn red and white.[75]

عَنْ أَنَسٍ أَنَّ النَّبِيَّ نَهَى عَنْ بَيْعِ ثَمَرِ التَّمْرِ حَتَّى يَزْهُوَ، فَقُلْنَا لِأَنَسٍ: مَا زَهْوُهَا؟ قَالَ: تَحْمَرُّ وَتَصْفَرُّ، أَرَأَيْتَ إِنْ مَنَعَ اللهُ الثَّمَرَةَ بِمَ تَسْتَحِلُّ مَالَ أَخِيكَ؟

According to Anas (may Allah be well pleased with him) that the Prophet (Allah bless him and give him peace) forbade selling dates until they were ripe. We asked Anas: "What is the sign of their ripeness?" He said: "They become red and yellow. If Allah afflicts the fruit, what right do you think that you have to your brother's money?"[76]

3.6.10 Sale and buy-back (bay' al-'īna)

Bank Negara Malaysia (BNM), the central bank of Malaysia, describes *bay' al-'īna* in the following words:

> *Bay' al-'īna* refers to an arrangement that involves sale of an asset to the purchaser on a deferred basis and subsequent purchase of the asset at a cash price lower than the deferred sale price or vice versa, and which complies with the specific requirements of *bay' al-'īna.*[77]

The International Financial Services Board, a standard-setting body for Islamic banks, describes *bay' al-'īna* as follows:

> A contract involving the sale and buy-back transaction of assets by a seller. A seller sells an asset to a buyer on a cash basis and later buys it back on a deferred payment basis where the price is higher than the cash price. It can also be applied when a seller sells an asset to a buyer on a deferred basis and later buys it back on a cash basis, at a price which is lower than the deferred price."[78]

Most classical schools of law proscribe *bay' al-'īna* on the ground that it is employed to circumvent the prohibition of usury. As an artificial sale, it is regarded as a devious means of justifying an interest-bearing debt. However, *bay' al-'īna* is valid in the Shafi'ī school and is considered legal in Malaysia.

3.6.11 Trade of stolen property

From ethical and social perspectives, commercial transactions in stolen property are an offence. That is why such offenders are prosecuted by courts.

It is not lawful for the faithful to purchase commodities that have been stolen or otherwise acquired without permission of the original owner. Because an individual cannot come into possession of stolen goods, he or she is not licensed to dispose of them. This point is affirmed in the following Prophetic Tradition.

لاَ تَبِعْ مَا لَيْسَ عِنْدَكَ.

Do not sell that which you do not possess.[79]

To purchase such an item is abetting and helping a thief – something that the Qur'ān prohibits,

وَتَعَاوَنُواْ عَلَى الْبِرِّ وَالتَّقْوَى وَلاَ تَعَاوَنُواْ عَلَى الإِثْمِ وَالْعُدْوَانِ

"And always support one another in (the works of) righteousness and piety, but do not become accomplices in (works of) sin and transgression."[80]

Thieves commit cardinal sins by stealing. Such offenders are liable to severe penalty, as the following verse states.

﴿وَالسَّارِقُ وَالسَّارِقَةُ فَاقْطَعُواْ أَيْدِيَهُمَا جَزَاءً بِمَا كَسَبَا نَكَالًا مِّنَ اللهِ﴾

(After proper judicial trial as per law,) cut off the hands of both the man as well as the woman who steal, in retribution of (the offence) which they have committed, a deterring punishment from Allah.[81]

If an individual's stolen property is found with someone, the real owner has the right to claim his or her goods, and the person with whom the goods are found should give them to its rightful owner and claim his or her loss from the thief who sold the things. Stolen goods are thus prohibited to trade.

The Holy Prophet (Allah bless him and give him peace) said:

مَنِ اشْتَرَى سَرِقَةً وَهُوَ يَعْلَمُ أَنَّهَا سَرِقَةٌ، فَقَدْ شَرِكَ فِي عَارِهَا وَإِثْمِهَا.

If any person buys a stolen good knowing it for what it is, that person is a partner in the ignominy and sin.[82]

3.6.12 Sale of items not in one's possession

Selling something that is not in one's possession is unlawful in Islam. The rationale behind this prohibition is very simple: one may not guarantee the quality of an item without seeing it in a tangible form. There is every likelihood that such an ambiguous transaction will raise questions on the integrity of the seller. The following Traditions establish the point that it is invalid to sell commodities before taking possession of them.

It is reported that Ibn 'Umar (may Allah be well pleased with him and his father) said:

أَنَّهُمْ كَانُوْا يَشْتَرُوْنَ الطَّعَامَ مِنَ الرُّكْبَانِ عَلَى عَهْدِ النَّبِيِّ a، فَيَبْعَثُ عَلَيْهِمْ مَنْ يَمْنَعُهُمْ أَنْ يَبِيْعُوْهُ حَيْثُ اشْتَرَوْهُ حَتَّ يَنْقُلُوهُ حَيْثُ يُبَاعُ الطَّعَامُ.

They used to buy foodstuffs direct from caravans during the time of the Prophet (Allah bless him and give him peace) and he sent someone to them forbidding them to sell it where they had bought it until they had moved it to where food was usually sold.[83]

Also Ibn 'Umar (may Allah be well pleased with him and his father) related:

نَهَى النَّبِيُّ أَنْ يُبَاعَ الطَّعَامُ إِذَا اشْتَرَاهُ حَتَّ يَسْتَوْفِيَهُ.

The Prophet (Allah bless him and give him peace) forbade foodstuffs to be sold after they had been bought until the whole amount had been received.[84]

It is reported that Ibn 'Umar (may Allah be well pleased with him and his father) was heard saying that the Prophet (Allah bless him and give him peace) said:

مَنِ ابْتَاعَ طَعَامًا فَلاَ يَبِعْهُ حَتَّ يَقْبِضَهُ.

When someone buys food he should not sell it until he has taken delivery of it.[85]

According to Ibn 'Abbās (may Allah be pleased with him), Allah's Messenger (Allah bless him and give him peace) said:

مَنِ ابْتَاعَ طَعَامًا فَلاَ يَبِعْهُ حَتَّ يَكْتَالَهُ.

Whoever buys food should not sell it until he has measured it.

Sālim's father reported:

رَأَيْتُ الَّذِيْنَ يَشْتَرُوْنَ الطَّعَامَ مُجَازَفَةً يُضْرَبُونَ عَلَى عَهْدِ رَسُوْلِ اللّٰهِ a أَنْ يَبِيْعُوْهُ حَتَّى يُؤْوُوْهُ إِلَى رِحَالِهِمْ.

In the time of Allah's Messenger (Allah bless him and give him peace), I saw that those who bought food without it being measured or weighed were beaten (as a disciplinary punishment) if they sold it before they had taken it to their homes.[86]

It is narrated from Ibn 'Umar (Allah be well pleased with him and his father), who said:

اِبْتَعْتُ زَيْتًا بِالسُّوْقِ، فَلَمَّا اسْتَوْجَبْتُهُ لَقِيَنِيْ رَجُلٌ فَأَعْطَانِيْ بِهِ رِبْحًا حَسَنًا، فَأَرَدْتُ أَنْ أَضْرِبَ عَلَى يَدِهِ، فَأَخَذَ رَجُلٌ مِنْ خَلْفِيْ بِذِرَاعِيْ، فَالْتَفَتُّ إِلَيْهِ، فَإِذَا زَيْدُ بْنُ ثَابِتٍ، فَقَالَ: لَا تَبِعْهُ حَيْثُ ابْتَعْتَهُ حَتَّى تَحُوْزَهُ إِلَى رَحْلِكَ؛ فَإِنَّ رَسُوْلَ اللهِ نَهَى أَنْ تُبَاعَ السِّلَعُ حَيْثُ تُبْتَاعُ حَتَّى يَحُوْزَهَا التُّجَّارُ إِلَى رِحَالِهِمْ.

I bought some olive oil in the marketplace, and when it came into my possession I was met by a man who offered me a good profit for it, and I wanted to make a deal with him, but a man behind me took hold of my arm. I turned around and saw that it was Zayd b. Thābit (may Allah be pleased with him). He said: "Do not sell it where you bought it until you take it to your place, for Allah's Messenger (Allah bless him and give him peace) forbade selling merchandise where it were bought, before the merchants moved them to their places."[87]

Ḥakīm b. Ḥizām (may Allah be pleased with him) narrated:

أَتَيْتُ رَسُوْلَ اللهِ فَقُلْتُ: يَأْتِيْنِيْ الرَّجُلُ يَسْأَلُنِيْ مِنَ الْبَيْعِ مَا لَيْسَ عِنْدِي، أَبْتَاعُ لَهُ مِنَ السُّوْقِ ثُمَّ أَبِيْعُهُ، قَالَ: لَا تَبِعْ مَا لَيْسَ عِنْدَكَ.

I went to Allah's Messenger (Allah bless him and give him peace) and said: "A man comes to me asking to buy something that I do not have. Can I buy it from the market for him and then give it to him?" The Messenger (Allah bless him and give him peace) said: "Do not sell what is not with you."[88]

3.6.13 Sale on sale

The faithful are forbidden to put an offer on a commodity that has been principally sold to someone else.

'Abd Allāh b. 'Umar (may Allah be well pleased with him and his father) narrated that Allah's Messenger (Allah bless him and give him peace) said:

لَا يَبِعْ بَعْضُكُمْ عَلَى بَيْعِ بَعْضٍ وَلَا تَلَقَّوُا السِّلَعَ حَتَّى يُهْبَطَ بِهَا الْأَسْوَاقَ.

Do not buy in opposition to another's purchase, and do not intercept the products until they arrive in the marketplace.[89]

This prohibition refers to a situation where someone has already negotiated for a purchase and the deal has been closed in an auction sale. Suddenly, another customer shows up and offers better price to the seller for the commodity which has already been sold to someone else for less, and instigates the seller to revert from the closed deal for some extra monetary benefit. The following Prophetic Tradition establishes that sale on sale is outlawed.

According to Abū Hurayra (may Allah be pleased with him), Allah's Messenger (Allah bless him and give him peace) said:

لَا تَحَاسَدُوْا وَلَا تَنَاجَشُوْا، وَلَا تَبَاغَضُوْا وَلَا تَدَابَرُوْا، وَلَا يَبِعْ بَعْضُكُمْ عَلَى بَيْعِ بَعْضٍ. وَكُوْنُوْا عِبَادَ اللهِ إِخْوَانًا. الْمُسْلِمُ أَخُو الْمُسْلِمِ؛ لَا يَظْلِمُهُ وَلَا يَخْذُلُهُ وَلَا يَحْقِرُهُ. اَلتَّقْوَى هَاهُنَا (وَيُشِيرُ إِلَى صَدْرِهِ ثَلَاثَ مَرَّاتٍ). بِحَسْبِ امْرِيءٍ مِنَ الشَّرِّ أَنْ يَحْقِرَ أَخَاهُ الْمُسْلِمَ. كُلُّ الْمُسْلِمِ عَلَى الْمُسْلِمِ حَرَامٌ دَمُهُ وَمَالُهُ وَعِرْضُهُ.

> You must not be jealous of one another, you must not outbid one another, you must not have spite against one another, you must not turn your backs on one another, and one of you must not buy in opposition to another's purchase. Servants of Allah! Become brothers to one another. The Muslim is the brother of the Muslim; he does not wrong him, he does not forsake him, and he does not scorn him. God wariness is here (and Allah's Messenger pointed to his sacred breast three times). It is evil enough for a Muslim to scorn his Muslim brother. The Muslim's blood, his property and his honour are forbidden (and inviolable) for the other Muslim.[90]

In a related point, if a dispute arises about a commodity which is claimed to be bought by two independent buyers, Shariah Law suggests that the decision would be made in favour of the one who proves to be the first one among two to buy that item. Al-Shawkānī comments on this score:

> There is a reason in it that any person who sold out an article to an individual, and then he sold it out to another person, the sale will not be for the second person; it will be for the first. It will become unlawful for the second person. It is because he has sold the thing that was beyond his jurisdiction.[91]

If the auction sale has not been closed, then would-be purchasers may outbid one another – and this is legally permissible. Sale by bidding is approved by the normative practice of the Messenger (Allah bless him and give him peace).

عَنْ أَنَسِ بْنِ مَالِكٍ أَنَّ رَسُوْلَ اللهِ بَاعَ حِلْسًا وَقَدَحًا، وَقَالَ: مَنْ يَشْتَرِيْ هَذَا الْحِلْسَ وَالْقَدَحَ؟ فَقَالَ رَجُلٌ: أَخَذْتُهُمَا بِدِرْهَمٍ، فَقَالَ النَّبِيُّ: مَنْ يَزِيدُ عَلَى دِرْهَمٍ؟ مَنْ يَزِيدُ عَلَى دِرْهَمٍ؟ فَأَعْطَاهُ رَجُلٌ دِرْهَمَيْنِ، فَبَاعَهُمَا مِنْهُ.

> Anas b. Mālik (may Allah be pleased with him) related that Allah's Messenger (Allah bless him and give him peace) sold a saddle blanket and a drinking bowl. He asked: "Who will buy this saddle blanket and drinking bowl?" whereupon a man offered: "I will take them for a *dirham*." So the Prophet (Allah bless him and give him peace) asked: "Who will give more than a *dirham*? Who will give more than a *dirham*?" A man agreed to give him two *dirhams*, so he sold them to him.[92]

3.6.14 Animals that feed on impurities (al-jallāla)

An animal that feeds on impurities is called *al-jallāla*. It consistently eats the droppings of other animals and impurities. The title *al-jallāla* is applied to an animal when the consumption of impurities changes its protein, structure, odour, colour and even taste. Consuming meat and drinking milk from such animals –including livestock, camels, cows, goats or hens that feed on impurities – is prohibited. Nor can we sacrifice them on the occasion of 'Īd (Muslims' festival).

عَنِ ابْنِ عُمَرَ ، قَالَ: نَهَى رَسُوْلُ اللهِ عَنْ أَكْلِ الجَلاَّلَةِ وَأَلْبَانِهَا.

> According to Ibn 'Umar (Allah be well pleased with him and his father): "Allah's Messenger (Allah bless him and give him peace) prohibited eating *al-jallāla* and milking it."[93]

In the Hadith given next, the Prophet (Allah bless him and give him peace) proscribed riding *al-jallāla*.

عَنِ ابْنِ عُمَرَ قَالَ: نَهَى رَسُوْلُ اللهِ عَنِ الجَلاَّلَةِ فِيْ الْإِبِلِ أَنْ يُرْكَبَ عَلَيْهَا أَوْ يُشْرَبَ مِنْ
أَلْبَانِهَا.

> Ibn 'Umar (Allah be well pleased with him and his father) said: "Allah's Messenger (Allah bless him and give him peace) forbade riding or drinking the milk of *al-jallāla* camels."[94]

Such an animal does not become unlawful for all eternity. Jurists suggest that such animals be tied at one place for a period of three days and given a diet of clean food so that their meat becomes wholesome and worthy of consumption.

Most of the time we focus on killing lawful animals in a manner that Islam prescribes. The meat of such animals alone is consumed. However, we neglect the way an animal is raised. At present, it is very important to know what animals feed on. Many poultry farms raise their animals on animal protein and animal by-products because of the low cost. In order to do a roaring trade, dairy farm owners feed their animals the by-products of unlawful animals – dogs, pigs and cats – because they cannot afford to raise their animals with organic feed. If a

Muslim knows that he or she is being offered the flesh of *al-jallāla*, he or she must not touch it.

Moreover, the faithful may consume herbivores (animals that survive on plants, fruits, leaves, and other natural food sources) as they are wholesome, whilst carnivores (animals that eat meat) are prohibited.

3.6.15 Lotteries and gambling (maysir)

Literally, *maysir* is a means of getting a profit without working for it. It refers to a game of chance, the acquisition of wealth without effort, whether or not this deprives another of his or her rights. Technically, *maysir* is defined as gambling and any form of business activity where financial gains are acquired from mere chance, speculation or conjecture. Since a lottery is one of the forms of gambling, it is proscribed. The reason for the unlawfulness of *maysir* is that it excites enmity and hatred among people. In reference to gambling, Allah says in the Qur'ān:

﴿يَا أَيُّهَا الَّذِينَ آمَنُواْ إِنَّمَا الْخَمْرُ وَالْمَيْسِرُ وَالأَنصَابُ وَالأَزْلاَمُ رِجْسٌ مِّنْ عَمَلِ الشَّيْطَانِ فَاجْتَنِبُوهُ لَعَلَّكُمْ تُفْلِحُونَ﴾

O believers! Wine and gambling and idols mounted (for worship) and divining arrows (for seeking luck – all) are filthy works of Satan. So turn away from them (completely) so that you may prosper.[95]

The following Tradition is on the prohibition of *maysir* (gambling), the lottery being its modern form.

عَنْ عَبْدِ اللهِ بْنِ عَمْرٍو أَنَّ نَبِيَّ اللهِ نَهَى عَنِ الْخَمْرِ وَالْمَيْسِرِ، وَالْكُوبَةِ وَالْغُبَيْرَاءِ، وَقَالَ: كُلُّ مُسْكِرٍ حَرَامٌ.

According to 'Abd Allāh b. 'Amr (may Allah be well pleased with him), Allah's Prophet (Allah bless him and give him peace) forbade wine, gambling, *al-kūba* (a type of musical drum) and *ghubayrā'* (an intoxicating drink made from millet) and said: "All intoxicants are prohibited."[96]

To understand the rationale behind the prohibition of lotteries, we need to familiarise ourselves with the custom of pagan Arabs with regard to practising lotteries. The most familiar form of gambling among the pagan Arabs was casting lots with arrows drawn from a bag. Some were blank and those who drew them got nothing at all. Other arrows indicated prizes. Whether or not one got anything depended on pure luck.

The principle on which gambling is prohibited is that one makes a profit without effort or suffer loss, on a mere chance. Lotteries, dice, wager and betting on horse races are all different forms of gambling.

3.6.16 Bitcoin

One of the hottest contemporary topics in business and trade from both the secular and the Islamic viewpoint has been Bitcoin. Traders in Bitcoin consider themselves lucky as their investments have turned out to be lucrative. If the current trend does not break, multiple rewards are expected from Bitcoin. Due to its huge popularity, many Muslims are enquiring whether Bitcoin it complies with Islam.

Buying and trading Bitcoin is not lawful, in my opinion, for the following reasons:

1 Bitcoin has no intrinsic value, whilst the value of a reliable currency may be durable for a long period of time. The narrative of the Seven Sleepers of the Cave demonstrates that valuable currency may be used even after 300 years.[97] The currency with an intrinsic value is gold and silver.[98]
2 Bitcoin is not issued by a state or a competent authority, and the overwhelming majority of institutions are still ambivalent about its future. Legally speaking, Bitcoin has no validity. Its uncertain future drives away many people, even ambitious people, because they do not want to gamble away their money. The general public – and even economists – feel that as the value of Bitcoin skyrocketed, it may also fall in the same fashion. This craze may fizzle sooner rather than later. On this score, Allah's Messenger (Allah bless him and give him peace) prohibited the *al-gharar* sale (a business contract which entails an element of uncertainty or hazard).[99]
3 No central bank guarantees Bitcoin as a valid currency. Perhaps there may never be one: many people purchase it because of the anonymity of its ownership. The possession of this currency is masked cleverly so that the owner may not pay any tax. Evading taxes is a crime against society and the government.[100]
4 From the Islamic perspective, all those who benefit from state services – for example, as every resident of a state uses public roads – and do not pay taxes are dishonest citizens. By living in a certain country, you actually enter into a contract that you will abide by its laws. Fulfilment of commitments is an obligation, as per the Qur'ān:

ا أَيُّهَا الَّذِينَ آمَنُوا أَوْفُوا بِالْعُقُودِ

"O believers! Fulfil (your) promises."[101]

5 Islamic economic thought calls attention to real economic activity based on physical assets in order to provide for oneself and one's family. Regarding trade and business, the Muslim Scripture states:

أَحَلَّ اللَّهُ الْبَيْعَ

"Allah has declared trade (i.e., buying and selling) lawful."[102]

How can one make money through Bitcoin or any other form of cryptocurrency when they cannot be held in any tangible form?

6 Exchanged only anonymously, this virtual currency paves the way for fraud, corruption and criminal activities. The prohibition of all forms of corruption stems from the following verse:

أَوْفُوا الْكَيْلَ وَلَا تَكُونُوا مِنَ الْمُخْسِرِينَ وَزِنُوا بِالْقِسْطَاسِ الْمُسْتَقِيمِ وَلَا تَبْخَسُوا النَّاسَ
أَشْيَاءَهُمْ وَلَا تَعْثَوْا فِي الْأَرْضِ مُفْسِدِينَ

> *Always fill up full measure and do not become injurious (to the rights of the people). And weigh with a straight balance. And do not give to the people their things (weighing) less than what is due, nor provoke strife in the land (by such moral, economic and social corruption and fraud).*[103]

7 Because of bad press, the value of Bitcoin is unstable. Because of its high volatility, cryptocurrencies are not reliable. Some regard Bitcoin's surge as very turbulent. Islam does not approve of such ambiguity and insecurity in financial matters.[104]

8 When trading Bitcoin, you may accumulate a lot of wealth in a short time, but you may also lose the whole of it. This is precisely what happens at casinos. On the illegality of gambling, the following verse reads:

يَا أَيُّهَا الَّذِينَ آمَنُواْ إِنَّمَا الْخَمْرُ وَالْمَيْسِرُ وَالأَنصَابُ وَالأَزْلاَمُ رِجْسٌ مِّنْ عَمَلِ الشَّيْطَانِ
فَاجْتَنِبُوهُ لَعَلَّكُمْ تُفْلِحُونَ

> *O believers! Wine and gambling and idols mounted (for worship) and divin arrows (for seeking luck – all) are filthy works of Satan. So turn away from them (completely) so that you may prosper.*[105]

Notes

1 Cited by al-Ghazālī in *Iḥyā' al-'ulūm*, 2:64.
2 Qur'ān 2:168.
3 Ibid., 5:88.
4 Ibid., 7:157.
5 Narrated by al-Bayhaqī in *al-Sunan al-kubrā*, 6:128 §11695; al-Quḍā'ī in *Musnad al-Shihāb*, 1:104 §121; al-Daylamī in *al-Firdaws bi-Ma'thūr al-Khiṭāb*, 2:441 §3918; and Abū Nu'aym in *ḥilya al-Awliyā'*, 7:126.
6 Narrated al-Ḥākim in *al-Mustadrak*, 2:7 §2134.
7 Narrated by al-Ḥākim in *al-Mustadrak*, 4:141 §7164.

8 Narrated by al-Bukhārī in *al-Ṣaḥīḥ*: *al-Īmān* [Faith], Ch.: On the excellence of the one who exercises prudence in his religion, 1:28 §52.
9 Narrated by Imam Muslim in *al-Ṣaḥīḥ*: *al-Zakāt* [The Alms-due], Ch.: Acceptance of charity that comes from good earnings and the growth thereof, 2:703 §1015.
10 Basic Principles of Halal and Haram, https://mjchalaaltrust.co.za/halal-standards-basic-principles/
11 Narrated by Imam Muslim in *al-Ṣaḥīḥ*: Hunting, sacrificing animals, and which part of the animal is edible, Ch.: The injunction to perform the slaughter and cutting well, and to sharpen the cutting blade, 3:1548 §1955; and al-Tirmidhī in *al-Sunan*: Blood-money payments, Ch.: What has come to us about the prohibition of mutilation, 4:23 §1409.
12 Narrated byAbū Dāwūd in *al-Sunan*: *al-Dhabā'iḥ* [Slaughter animals], Ch.: Slaughtering with *marwa* (a type of stone, like marble or granite), 3:102 §2821.
13 Narrated by al-Tirmidhī in *al-Sunan*: *al-Aṭ'ima* [Foodstuffs], Ch.: What has been related about consuming the flesh of the *al-jallāla* and milking it, 4:270 §1825.
14 Qur'ān 5:3.
15 Ibid., 6:121.
16 Ibid., 5:5.
17 What is Halal: A Guide for Non-Muslims, www.icv.org.au/about/about-islam-overview/what-is-halal-a-guide-for-non-muslims/
18 Qur'ān 6:121.
19 Ibid., 5:1.
20 Narrated by Ibn Abī Shayba in *al-Muṣannaf*, 4:287 §20209.
21 Narrated by al-Bukhārī in *Khalqaf'āl al-'ibād*, 1:66.
22 Narrated by al-Bayhaqī in *al-Sunan al-Kubrā*, 6:16 §10847.
23 Qur'ān 2:79.
24 Ibid., 7:26.
25 Narrated by al-Nasā'ī in *al-Sunan al-Kubrā*, 5:437 §9450.
26 Narrated by al-Bukhārī in *al-Ṣaḥīḥ*: *al-Janā'iz* [Funeral ceremonies], Ch.: The order to join funeral processions, 1:417 §1182.
27 Narrated by Ibn Mājah in *al-Sunan*: *Kitab ul Janai'z*. The chapters on what has been narrated regarding funerals, Ch.: What was narrated concerning washing the disease, 1:469 §1460.
28 Narrated by al-Bukhārī in *al-Ṣaḥīḥ*: *al-Buyū'* [Sales], Ch.: When one of the parties gives his companion the option to withdraw after a sale has been concluded, the sale becomes binding, 2:744 §2006.
29 Narrated by al-Bukhārī in *al-Ṣaḥīḥ*: *al-Buyū'* [Sales], Ch.: A buyer and seller making things clear and not concealing anything and showing good faith, 2:732 §1973.
30 Islamic Question & Answer, https://islamqa.info/en/13973
31 Narrated by al-Bukhārī in *al-Ṣaḥīḥ*: *al-Buyū'* [Sales], The Prophet (Allah bless him and give him peace) buying on credit, 2:729 §1962.
32 Narrated by al-Bukhārī in *al-Ṣaḥīḥ*: *al-Buyū'* [Sales], Ch.: When unlawful conditions are stipulated in a sale, 2:759 §2060.
33 Narrated by al-Bukhārī in *al-Ṣaḥīḥ*: *al-Salam* [The *Salam* sale (a sale in which the price is paid in advance for goods to be delivered later)], Ch.: The *salam* in respect of a specified measure, 2:781 §2124.
34 Narrated by Abū Dāwūd in *al-Sunan*: *al-Ijāra* [Employment], Ch.: Regarding a man selling what he does not possess, 3:283 §3503.
35 Qur'ān 17:70.
36 Qur'ān 5:32
37 Ibid., 5:3.
38 Narrated by Ibn Ḥibbān in *al-Ṣaḥīḥ*, 11:312 §4938; Aḥmad b. Ḥanbal in *al-Musnad*, 1:293 §2678; and al-Dāraquṭnī in *al-Sunan*, 3:7 § 20.

39 Narrated by al-Bukhārī in *al-Ṣaḥīḥ*: *al-Buyū'* [Sales], Ch.: Selling carrion and idols, 2:779 §2121; Muslim in *al-Ṣaḥīḥ*: *al-Musāqāt* [Sharecropping], Ch.: The prohibition of selling wine, dead meat, pork and idols, 3:1207 §1581; and al-Tirmidhī in *al-Sunan*: *al-Buyū'* [Sales], Ch.: What has been related about selling skins of dead animals and idols, 3:591 §1297.

40 Qur'ān 35:10.

41 Narrated by al-Bukhārī in *al-Ṣaḥīḥ*: *al-Īmān* [Faith], Ch.: What has come to inform us that actions are judged according to one's intention and sincerity, and every man is credited with what he intended, 1:30 §54; and Muslim in *al-Ṣaḥīḥ*: *al-Imāra* [The emirate], Ch.: His saying: "Actions are judged according to the intention," and that he included in it the military campaign and other actions, 3:1515 §1907.

42 Ayatollah & Fadlollah, 2006. Islamic Rulings, a Guide of Islamic Practice, https://www.arabicbookshop.net/islamic-rulings/163-184

43 Narrated by Abū Dāwūd in *al-Sunan*: *al-Ijāra* [Employment], Ch.: Regarding a man selling what he does not possess, 3:283 §3503.

44 Narrated by Abū Dāwūd in *al-Sunan*: *al-Ijāra* [Employment], Ch.: Regarding selling food before taking possession of it, 3:282 §3499.

45 Narrated by al-Tirmidhī in *al-Sunan*: *al-Buyū'* [Sales], Ch.: What has been related about it being disliked to sell what one does not have, 3:534 §1232.

46 Qur'ān 2:282.

47 Narrated by al-Bukhārī in *al-Ṣaḥīḥ*: *al-Buyū'* [Sales], The Prophet (Allah bless him and give him peace) buying on credit, 2:729 §1962.

48 Narrated by Imam Muslim in *al-Ṣaḥīḥ*: *al-Ḥudūd [*The prescribed punishments], Ch.: Cutting off the hand of a thief from the nobility and others; the prohibition of interceding with regard to the prescribed punishments, 3:1315 §1688; al-Bukhārī in *al-Ṣaḥīḥ*: *Faḍā'il al-Ṣaḥāba* [The excellent merits of the Companions], Ch.: Concerning Usāma b. Zayd, 3:1366 §3526; and al-Tirmidhī in *al-Sunan*: *al-Ḥudūd* [The prescribed punishments], Ch.: What has been related about the abhorrence of interceding in the legal punishments, 4:37 §1430.

49 Ibn Rushd, *Bidāyat al-mujtahid*, 2:299.

50 Qur'ān 4:105–109.

51 Ibid., 3:75.

52 Narrated by Abū Dāwūd in *al-Sunan*: *al-Salām* [Well-being], Ch.: Regarding kissing the body, 4:356 §5224.

53 Cited by al-Sarkhasī in *al-Mabsūṭ*, 12:194.

54 Al-Jurjānī, *al-Ta'rifāt*, p. 208.

55 Narrated by al-Bukhārī in *al-Ṣaḥīḥ*: *al-Buyū'* [Sales], Ch.: Selling fresh dates before it is clear that they are sound, 2:766 §2082.

56 Previously we have discussed the sale of she-camel that is pregnant, the fetus of a came still in the womb of a she-camel. However, the sale of *ḥabal al-ḥabāla* (unborn animals) is different from it as it only discusses the sale of fetus without selling its mother alone.

57 Narrated by Imam Muslim in *al-Ṣaḥīḥ*: *al-Buyū'* [Sales], Ch.: The prohibition of *ḥabal al-ḥabāla* (selling the offspring of the offspring that is still in the womb of the camel), 3:1153 §1514.

58 Narrated by al-Ṭabarānī in *al-Mu'jam al-Kabīr*, 11:230 §11581.

59 Narrated by Ibn Mājah in *al-Sunan*: Ch.: Prohibition of buying what is in the wombs and udders of cattle and whatever a diver is going to bring up, 3:2196.

60 Narrated by al-Tirmidhī in *al-Sunan*: *al-Buyū'* [Sales], Ch.: What has been related about sales of *al-gharar* (a sale involving uncertainty or deceit) are disliked, 3:532 §1230.

61 Ibid.

62 Narrated by al-Bukhārī in *al-Ṣaḥīḥ*: *al-Buyū'* [Sales], Ch.: The *al-munābadha* sale, 2:754 §2039.

63 Narrated by al-Tirmidhī in *al-Sunan*: *al-Buyū'* [Sales], Ch.: What has been related about *al-munābadha* and *al-mulāmasa*, 3:601 §1310.
64 Narrated by Mālik in *al-Muwaṭṭa'*, 2:667.
65 Narrated by al-Bukhārī in *al-Ṣaḥīḥ*: *al-Buyū'* [Sales], Ch.: The *al-mulāmasa* sale, 2:754 §2037.
66 Narrated by Abū Dāwūd in *al-Sunan*: *al-Tijārāt* [Trade], Ch.: Regarding selling crops years in advance, 3:254 §3374.
67 Narrated by Imam Muslim in *al-Ṣaḥīḥ*: *al-Buyū'* [Sales], Ch.: The prohibition of *al-muḥāqala* and *al-muzābana*, and *al-mukhābara*, and selling produce before its goodness appears, and *al-mu'āwama*, which he is selling years in advance, 3:1174 §1536.
68 Ibid., 3:1175 §1536.
69 Narrated by Abū Dāwūd in *al-Sunan*: *al-Buyū'* [Sales], Ch.: Regarding the stern warning concerning that, 3:261 §3400.
70 Narrated by Imam Muslim in *al-Ṣaḥīḥ*: *al-Buyū'* [Sales], Ch.: The prohibition of selling fresh dates in exchange for dry dates except in the case of *al-arāyā* (a kind of sale in which the owner of dates that are still on the tree can sell them for dried dates by estimation), 3:1168 §1539.
71 Narrated by al-Tirmidhī in *al-Sunan*: *al-Buyū'* [Sales], Ch.: What has been related about the prohibition from making exceptions, 3:585 §1290.
72 Narrated by al-Ṭabarānī in *al-Mu'jam al-Awsaṭ*, 6:43 §5744.
73 Narrated by al-Bukhārī in *al-Ṣaḥīḥ*: *al-Zakāt* [The stipulated amount of alms], Ch.: Someone selling his fruit, palm trees, land or crops when *'ushr* (one-tenth of the produce of land) or obligatory charity is due on them and then paying the obligatory charity he owes from something else, or selling his fruit before obligatory charity is due on it, 2:541 §1415.
74 Narrated by Imam Muslim in *al-Ṣaḥīḥ*: *al-Buyū'* [Sales], Ch.: The prohibition of selling produce before its goodness appears, 3:1165 §1535.
75 Narrated by al-Ḥākim in *al-Mustadrak*, 2:23 §1292.
76 Narrated by al-Bukhārī in *al-Ṣaḥīḥ*: *al-Buyū'* [Sales], Ch.: The *mukhādara* sale (selling fruits and grains while still green), 2:768 §2094.
77 Kureshi & Hayat, 2015, *Contracts and Deals in Islamic Finance: A User's Guide to Cash Flows, Balance Sheets, and Capital Structures*, Wiley, USA, ISBN: 978-1-119-02056-1
78 Compilation Guide on Prudential and Structural Islamic Finance Indicators,www.ifsb.org/PSIFI_08/download/compilation_guide%202007.pdf
79 Narrated by Abū Dāwūd in *al-Sunan*: *al-Ijāra* [Employment], Ch.: Regarding a man selling what he does not possess, 3:283 §3503.
80 Qur'ān 5:2.
81 Ibid., 5:38.
82 Narrated by al-Ḥākim in *al-Mustadrak*, 2:41 §2253.
83 Narrated by al-Bukhārī in *al-Ṣaḥīḥ*: *al-Buyū'* [Sales], Ch.: What is mentioned about markets, 2:747 §2017.
84 Ibid.
85 Narrated by al-Bukhārī in *al-Ṣaḥīḥ*: *al-Buyū'* [Sales], Ch.: What is mentioned about selling food and hoarding, 2:750 §2026.
86 Ibid., 2:750 §2024.
87 Narrated by Abū Dāwūd in *al-Sunan*: *al-Ijāra* [Employment], Ch.: Regarding selling food before taking possession of it, 3:282 §3499.
88 Narrated by al-Tirmidhī in *al-Sunan*: *al-Buyū'* [Sales], Ch.: What has been related about it being disliked to sell what one does not have, 3:534 §1232.
89 Narrated by Abū Dāwūd in *al-Sunan*: *al-Ijāra* [Employment], Ch.: Regarding meeting merchants outside the city, 3:269 §3436.
90 Narrated by Imam Muslim in *al-Ṣaḥīḥ*: Al-bir, wa al-*Ṣilat wa al-ādāb*, Piety, affinity and good manners, Ch.: The prohibition of wronging the Muslim, deserting him, and

despising him, his goods, his blood and his wealth, 4:1986 §2564; 'Abd b. Ḥumayd in *al-Musnad*, 1:420 §1442; and Ibn Ḥajar al-'Asqalānī in *Fatḥ al-Bārī*, 10:483.
91 Narrated by al-Shawkānī in *Nayl al-Awtār*, 5:254.
92 Narrated by al-Tirmidhī in *al-Sunan*: *al-Buyū'* [Sales], Ch.: What has been related about auctioning, 3:522 §1218; and Ibn Qudāma in *al-Mughnī*, 4:149.
93 Narrated by al-Tirmidhī in *al-Sunan*: *al-Aṭ'ima* [Foodstuffs], Ch.: What has been related about consuming the flesh of the *al-jallāla* and milking it, 4:270 §1824.
94 Narrated by Abū Dāwūd in *al-Sunan*: *al-Aṭ'ima* [Foodstuffs], Ch.: What has been related about consuming the flesh of the *al-jallāla* and milking it, 3:351 §3787.
95 Qur'ān 5:90.
96 Narrated by Abū Dāwūd *al-Sunan*: *al-Ashriba* [Beverages], Ch.: What has been reported regarding intoxicants, 3:328 §3685.
97 Qur'ān 18:19.
98 Ibid., 3:14.
99 Narrated by al-Tirmidhī in *al-Sunan*: *al-Buyū'* [Sales], Ch.: What has been related about sales of *al-gharar* (a sale involving uncertainty or deceit) are disliked, 3:532 §1230.
100 Ibid.
101 Qur'ān 5:1.
102 Ibid., 2:275.
103 Ibid., 26:181–183.
104 Narrated by al-Tirmidhī in *al-Sunan*: *al-Buyū'* [Sales], Ch.: What has been related about sales of *al-gharar* (a sale involving uncertainty or deceit) are disliked, 3:532 §1230.
105 Qur'ān 5:90.

Bibliography

The Holy Qur'ān

'Abd b. Ḥumayd, Abū Muhammad b. Naṣr al-Kasī (d. 249/863). *Al-Musnad*. Cairo, Egypt: Maktaba al-Sunna, 1408/1988.

Abū Dāwūd, Sulaymān b. Ash'ath b. Isḥāq b. Bashīr al-Sijistānī (202–275/817–889). *Al-Sunan*. Beirut, Lebanon: Dār al-Fikr, 1414/1994.

Abū Nu'aym, Aḥmad b. 'Abd Allāh b. Aḥmad b. Isḥāq b. Mūsā b. Mihrān al-Aṣbahānī (336–430/948–1038). *ḥilya al-Awliyā'waṬabaqāt al-Aṣfiyā'*. Beirut, Lebanon: Dār al-Kitāb al-'Arabī, 1400/1980.

'Asqalānī, Ibn Ḥajar Aḥmad b. *Fatḥ al-Bārīsharḥ Ṣaḥīḥ al-Bukhārī*. Beirut, Lebanon: Dār al-Ma'rifa, 1379AH.

Basic Principles of Halal and Haram, https://mjchalaaltrust.co.za/*halal*-standards-basic-principles/

Bayhaqī, Aḥmad b. al-Ḥusayn al-. *Al-Sunan al-Kubrā*. Mecca, Saudi Arabia: Maktaba Dār al-Bāz, 1994.

Bukhārī, Abū'Abd Allāh Muhammad b. Ismā'īl b. Ibrahīm b. Mughīra al-. (194–256/810–870). *Al-Ṣaḥīḥ*. Beirut, Lebanon, Damascus, Syria: Dār al-Qalam, 1401/1981.

Compilation Guide on Prudential and Structural Islamic Finance Indicators, www.ifsb.org/PSIFI_08/download/compilation_guide%202007.pdf

Dāraquṭnī, 'Alī b. 'Umar al-. *Al-Sunan*. Beirut, Lebanon: Dār al-Ma'rifa, 1966.

Daylamī, Abū Shujā'Shīrawayh. *Al-Firdaws bi ma'thūr al-khiṭāb*. Mecca, Saudi Arabia: Dar al-Kotob al-Ilmiyah, 1986.

Ghazālī, Abūḥāmid Muhammad b. Muhammad al-Ghazālī al- (450–505AH). *Iḥyā 'al-'Ulūm*. Beirut, Lebanon: Dār al-Ma'rifa, 2001.
ḥākim, Muhammad b. 'Abd Allāh al-. *Al-Mustadrak 'alā al-ṣaḥīḥayn*. Beirut, Lebanon: Dar al-Kotob al-Ilmiyah, 1990.
Ḥanbal, Aḥmad b. *Al-Musnad*. Beirut, Lebanon: Dar al-Kotob al-Ilmiyah, 1986.
Ibn Abī Shayba, 'Abd Allāh b. Muhammad. *Al-Muṣannaf*. Riyadh: Maktaba al-Rushd, 1409AH.
Ibn Ḥibbān, Abūḥātim Muhammad. *Al-Ṣaḥīḥ*. Beirut, Lebanon: Mu'assasa al-Risāla, 1993.
Ibn Kathīr, Abū al-Fidā'Ismā'īl b. 'Umar. *Tafsīr al-Qur'ān al-'Aẓīm*. Beirut, Lebanon: Dar al-Fikr, 1401AH.
Ibn Mājah, Abū'Abd Allāh Muhammad b. Yazīd al-Qazwīnī (209–273/824–887). *Al-Sunan*. Beirut, Lebanon: Dār al-Kutub al-'Ilmiyya, 1419/1998.
Ibn Qudāma al-Maqdisī. *Al-Mughnīfīfiqh al-Imām Aḥmad b. Ḥanbal al-Shaybānī*. Beirut, Lebanon: Dar al-Fikr, 1405AH.
Ibn Rushd, Muhammad b. Aḥmad. *Bidāyat al-Mujtahid*. Beirut, Lebanon: Dar al-Fikr, n.d.
Islamic Question & Answer, https://islamqa.info/en/13973
Jurjānī, 'Alī b. Muhammad b. 'Alī Sayyid Sharīf al- (740–816 AH). *Al-Ta'rifāt*. Beirut, Lebanon: 'ālim al-Kutub, 1416/1996.
Mālik, Ibn Anas b. Mālik b. Abī'āmir b. 'Amr b. Ḥārith al-Aṣbaḥī (93–179/712–795). *Al-Muwaṭṭā'*. Beirut, Lebanon: Dār Iḥyā' al-Turāth al-'Arabī, 1990.
Muslim, Ibn al-*Ḥajjāj* Abū al-Ḥasan al-Qushayrī al-Naysābūrī (206–261/821–875). *Al-Mu'jam al-kabīr*. Mosul: Maktaba al-'Ulūmwa al-ḥikam, 1983.
Nasā'ī, Aḥmad b. Shu'ayb Abū'Abd al-Raḥmān al- (215–303/830–915). *'Amal al-Yawmwa al-Layla*. Beirut, Lebanon: Mu'assisa al-Risāla, 1407/1987.
Sarakhsī, Shams al-Dīn al-. *Al-Mabsūṭ*. Beirut, Lebanon: Dār al-Ma'rifa, 1978.
Shawkānī, Muhammad b. 'Alī al-. *Nayl al-awṭārsharḥMuntaqā al-akhbār*. Beirut, Lebanon: Dār al-Jīl, 1973.
Ṭabarānī, Sulaymān b. Aḥmad al-. *Al-Mu'jam al-awsaṭ*. Cairo: Dār al-Ḥaramayn, 1415AH.
———. *Al-Mu'jam al-kabīr*. Mosul: Maktaba al-'Ulūmwa al-ḥikam, 1983.
Tirmidhī, Abū 'Īsā Muhammad b. 'Īsā al-. *Al-Sunan*. Beirut, Lebanon: Dār Iḥyā' al-Turāth al-'Arabī, n.d.
What is Halal: A Guide for Non-Muslims, www.icv.org.au/about/about-islam-overview/what-is-*halal*-a-guide-for-non-muslims/

4 Sharia rules on usury (*ribā*)

Literally, *ribā* (usury) means an increase, expansion, growth or addition in a particular item. The term refers to unjust, exploitative gains made in trade or business. Technically, *ribā* is an addition in the principal amount, paid by the borrower to the lender, that is stipulated in a loan transaction.

In the light of this definition, anything chargeable besides the principal amount as a contractual obligation falls into the category of *ribā. Ribā* in barter loans also falls into the category of *ribā*, as is evident from Prophetic Traditions,. When any of the six commodities – gold, silver, wheat, barley, dates and salt – are exchanged using a system of barter with a time lag in equal or unequal measures, this constitutes *ribā*.

4.1 Prohibition of *ribā* in the Qur'ān

Under the system of religious laws that Muslims practise, making money from money is usury, which is a major sin. Since usury is a means of exploitation, Allah has condemned and proscribed it in the following Qur'ānic verses:

الَّذِينَ يَأْكُلُونَ الرِّبَا لَا يَقُومُونَ إِلَّا كَمَا يَقُومُ الَّذِي يَتَخَبَّطُهُ الشَّيْطَانُ مِنَ الْمَسِّ ذَلِكَ
بِأَنَّهُمْ قَالُوا إِنَّمَا الْبَيْعُ مِثْلُ الرِّبَا وَأَحَلَّ اللهُ الْبَيْعَ وَحَرَّمَ الرِّبَا فَمَن جَاءَهُ مَوْعِظَةٌ مِّن رَّبِّهِ
فَانتَهَى فَلَهُ مَا سَلَفَ وَأَمْرُهُ إِلَى اللهِ وَمَنْ عَادَ فَأُولَئِكَ أَصْحَابُ النَّارِ هُمْ فِيهَا خَالِدُونَ

Those who live on usury will not be able to stand (on the Day of Judgment), but like the one whom Satan has made insane with his touch (i.e., damnation). This is because they used to say that trade (i.e., buying and selling) is similar to usury, whereas Allah has declared trade (i.e., buying and selling) lawful and usury unlawful. So, if someone refrains (from usury) on receiving admonition from his Lord, then he can keep whatever he took in the past and his case is with Allah. But those who continued with usury (despite the admonition) would be the inmates of Hell. They will abide there permanently.[1]

يَمْحَقُ اللهُ الرِّبَا وَيُرْبِي الصَّدَقَاتِ وَاللهُ لَا يُحِبُّ كُلَّ كَفَّارٍ أَثِيمٍ

Allah eliminates usury (i.e., deprives usurious profits of prosperous growth) and multiplies alms gifts (i.e., increases blessings of clean wealth manifold through charity donations). And Allah does not like anyone who is ungrateful and disobedient.[2]

يَا أَيُّهَا الَّذِينَ آمَنُواْ لاَ تَأْكُلُواْ الرِّبَا أَضْعَافًا مُّضَاعَفَةً وَاتَّقُواْ اللّهَ لَعَلَّكُمْ تُفْلِحُونَ

O believers! Do not live on usury doubled and redoubled, and keep fearing Allah so that you may prosper.[3]

يَا أَيُّهَا الَّذِينَ آمَنُواْ اتَّقُواْ اللّهَ وَذَرُواْ مَا بَقِيَ مِنَ الرِّبَا إِن كُنتُم مُّؤْمِنِينَ○ فَإِن لَّمْ تَفْعَلُواْ فَأْذَنُواْ
بِحَرْبٍ مِّنَ اللّهِ وَرَسُولِهِ وَإِن تُبْتُمْ فَلَكُمْ رُؤُوسُ أَمْوَالِكُمْ لاَ تَظْلِمُونَ وَلاَ تُظْلَمُونَ○

O believers! Fear Allah and write off whatever balance remains of usury if you are believers (true to the core of your hearts). But if you do not do so, then be warned of the declaration of war from Allah and His Holy Messenger (peace and blessings be upon him). And if you repent, then your principal amounts are (lawfully) yours. (In this case) you will neither do any wrong, nor be wronged.[4]

Certain civilisations were forbidden from practising the evil of charging interest, but they did not heed the Divine commandment, so they risked chastisement.

وَأَخْذِهِمُ الرِّبَا وَقَدْ نُهُواْ عَنْهُ وَأَكْلِهِمْ أَمْوَالَ النَّاسِ بِالْبَاطِلِ وَأَعْتَدْنَا لِلْكَافِرِينَ مِنْهُمْ عَذَابًا أَلِيمًا○

And (also) because of their taking usury, despite that they were forbidden to do it, and because of their usurping others' wealth wrongfully (they were punished). And we have prepared a torturous torment for those of them who disbeliever[5]

4.2 Prohibition of *ribā* in Hadith

The Holy Prophet (Allah bless him and give him peace) also condemned *ribā* (usury) as an evil that the Muslim traders and the common people in a Muslim social fabric must shun.

According to Jābir (may Allah be well pleased with him):

لَعَنَ رَسُوْلُ اِللهِ ○آكِلَ الرِّبَا، وَمُوْكِلَهُ، وَكَاتِبَهُ، وَشَاهِدَيْهِ، وَقَالَ: هُمْ سَوَاءٌ.

Allah's Messenger (Allah bless him and give him peace) cursed the one who consumes *ribā* (usury) and the one who pays for it, the one who writes it down and the two who witness it. And the Prophet (Allah bless him and give him peace) said: "They are all the same."[6]

Elsewhere the Prophet (Allah bless him and give him peace) condemned usury in the strongest possible terms:

اَلرِّبَاَ سَبْعُوْنَ حُوْباً، أَيْسَرُهَا أَنْ يَنْكِحَ الرَّجُلُ أُمَّهُ.

There are seventy degrees of usury, the least of which is equivalent to a man having intercourse with his mother.[7]

On the night of ascension to heaven, the Prophet (Allah bless him and give him peace) saw usurers being tormented.

According to Abū Hurayra (may Allah be pleased with him), the Prophet (Allah bless him and give him peace) said:

أَتَيْتُ لَيْلَةَ أُسْرِيَ بِيْ عَلَى قَوْمٍ، بُطُونُهُمْ كَالْبُيُوتِ، فِيهَا الْحَيَّاتُ تُرَى مِنْ خَارِجِ
بُطُونِهِمْ، فَقُلْتُ: مَنْ هَؤُلاَءِ يَاَ جِبْرَائِيلُ؟ قَالَ: هَؤُلاَءِ أَكَلَةُ الرِّباَ.

On the night of Ascension I came upon people whose stomachs were like houses with snakes visible from the outside. I said: "Who are these, Jibrā'īl?" He said: "They are the ones who consumed usury."[8]

'Abd Allāh b. Mas'ūd (may Allah be well pleased with him) narrates that the Prophet (Allah bless him and give him peace) said:

الرِّباَ بِضْعٌ وَسَبْعُوْنَ باَباً، وَالشِّرْكُ مِثْلُ ذَلِكَ.

There are seventy-odd grades of usury with suchlike grades of polytheism.[9]

'Abd Allāh b. Ḥanzala (may Allah be well pleased with him), a Companion martyred at Uḥud and bathed by angels, narrated the Prophetic Tradition:

دِرْهَمٌ رِباً يْأَكُلُهُ الرَّجُلُ وَهُوَ يَعْلَمُ أَشَدُّ مِنْ سِتَّةٍ وَثَلاَثِيْنَ زَنْيَةً.

A man's knowingly consuming one *dirham* of usury is worse than thirty-six incestuous acts.[10]

Ibn Mas'ūd (may Allah be pleased with him) reported that Allah's Prophet (Allah bless him and give him peace) said:

مَا أَحَدٌ أَكْثَرَ مِنَ الرِّبَاَ إِلاَّ كَانَ عَاقِبَةُ أَمْرِهِ إِلَى قِلَّةٍ.

There is no one who deals in usury a great deal but he will end up with little (i.e., his wealth will decrease since there will be no blessing in it).[11]

4.3 Usury (*ribā*) and its kinds

There are two main kinds of *ribā*: *ribā al-duyūn* (interest earned on lending money to another party) and *ribā al-buyū'* (a sale transaction in which a commodity is exchanged for an unequal amount of the same commodity and supply is postponed). *Ribā al-buyū'* is divided into two types: *ribā al-faḍl* and *ribā al-nasī'a*. This section provides the details of both kinds.

4.3.1 Ribā al-faḍl *(surplus interest)*

Ribā al-faḍl is the selling of one commodity for another of the same kind on the spot and in excess. An example of this is exchanging one kilo of a fine type of dates for two kilos of low-quality dates.

The Qur'ān categorically denounced and disallowed *ribā* but did not characterize it. The definition of this *ribā* has come from Prophetic Traditions. The following Traditions define and interdict *ribā al-faḍl* (surplus interest).

Abū Sa'īd al-Khudrī and Abū Hurayra (may Allah be well pleased with them) reported:

أَنَّ رَسُولَ اللَّهِ اسْتَعْمَلَ رَجُلًا عَلَى خَيْبَرَ فَجَاءَهُ بِتَمْرٍ جَنِيْبٍ، فَقَالَ رَسُوْلُ اللَّهِ: أَكُلُّ تَمْرِ خَيْبَرَ هَكَذَا؟ قَالَ: لَا وَاللَّهِ يَا رَسُوْلَ اللَّهِ، إِنَّا لَنَأْخُذُ الصَّاعَ مِنْ هَذَا بِالصَّاعَيْنِ وَالصَّاعَيْنِ بِالثَّلَاثَةِ، فَقَالَ رَسُوْلُ اللَّهِ: لاَ تَفْعَلْ، بِعِ الجَمْعَ بِالدَّرَاهِمِ، ثُمَّ ابْتَعْ بِالدَّرَاهِمِ جَنِيبًا.

Allah's Messenger (Allah bless him and give him peace) appointed a man as an agent in Khaybar who brought him some dates of a really excellent kind. Allah's Messenger (Allah bless him and give him peace) said: "Are all the dates of Khaybar like this?" He said: "No, Messenger of Allah. We take one *ṣā'* of this kind for two *ṣā's* and two *ṣā's* for three *ṣā's*." Allah's Messenger (Allah bless him and give him peace) said: "Do not do that. Sell the worse ones for *dirhams* and then buy the good ones with those *dirhams*."[12]

According to Abū Sa'īd al-Khudrī (may Allah be pleased with him), Allah's Messenger (Allah bless him and give him peace) said:

لَا تَبِيعُوْا الذَّهَبَ بِالذَّهَبِ إِلَّا مِثْلًا بِمِثْلٍ، وَلَا تُشِفُّوْا بَعْضَهَا عَلَى بَعْضٍ، وَلَا تَبِيعُوا الْوَرِقَ بِالْوَرِقِ إِلاَّ مِثْلاً بِمِثْلٍ، وَلاَ تُشِفُّوْا بَعْضَهَا عَلَى بَعْضٍ، وَلاَ تَبِيعُوْا مِنْهَا غَائِبًا بِنَاجِزٍ.

Do not sell gold for gold except like for like, and do not give more of one and less of the other. Do not sell silver except like for like, and do not give more of one and less of the other. And do not exchange something to be given later for something to be given now.[13]

According to 'Uthmān b. 'Affān (may Allah be pleased with him), Allah's Messenger (Allah bless him and give him peace) said:

لاَ تَبِيْعُوا الدِّيْنَارَ بِالدِّيْنَارَيْنِ وَلاَ الدِّرْهَمَ بِالدِّرْهَمَيْنِ.

Do not sell one *dinar* for two *dinars*, or one *dirham* for two *dirhams*.[14]

According to Abū Sa'īd al-Khudrī (may Allah be pleased with him), Allah's Messenger (Allah bless him and give him peace) said:

اَلذَّهَبُ بِالذَّهَبِ، وَالْفِضَّةُ بِالْفِضَّةِ، وَالْبُرُّ بِالْبُرِّ، وَالشَّعِيرُ بِالشَّعِيْرِ، وَالتَّمْرُ بِالتَّمْرِ، وَالْمِلْحُ بِالْمِلْحِ مِثْلاً بِمِثْلٍ يَدًا بِيَدٍ، فَمَنْ زَادَ أَوِ اسْتَزَادَ فَقَدْ أَرْبَى، الْآخِذُ وَالْمُعْطِي فِيْهِ سَوَاءٌ.

Gold for gold, silver for silver, wheat for wheat, barley for barley, dates for dates, salt for salt, like for like, hand to hand. Whoever gives more or asks for more, he has engaged in *ribā*, and the taker and the giver are the same.[15]

In business transactions, if gold is sold for gold and silver for silver, their quantities must be equivalent and the transaction must take place on the spot, otherwise this will be a usurious deal.

عَنْ مَعْمَرِ بْنِ عَبْدِ اللهِ أَنَّهُ أَرْسَلَ غُلَامَهُ بِصَاعِ قَمْحٍ، فَقَالَ: بِعْهُ ثُمَّ اشْتَرِ بِهِ شَعِيرًا، فَذَهَبَ الْغُلَامُ فَأَخَذَ صَاعًا وَزِيَادَةَ بَعْضِ صَاعٍ فَلَمَّا جَاءَ مَعْمَرًا أَخْبَرَهُ بِذَلِكَ، فَقَالَ لَهُ مَعْمَرٌ: لِمَ فَعَلْتَ ذَلِكَ؟ انْطَلِقْ فَرُدَّهُ، وَلَا تَأْخُذَنَّ إِلَّا مِثْلًا بِمِثْلٍ، فَإِنِّي كُنْتُ أَسْمَعُ رَسُوْلَ اللهِ يَقُولُ: الطَّعَامُ بِالطَّعَامِ مِثْلًا بِمِثْلٍ، قَالَ: وَكَانَ طَعَامُنَا يَوْمَئِذٍ الشَّعِيرُ، قِيْلَ لَهُ: فَإِنَّهُ لَيْسَ بِمِثْلِهِ، قَالَ: إِنِّي أَخَافُ أَنْ يُضَارِعَ.

Ma'mar b. 'Abd Allāh narrated that he sent his slave with a *ṣā'* of wheat and he said: "Sell it, then buy barley." The slave went and took a *ṣā'* and part of a *ṣā'* more. When he came to Ma'mar he told him about that, and Ma'mar said to him: "Why did you do that? Go and give it back, and do not take anything but like for like, for I used to hear Allah's Messenger (Allah bless him and give him peace) say: 'Food for food, like for like.' And our food at that time was barley." It was said to him: "It is not like it." He said: "I am afraid that it may be similar."[16]

Faḍāla b. 'Ubayd (may Allah be pleased with him) narrated:

اِشْتَرَيْتُ يَوْمَ خَيْبَرَ قِلَادَةً بِاثْنَيْ عَشَرَ دِينَارًا، فِيْهَا ذَهَبٌ وَخَرَزٌ، فَفَصَّلْتُهَا فَوَجَدْتُ فِيْهَا أَكْثَرَ مِنَ اثْنَيْ عَشَرَ دِينَارًا، فَذَكَرْتُ ذَلِكَ لِلنَّبِيِّ ﷺ، فَقَالَ: لَا تُبَاعُ حَتَّى تُفَصَّلَ.

On the Day of Khaybar, I bought a necklace for twelve dinars, in which there were gold and pearls. I separated them and I found (it worth) more than twelve dinars in it. I mentioned that to the Prophet (Allah bless him and give him peace) and he said: "It should not be sold until they are separated."[17]

4.3.2 Ribā al-nasī'a *(interest charged on loans)*

Ribā al-nasī'a is derived from the Arabic root *nasī'a*, which means to "delay," "postpone" or "defer." *Ribā al-nasī'a* refers to the time that is allowed to the borrower to pay off the loan, in return for the "addition" or the "premium." Hence it is equal to the interest charged on loans.

The following Hadith reports define and prohibit *ribā al-nasī'a.*

عَنْ سُلَيْمَانَ بْنِ عَمْرٍو عَنْ أَبِيْهِ قَالَ: سَمِعْتُ رَسُوْلَ اللهِ فِيْ حَجَّةِ الْوَدَاعِ يَقُوْلُ: أَلَا إِنَّ كُلَّ رِبًا مِنْ رِبَا الْجَاهِلِيَّةِ مَوْضُوْعٌ، لَكُمْ رُؤُوْسُ أَمْوَالِكُمْ، لَا تَظْلِمُوْنَ وَلَا تُظْلَمُوْنَ، أَلَا وَإِنَّ كُلَّ دَمٍ مِنْ دَمِ الْجَاهِلِيَّةِ مَوْضُوْعٌ، وَأَوَّلُ دَمٍ أَضَعُ مِنْهَا دَمُ الْحَارِثِ بْنِ عَبْدِ الْمُطَّلِبِ، كَانَ مُسْتَرْضِعًا فِيْ بَنِيْ لَيْثٍ فَقَتَلَتْهُ هُذَيْلٌ، قَالَ: اللَّهُمَّ، هَلْ بَلَّغْتُ؟ قَالُوْا: نَعَمْ، ثَلَاثَ مَرَّاتٍ، قَالَ: اللَّهُمَّ اشْهَدْ، ثَلَاثَ مَرَّاتٍ.

Sulaymān b. 'Amr narrated that his father said: "I heard Allah's Messenger (Allah bless him and give him peace), during his Farewell Pilgrimage, say: 'All *ribā* of the Era of Ignorance is abolished; you will have your capital sums. Do not deal unjustly, and you will not be dealt with unjustly. All blood feuds of the Era of Ignorance are abolished, and the first blood feud that I abolish is the blood feud of al-Ḥarith b. 'Abd al-Muṭṭalib who was nursed among Banū Layth and killed by Hudhayl.' He said: 'Allah, have I conveyed (Your message)?' and they said three times: 'Yes.' The Messenger (Allah bless him and give him peace) said: 'Allah, bear witness!' three times."[18]

'Abd Allāh b. Salām (may Allah be pleased with him) said to Abū Burda (may Allah be pleased with him):

إِنَّكَ بِأَرْضٍ، الرِّبَا بِهَا فَاشٍ، إِذَا كَانَ لَكَ عَلَى رَجُلٍ حَقٌّ فَأَهْدَى إِلَيْكَ حِمْلَ تِبْنٍ أَوْ حِمْلَ شَعِيْرٍ أَوْ حِمْلَ قَتٍّ فَلَا تَأْخُذْهُ فَإِنَّهُ رِبًا.

You are in a land where usury is widespread. If a man owes you something and gives you a load of straw or a load of barley or a load of fodder, do not take it from him. It is usury.[19]

Yaḥya b. Abū Isḥāq al-Hunā'ī narrated that he asked Anas b. Mālik (may Allah be pleased with him): "What if a man gives his brother a loan, then (the borrower) gives him a gift?" Anas b. Mālik (may Allah be pleased with him) said in answer that Allah's Messenger (Allah bless him and give him peace) said:

إِذَا أَقْرَضَ أَحَدُكُمْ قَرْضًا فَأَهْدَى لَهُ أَوْ حَمَلَهُ عَلَى الدَّابَّةِ، فَلَا يَرْكَبْهَا وَلَا يَقْبَلْهُ، إِلَّا أَنْ يَكُوْنَ جَرَى بَيْنَهُ وَبَيْنَهُ قَبْلَ ذَلِكَ.

If any one of you borrows something then he gives (the lender) a gift or gives him a ride on his riding-beast, he should not accept the gift or the ride, unless they used to treat each other in that manner beforehand.[20]

Abū 'l-Minhāl related that he asked al-Barā' b. 'Āzib and Zayd b. Arqam about money-changing and they said:

كُنَّا تَاجِرَيْنِ عَلَى عَهْدِ رَسُولِ اللهِ فَسَأَلْنَا رَسُوْلَ اللهِ عَنِ الصَّرْفِ، فَقَالَ: إِنْ كَانَ يَدًا بِيَدٍ فَلَا بَأْسَ، وَإِنْ كَانَ نَسَاءً فَلَا يَصْلُحُ.

We used to be merchants during the time of Allah's Messenger (Allah bless him and give him peace) and we asked Allah's Messenger (Allah bless him and give him peace) about money-changing and he said: "There is no harm if it is hand to hand. If there is a delay, then it is not proper."[21]

Both types of *ribā* discussed represent an additional unjust and impermissible gain that is paid by one party to another.

Notes

1 Qur'ān 2:275.
2 Ibid., 2:276.
3 Ibid., 3:130.
4 Ibid., 2:278–279.
5 Ibid., 4:161.
6 Narrated by Imam Muslim in *al-Ṣaḥīḥ*: *al-Musāqāt* [Sharecropping], Ch.: Cursing the one who consumes *ribā* and the one who pays it, 3:1219 §1598; and Ibn Mājah in *al-Sunan*: *al-Tijārāt* [Trade], Ch.: Emphatic prohibition of usury, 2:764 §2277.
7 Narrated by Ibn Mājah in *al-Sunan*: *al-Tijārāt* [Trade], Ch.: Emphatic prohibition of usury, 2:764 §2274; and al-Mundhirī in *al-Targhībwa al-Tarhīb*, 3:6 §2584.
8 Narrated by Ibn Mājah in *al-Sunan*: *al-Tijārāt* [Trade], Ch.: Emphatic prohibition of usury, 2:763 §2273.
9 Narrated by al-Bazzār in *al-Musnad*, 5:318 §1935; al-Mundhirī, *al-Targhībwa al-Tarhīb*, 3:5 §2846; and al-Haythamī in *Majma' al-Zawā'id*, 4:117.
10 Narrated by Aḥmad b. Ḥanbal in *al-Musnad*, 5:225 §22007; al-Ṭabarānī in *al-Mu'jam al-Awsaṭ*, 3:125 §2682; and al-Dāraquṭnī in *al-Sunan*, 3:16 §48.

11 Narrated by Ibn Mājah in *al-Sunan*: *al-Tijārāt* [Trade], Ch.: Emphatic prohibition of usury, 2:765 §2279.
12 Narrated by al-Bukhārī in *al-Ṣaḥīḥ*: *al-Buyū'* [Sales], Ch.: When someone wants to sell one kind of dates for a better kind, 2:767 §2089.
13 Narrated by Imam Muslim in *al-Ṣaḥīḥ*: *al-Musāqāt* [Sharecropping], Ch.: *Ribā* (usury/interest), 3:1208 §1584.
14 Ibid., 3:1209 §1585.
15 Narrated by Imam Muslim in *al-Ṣaḥīḥ*: *al-Musāqāt* [Sharecropping], Ch.: Exchange and selling gold for silver on the spot, 3:1211 §1584.
16 Narrated by Imam Muslim in *al-Ṣaḥīḥ*: *al-Musāqāt* [Sharecropping], Ch.: Selling food like for like, 3:1214 §1592.
17 Narrated by Abū Dāwūd in *al-Sunan*: *al-Buyū'* [Sales], Ch.: Regarding jewelry on swords being sold for dirhams, 3:249 §3352.
18 Narrated by Abū Dāwūd in *al-Sunan*: *al-Buyū'* [Sales], Ch.: Regarding the abolition of *ribā*, 3:244 §3334; and al-Bayhaqī in *al-Sunan al-Kubrā*, 5:275 §10245.
19 Narrated by al-Bukhārī in *al-Ṣaḥīḥ*: *Faḍā'il al-Ṣaḥāba* [The Excellent Merits of the Companions], Ch.: The virtues of 'Abd Allāh b. Salām (well pleased), 3:1388 §3603.
20 Narrated by Ibn Mājah in *al-Sunan*: *al-Ṣadaqāt* [Charitable donations], Ch.: Lending, 2:813 §2432.
21 Narrated by al-Bukhārī in *al-Ṣaḥīḥ*: *al-Buyū'* [Sales], Ch.: Trading by land, 2:726 §1955.

Bibliography

The Holy Qur'ān

Abū Dāwūd, Sulaymān b. Ash'ath b. Isḥāq b. Bashīr al-Sijistānī (202–275/817–889). *Al-Sunan*. Beirut, Lebanon: Dār al-Fikr, 1414/1994.

Bayhaqī, Aḥmad b. al-Ḥusayn al-. *Al-Sunan al-kubrā*. Mecca, Saudi Arabia: Maktaba Dār al-Bāz, 1994.

Bazzār, Aḥmad b. 'Amr al-. *Al-Musnad* (*al-Baḥr al-zakhār*). Beirut, Lebanon: Mu'assasa' Ulūm al-Qur'ān, 1409AH.

Bukhārī, Abū' Abd Allāh Muhammad b. Ismā'īl b. Ibrahīm b. Mughīra al-. (194–256/810–870). *Al-Ṣaḥīḥ*. Beirut, Lebanon, Damascus, Syria: Dār al-Qalam, 1401/1981.

Dāraquṭnī, 'Alī b. 'Umar al-. *Al-Sunan*. Beirut, Lebanon: Dār al-Ma'rifa, 1966.

Ḥanbal, Aḥmad b. *Al-Musnad*. Beirut, Lebanon: Dar al-Kotob al-Ilmiyah, 1986.

Haythamī, Nūr al-Dīn Abū al-Ḥasan'Alī al-. *Majma' al-zawā'idwamanba' al-fawā'id*. Cairo: Dār al-Rayān li al-Turāth, 1987.

Ibn Mājah, Abū 'Abd Allāh Muhammad b. Yazīd al-Qazwīnī (209–273/824–887). *Al-Sunan*. Beirut, Lebanon: Dār al-Kutub al-'Ilmiyya, 1419/1998.

Mundhirī, 'Abd al-'Aẓīm al-. *Al-Targhībwa al-tarhīb*. Beirut, Lebanon: Dar al-Kotob al-Ilmiyah, 1417AH.

Muslim, Ibn al-*Ḥajj*āj Abū al-Ḥasan al-Qushayrī al-Naysābūrī (206–261/821–875). *Al-Ṣaḥīḥ*. Beirut, Lebanon: Dār al-Iḥyā' al-Turāth al-'Arabī, 1997.

Ṭabarānī, Sulaymān b. Aḥmad al-. *Al-Mu'jam al-awsaṭ*. Cairo: Dār al-Ḥaramayn, 1415AH.

5 Restrictions for the business class

The basic law for things is that they are permitted, unless there is clear proof that establishes prohibition; this is a mark of Allah 's mercy to the community of the Prophet Muhammad (Allah bless him and give him peace). This jurisprudential maxim is reinforced by Divine decree:

هوَ الَّذِي خَلَقَ لَكُم مَّا فِي الأَرْضِ جَمِيعاً

He is the One Who created for you all that is in the earth.[1]

The principle of permissibility of all things is applicable to sale, trade and business activities. The only practices forbidden are those that do not conform to some Divine ordinance or the normative practice of the Messenger (Allah bless him and give him peace). The factors which invalidate a business activity are limited.

> Forbidden or proscribed things, called *ḥarām*, by Islamic law are which the faithful is commanded to avoid.[2]

Some people commit evils, know well that they have fallen into sin, and confess their transgression. Ashamed, they feel they have rebelled against Allah. On the contrary, some commit lewdness, abomination and wickedness and, instead of feeling remorse, come up with flimsy excuses so as to justify their iniquity. The latter conduct is more reprehensible than the former. This was precisely the type of behaviour that previous communities displayed. For example, the Jews were obliged to refrain from every activity on the Sabbath day, but they breached its sanctity.

وسْأَلْهُمْ عَنِ الْقَرْيَةِ الَّتِي كَانَتْ حَاضِرَةَ الْبَحْرِ إِذْ يَعْدُونَ فِي السَّبْتِ إِذْ تَأْتِيهِمْ حِيتَانُهُمْ يَوْمَ
سَبْتِهِمْ شُرَّعاً وَيَوْمَ لَا يَسْبِتُونَ لَا تَأْتِيهِمْ كَذَلِكَ نَبْلُوهُم بِمَا كَانُوا يَفْسُقُونَ

And enquire of them the plight of the town which was situated on the seashore when they transgressed (the commandments with regard to the Sabbath) Saturday. (This occurred) when the fish swarmed from all sides, appearing to (the surface of) water on their (venerated) Saturday. And (the fish) would not come to them on (the rest of) the days, which they did not revere like Saturday. We were trying them this way because they were disobedient.[3]

Imam Ibn Kathīr explains how the Jews transgressed their religious law in pursuit of worldly gains.

> Allah sent His torment on the village that disobeyed Him and broke their pledge and their covenant to observe the sanctity of the Sabbath. They began using deceitful means to avoid honouring the Sabbath by placing nets, ropes and artificial pools of water for the purpose of fishing before the Sabbath. When the fish came in abundance on Saturday as usual, they were caught in the ropes and nets for the rest of Saturday. During the night, the Jews collected the fish after the Sabbath ended. When they did that, Allah changed them from humans into monkeys, the animals having the form closest to humans. Their evil deeds and deceit appeared lawful on the surface, but they were in reality wicked. This is why their punishment was compatible with their crime.[4]

The following Tradition tells us how the Jews benefited from the unlawful by concocting a justification for their actions.

It is related that Ibn 'Abbās (may Allah be pleased with him) was heard saying:

بَلَغَ عُمَرَ بْنَ الْخَطَّابِ أَنَّ فُلَانًا بَاعَ خَمْرًا فَقَالَ: قَاتَلَ اللّٰه فُلَانًا أَلَمْ يَعْلَمْ أَنَّ رَسُوْلَ اللّٰه a
قَالَ: قَاتَلَ اللّٰه الْيَهُوْدَ حُرِّمَتْ عَلَيْهِمُ الشُّحُوْمُ فَجَمَلُوْهَا فَبَاعُوْهَا.

'Umar b. al-Khaṭṭāb (may Allah be pleased with him) heard that a certain person had sold wine. He said: "May Allah fight so-and so! Does he not know that Allah's Messenger (Allah bless him and give him peace) said: 'May Allah fight the Jews! Fat was made unlawful for them but they melted and sold it.'"[5]

Changing the name of an unlawful article when its essence remains the same is not legitimate in Sharia. This devious tactic carries a double burden of sin. Some people coin new terms in order to deal in usury, consume alcohol, and yet the evil of engaging in usurious transactions and drinking persists. Allah's Messenger (Allah bless him and give him peace) prophesied that some people would legalise the consumption of alcoholic drinks by modifying their names. Abū Mālik al-Ash'arī (may Allah be pleased with him) reported that the Messenger (Allah bless him and give him peace) said:

لَيَشْرَبَنَّ نَاسٌ مِنْ أُمَّتِي الْخَمْرَ يُسَمُّوْنَهَا بِغَيْرِ اسْمِهَا، يُعْزَفُ عَلَى رُءُوْسِهِمْ بِالْمَعَازِفِ
وَالْمُغَنِّيَاتِ، يَخْسِفُ اللّٰه بِهِمُ الْأَرْضَ، وَيَجْعَلُ مِنْهُمُ الْقِرَدَةَ وَالْخَنَازِيرَ.

> Undoubtedly, people among my nation will drink wine, calling it by another name, and musical instruments will be played for them and singing girls (will sing for them). Allah will cause the earth to swallow them up, and will turn them into monkeys and pigs.[6]

Another Tradition mentions some further misdeeds which people will validate:

لَيَكُونَنَّ مِنْ أُمَّتِي أَقْوَامٌ يَسْتَحِلُّونَ الحِرَ وَالحَرِيرَ وَالخَمْرَ وَالْمَعَازِفَ.

> From among my followers, certainly there will be some people who will consider fornication, silk, wine and musical instruments to be lawful.[7]

At present, through their own impiety, wickedness and love of pleasure, transgressors call usury "interest," dance and vulgarity "art and culture," and liquor "spirits."

Some additional business-related prohibitions are explained in this chapter.

5.1 Cheating

Misconduct, trickery, falsehood and betrayal are forms of unethical conduct. If individuals who take unfair advantage of others through these crooked means upset the social equilibrium, they are guilty of fraud in the eyes of the law. Allah Almighty condemns this ugly social evil.

These forms of unethical behaviour damage society as well as businesses. Sellers who give into the temptation to cheat are enemies of society. What is more, they hurt themselves more than others by undermining their own credibility in the end. Allah, the Exalted, destroyed previous nations when they wronged people by not giving full measure and weight. On the prohibition of cheating, the Qur'ān says:

وَيْلٌ لِّلْمُطَفِّفِينَ○ الَّذِينَ إِذَا اكْتَالُوا عَلَى النَّاسِ يَسْتَوْفُونَ○ وَإِذَا كَالُوهُمْ أَو وَّزَنُوهُمْ يُخْسِرُونَ○

> *Woe to those who give less in measure or weight! When (they) take by measure from others, they take (from them) full. And when they (themselves) give by measure or weigh to others, they give them less.*[8]

Dishonest shopkeepers might take the issue of cheating in measurement and weight lightly, but the Almighty warns them that it is not a trivial matter. Condemning this evil, the Qur'ān says:

أَلَا يَظُنُّ أُولَٰئِكَ أَنَّهُم مَّبْعُوثُونَ○ لِيَوْمٍ عَظِيمٍ○ يَوْمَ يَقُومُ النَّاسُ لِرَبِّ الْعَالَمِينَ○

> *Do they not believe that they will be raised up (again after death), for a Terrible Day, the Day when all mankind will stand before the Lord of all the worlds?*[9]

The wretched people of the Prophet Shu'ayb (peace be upon him) habitually cheated in trade in spite of the fact that the Lord had granted them goodly provisions. The Prophet (Allah bless him and give him peace) enjoined them to resist:

قَدْ جَاءَتْكُم بَيِّنَةٌ مِّن رَّبِّكُمْ فَأَوْفُواْ الْكَيْلَ وَالْمِيزَانَ وَلَا تَبْخَسُواْ النَّاسَ أَشْيَاءَهُمْ

Indeed, there has come to you from your Lord a clear sign. So give full measure and weight, and do not decrease whilst giving people their things.[10]

They, the champions of deception and corruption, did not heed his exhortations. Mocking their Prophet's call to observe the Divine regulations in conducting business, the dwellers of Madyan (Shu'ayb's nation) said:

يَا شُعَيْبُ أَصَلاَتُكَ تَأْمُرُكَ أَن نَّتْرُكَ مَا يَعْبُدُ آبَاؤُنَا أَوْ أَن نَّفْعَلَ فِي أَمْوَالِنَا مَا نَشَاءُ إِنَّكَ لَأَنتَ الْحَلِيمُ الرَّشِيدُ

O Shu'ayb, does your prayer only command you that we forsake those (gods) which our fathers have been worshipping, or that we refrain from doing with our wealth what we like? Surely, you (alone) must be the most tolerant and guided one![11]

The Messenger (Allah bless him) of the people of Madyan kept on exhorting them to mend their ways, and follow the divinely prescribed business practices, yet they did not take his counsel. Allah Almighty seized them for their iniquity and a mighty blast struck the wrongdoers from among them.

وَلَمَّا جَاءَ أَمْرُنَا نَجَّيْنَا شُعَيْبًا وَالَّذِينَ آمَنُواْ مَعَهُ بِرَحْمَةٍ مِّنَّا وَأَخَذَتِ الَّذِينَ ظَلَمُواْ الصَّيْحَةُ فَأَصْبَحُواْ فِي دِيَارِهِمْ جَاثِمِينَ كَأَن لَّمْ يَغْنَوْاْ فِيهَا أَلَا بُعْدًا لِّمَدْيَنَ كَمَا بَعِدَتْ ثَمُودُ

And when Our command (of torment) came We saved Shu'aib and the believers with him through Our Mercy but a dreadful Blast seized the wrongdoers. So they reached the morning (as dead) lying prostrate in their homes –. As if they had never put up there. Listen! (The people of) Madyan are doomed as were doomed (the people of) Thamud.[12]

The extermination of the people of Shu'ayb cautions us against cheating and deceiving customers, employees, employers and anyone who confides in us.

The shopkeepers and the businesspeople who swindle buyers may think that their wealth will immortalise them. But on the contrary, the Qur'ān directs people to engage in fair dealings with their fellows and render them their due; what is left will be enough to meet their material needs. Traders must take into consideration the fact that the fruit of righteous dealings is good in the sight of the Sustainer.

بَقِيَّتُ اللَّهِ خَيْرٌ لَّكُمْ إِن كُنتُم مُّؤْمِنِينَ وَمَا أَنَا عَلَيْكُم بِحَفِيظٍ

That which is left over from Allah's provision (only that) is better for you if you have faith.[13]

A Prophetic Tradition reinforces the theme of the cited verse. According to Abū al-Dardā' (may Allah be pleased with him), Allah's Messenger (Allah bless him and give him peace) said:

مَامِنْ يَوْمٍ طَلَعَتْ فِيْهِ الشَّمْسُ إِلَّا وَبِجَنْبَيْهَا مَلَكَانِ يُنَادِيَانِ يَسْمَعُهُ خَلْقُ اللهِ كُلُّهُمْ إِلَّا الثَّقَلَيْنْ: يَا أَيُّهَا النَّاسُ هَلُمُّوْا إِلَى رَبِّكُمْ، إِنَّ مَا قَلَّ وَكَفَى خَيْرٌ مِمَّا كَثُرَ وَأَلْهَى.

Every day in which the sun rises two angels descend. What they proclaim all Allah's creatures hear aside from jinn and humans: "People! Come to your Lord! No doubt what is little and sufficient is better than abundance that distracts."[14]

In order to build a moral society, Muhammad, Allah's Messenger (Allah bless him and give him peace) forbade all forms of deceiving in business. Cheating while buying and selling is such an enormity that the Prophet (Allah bless him and give him peace) dissociated himself from the people who deceive.

لَيْسَ مِنَّا مَنْ غَشَّ.

He who cheats is not one of us.[15]

In another Tradition, the Messenger (Allah bless him and give him peace) condemned dishonesty and betrayal as the traits of the inmates of Hell. He said:

وَأَهْلُ النَّارِ خَمْسَةٌ: الضَّعِيْفُ الَّذِيْ لَا زَبْرَ لَهُ، الَّذِيْنَ هُمْ فِيْكُمْ تَبَعًا لَا يَبْتَغُوْنَ أَهْلًا وَلَا مَالًا، وَالْخَائِنُ الَّذِيْ لَا يَخْفَى لَهُ طَمَعٌ وَإِنْ دَقَّ إِلَّا خَانَهُ، وَرَجُلٌ لَا يُصْبِحُ وَلَا يُمْسِيْ إِلَّا وَهُوَ يُخَادِعُكَ عَنْ أَهْلِكَ وَمَالِكَ وَذَكَرَ الْبُخْلَ أَوِ الْكَذِبَ، وَالشِّنْظِيْرُ الْفَحَّاشُ.

"And the people of the Fire are of five types: A weak man who lacks the wisdom (to avoid evil); those who are your followers that do not have any care for family and wealth; one who is dishonest and is a miser even for a little; a man who will betray you morning and evening with regard to your family and your wealth" – and he mentioned miserliness or lying – "and the one whose language is obscene."[16]

Many people may take cheating lightly, but a study of the primary sources of Islam and the Hadith that have been quoted establish that this practice in particular leads one to damnation.

Some further Traditions condemn cheating.

Ḥakīm b. Ḥizām (may Allah be pleased with him) reported that the Prophet (Allah bless him and give him peace) said:

الْبَيِّعَانِ بِالْخِيَارِ مَا لَمْ يَتَفَرَّقَا، أَوْ قَالَ: حَتَّى يَتَفَرَّقَا، فَإِنْ صَدَقَا وَبَيَّنَا بُورِكَ لَهُمَا فِي بَيْعِهِمَا، وَإِنْ كَتَمَا وَكَذَبَا مُحِقَتْ بَرَكَةُ بَيْعِهِمَا.

The seller and the buyer have the option (to revoke the sale) as long as they have not separated (or he said: "until they separate"). If they speak the truth and make things clear, they will be blessed in their sale. If they conceal and lie, the blessing of their transaction will be obliterated.[17]

'Uqba b. 'Āmir (may Allah be pleased with him) said:

لاَ يَحِلُّ لِامْرِئٍ يَبِيعُ سِلْعَةً يَعْلَمُ أَنَّ بِهَا دَاءً إِلاَّ أَخْبَرَهُ.

It is not lawful for a Muslim to sell goods knowing that there is a defect in them without mentioning it.[18]

Will a Muslim give short measure or weight if he or she bears in mind the message contained in the following Tradition of the Prophet (Allah bless him)?

زِنْ وَأَرْجِحْ.

Weigh and add more.[19]

Islam does not tolerate practising dishonesty while selling objects of sale:

عَنْ أَبِي هُرَيْرَةَ أَنَّ رَسُوْلَ اللهِ a مَرَّ عَلَى صُبْرَةِ طَعَامٍ، فَأَدْخَلَ يَدَهُ فِيْهَا فَنَالَتْ أَصَابِعُهُ بَلَلًا، فَقَالَ: مَا هَذَا يَا صَاحِبَ الطَّعَامِ؟ قَالَ: أَصَابَتْهُ السَّمَاءُ يَا رَسُوْلَ اللهِ، قَالَ: أَفَلَا جَعَلْتَهُ فَوْقَ الطَّعَامِ كَيْ يَرَاهُ النَّاسُ؟ مَنْ غَشَّ فَلَيْسَ مِنِّي.

Abū Hurayra (may Allah be pleased with him) narrated that Allah's Messenger (Allah bless him and give him peace), passing by a pile of foodstuff, put his hand (deep) in it and found that it had got wet. He said: "What is this, seller of the foodstuff?" He said: "It got rained on, Messenger of Allah (Allah bless him and give him peace)." He said: "Why do you not put it on top of the food so that people can see it? Whoever deceives does not pertain to me."[20]

In the aforementioned Hadith, the words of the man "it got rained on" indicate that the seller did not make the pile of foodstuff wet, but he was guilty of hiding the moist part, hence the Prophet's expression of disapproval. In like manner, giving less measure in dim light and displaying good vegetables but selling stale vegetables are dishonest ways to make money.

According to 'Alī (may Allah be pleased with him), the Blessed Prophet (Allah bless him and give him peace) said:

غَبْنُ الْمُسْتَرْسِلِ رِباً.

Deceiving an *al-mustarsal* (an ignorant entrant into the market) is usury.[21]

A contract must be free from *tadlīs* (fraud). Islamic law addresses each difficulty of human beings, and it has offered a solution to a case where one of the contracting parties cheats the other by concealing a defect in a commodity, asset or property while putting up for sale: the harmed party has every right to invalidate the contract by exercising his or her legal right.

5.2 Oath-taking

To earn good profits, some shopkeepers bear witness, using Allah's name, that their commodities are flawless. At times they assure customers very solemnly that they were offered a higher amount of money a few moments ago, yet they did not sell. Through such tricks they might entrap customers. On realising the nature of such a shopkeeper, customers disregard his or her words. A great many oath-takers unwittingly damage their business and industry in this way.

Wild exaggerations, false oaths and gross misstatements are employed to deceive clients into buying articles. Though swearing oaths may win the confidence of some customers, yet the gains are denuded of Divine blessings. Such earnings, though much, seem paltry. In the following Tradition, the Messenger (Allah bless him and give him peace) warned the faithful to beware swearing oaths when selling a commodity.

On the prohibition of giving oaths while selling commodities, Abū Hurayra (may Allah be pleased with him) reported Allah's Messenger (Allah bless him and give him peace) as saying:

اَلْحَلِفُ مُنَفِّقَةٌ لِلسِّلْعَةِ مُمْحِقَةٌ لِلْبَرَكَةِ.

Taking oaths hastens the sale of goods but eradicates the blessings.[22]

The theme of avoidance of taking oaths in business transactions and selling is echoed in another Hadith. Abū Qatāda al-Ansārī (may Allah be pleased with him) reported that he heard Allah's Messenger (Allah bless him and give him peace) say:

إِيَّاكُمْ وَكَثْرَةَ الْحَلِفِ فِي الْبَيْعِ، فَإِنَّهُ يُنَفِّقُ ثُمَّ يَمْحَقُ.

Beware of swearing a great deal when selling, for it brings about a sale, then erases (the blessing of the profit).[23]

Giving one's word in the Name of Allah when not lying is a minor offence, whereas employing His sacred Name in order to deceive others is a major offense.[24] Shopkeepers, therefore, must not swear falsely so that they may do a roaring trade. Swearing false oaths in the Name of Allah is as good as swindling. Allah will not cleanse such people of sins as they profane the name of the Divine on the Day of Accountability (Resurrection).

عَنْ أَبِيْ ذَرٍّ عَنِ النَّبِيِّ قَالَ: ثَلَاثَةٌ لَا يُكَلِّمُهُمُ اللّٰهُ يَوْمَ الْقِيَامَةِ وَلَا يَنْظُرُ إِلَيْهِمْ وَلَا يُزَكِّيْهِمْ وَلَهُمْ عَذَابٌ أَلِيْمٌ، قَالَ: فَقَرَأَهَا رَسُوْلُ اللّٰهِ a ثَلَاثَ مِرَارًا. قَالَ أَبُو ذَرٍّ: خَابُوْا وَخَسِرُوْا، مَنْ هُمْ يَا رَسُوْلَ اللّٰهِ؟ قَالَ: الْمُسْبِلُ، وَالْمَنَّانُ، وَالْمُنَفِّقُ سِلْعَتَهُ بِالْحَلْفِ الْكَاذِبِ.

It is narrated from Abū Dharr (may Allah be pleased with him) that the Prophet (Allah bless him and give him peace) said: "There are three to whom Allah will not speak on the Day of Resurrection, nor will He look at them nor sanctify them, and theirs will be a painful torment." Allah's Messenger (Allah bless him and give him peace) repeated it three times. Abū Dharr (may Allah be pleased with him) said: "May they be lost and doomed! Who are they, Messenger of Allah?" He said: "The one who lets his lower garment hang below his ankles, the one who reminds others (of his gifts), and the one who sells his product by means of a false oath."[25]

Enticing people to buy one's goods is normal in society, yet Islamic tradition and thought abhor this practice, as evidenced by the following Prophetic Tradition.

عَنْ عَبْدِ اللّٰهِ بْنِ أَبِيْ أَوْفَى أَنَّ رَجُلًا أَقَامَ سِلْعَةً وَهُوَ فِي السُّوقِ فَحَلَفَ بِاللّٰهِ لَقَدْ أَعْطَى بِهَا مَا لَمْ يُعْطِ، لِيُوْقِعَ فِيْهَا رَجُلًا مِنَ الْمُسْلِمِيْنَ، فَنَزَلَتْ: ﴿إِنَّ الَّذِينَ يَشْتَرُونَ بِعَهْدِ اللّٰهِ وَأَيْمَانِهِمْ ثَمَنًا قَلِيلًا﴾.

It is related from 'Abd Allāh b. Abī Awfā (may Allah be pleased with him) that a man set up some goods in the market and swore by Allah that he had been offered for them an amount that he had not in fact been offered in order to entice a Muslim man into buying them. So it was revealed [Q.3:77]: *"Certainly, those who sell the promise of Allah and their own oaths for a small price."*[26]

Another Hadith also tells us what type of sinful conduct will ruin traders.

قَالَ رَسُوْلُ اللّٰهِ: إِنَّ التُّجَّارَ هُمُ الْفُجَّارُ. قَالَ: قِيلَ: يَا رَسُولَ اللّٰهِ، أَوَلَيْسَ قَدْ أَحَلَّ اللّٰهُ الْبَيْعَ؟ قَالَ: بَلَى، وَلَكِنَّهُمْ يُحَدِّثُوْنَ فَيَكْذِبُوْنَ، وَيَحْلِفُوْنَ وَيَأْثَمُوْنَ.

> Allah's Messenger (Allah bless him and give him peace) said, "Indeed, traders are wicked and sinful." He was asked: "Allah's Messenger, has Allah not permitted buying and selling?" The Prophet (Allah bless him and give him peace) said: "Of course (Allah has made buying and selling lawful)! But when they speak, they (in order to sell their commodities) lie and swear, and thus become fall into error."[27]

The Qur'ān warns the faithful of the penalty in the Hereafter for selling oaths.

إِنَّ الَّذِينَ يَشْتَرُونَ بِعَهْدِ اللهِ وَأَيْمَانِهِمْ ثَمَنًا قَلِيلاً أُوْلَئِكَ لاَ خَلاَقَ لَهُمْ فِي الْآخِرَةِ وَلاَ يُكَلِّمُهُمُ
اللّهُ وَلَا يَنظُرُ إِلَيْهِمْ يَوْمَ الْقِيَامَةِ وَلَا يُزَكِّيهِمْ وَلَهُمْ عَذَابٌ أَلِيمٌ

> *Certainly, those who sell the promise of Allah and their own oaths for a small price, it is they who will not have any share in the Hereafter. And on the Day of Resurrection Allah will neither speak to nor look at them, nor will He purify them, and for them will be painful torment.*[28]

Swearing a false oath which leads to someone's undeserved loss or one's undue profit is not permitted under any circumstance; it is one of the cardinal offences in the sight of Allah.

According to 'Abd Allāh b. Unays al-Juhanī (may Allah be pleased with him), Allah's Messenger (Allah bless him and give him peace) said:

إِنَّ مِنْ أَكْبَرِ الْكَبَائِرِ الشِّرْكُ بِاللّهِ، وَعُقُوْقُ الْوَالِدَيْنِ، وَالْيَمِيْنُ الْغَمُوْسُ، وَمَا حَلَفَ حَالِفٌ
بِاللّٰهِ يَمِيْنَ صَبْرٍ فَأَدْخَلَ فِيْهَا مِثْلَ جَنَاحِ بَعُوضَةٍ إِلاَّ جُعِلَتْ نُكْتَةً فِيْ قَلْبِهِ إِلَى يَوْمِ الْقِيَامَةِ.

> Indeed among the worst of the major sins is shirk (believing in multiple gods as partners) with Allah, disobeying the parents and (swearing) the false oath. No one insists on taking an oath in which he swears, including the like of a wing of a mosquito (of falsehood) in it except that a spot is placed in his heart until the Day of Resurrection.[29]

The atonement for false oaths is repenting to Allah in all sincerity, and then mending one's character.

5.3 Hoarding

Muslims are not allowed to collect and keep large amounts of food, money and valuable objects secretly so that other people will go without them. Though hoarding is illicit, one may keep goods for meeting personal needs, if it does not upset market equilibrium. In many contexts, depriving others from what they need is unethical and a violation of religious law.

On the prohibition of hoarding resources and not using them, Allah says in the Qur'ān:

وَلاَ يَحْسَبَنَّ الَّذِينَ يَبْخَلُونَ بِمَا آتَاهُمُ اللهُ مِن فَضْلِهِ هُوَ خَيْرًا لَّهُمْ بَلْ هُوَ شَرٌّ لَّهُمْ سَيُطَوَّقُونَ مَا بَخِلُواْ بِهِ يَوْمَ الْقِيَامَةِ

And those who are niggardly in giving away (from the wealth) which Allah has bestowed upon them out of His bounty must never consider this miserliness of any benefit to themselves; it is rather injurious to them. Soon on the Day of Resurrection, this wealth they are niggardly about will be put around (their necks) like a neck-fetter.[30]

Greedy folks who live in the lap of luxury and close their eyes to the needs of the downtrodden are forewarned of adverse consequences:

الَّذِي جَمَعَ مَالًا وَعَدَّدَهُ○يَحْسَبُ أَنَّ مَالَهُ أَخْلَدَهُ○كَلاَّ لَيُنبَذَنَّ فِي الْحُطَمَةِ○وَمَا أَدْرَاكَ مَا الْحُطَمَةُ○نَارُ اللهِ الْمُوقَدَةُ○الَّتِي تَطَّلِعُ عَلَى الْأَفْئِدَةِ○إِنَّهَا عَلَيْهِم مُّؤْصَدَةٌ○فِي عَمَدٍ مُّمَدَّدَةٍ○

(Woe to him) who accumulates wealth and keeps counting it! He thinks that his riches will keep him alive forever. By no means! He will certainly be cast into al-ḥuṭama *(the fire). And what will make you understand what* al-ḥuṭama *(the crushing up Fire) is? (It) is a fire kindled by Allah. That will rise over the hearts (with its torture). Indeed, that (fire) will be closed upon them all around, in towering columns (of fierce flames and they will not find any way to escape).*[31]

Muslim law instils a sense of fair play in people's minds and forbids them from hoarding:

وَالَّذِينَ يَكْنِزُونَ الذَّهَبَ وَالْفِضَّةَ وَلَا يُنفِقُونَهَا فِي سَبِيلِ اللهِ فَبَشِّرْهُم بِعَذَابٍ أَلِيمٍ○يَوْمَ يُحْمَى عَلَيْهَا فِي نَارِ جَهَنَّمَ فَتُكْوَى بِهَا جِبَاهُهُمْ وَجُنوبُهُمْ وَظُهُورُهُمْ هَذَا مَا كَنَزْتُمْ لِأَنفُسِكُمْ فَذُوقُواْ مَا كُنتُمْ تَكْنِزُونَ○

And those who hoard silver and gold and do not spend it in the cause of Allah, warn them of a grievous torment. The Day when this (gold, silver and wealth) will be heated in the Fire of Hell, their foreheads, sides and backs will be branded with this (heated material, and it will be said to them:) "This is the same (wealth) that you treasured for (the benefit of) your souls. So taste (this wealth) which you had been amassing."[32]

When shopkeepers or businesspeople store large amounts of things, they intend to sell goods at an inflated price so that they may overcharge. With a view to deterring his followers from hiding away commodities for public use, the Blessed Prophet (Allah bless him and give him peace) said:

مَنِ احْتَكَرَ فَهُوَ خَاطِئٌ.

Whoever hoards is a sinner.[33]

Ibn ‘Umar (may Allah be well pleased with him and his father) related that the Prophet (Allah bless him and give him peace) said:

مَنِ احْتَكَرَ طَعَامًا أَرْبَعِينَ لَيْلَةً، فَقَدْ بَرِئَ مِنَ اللهِ تَعَالَى، وَبَرِئَ اللهُ تَعَالَى، مِنْهُ.

If anyone withholds grain for forty nights (out of the desire for a high price), he is free from Allah’s obligation and Allah will renounce him.[34]

Ma’mar b. ‘Abd Allah (may Allah be well pleased with him) narrated that Allah’s Messenger (Allah bless him and give him peace) said:

لاَ يَحْتَكِرُ إِلاَّ خَاطِئٌ.

No one but a sinner hoards.[35]

Muā’dh b. Jabal (may Allah be well pleased with him) reported that Allah’s Messenger (Allah bless him and give him peace) said:

بِئْسَ الْعَبْدُ الْمُحْتَكِرُ، إِنْ أَرْخَصَ اللهُ الأَسْعَارَ حَزِنَ، وَإِنْ أَغْلاَهَا اللهُ فَرِحَ.

The man who hoards goods is evil. If Allah lowers prices, ṣ he is grieved, and if Allah raises prices, he is happy.[36]

In the preceding Traditions, the Messenger (Allah bless him and give him peace) denounced those individuals who, driven by sheer greed, acquire wealth at the expense of others by manipulating the prices of food items and other necessities of life.

The Prophet (Allah bless him and give him peace) blessed traders but cursed hoarders.

اَلْجَالِبُ مَرْزُوْقٌ، وَالْمُحْتَكِرُ مَلْعُوْنٌ.

He who brings goods to the market is blessed with provision, but he who withholds them is cursed.[37]

Hoarding is an unproductive and antisocial habit. A scarcity of certain goods even during stable economic times can be a big drain on customers’ personal finances. By outlawing hoarding, Islam closed the door to greed, avarice and exploitation. Nothing is more destructive to a believer's faith than getting caught up in the febrile pursuit of passion and basal desires.

The remedy to the evil of cheating is bearing in mind that Allah, the Exalted, is watching over us and that the reckoning will examine even the minutest deeds, good and evil.

إِنَّ رَبَّكَ لَبِالْمِرْصَادِ۝

Indeed, your Lord is Ever-Watchful (over them).[38]

5.4 Greed

Greedy people show a strong desire to gather material possessions. However, their wealth becomes like a cocoon from which they find it hard to disentangle themselves. Driven by insatiable desire and never content, they go on collecting treasures only to die among them. In this world, they labour fruitlessly seeing that they leave their wealth behind them in the form of inheritance, and in the Afterlife, they will be subjected to chastisement:

وَأَمَّا مَن بَخِلَ وَاسْتَغْنَىٰ۝ وَكَذَّبَ بِالْحُسْنَىٰ۝فَسَنُيَسِّرُهُ لِلْعُسْرَىٰ۝وَمَا يُغْنِي عَنْهُ مَالُهُ إِذَا تَرَدَّىٰ۝

But he who is (a) miser and disregards (spending in the cause of Allah), and (in this way) denies the good (the Dīn *[Religion] of truth and [the] afterlife), soon shall We facilitate his landing into hardship (advancing towards torment, so that punishment becomes his rightful due). And his wealth will not help him any way when he falls into (the pit of) destruction.*[39]

The Qur'ān allows the faithful to benefit from the material resources at their disposal.[40] Blessed are the souls that are not swayed by cupidity – but the word of Allah also warns them to be on guard against activities that distract them from the recollection of Allah Almighty. Believers use wealth so that they may be come free from worldly obligations and devote themselves to the Lord. Why should they accumulate unlimited sums of money? This will not follow them into the grave.

The Messenger (Allah bless him and give him peace) sought Allah's protection against the soul that wants more and more and is never satiated.

According to Zayd b. Arqam (may Allah be pleased with him), the Prophet (Allah bless him and give him peace) used to say:

اَللّٰهُمَّ، آتِ نَفْسِيْ تَقْوَاهَا، وَزَكِّهَا أَنْتَ خَيْرُ مَنْ زَكَّاهَا، أَنْتَ وَلِيُّهَا وَمَوْلَاهَا. اللّٰهُمَّ، إِنِّيْ أَعُوْذُ بِكَ مِنْ عِلْمٍ لَا يَنْفَعُ، وَمِنْ قَلْبٍ لَا يَخْشَعُ، وَمِنْ نَفْسٍ لَا تَشْبَعُ، وَمِنْ دَعْوَةٍ لَا يُسْتَجَابُ لَهَا.

> Allah, grant my soul its piety and purify it, for You are the best to purify it, You are its Guardian and its Lord. Allah, I seek refuge with You from knowledge that is not beneficial, a heart that is not humble (before You), a soul that is not satisfied and a prayer that is not answered.[41]

Those who earn material resources and expend them in obedience to Allah will experience contentment, while those with an excessive or inordinate desire for wealth never feel peace and serenity within. The Messenger (Allah bless him and give him peace) sought Divine protection against greediness:

عَنْ حَكِيْمِ بْنِ حِزَامٍ قَالَ: سَأَلْتُ رَسُوْلَ اللّٰه a فَأَعْطَانِيْ، ثُمَّ سَأَلْتُهُ فَأَعْطَانِيْ، ثُمَّ سَأَلْتُهُ فَأَعْطَانِيْ، ثُمَّ قَالَ: يَا حَكِيمُ، إِنَّ هَذَا الْمَالَ خَضِرَةٌ حُلْوَةٌ فَمَنْ أَخَذَهُ بِسَخَاوَةِ نَفْسٍ، بُوْرِكَ لَهُ فِيْهِ، وَمَنْ أَخَذَهُ بِإِشْرَافِ نَفْسٍ، لَمْ يُبَارَكْ لَهُ فِيْهِ، كَالَّذِيْ يَأْكُلُ وَلَا يَشْبَعُ. اَلْيَدُ الْعُلْيَا خَيْرٌ مِنْ الْيَدِ السُّفْلَى، قَالَ حَكِيْمٌ: فَقُلْتُ: يَا رَسُوْلَ اللّٰهِ، وَالَّذِيْ بَعَثَكَ بِالْحَقِّ، لَا أَرْزَأُ أَحَدًا بَعْدَكَ شَيْئًا حَتَّى أُفَارِقَ الدُّنْيَا، فَكَانَ أَبُوْ بَكْرٍ g يَدْعُوْ حَكِيْمًا إِلَى الْعَطَاءِ فَيَأْبَى أَنْ يَقْبَلَهُ مِنْهُ. ثُمَّ إِنَّ عُمَرَ g دَعَاهُ لِيُعْطِيَهُ فَأَبَى أَنْ يَقْبَلَ مِنْهُ شَيْئًا. فَقَالَ عُمَرُ: إِنِّيْ أُشْهِدُكُمْ يَا مَعْشَرَ الْمُسْلِمِيْنَ عَلَى حَكِيْمٍ، أَنِّيْ أَعْرِضُ عَلَيْهِ حَقَّهُ مِنْ هَذَا الْفَيْءِ فَيَأْبَى أَنْ يَأْخُذَهُ. فَلَمْ يَرْزَأْ حَكِيْمٌ أَحَدًا مِنْ النَّاسِ بَعْدَ رَسُولِ اللّٰه a حَتَّى تُوُفِّيَ.

> Ḥakīm b. Ḥizām (may Allah be pleased with him) reported: “I asked Allah’s Messenger and he gave to me and then I asked him and he gave to me and then I asked him again and he gave to me. Then he said: ‘Ḥakīm, this wealth is verdant and sweet. Anyone who takes it in a generous spirit will be blessed in it but anyone who takes it in an avaricious way will not be blessed in it, like someone who eats and is not satisfied. The upper hand is better than the lower hand.’” Ḥakīm (may Allah be well pleased with him) narrated: “I said: ‘Messenger of Allah, by the One who sent you with the truth, I will never again ask anyone for anything until I leave this world.’” Abū Bakr (may Allah be well pleased with him) called Ḥakīm to take his share and he refused to take it from him. Then ‘Umar (may Allah be well pleased with him) called him to give to him his share and he refused to accept anything from him either. ‘Umar (may Allah be well pleased with him) said: “I call on you to testify, company of Muslims, that I offered Ḥakīm his share of this booty and he refused to take it!” Ḥakīm (may Allah be well pleased with him) did not take anything from any person after Allah’s Messenger (Allah bless him and give him peace) until he died.[42]

Greed is a calamitous frame of mind. One’s desire knows no bounds if one does not seek and apply its cure.

Ibn ‘Abbās (may Allah be pleased with him) said that he heard the Prophet (Allah bless him and give him peace) say:

لَوْ أَنَّ لِابْنِ آدَمَ مِثْلَ وَادٍ مَالًا، لَأَحَبَّ أَنَّ لَهُ إِلَيْهِ مِثْلَهُ، وَلَا يَمْلَأُ عَيْنَ ابْنِ آدَمَ إِلَّا التُّرَابُ، وَيَتُوبُ اللهُ عَلَى مَنْ تَابَ.

> If the son of Adam had possessed a valley of wealth, he would want to have another. The eye of the son of Adam is only filled by earth. Allah turns to whoever turns in repentance to Him.[43]

If people love money with inordinate love instead of seeking the approbation of the Lord, this reduces their faith in Allah and severs them from the Almighty. Craving for wealth may lead one to pursue it through unlawful avenues.

عَنِ ابْنِ كَعْبِ بْنِ مَالِكٍ الْأَنْصَارِيِّ عَنْ أَبِيهِ قَالَ: قَالَ رَسُوْلُ اللهِ a: مَا ذِئْبَانِ جَائِعَانِ أُرْسِلَا فِي غَنَمٍ بِأَفْسَدَ لَهَا مِنْ حِرْصِ الْمَرْءِ عَلَى الْمَالِ وَالشَّرَفِ لِدِيْنِهِ.

> Ibn Ka'b b. Mālik al-Anṣārī narrated from his father that Allah's Messenger (Allah bless him and give him peace) said: "Two wolves free among sheep are no more destructive to them than a man's desire for wealth and honour is to his religion."[44]

An overwhelming desire to have more of something (such as money) than is actually needed causes one to belittle one's resources. It is essential for Muslim traders, therefore, that they purify themselves from this blind, fierce and all-consuming passion which causes discord between human beings. What is worse than alienating oneself from fellow creatures and from the Lord?

5.5 Concealing defects of a commodity

Disclosing the defect of a tradable product is a duty. The primary sources of Islam have spelt out the necessity of keeping business transactions free from unlawful acts such as fraud, deception, forgery and concealment of flaws which might cause loss to individuals and society. Sellers who practise this Islamic ordinance reap religious and material rewards: such conscientious shopkeepers earn the trust of purchasers and merit the approval of the Most High. Bringing the defect of a product to light is an act of honesty, an important quality of a Muslim's character.

Sellers, merchants and purveyors are under obligation to reveal the defects of the commodities they sell. 'Uqba b. 'Āmir (may Allah be pleased with him) narrated that he heard the Messenger of Allah (Allah bless him and give him peace) say:

اَلْمُسْلِمُ أَخُو الْمُسْلِمِ، لَا يَحِلُّ لِمُسْلِمٍ بَاعَ مِنْ أَخِيْهِ بَيْعًا، فِيْهِ عَيْبٌ، إِلَّا بَيَّنَهُ لَهُ.

> The Muslim is the brother of another Muslim; it is not permissible for a Muslim to sell his brother goods in which there is a defect, without pointing that out to him.[45]

If anyone sells a commodity with a defect without mentioning it, he or she earns the displeasure of Allah and is deprived of its blessing.

عَنْ وَاثِلَةَ بْنِ الْأَسْقَعِ، قَالَ: سَمِعْتُ رَسُوْلَ اللّٰه a يَقُولُ: مَنْ بَاعَ عَيْبًا لَمْ يُبَيِّنْهُ، لَمْ يَزَلْ فِيْ مَقْتِ اللّٰه، وَلَمْ تَزَلِ الْمَلَائِكَةُ تَلْعَنُهُ.

> It was narrated that Wāthila b. al-Asqa' (may Allah be pleased with him) said: "I heard Allah's Messenger (Allah bless him and give him peace) say: 'Whoever sells defective goods without pointing it out will remain subject to the wrath of Allah, and the angels will continue to curse him.'"[46]

According to the preceding Hadith, every Muslim should be a well-wisher of their fellows. Before selling a defective commodity, a trader must disclose its fault. A famous Prophetic Tradition reinforces this argument.

عَنْ أَبِيْ هُرَيْرَةَ أَنَّ رَسُوْلَ اللّٰهِ مَرَّ عَلَى صُبْرَةِ طَعَامٍ، فَأَدْخَلَ يَدَهُ فِيْهَا فَنَالَتْ أَصَابِعُهُ بَلَلًا، فَقَالَ: مَا هَذَا يَا صَاحِبَ الطَّعَامِ؟ قَالَ: أَصَابَتْهُ السَّمَاءُ يَا رَسُولَ اللّٰهِ، قَالَ: أَفَلَا جَعَلْتَهُ فَوْقَ الطَّعَامِ كَيْ يَرَاهُ النَّاسُ؟ مَنْ غَشَّ فَلَيْسَ مِنِّي.

> Abū Hurayra (may Allah be pleased with him) narrated that Allah's Messenger (Allah bless him and give him peace), passing by a pile of foodstuff, put his hand (deep) in it and found that it had got wet. He said: "What is this, seller of the foodstuff?" He said: "It got rained on, Messenger of Allah (Allah bless him and give him peace)." He said: "Why do you not put it on top of the food so that people can see it? Whoever deceives does not pertain to me."[47]

This event emphasises the importance of honesty in business. Among all the systems of beliefs, Islam is the only religion which places significant stress on ethics in business and also presents its Prophet (Allah bless him and give him peace) as a role model. On an occasion, the Prophet (Allah bless him and give him peace) said:

اَلْبَيِّعَانِ بِالْخِيَارِ مَا لَمْ يَتَفَرَّقَا، أَوْ قَالَ: حَتَّى يَتَفَرَّقَا، فَإِنْ صَدَقَا وَبَيَّنَا بُوْرِكَ لَهُمَا فِيْ بَيْعِهِمَا، وَإِنْ كَتَمَا وَكَذَبَا مُحِقَتْ بَرَكَةُ بَيْعِهِمَا.

> The seller and the buyer have the option (to revoke the sale) as long as they have not separated (or he said: "until they separate"). Should they speak the truth and make things clear, they will be blessed in their sale. Should they conceal and lie, the blessing of their transaction will be obliterated.[48]

Any trade that is inconsistent with the teachings and instructions of sanctioned ethics is not lawful. If the business community is in doubt as to the ethics of its conduct in a certain case, it should not engage in it, irrespective of any economic benefits that would accrue.

At present in Muslim lands, fixing systems is the biggest challenge. If systems go on malfunctioning, they will affect individual survival and bring national economic performance to a standstill. The solution to economic troubles lies in the integrity of one's work. Scores of examples in Hadith books explain that dishonesty in business results in scarcity; a corrupt person feels that his or her income has shrunk.

5.6 Aiding and abetting evils

In order to merit forgiveness and recompense, the faithful must abide by the commandments and the prohibitions contained in the primary sources of Islam. All their life is devoted to the propagation of virtues and the prevention of evils.

وَتَعَاوَنُواْ عَلَى الْبِرِّ وَالتَّقْوَى وَلاَ تَعَاوَنُواْ عَلَى الإِثْمِ وَالْعُدْوَانِ وَاتَّقُواْ اللّهَ إِنَّ اللّهَ شَدِيدُ الْعِقَابِ

> *And always support one another in (the works of) righteousness and piety, but do not become accomplices in (works of) sin and transgression. And fear Allah persistently. Indeed, Allah awards severe punishment (to those who disobey and defy).*[49]

When one of their coreligionists falls ill, the adherents of the Muslim religion, rather than leaving them to their own fate and devices, extend help to the distressed.

Abū Hurayra (may Allah be pleased with him) narrated that the Prophet (Allah bless him and give him peace) said:

> If anyone relieves a believer of the agony of this world, Allah will relieve him of one of the agonies of the Day of Rising. If anyone makes life easy for a person in distress, Allah will make life easy for him in this world and the Next. If anyone covers the faults of a Muslim in this world, Allah will cover his faults in this world and in the Next. Allah does not cease extending help to His servant as long as His servant continues extending help to his brother.[50]

On the prohibition of standing by an oppressor, Allah's Messenger (Allah bless him and give him peace) said:

مَنْ مَشَى مَعَ ظَالِمٍ لِيُعِينَهُ وَهُوَ يَعْلَمُ أَنَّهُ ظَالِمٌ، فَقَدْ خَرَجَ مِنَ الإِسْلاَمِ.

> If anyone marches with an oppressor so as to abet him, knowing that he is an oppressor, then he has exited from Islam.[51]

The injunction to cooperate in matters of righteousness while withholding cooperation in matters of sinfulness extends to business activities.

According to Ibn Ḥajar al-'Asqalānī, selling weapons to rebels and miscreants during a time of civil unrest is undesirable – but there is no harm in selling arms to the rightful party in such circumstances.[52]

Notes

1 Qur'ān 2:29.
2 Ibid., 2:173.
3 Ibid., 7:163.
4 Ibn Kathīr in *Tafsīr al-Qur'ān al-'Aẓīm*, 4:258–259.
5 Narrated by al-Bukhārī in *al-Ṣaḥīḥ*: *al-Buyū'* [Sales], Ch.: The fat of carrion should not be melted down nor should its fat be sold, 2:774 §2110.
6 Narrated by Ibn Mājah in al-Sunan: al-Fitan [Troubles], Ch.: Punishments, 2:1333 §4020.
7 Narrated by al-Bukhārī in *al-Ṣaḥīḥ*: *al-Ashriba* [Beverages], Ch.: What has come about someone who considers wine to be lawful and calls it by a different name, 5:2123 §5286.
8 Qur'ān 83:1–3.
9 Ibid., 83:4–6.
10 Ibid., 7:85.
11 Ibid., 11:87.
12 Ibid., 11:94–95.
13 Ibid., 11:86
14 Narrated by Ibn Kathīr in *Tafsīr al-Qur'ān al-'Aẓīm*, 2:415.
15 Narrated by Abū Dāwūd in *al-Sunan*: *al-Ijāra* [Employment], Ch.: Regarding the prohibition of deception, 3:272 §3452.
16 Narrated by Imam Muslim in *al-Ṣaḥīḥ*: *al-Janat wa Ṣifāthā wa ahluhā*The quality of the garden of Paradise and its felicity and its people, Ch.: Attributes by which the people of Paradise and the people of the Fire may be recognized in this world, 4:2197 §2865.
17 Narrated by al-Bukhārī in *al-Ṣaḥīḥ*: *al-Buyū'* [Sales], Ch.: A buyer and seller making things clear and not concealing anything and showing good faith, 2:732 §1973.
18 Ibid., 2:731 §1972.
19 Narrated by al-Tirmidhī in *al-Sunan*: *al-Buyū'* [Sales], Ch.: What has been related about giving more in weights, 3:598 §1305; and Abū Dāwūd in *al-Sunan*: *al-Buyū'* [Sales], Ch.: Regarding giving a little more when weighing, and weighing for a fee, 3:245 §3336.
20 Narrated by Imam Muslim in *al-Ṣaḥīḥ*: *al-Īmān* [Faith], Ch.: The saying of the Prophet (Allah bless him and give him peace), "Whoever deceives us is not one of us," 1:99 §102.
21 Narrated by al-Bayhaqī in *al-Sunan al-Kubrā*, 5:348 §10707.
22 Narrated by al-Bukhārī in *al-Ṣaḥīḥ*: *al-Buyū'* [Sales], Ch.: What is disliked regarding swearing when buying and selling, 2:735 §1981; Muslim in *al-Ṣaḥīḥ*: *al-Buyū'* [Sales], Ch.: The prohibition of swearing oaths when buying and selling, 3:1228 §1606; and Abū Dāwūd in *al-Sunan*: *al-Libās* [Clothing], Ch.: The abhorrence of swearing oaths when buying and selling, 3:245 §3335.
23 Narrated by Imam Muslim in *al-Ṣaḥīḥ*: *al-Musāqāt* [Sharecropping], Ch.: The prohibition of swearing oaths when selling, 3:1228 §1607.
24 Al-'Asqalānī, *Fatḥ al-bārī*, 4:100.
25 Narrated by Imam Muslim in *al-Ṣaḥīḥ*: *al-Īmān* [Faith], Ch.: Clarifying the emphatic prohibition of letting one's garment hang below the ankles, reminding others of one's gift and selling goods by means of a false oath; mention of the three to whom Allah, Most High, will not speak on the Day of Resurrection, nor look at them, nor sanctify them, and theirs will be a painful torment, 1: 102 §106.

26 Narrated by al-Bukhārī in *al-Ṣaḥīḥ*: *al-Buyū'* [Sales], Ch.: The disapproved nature of swearing oaths while selling, 2:735 §1982.
27 Narrated by Aḥmad b. Ḥanbal in *al-Musnad*, 3:428 §15569.
28 Qur'ān 3:77.
29 Narrated by al-Tirmidhī in *al-Sunan*: *Tafsīr al-Qur'ān* [Interpretation of the Qur'ān], Ch.: From *Sūra al-Nisā'*, 5:236 §3020.
30 Qur'ān 3:180.
31 Ibid., 104:2–9.
32 Ibid., 9:34–35.
33 Narrated by Imam Muslim in *al-Ṣaḥīḥ*: *al-Musāqāt* [Sharecropping], Ch.: The prohibition of hoarding staple foods, 3:1227 §1605; al-Ṭabarānī in *al-Mu'jam al-Kabīr*, 20:445 §1086; and al-Bayhaqī in *al-Sunan al-Kubrā*, 6:29 §10930.
34 Narrated by Aḥmad b. Ḥanbal in *al-Musnad*, 2:33 §4880.
35 Narrated by Imam Muslim in *al-Ṣaḥīḥ*: *al-Musāqāt* [Sharecropping], Ch.: The prohibition of hoarding staple foods, 3:1228 §1605.
36 Narrated by al-Ṭabarānī in *al-Mu'jam al-Kabīr*, 20:95 §186.
37 Narrated by Ibn Mājah in *al-Sunan*: *al-Tijārāt* [Trade], Ch.: Hoarding and importing, 2:728 §2153; al-Dārimī in *al-Sunan*, 2:324 §2544; and al-Bayhaqī in *al-Sunan al-Kubrā*, 6:30 §10934.
38 Qur'ān 89:14.
39 Ibid., 92:8–11.
40 Ibid., 2:29.
41 Narrated by Imam Muslim in *al-Ṣaḥīḥ*: *Dhikr, du'ā', tawba wa istighfār*Remembrance [*dhikr*], supplication [*du'ā'*], repentance [*tawba*] and seeking forgiveness [*istighfār*], Ch.: Supplications, 4:2088 §2722.
42 Narrated by al-Bukhārī in *al-Ṣaḥīḥ*: *al-Zakāt* [The Alms-Due], Ch.: Refraining from begging, 2:535 §1403.
43 Narrated by al-Bukhārī in *al-Ṣaḥīḥ*: *al-Riqāq* [The softening of hearts], Ch.: The affliction of wealth about which one should be careful, 5:2364 §6073.
44 Narrated by al-Tirmidhī in *al-Sunan*: *al-Zuhd* [Abstinence], Ch.: (43), 4:588 §2376.
45 Narrated by Ibn Mājah in *al-Sunan*: *al-Tijārāt* [Trade], Ch.: One who sells defective goods should point out the defect, 2:2246.
46 Narrated by Ibn Mājah in *al-Sunan*: *al-Tijārāt* [Trade], Ch.: One who sells defective goods should point out the defect, 2:755 §2247.
47 Narrated by Imam Muslim in *al-Ṣaḥīḥ*: *al-Īmān* [Faith], Ch.: The saying of the Prophet (Allah bless him and give him peace), "Whoever bilks us is not one of us," 1:99 §102.
48 Narrated by al-Bukhārī in *al-Ṣaḥīḥ*: *al-Buyū'* [Sales], Ch.: A buyer and seller making things clear and not concealing anything and showing good faith, 2:732 §1973.
49 Qur'ān 5:2.
50 Narrated by Imam Muslim in *al-Ṣaḥīḥ*: *Dhikr, du'ā', tawba wa istighfār*Remembrance [*dhikr*], supplication [*du'ā'*], repentance [*tawba*] and seeking forgiveness [*istighfār*], Ch.: The excellent merit of assembling at the recitation of the Qur'ān, 4:2074 §2699; and Abū Dāwūd in *al-Sunan*, *al-Adab* [Proper conduct], Ch.: Assistance for the Muslim, 4:287 §4946.
51 Narrated by al-Shaybānī in *al-Āḥādwa al-Mathānī*, 5:347 §2918; al-Munāwī in *Fayḍ al-Qadīr*, 6:229; and al-'Asqalānī in *al-Iṣāba*, 1:155 §341.
52 Al-'Asqalānī, *Fatḥ al-bārī*, 4:408.

Bibliography

The Holy Qur'ān

Abū Dāwūd, Sulaymān b. Ash'ath b. Isḥāq b. Bashīr al-Sijistānī (202–275/817–889). *Al-Sunan*. Beirut, Lebanon: Dār al-Fikr, 1414/1994.

'Asqalānī, Ibn Ḥajar Aḥmad b. 'Alī al-. *Al-Iṣābafītamyīz al-Ṣaḥāba*. Beirut, Lebanon: Dār al-Jīl, 1412AH.

———. *Fatḥ al-Bārīsharḥ Ṣaḥīḥ al-Bukhārī*. Beirut, Lebanon: Dār al-Ma'rifa, 1379AH.

Bayhaqī, Aḥmad b. al-Ḥusayn al-. *Al-Sunan al-kubrā*. Mecca, Saudi Arabia: Maktaba Dār al-Bāz, 1994.

Bukhārī, Abū'Abd Allāh Muhammad b. Ismā'īl b. Ibrahīm b. Mughīra al-. (194–256/810–870). *Al-Adab al-Mufrad*. Beirut, Lebanon: Dār al-Bashā'ir al-Islāmiyya, 1409/1989.

Dārimī, 'Abd Allāh al-. *Al-Sunan*. Beirut, Lebanon: Dār al-Kitāb al-'Arabī, 1407.

Ḥanbal, Aḥmad b. *Al-Musnad*. Beirut, Lebanon: Dar al-Kotob al-Ilmiyah, 1986.

Ibn Kathīr, Abū al-Fidā' Ismā'īl b. 'Umar. *Tafsīr al-Qur'ān al-'Aẓīm*. Beirut, Lebanon: Dar al-Fikr, 1401AH.

Ibn Mājah, Abū 'Abd Allāh Muhammad b. Yazīd al-Qazwīnī (209–273/824–887). *Al-Sunan*. Beirut, Lebanon: Dār al-Kutub al-'Ilmiyya, 1419/1998.

Munāwī, 'Abd al-Ra'ūf b. *Tāj al-Dīn al-.al-Taysīr bi-sharḥ al-Jāmi' al-ṣaghīr*. Saudi Arabia, Riyadh: Maktaba al-Imām al-Shāfi'ī, 1408/1988 ad.

Muslim, Ibn al-*Ḥajj*āj Abū al-Ḥasan al-Qushayrī al-Naysābūrī (206–261/821–875). *Al-Ṣaḥīḥ*. Beirut, Lebanon: Dār al-Iḥyā' al-Turāth al-'Arabī, 1997.

Shaybānī, Abū Bakr Aḥmad b. 'Amr b. al-Ḍaḥḥāk b. Makhlad al- (206–287/822–900). *Al-āḥād wa al-Mathānī*. Riyadh, Saudi Arabia: Dār al-Rāya, 1411/1991.

Ṭabarānī, Sulaymān b. Aḥmad al-. *Al-Mu'jam al-kabīr*. Mosul: Maktaba al-'Ulūmwa al-ḥikam, 1996.

Tirmidhī, Abū 'Īsā Muhammad b. 'Īsā al-. *Al-Sunan*. Beirut, Lebanon: Dār Iḥyā' al-Turāth al-'Arabī, n.d.

6 Seven highly destructive practices of traders

In Islam there are two types of sins; major sins (*kabā'ir*) and minor sins (*ṣaghā'ir*).[1] What are the major sins? Al-Dhahabī, a leading Shafi'ī traditionalist and historian of Islam, describes *kabā'ir*, or grave sins: if the Glorious Qur'ān and the Prophetic Traditions prescribe a penalty for a certain crime, issue a severe warning of chastisement in the eternal world or invoke a curse on its perpetrator, then this defiance falls into the category of major sins.[2]

The following verse mentions cardinal acts of disobedience.

إِن تَجْتَنِبُواْ كَبَآئِرَ مَا تُنْهَوْنَ عَنْهُ نُكَفِّرْ عَنكُمْ سَيِّئَاتِكُمْ وَنُدْخِلْكُم مُّدْخَلاً كَرِيمًا

If you keep abstaining from major sins that you are forbidden to do, We shall remove from you your minor sins and shall admit you to a place of honour.[3]

The faithful who avoid grave sins and shameful deeds, even though they may occasionally stumble into small faults, will be excused by the Lord.

الَّذِينَ يَجْتَنِبُونَ كَبَائِرَ الْإِثْمِ وَالْفَوَاحِشَ إِلاَّ اللَّمَمَ إِنَّ رَبَّكَ وَاسِعُ الْمَغْفِرَةِ

Those who guard against grave sins and indecencies excepting small sins (and omissions), surely your Lord has vast prospects of forgiveness (for them).[4]

Praising the faithful, Qur'ān defines them:

وَالَّذِينَ يَجْتَنِبُونَ كَبَائِرَ الْإِثْمِ وَالْفَوَاحِشَ

/And those who refrain from major sins and the indecencies.[5]

A Prophetic Hadith enumerated seven deadly sins, which are described on the following sections.

عَنْ أَبِي هُرَيْرَةَ، أَنَّ رَسُولَ اللَّهِ صلى الله عليه وسلم قَالَ " اجْتَنِبُوا السَّبْعَ الْمُوبِقَاتِ ". قِيلَ يَا رَسُولَ اللَّهِ مَا هِيَ قَالَ " الشِّرْكُ بِاللَّهِ وَالشُّحُّ وَقَتْلُ النَّفْسِ الَّتِي حَرَّمَ اللَّهُ إِلاَّ بِالْحَقِّ وَأَكْلُ الرِّبَا وَأَكْلُ مَالِ الْيَتِيمِ وَالتَّوَلِّي يَوْمَ الزَّحْفِ وَقَذْفُ الْمُحْصَنَاتِ الْغَافِلاَتِ الْمُؤْمِنَاتِ "

According to Abu, 'Hurayra', 'Prophet Muhammad (Allah bless him and give him peace), said: avoid the seven sins that doom one to Hell. "It was said: 'O Messenger of Allah, what are they?' He said: 'Associating others with Allah (Shirk), magic, killing a soul whom Allah has forbidden killing, except in cases dictated by Islamic law, consuming *Riba*, consuming the property of orphans, fleeing on the day of the march (to battlefield), and slandering chaste women who never even think of anything touching their chastity and are good believers.'"[6]

The doors of repentance are open for everyone, no matter how seasoned a criminal.

Ibn 'Umar (may Allah be well pleased with him and his father) reported that the Messenger (Allah bless him and give him peace) said:

إِنَّ اللَّه يَقْبَلُ تَوْبَةَ الْعَبْدِ مَا لَمْ يُغَرْغِرْ

Indeed Allah accepts the repentance of a slave as long as his soul does not reach his throat.[7]

6.1 Worshipping others with Allah

Some business owners madly pursue material resources and their lust for building wealth knows no bounds. Such people love wealth with a passion, as the Qur'ān indicates:

وَتُحِبُّونَ الْمَالَ حُبًّا جَمًّا○

And you love wealth and riches inordinately.[8]

In order to expand their business or avoid losses, these people transgress Divine limits. They may resort to practices which border on acts of polytheism to grow affluent. Instead of stooping so low, they should rely on Allah Almighty, supplicate to Him for prosperity, and put their heart and soul in their work.

The Muslim religion knows no greater sin than *shirk*, the association of other deities with Allah, the Exalted. The Islamic Scripture warns against falling into the sin of practising idolatry, since through this cardinal sin polytheists will become the dwellers of Hellfire on the Day of Resurrection.

إِنَّكُمْ وَمَا تَعْبُدُونَ مِن دُونِ اللَّهِ حَصَبُ جَهَنَّمَ أَنتُمْ لَهَا وَارِدُونَ

Surely you and the (idols) you worship besides Allah (all) are the fuel of Hell. You are going to enter it.[9]

If anyone dies while committing pure and blatant polytheism, he or she will abide forever in Hellfire. Allah says in the Qur'ān:

إِنَّهُ مَن يُشْرِكْ بِاللَّهِ فَقَدْ حَرَّمَ اللَّهُ عَلَيهِ الْجَنَّةَ وَمَأْوَاهُ النَّارُ وَمَا لِلظَّالِمِينَ مِنْ أَنصَارٍ

Indeed, Allah has forbidden Paradise to him who associates partners with Him. And Hell is his abode and the wrongdoers will not find any helpers.[10]

If anyone commits the deadly sin of ascribing a partner to Allah, all his or her works will be nullified.

وَلَقَدْ أُوحِيَ إِلَيْكَ وَإِلَى الَّذِينَ مِنْ قَبْلِكَ لَئِنْ أَشْرَكْتَ لَيَحْبَطَنَّ عَمَلُكَ وَلَتَكُونَنَّ مِنَ الْخَاسِرِينَ

And in truth (this) revelation has been sent to you and to those (Messengers as well) who were (raised) before you: "(O man,) if you associate partners with Allah, then all your work will go to waste, and you will certainly be amongst the losers."[11]

The same emphasis echoes elsewhere in the Qur'ān.

مَا كَانَ لِلْمُشْرِكِينَ أَن يَعْمُرُوا مَسَاجِدَ اللهِ شَاهِدِينَ عَلَى أَنفُسِهِمْ بِالْكُفْرِ أُوْلَئِكَ حَبِطَتْ أَعْمَالُهُمْ وَفِي النَّارِ هُمْ خَالِدُونَ

It is not for the polytheists to maintain and frequent the mosques of Allah, whereas they themselves bear witness to their disbelief. All their deeds have become void and in Hell they shall dwell forever.[12]

6.2 Black magic

When corporations become larger and larger, the only concern of their owners is big profits, so they may develop malice towards rivals in the business. They may resort to the unethical practice of harming or destroying the competitor through the use of black magic.

From a religious perspective, sorcery, known in Arabic as *siḥr*, is prohibited. Some shopkeepers and traders stoop so low as to destroy the businesses of their rivals. For this purpose, they may resort to black magic – a cardinal sin.

The use of magic is forbidden because of the concern for the welfare of human beings. Witchcraft can damage relationships among individuals and families, affecting them psychologically and physically. On this score the Qur'ān says:

فَيَتَعَلَّمُونَ مِنْهُمَا مَا يُفَرِّقُونَ بِهِ بَيْنَ الْمَرْءِ وَزَوْجِهِ

They (the Jews) used to learn such (magic) from both of them by which they caused separation between husband and wife.[13]

In some cases this devilish action causes illness and death. The Holy Qur'ān warns against practising magic by highlighting its inherent evil:

وَلَقَدْ عَلِمُواْ لَمَنِ اشْتَرَاهُ مَا لَهُ فِي الآخِرَةِ مِنْ خَلاَقٍ وَلَبِئْسَ مَا شَرَوْاْ بِهِ أَنفُسَهُمْ

And surely they (also) knew that he who would buy this (sorcery or disbelief) would not have any share in the Hereafter. And most evil is that for which they sold (the real well-being or the success of) their souls (in the Hereafter).[14]

A whole chapter of the Qur'ān, titled *al-Falaq*, condemns witchcraft.

قُلْ أَعُوذُ بِرَبِّ الْفَلَقِ۝مِن شَرِّ مَا خَلَقَ۝ وَمِن شَرِّ غَاسِقٍ إِذَا وَقَبَ۝وَمِن شَرِّ النَّفَّاثَاتِ فِي الْعُقَدِ۝وَمِن شَرِّ حَاسِدٍ إِذَا حَسَدَ۝

Beseech: "I seek refuge with the Lord of daybreak (or Who brought the universe into existence with an explosion extremely fast), from the evil influence (and harmfulness) of everything that He has created, and (in particular) from the evil of the murky night when (its) darkness prevails, and from the evil of those women (and men) who practise magic on knots by blowing, and from the mischief of every envious person when he envies. The faithful rehearse the above chapter of the Qur'ān to protect themselves for the evil effects of sorcery."[15]

Magicians deceive and create great mischief. They can strike fear into people by creating an illusion that something exists. This is exemplified by the sorcerers of Pharaoh who played a clever trick on the people:

فَإِذَا حِبَالُهُمْ وَعِصِيُّهُمْ يُخَيَّلُ إِلَيْهِ مِن سِحْرِهِمْ أَنَّهَا تَسْعَى

Suddenly their cords and rods, by the effect of their magic, seemed to Mūsā (Moses) as if they were slithering (on the ground).[16]

Elsewhere the Qur'ān tells us:

قَالُواْ يَا مُوسَى إِمَّا أَن تُلْقِيَ وَإِمَّا أَن نَّكُونَ نَحْنُ الْمُلْقِينَ۝قَالَ أَلْقُوْاْ فَلَمَّا أَلْقَوْاْ سَحَرُواْ أَعْيُنَ النَّاسِ وَاسْتَرْهَبُوهُمْ وَجَاءُوا بِسِحْرٍ عَظِيمٍ

> *(The magicians) said: "Mūsā (Moses)! Either you throw (your object) or we become (the first) to throw." Mūsā (Moses) said: "You throw (first)." So when they threw (their strings and sticks on the ground), they bewitched the eyes of the people, and struck them with awe, and brought (forth) an extremely effective magic.*[17]

In the following Hadith, the Prophet Muhammad (Allah bless him and give him peace) commanded his followers to avoid the seven destructive sins, one sin being practising sorcery.

الشِّرْكُ بِاللهِ وَالشُّحُّ وَقَتْلُ النَّفْسِ الَّتِي حَرَّمَ اللَّهُ إِلاَّ بِالْحَقِّ وَأَكْلُ الرِّبَا وَأَكْلُ مَالِ الْيَتِيمِ
وَالتَّوَلِّي يَوْمَ الزَّحْفِ وَقَذْفُ الْمُحْصَنَاتِ الْغَافِلَاتِ الْمُؤْمِنَاتِ

> Making anyone or anything a partner with Allah; practising sorcery; killing a living being without justification whose life has been declared sacred by Allah; practising usury; misappropriating the property of an orphan; running away in a battle; and slandering chaste, innocent, believing women.[18]

When practitioners of witchery and wizardry cause damage to life and property, and their offence is established in a court of law, it is obligatory for the ruler of the Muslims to award the criminals an exemplary punishment.

6.3 Murder

Due to their obsession with the rapid growth of their fortune, people in the corporate sector can go to any length. The owners of plazas, firms and multinational companies at times orchestrate and execute the murder of their own partners through contract killing. Even some shopkeepers and traders stoop so low as to destroy the businesses of their rivals by means of all types of unfair means.

Hell is the just retribution of these slayers. The punishment of murderers who intentionally take the lives of the faithful can be well understood from this Scriptural verse, wherein Allah states that Hell is the recompense for such characters.

وَمَن يَقْتُلْ مُؤْمِنًا مُّتَعَمِّدًا فَجَزَآؤُهُ جَهَنَّمُ خَالِدًا فِيهَا وَغَضِبَ اللهُ عَلَيْهِ وَلَعَنَهُ وَأَعَدَّ لَهُ عَذَابًا
عَظِيمًا

> *But he who kills a Muslim deliberately, his sentence will be Hell wherein will he abide for ages. Allah will afflict him with His wrath and will cast His curse on him. And He has prepared for him a dreadful torment.*[19]

The previous quotation describes the shameful doom that awaits a person who has killed on purpose. However, such an individual cannot escape legal consequences – a life should be taken for a life destroyed – as is mentioned elsewhere in the Qur'ān:

يَا أَيُّهَا الَّذِينَ آمَنُواْ كُتِبَ عَلَيْكُمُ الْقِصَاصُ فِي الْقَتْلَى الْحُرُّ بِالْحُرِّ وَالْعَبْدُ بِالْعَبْدِ وَالأُنثَى بِالأُنثَى فَمَنْ عُفِيَ لَهُ مِنْ أَخِيهِ شَيْءٌ فَاتِّبَاعٌ بِالْمَعْرُوفِ وَأَدَاءٌ إِلَيْهِ بِإِحْسَانٍ ذَلِكَ تَخْفِيفٌ مِّن رَّبِّكُمْ وَرَحْمَةٌ فَمَنِ اعْتَدَى بَعْدَ ذَلِكَ فَلَهُ عَذَابٌ أَلِيمٌ

O believers! Retribution (the law of equality in punishment) is prescribed for you in the case of those who are unjustly slain: a free man for a free man, a slave for a slave and a woman for a woman. Then, if he (the murderer) is granted some remission (in retribution) by his brother (the victim's heir), that should be executed fairly according to the law, and (retribution) should be paid (to the heirs of the slain) in a graceful manner. This is a concession and kindness from your Lord. So anyone who transgresses after that, there is painful torment for him.[20]

A Hadith report says that the killing of an individual, without legal authority, is a tragedy more serious than the passing away of the entire world.

Al-Barā' b. 'āzib (may Allah be pleased with him) narrated that Allah's Messenger (Allah bless him and give him peace) said:

لَزَوَالُ الدُّنْيَا جَمِيْعًا أَهْوَنُ عِنْدَ اللهِ مِنْ سَفْكِ دَمٍ بِغَيْرِ حَقٍّ.

Surely, in the estimation of Allah, the passing away of the whole world is lighter than unjustly shedding the blood of a human being.[21]

While delivering his Last Sermon on the eve of the final pilgrimage, Allah's Messenger (Allah bless him and give him peace) made clear the unlawfulness of killing and pointed out its enormity. He said:

إِنَّ دِمَاءَكُمْ وَأَمْوَالَكُمْ وَأَعْرَاضَكُمْ عَلَيْكُمْ حَرَامٌ، كَحُرْمَةِ يَوْمِكُمْ هَذَا، فِيْ شَهْرِكُمْ هَذَا، فِيْ بَلَدِكُمْ هَذَا، إِلَى يَوْمِ تَلْقَوْنَ رَبَّكُمْ. أَلَا، هَلْ بَلَّغْتُ؟ قَالُوْا: نَعَمْ. قَالَ: اَللَّهُمَّ اشْهَدْ، فَلْيُبَلِّغِ الشَّاهِدُ الْغَائِبَ، فَرُبَّ مُبَلَّغٍ أَوْعَى مِنْ سَامِعٍ، فَلَا تَرْجِعُوْا بَعْدِيْ كُفَّارًا يَضْرِبُ بَعْضُكُمْ رِقَابَ بَعْضٍ.

"Indeed your blood, your property and your honour are inviolable for you, like the inviolability of this day of yours and this month of yours and this land of yours, until the day you meet your Lord. Listen, have I conveyed the message?" The Companions replied, "Yes." He said, "Allah, bear witness. Let the one present inform those who are absent, for perhaps the one to whom it is conveyed will retain it better than he who hears it (directly). Do not revert as disbelievers after me, striking each other's necks."[22]

Abū Sa'īd al-Khudrī and Abū Hurayra (may Allah be well pleased with them) narrated that the Blessed Messenger (Allah bless him and give him peace) said regarding the murder of a believing Muslim:

لَوْ أَنَّ أَهْلَ السَّمَاءِ وَأَهْلَ الْأَرْضِ اشْتَرَكُوْا فِيْ دَمِ مُؤْمِنٍ، لَأَكَبَّهُمُ اللهُ فِي النَّارِ.

Even if all the inhabitants of the heavens and the earth gathered together to shed the blood of a single believer, Allah would cast them all into Hellfire.[23]

'Abd Allāh b. Mas'ūd (may be Allah be pleased with him) narrated that the Messenger (Allah bless him and give him peace) said while describing the enormity of shedding blood unlawfully:

أَوَّلُ مَا يُقْضَى بَيْنَ النَّاسِ يَوْمَ الْقِيَامَةِ فِي الدِّمَاءِ.

The first issue that will be judged between people on the Day of Resurrection is that of blood (i.e., murder).[24]

Ibn 'Umar (may Allah be well pleased with him and his father) reported that the Holy Prophet (Allah bless him and give him peace) warned about the disastrous consequences of fighting and bloodshed:

إِنَّ مِنْ وَرَطَاتِ الْأُمُورِ الَّتِي لَا مَخْرَجَ لِمَنْ أَوْقَعَ نَفْسَهُ فِيهَا، سَفْكُ الدَّمِ الْحَرَامِ بِغَيْرِ حِلِّهِ.

Of the serious matters from which no one who brings it upon himself and falls into it will escape is that of blood that was shed unlawfully.[25]

Allah Almighty does not chastise murderers and wrongdoers immediately for their misdeeds. Thus the Lord gives them time to right their wrong. If they choose not to mend their character and persist in transgression, He seizes them with painful torment.

6.4 *Ribā* (usury)

In business, people should work diligently to earn and build wealth. Some people fall into the temptation of partaking in usurious transitions and assume that their possessions and wealth will multiply. Muslim merchants should heed Allah Almighty's message that He is displeased with usury.

Literally, *ribā* means an "increment" or "addition." In Islamic jurisprudence, consuming *ribā* refers to a practice of increment in borrowing or lending money, paid in kind or in money above the principal amount of debt. Through this unjust practice, the borrower's debt doubles and redoubles and the lender accumulates unearned profit.

The Qur'ān prohibits *ribā* and condemns it as a great impediment to social justice and development.

١- الَّذِينَ يَأْكُلُونَ الرِّبَا لاَ يَقُومُونَ إِلاَّ كَمَا يَقُومُ الَّذِي يَتَخَبَّطُهُ الشَّيْطَانُ مِنَ الْمَسِّ ذَلِكَ
بِأَنَّهُمْ قَالُواْ إِنَّمَا الْبَيْعُ مِثْلُ الرِّبَا وَأَحَلَّ اللهُ الْبَيْعَ وَحَرَّمَ الرِّبَا فَمَن جَاءَهُ مَوْعِظَةٌ مِّن رَّبِّهِ
فَانتَهَى فَلَهُ مَا سَلَفَ وَأَمْرُهُ إِلَى اللهِ وَمَنْ عَادَ فَأُوْلَئِكَ أَصْحَابُ النَّارِ هُمْ فِيهَا خَالِدُونَ

Those who live on usury will not be able to stand (on the Day of Judgment), but like the one whom Satan has made insane with his touch (i.e., damnation). This is because they used to say that trade (i.e., buying and selling) is similar to usury, whereas Allah has declared trade (i.e., buying and selling) lawful and usury unlawful. So, if someone refrains (from usury) on receiving admonition from his Lord, then he can keep whatever he took in the past and his case is with Allah. But those who continued with usury (despite the admonition) would be the inmates of Hell. They will abide there permanently.[26]

٢- يَمْحَقُ اللهُ الْرِّبَا وَيُرْبِي الصَّدَقَاتِ وَاللهُ لاَ يُحِبُّ كُلَّ كَفَّارٍ أَثِيمٍ

Allah eliminates usury (i.e., deprives usurious profits of prosperous growth) and multiplies alms gifts (i.e., increases blessings of clean wealth manifold through charity donations). And Allah does not like anyone who is ungrateful and disobedient.[27]

٣- يَا أَيُّهَا الَّذِينَ آمَنُواْ لاَ تَأْكُلُواْ الرِّبَا أَضْعَافًا مُّضَاعَفَةً وَاتَّقُواْ اللهَ لَعَلَّكُمْ تُفْلِحُونَ

O believers! Do not live on usury doubled and redoubled, and keep fearing Allah so that you may prosper.[28]

٤- يَا أَيُّهَا الَّذِينَ آمَنُواْ اتَّقُواْ اللَّهَ وَذَرُواْ مَا بَقِيَ مِنَ الرِّبَا إِن كُنتُم مُّؤْمِنِينَ فَإِن لَّمْ تَفْعَلُواْ
فَأْذَنُواْ بِحَرْبٍ مِّنَ اللهِ وَرَسُولِهِ وَإِن تُبْتُمْ فَلَكُمْ رُؤُوسُ أَمْوَالِكُمْ لاَ تَظْلِمُونَ وَلاَ تُظْلَمُونَ

O believers! Fear Allah and write off whatever balance remains of usury if you are believers (true to the core of your hearts). But if you do not do so, then be warned of the declaration of war from Allah and His Holy Messenger (Allah bless him and give him peace). And if you repent, then your principal amounts are (lawfully) yours. (In this case) you will neither do any wrong, nor be wronged.[29]

Charging interest is one of the seven sins which dooms a person to the Fire. The Blessed Prophet (Allah bless him and give him peace) denounced usurious transactions as they result in moral, social, economic and religious ills. Some Traditions are cited next to establish the evil of this social practice.

According to Jābir (may Allah be pleased with him):

لَعَنَ رَسُوْلُ اللهِ آكِلَ الرِّبَا، وَمُؤْكِلَهُ، وَكَاتِبَهُ، وَشَاهِدَيْهِ، وَقَالَ: هُمْ سَوَاءٌ.

Allah's Messenger (Allah bless him and give him peace) cursed the one who consumes *ribā*(usury) and the one who pays for it, the one who writes it down and the two who witness it and he said: "They are all the same."[30]

Elsewhere the Prophet (Allah bless him and give him peace) denounced usury in these words:

الرِّبَا سَبْعُوْنَ حُوْباً، أَيْسَرُهَا أَنْ يَنْكِحَ الرَّجُلُ أُمَّهُ.

There are seventy degrees of usury, the least of which is equivalent to a man having intercourse with his mother.[31]

The faithful are under obligation to make a profit through their own exertions, not through exploiting other people who happen to be in need of money.

6.5 Consuming orphans' wealth

Fatherless and/or motherless children are deserving of affection and monetary help to live honourably. However, some men of means prove so callous after the demise of their brothers, sisters or uncles that they – illegally in the eyes of Allah Almighty and the law of the land – take possession of the orphan's property. What such selfish people snatch for their inheritance is just fuel for Hellfire. Oppressors should fear that the orphans' cries may doom them in both worlds.

Islam enjoins the guardians of orphans to take care of the welfare of their wards and maintain their property. A verse of the Qur'ān reinforces this theme:

وَيَسْأَلُونَكَ عَنِ الْيَتَامَى قُلْ إِصْلاَحٌ لَّهُمْ خَيْرٌ وَإِنْ تُخَالِطُوهُمْ فَإِخْوَانُكُمْ وَاللهُ يَعْلَمُ الْمُفْسِدَ
مِنَ الْمُصْلِحِ وَلَوْ شَاءَ اللهُ لَأَعْنَتَكُمْ إِنَّ اللهَ عَزِيزٌ حَكِيمٌ

And they ask you about orphans. Say: "It is meritorious to set (their affairs) right. And if you associate them with yourselves (in subsistence and business), then they are also your brothers. And Allah distinctly recognizes the one who is destructive from the other who is constructive. And if Allah willed, He would put you in distress. Verily, Allah is All-Mighty, All-Wise."[32]

The Scripture stipulates that the guardians must promote and protect the interest of minors and treat them with kindness.

وَلاَ تُؤْتُواْ السُّفَهَاءَ أَمْوَالَكُمُ الَّتِي جَعَلَ اللّهُ لَكُمْ قِيَاماً وَارْزُقُوهُمْ فِيهَا وَاكْسُوهُمْ وَقُولُواْ لَهُمْ قَوْلاً مَّعْرُوفًا

And do not entrust to the mentally deficient your (or their) assets which Allah has made a means of stability for your economy. However, feed them out of it and clothe them, and say to them good and nice words.[33]

Guardians who squander the orphans' resources wastefully are subject to a stern warning.

وَابْتَلُواْ الْيَتَامَى حَتَّىَ إِذَا بَلَغُواْ النِّكَاحَ فَإِنْ آنَسْتُم مِّنْهُمْ رُشْدًا فَادْفَعُواْ إِلَيْهِمْ أَمْوَالَهُمْ وَلاَ تَأْكُلُوهَا إِسْرَافًا وَبِدَارًا أَن يَكْبَرُواْ وَمَن كَانَ غَنِيًّا فَلْيَسْتَعْفِفْ وَمَن كَانَ فَقِيرًا فَلْيَأْكُلْ بِالْمَعْرُوفِ فَإِذَا دَفَعْتُمْ إِلَيْهِمْ أَمْوَالَهُمْ فَأَشْهِدُواْ عَلَيْهِمْ وَكَفَى بِاللّهِ حَسِيبًا

And evaluate and test the orphans (for the sake of their training) till they attain to (the age of) marriage. Then if you discern in them ingenuity (and the knack of planning), hand over their assets to them. And devour not their wealth spending it wastefully and in haste (fearing that after) they grow mature (they will take it back). The one who is affluent must absolutely abstain (from the orphan's property), but he who is indigent (himself) should consume but a fair portion of it (only). And when you return to them their assets, take witnesses over them. And Sufficient is Allah at reckoning.[34]

Well-off guardians should claim no remuneration, however, poor guardians may take from the orphan's property a just and reasonable amount in return for their guardianship. Using the wealth of an orphan in one's care is admissible as a business activity, provided that one intends to increase the wealth of the ward. In this case it is a virtuous deed.

According to 'Amr b. Shu'āyb, on the authority of his father, his grandfather (may Allah be pleased with him) said:

> A man came to the Prophet (Allah bless him and give him peace) and said: "I am a poor person, I have nothing with me, and I have an orphan." He said: "Eat from the wealth of your orphan without extravagance, haste, or using it for trade."[35]

Islam treats unlawfully taking for oneself the wealth of an orphan under one's care as a mortal sin that sends one to the blazing fires of Hell.

إِنَّ الَّذِينَ يَأْكُلُونَ أَمْوَالَ الْيَتَامَى ظُلْمًا إِنَّمَا يَأْكُلُونَ فِي بُطُونِهِمْ نَارًا وَسَيَصْلَوْنَ سَعِيرًا

Indeed, those who eat up the property of orphans unjustly fill their bellies but with fire, and soon will they fall into a Blazing Fire.[36]

6.6 Fleeing from the battlefield

The battlefield of merchants is their trade. For them diligence is the way to achieve growth and prosperity. Blessed are the people who exercise their mental and physical energies, so as to raise their families. The Messenger (Allah bless him and give him peace) said:

مَا كَسَبَ الرَّجُلُ كَسْبًا أَطْيَبَ مِنْ عَمَلِ يَدِهِ وَمَا أَنْفَقَ الرَّجُلُ عَلَى نَفْسِهِ وَأَهْلِهِ وَوَلَدِهِ
وَخَادِمِهِ فَهُوَ صَدَقَةٌ

No man earns anything better than that which he earns with his own hands. What a man spends on himself, his wife, his child and his servant is charity.[37]

If hard times ever come their way, they should recall the words of the Prophet (Allah bless him and give him peace):

There are sins that are remitted by nothing save the care for seeking sustenance.[38]

Some people, instead of focusing all their energy on building their business, seek to use unfair means so as to increase their possessions. Instead of facing troubles coming their way, they try to flee away from them and indulge in malpractices and conspiracies. This is like fleeing away from the battlefield and not facing their enemies with bravery and confidence. On fleeing from the battlefield, Allah warns the faithful,

يَا أَيُّهَا الَّذِينَ آمَنُواْ إِذَا لَقِيتُمُ الَّذِينَ كَفَرُواْ زَحْفاً فَلاَ تُوَلُّوهُمُ الأَدْبَارَ

O believers! When you combat the disbelievers (in the battlefield), never turn your backs on them (even if they are) a large army.[39]

Those who desert their posts are warned by Allah. If any believer flees for any reason other than those mentioned next, he or she commits a major sin.

وَمَن يُوَلِّهِمْ يَوْمَئِذٍ دُبُرَهُ إِلاَّ مُتَحَرِّفاً لِّقِتَالٍ أَوْ مُتَحَيِّزاً إِلَى فِئَةٍ فَقَدْ بَاءَ بِغَضَبٍ مِّنَ اللهِ وَمَأْوَاهُ جَهَنَّمُ وَبِئْسَ الْمَصِيرِ

And he who turns his back on them that day, except he who is manoeuvring in the fight, or he who wants to join one of his own troops (for support), certainly he returns with the wrath of Allah and Hell is his abode and that is (the most) evil abode.[40]

Hadith literature also states the same theme. Abū Hurayra (may Allah be pleased with him) reported that the Prophet (Allah bless him and give him peace) said, "Avoid the seven destroyers." The listeners asked: "Messenger of Allah, what are they?" The Prophet (Allah bless him and give him peace) then explained:

اَلشِّرْكُ بِاللهِ، وَالسِّحْرُ، وَقَتْلُ النَّفْسِ الَّتِيْ حَرَّمَ اللهُ إِلَّا بِالْحَقِّ، وَأَكْلُ الرِّبَا، وَأَكْلُ مَالِ الْيَتِيْمِ، وَالتَّوَلِّي يَوْمَ الزَّحْفِ، وَقَذْفُ الْمُحْصَنَاتِ الْغَافِلاَتِ الْمُؤْمِنَاتِ.

Making anyone or anything a partner with Allah; practising sorcery; killing a living being without justification whose life has been declared sacred by Allah; practising usury; misappropriating the property of an orphan; running away in a battle; and slandering chaste, innocent, believing women.[41]

6.7 Slandering chaste, innocent, faithful women

Woe to traders who indulge in personal attacks and character assassination of women! Such blame might temporarily work out in their favour but, in the long run, they face the consequences of their vile actions. Accusers must bear in their mind that the blame game and dirty accusations may rebound on their own families one day.

People who launch a charge against chaste women without supporting it with evidence are strongly disapproved by Allah Almighty. Four witnesses are required to support any allegation. Moreover, accusing virtuous women falsely will bring a grievous penalty in the Hereafter:

إِنَّ الَّذِينَ يَرْمُونَ الْمُحْصَنَاتِ الْغَافِلَاتِ الْمُؤْمِنَاتِ لُعِنُوا فِي الدُّنْيَا وَالْآخِرَةِ وَلَهُمْ عَذَابٌ عَظِيمٌ

Verily, those who falsely accuse chaste, believing women who are unaware of, and unacquainted (with, even the very idea of indecency and evil) are cursed in this world and in the Hereafter. And for them is woeful punishment.[42]

Though the verse has laid down the punishment for traducing virtuous, believing women, it also applies to falsely stigmatising chaste men. Virtuous women have been specially mentioned because generally women are more often accused of behaving immodestly or unchastely. Moreover, the unjust accusation of pure and chaste women is one of the mortal sins according to the Prophetic Traditions.

6.8 The cure for deadly trading practices

Perhaps at the bottom of all the previously mentioned major sins lies pangs of envy. Envious businesspeople may think themselves more deserving of Divine bounties than their fellow beings. Unable to enjoy the good things of life, they plot to deprive others of them. This type of mentality brings about much destruction and death in the world.

In order to overcome the resentful feelings caused by desiring status, success and fortune, jealous people must bear in mind the words of the Divine:

ذَٰلِكَ فَضْلُ اللهِ يُؤْتِيهِ مَن يَشَاءُ وَاللهُ وَاسِعٌ عَلِيمٌ

> *This is the grace of Allah which He grants whom He wills, and Allah is Infinite, All-Knowing.*[43]

Going green with envy on observing someone's good fortune and personal effects does not behoove the faithful: none but Allah is the distributor of the means of sustenance. So resentment against another person's social standing is, in reality, taking exception to the profound sagacity of the Lord. An envier may not confess that he or she is displeased with Divine distribution.

أَهُمْ يَقْسِمُونَ رَحْمَةَ رَبِّكَ نَحْنُ قَسَمْنَا بَيْنَهُم مَّعِيشَتَهُمْ فِي الْحَيَاةِ الدُّنْيَا

> *We distribute amongst them (the resources of) economy in the life of this world, and We alone raise some of them in grades (of wealth and resources) over the others.*[44]

This blameworthy trait is a disease which severs one's faith. To get rid of this inward evil, one should supplicate to Allah Almighty with a sincere heart. Another way of purifying one's heart is by making gifts to the individual who is an object of envy and treating them well. On this score, the Messenger (Allah bless him and give him peace) said:

تَصَافَحُوْا، يَذْهَبِ الْغِلُّ، وَتَهَادَوْا، تَحَابُّوْا وَتَذْهَبِ الشَّحْنَاءُ.

> Shake hands, for this will dispel rancour, and exchange gifts and love one another, for this will dispel hatred.[45]

Elsewhere the Messenger (Allah bless him and give him peace) encouraged people to present gifts mutually, as they remove bad feelings. He said:

تَهَادَوْا، فَإِنَّ الْهَدِيَّةَ تُذْهِبُ وَحَرَ الصَّدْرِ.

> Give gifts, for indeed the gift removes bad feelings from the chest.[46]

It is obvious that those who practise jealousy first nurse hatred within. This is a sure way to kill one's inner happiness and peace of mind. Islam urges a course of action alternative to envy – "one of the most potent causes of unhappiness" in the estimation of Bertrand Russell.

According to 'Abd Allāh b. 'Umar (may Allah be well pleased with him and his father), he heard Allah's Messenger (Allah bless him and give him peace) say:

> There is no reason to be envious except of these two: (1) a man to whom Allah has brought the Book, and he recites it in the night vigil, and (2) a man to whom Allah has given wealth, so he devotes it to charity during the night and the day.[47]

Notes

1 Cited by al-Ghazālī in *Iḥyā' al-'ulūm*, 4:11.
2 Al-Dhahabī, *al-Kabā'ir*, p. 13.
3 Qur'ān 4:31.
4 Ibid., 53:32.
5 Ibid., 42:37.
6 Nasā'ī, Aḥmad b. Shu'ayb Abū'Abd al-Raḥmān al- (215–303/830–915). al-Sunan. Ch: Avoiding Consuming The Orphan's Property, Beirut, Lebanon: Dār al-Kutub al-'Ilmiyya, 1416/1995.
7 Narrated by al-Tirmidhī in *al-Sunan*: *al-Da'awāt* [Supplications], Ch.: Indeed, Allah accepts the repentance of a slave as long as his soul does not reach his throat, 5:547 §3537.
8 Qur'ān 89:20.
9 Ibid., 21:98.
10 Ibid., 5:72.
11 Ibid., 39:65.
12 Ibid., 9:17.
13 Ibid., 2:102.
14 Ibid.
15 Ibid., 113:1–5.
16 Ibid., 20:66.
17 Ibid., 7:115–116.
18 Narrated by al-Bukhārī in *al-Ṣaḥīḥ*: Bk.:al-Waṣāya [Wills], Ch.: The words of Almighty Allah: "*Indeed, those who eat up the property of orphans unjustly fill their bellies but with fire, and soon will they fall into a Blazing Fire*" [Q.4:10], 3:1017 §2615.
19 Qur'ān 4:93.
20 Ibid., 2:178.
21 Narrated by Ibn Abī al-Dunyā in *al-Ahwāl*, p. 190 §183; Ibn Abī'Āṣim in *al-Diyāt*, p. 2 §2; and al-Bayhaqī in *Shu'ab al-Īmān*, 4:345 §5344.

22 Narrated by al-Bukhārī in *al-Ṣaḥīḥ*: *al-Ḥajj* [Pilgrimage], 2:620 §1654, and *al-'Ilm* [Knowledge], Ch.: The saying of the Prophet (Allah bless him and give him peace), "Many a person to whom something is conveyed retains it better than the one who heard it," 1:37 §67; and Muslim in *al-Ṣaḥīḥ*, 3:1305–1306 §1679.
23 Narrated by al-Tirmidhī in *al-Sunan*: *al-Diyāt* [Blood Money], Ch.: The legal ruling concerning blood, 4:17 §1398; al-Rabī' in *al-Musnad*, 1:292 §757; and al-Daylamī in *Musnad al-firdaws*, 3:361 §5089.
24 Narrated by al-Bukhārī in *al-Ṣaḥīḥ*: *al-Diyāt* [Blood Money], Ch.: Whoever kills a believer intentionally, 6:2517 §6471; Muslim in *al-Ṣaḥīḥ*, 3:1304 §1678; al-Nasā'ī in *al-Sunan*: *Taḥrīm al-dam* [The Prohibition of Bloodshed], Ch.: The sanctity of blood, 7:83 §3994; and Aḥmad b. Ḥanbal in *al-Musnad*, 1:442.
25 Narrated by al-Bukhārī in *al-Ṣaḥīḥ*: *al-Diyāt* [Blood Money], Ch.: Whoever kills a believer intentionally, 6:2517 §6470; and al-Bayhaqī in *al-Sunan al-kubrā*, 8:21 §15637.
26 Qur'ān 2:275.
27 Ibid., 2:276.
28 Ibid., 3:130.
29 Ibid., 2:278–279.
30 Narrated by Imam Muslim in *al-Ṣaḥīḥ*: *al-Musāqāt* [Sharecropping], Ch.: Cursing the one who consumes *ribā* and the one who pays it, 3:1219 §1598; and Ibn Mājah in *al-Sunan*: *al-Tijārāt* [Trade], Ch.: Emphatic prohibition of usury, 2:764 §2277.
31 Narrated by Ibn Mājah in *al-Sunan*: *al-Tijārāt* [Trade], Ch.: Emphatic prohibition of usury, 2:764 §2274; and al-Mundhirī in *al-Targhībwa al-Tarhīb*, 3:6 §2584.
32 Qur'ān 2:220.
33 Ibid., 4:5.
34 Ibid., 4:6.
35 Narrated by Abū Dāwūd in *al-Sunan*: Bk.:*al-Waṣāya* [Wills], Ch.: What has been related about what is allowed for the guardian of the orphan to take from his wealth, 3:115 §2872.
36 Qur'ān 4:10.
37 Narrated by Ibn Mājah in *al-Sunan*: *al-Tijārāt* [Trade], Ch.: Urging the acquisition of profits, 2:723 §2138; and al-Mundhirī in *al-Targhībwa al-Tarhīb*, 2:333 §2602.
38 Narrated by al-Ṭabarānī in *al-Mu'jam al-awsaṭ*, 1:38 §102; and al-Haythamī in *Majma' al-zawā'id*, 2:291.
39 Qur'ān 8:15.
40 Ibid., 8:16.
41 Narrated by al-Bukhārī in *al-Ṣaḥīḥ*: Bk.:al-Waṣāya [Wills], Ch.: The words of Almighty Allah: "*Indeed, those who eat up the property of orphans unjustly fill their bellies but with fire, and soon will they fall into a Blazing Fire*" [Q.4:10],3:1017 §2615.
42 Qur'ān., 24:23.
43 Ibid., 5:54.
44 Ibid., 43:32.
45 Narrated by Mālik in *al-Muwaṭṭa'*, 2:908 §1617; and al-Suyūṭī in *Tanwīr al-ḥawālikSharḥMuwaṭṭa'Mālik*, 2:214 §1617.
46 Narrated by al-Tirmidhī in *al-Sunan*: *al-Walā'wa al-hiba* [Inheritance and gifts], Ch.: Regarding the Prophet's encouraging gifts, 4:441 §2130; and al-Zayla'ī in *Naṣb al-Rāya*, 4:121.
47 Narrated by al-Bukhārī in *al-Ṣaḥīḥ*: *Faḍā'il al-Qur'ān* [The excellent merits of the Qur'ān], Ch.: Envy for the one deeply attached to the Qur'ān, 4:1919 §4737; Muslim in *al-Ṣaḥīḥ*: *Ṣalāt al-Musāfirīnwa Qaṣru-hā* [The ritual prayer of the travellers and its curtailment], Ch.: The excellent merit of someone who studies the Qur'ān and teaches it, and the excellent merit of someone who learns wisdom from jurisprudence or something else, then acts upon it and teaches it, 1:558–9 §815; Ibn Abī Shayba in *al-Muṣannaf*, 6:153 §30281–2; and Abū Ya'lā in *al-Musnad*, 9:291 §5417.

Bibliography

The Holy Qur'ān

Abū Dāwūd, Sulaymān b. Ash'ath b. Isʜāq b. Bashīr al-Sijistānī (202–275/817–889). *Al-Sunan*. Beirut, Lebanon: Dār al-Fikr, 1414/1994.

Abū Ya'lā, Aʜmad b. 'Alī b. Mathnā b. Yaʜyā b. 'Īsā b. al-Hilāl al-Mūṣilī al-Tamīmī (210–307/825–919). *Al-Musnad*. Damascus, Syria: Dār al-Ma'mūn li al-Turāth, 1404/1984.

Bayhaqī, Aḥmad b. al-Ḥusayn al-. *Al-Sunan al-kubrā*. Mecca, Saudi Arabia: Maktaba Dār al-Bāz, 1994.

———. *Shu'ab al-Īmān*. Beirut, Lebanon: Dar al-Kotob al-Ilmiyah, 1990.

Bukhārī, Abū'Abd Allāh Muhammad b. Ismā'īl b. Ibrahīm b. Mughīra al-. (194–256/810–870). *Al-Adab al-Mufrad*. Beirut, Lebanon: Dār al-Bashā'ir al-Islāmiyya, 1409/1989.

Daylamī, Abū Shujā'Shīrawayh. *Al-Firdaws bi ma'thūr al-khiṭāb*. Mecca, Saudi Arabia: Dar al-Kotob al-Ilmiyah, 1986.

Dhahabī, Shams al-Dīn Muhammad b. Aḥmad al-. *Al-Kabā'ir*. Beirut, Lebanon: Dār al-Nadwa al-Jadīda, n.d.

Ghazālī, Abūḥāmid Muhammad b. Muhammad al-Ghazālī al- (450–505ᴀʜ). *Iḥyā'al-'Ulūm*. Beirut, Lebanon: Dār al-Ma'rifa, 2001.

Ḥanbal, Aḥmad b. *Al-Musnad*. Beirut, Lebanon: Dar al-Kotob al-Ilmiyah, 1986.

Haythamī, Nūr al-Dīn Abū al-Ḥasan'Alī al-. *Majma' al-zawā'idwamanba' al-fawā'id*. Cairo: Dār al-Rayān li al-Turāth, 1987.

Ibn Abī al-Dunyā, Abū Bakr 'Abd Allāh b. Muhammad b. al-Qurashī (208–281ᴀʜ). *al-Ahwāl*. Egypt: Maktaba āl Yāsir, 1413ᴀʜ.

Ibn Abī Shayba, 'Abd Allāh b. Muhammad. *Al-Muṣannaf*. Riyadh: Maktaba al-Rushd, 1409ᴀʜ.

Ibn Mājah, Abū 'Abd Allāh Muhammad b. Yazīd al-Qazwīnī (209–273/824–887). *Al-Sunan*. Beirut, Lebanon: Dār al-Kutub al-'Ilmiyya, 1419/1998.

Mālik, Ibn Anas b. Mālik b. Abī'āmir b. 'Amr b. Ḥārith al-Aṣbaʜī (93–179/712–795). *Al-Muwaṭṭā'*. Beirut, Lebanon: Dār Iḥyā' al-Turāth al-'Arabī, 1990.

Mundhirī, 'Abd al-'Aẓīm al-. *Al-Targhībwa al-tarhīb*. Beirut, Lebanon: Dar al-Kotob al-Ilmiyah, 1417ᴀʜ.

Muslim, Ibn al-Ḥajjāj Abū al-Ḥasan al-Qushayrī al-Naysābūrī (206–261/821–875). *Al-Ṣaʜīʜ*. Beirut, Lebanon: Dār al-Iʜyā' al-Turāth al-'Arabī, 1997.

Nasā'ī, Aʜmad b. Shu'ayb Abū 'Abd al-Raʜmān al- (215–303/830–915). *al-Sunan*. Beirut, Lebanon: Dār al-Kutub al-'Ilmiyya, 1416/1995.

Suyūṭī, Jalāl al-Dīn Abū al-Faḍl 'Abd al-Raʜmān b. Abī Bakr b. Muhammad b. Abī Bakr b. 'Uthmān al- (849–911/1445–1505). *Tanwīr al-ḥawālik Sharḥ Muwaṭṭa' Mālik*. Egypt: Maktaba al-Tajjāriyya al-Kubrā, 1389/1969.

Ṭabarānī, Sulaymān b. Aḥmad al-. *Al-Mu'jam al-awsaṭ*. Cairo: Dār al-Ḥaramayn, 1415ᴀʜ.

Tirmidhī, Abū 'Īsā Muhammad b. 'Īsā al-. *Al-Sunan*. Beirut, Lebanon: Dār Iḥyā' al-Turāth al-'Arabī, n.d.

Zayla'ī, Abū Muhammad 'Abd Allāh b. Yūsuf al-Ḥanafī al- (d. 762/1360). *Naṣb al-Rāya li-Aʜadīth al-Hidāya*. Egypt: Dār al-Ḥadīth, 1357/1938.

7 The legal status of contracts

7.1 Mortgages

Mortgages for household, commercial or personal needs in non-Muslim societies are based on interest. What Allah has prohibited no one may legalise. If an individual attempts to legalise interest or any one of the Divine prohibitions, he or she is no longer within the ambit of Islam. In non-Muslim countries where Muslims are small in numbers, the issue of mortgage for them becomes an issue of *ijtihād* (independent reasoning of a jurist's mental faculty in deducing a solution to a legal question).

A pertinent juristic maxim worth citing here is that "injunctions change with the change of circumstances, places and ages."[1] As the conditions of Muslim minorities living in non-Muslim countries change and there is no alternative system available, the legal status of the prohibited thing becomes different. According to jurists, if Muslims are residents of a land where the rules of Sharia are not in force – when they also pay taxes to the non-Muslim government – then they may make use of the available facilities. In such a situation, forbidden interest will not become lawful, but this injunction will not be applicable. To sum up, interest-based mortgages are acceptable until a viable Islamic solution is available, even though the status of interest remains categorically forbidden.[2]

7.2 Insurance

There is no harm in entering into an insurance policy with one of the numerous Islamic insurance companies that strictly observe Sharia-compliant standards.

Conventional insurance as practised in the advanced industrial societies is generally considered to be illegal by the majority of Islamic scholars. However, holding an insurance policy is allowable, according to some scholars. Still, it is better for the faithful to avoid this business, putting their trust in the Almighty, instead of putting faith in the insurance company and assuming that it would come to their rescue if there is a disaster.

An insurance policy provided by conventional banks and insurance companies has been receiving criticism among a number of Muslim scholars. Alternatively, Muslim jurists have introduced an alternative: *takaful*, an insurance system which complies with the principles of Sharia.

7.3 *Takaful*: an alternative to conventional insurance

The English terms for *takaful* are "solidarity," "mutual guarantee" or "guaranteeing each other." Based on "social solidarity, cooperation and joint indemnification of losses of the members,"[3] *takaful* is Islamic insurance as it is run under the principles of Islamic finance. The system is a communal enterprise in which members pool their resources and help each other in case of loss or casualty. *Takaful* is Sharia-compliant insurance, a modern approach to reducing one's exposure to risks and ensuring social welfare.

Technically *takaful* means "a mutual guarantee or assurance based on the principles of *al-aqd* (contract) provided by a group of people living in the same society, against a defined risk or catastrophe befalling life, property or any form of valuable asset."[4] Ayub defined the term *takaful* as follows,

> A form of Islamic insurance based on the principle of *Ta'awon* or mutual assistance. It provides for mutual assistance in cases of loss to life, assets and property and offers joint risk-sharing in the event of a loss incurred by one of the pool members.[5]

7.3.1 Takaful *and risk mitigation*

Takaful, an alternative to conventional insurance, is a means of mitigating the financial risk of loss through accidents, injuries and misfortunes. Muslims avoid taking precautionary measures before any undesired situation reaches them; this is because of their unveiled understanding of Allah's desire. The following verse explains the desire of Allah Almighty in relation to the knowledge of people worldly affairs.

إِنَّ اللَّه لَا يُغَيِّرُ مَا بِقَوْمٍ حَتَّىٰ يُغَيِّرُوا۟ مَا بِأَنْفُسِهِمْ

> *Verily, Allah does not change the state of a people until they bring about a change in themselves.*[6]

The verse cited and the following Tradition instil the importance of hard work and endeavouring to find a means of avoiding unpleasant circumstances and lessen the risk of adverse conditions. Reliance on the Almighty means exerting oneself and then committing one's affairs to Him.

One day Allah's Messenger (Allah bless him and give him peace) noticed a Bedouin who left his camel without tying it. The Bedouin asked:

يَا رَسُوْلَ اللَّه، أَعْقِلُهَا وَأَتَوَكَّلُ، أَوْ أُطْلِقُهَا وَأَتَوَكَّلُ؟

> Messenger of Allah, shall I tie it and rely (upon Allah), or shall I leave it loose and rely (upon Allah)?

He replied:

اِعْقِلْهَا وَتَوَكَّلْ.

Tie your camel (first), then put your trust in Allah.[7]

So the real meaning of reliance on Allah Almighty means making careful plans to attain good and avert misfortune to the best of one's ability. The Qur'ān tells us that the Prophet Yūsuf (Allah bless him and give him peace) worked out a carefully considered strategy to save the citizens of Egypt from imminent famine.

قَالَ تَزْرَعُونَ سَبْعَ سِنِينَ دَأَباً فَمَا حَصَدتُّمْ فَذَرُوهُ فِي سُنبُلِهِ إِلاَّ قَلِيلاً مِّمَّا تَأْكُلُونَ○ثُمَّ يَأْتِي مِن بَعْدِ ذَلِكَ سَبْعٌ شِدَادٌ يَأْكُلْنَ مَا قَدَّمْتُمْ لَهُنَّ إِلاَّ قَلِيلاً مِّمَّا تُحْصِنُونَ○ثُمَّ يَأْتِي مِن بَعْدِ ذَلِكَ عَامٌ فِيهِ يُغَاثُ النَّاسُ وَفِيهِ يَعْصِرُونَ○

Yūsuf (Joseph) said: "You will cultivate as usual, consecutively for seven years. So whatever you reap, keep it (in storage), leaving the grains in their ears except a small quantity (to thresh) for your (yearly) consumption. Then after this, there will come seven hard years (of drought) which will consume that (store) which you will have laid up for these years except a small quantity (which will fall surplus and) which you will keep in reserve. Then, following this, will come a year during which people will be blessed with (plenty of) rain, and (the yield of fruits will be such as) they will press juices (of fruits that year)."[8]

7.3.2 Sharia basis

The Muslim Scripture charges its believers to cooperate with each other:

وَتَعَاوَنُواْ عَلَى الْبِرِّ وَالتَّقْوَى

And always support one another in (the works of) righteousness and piety.[9]

Allah describes the character of the faithful in these words:

وَالْمُؤْمِنُونَ وَالْمُؤْمِنَاتُ بَعْضُهُمْ أَوْلِيَاءُ بَعْضٍ

The believers, men and women, are helpers and friends to one another.[10]

In ancient Arabia, it was a common practice for tribes to put their resources together to pay for blood money, the basis of Islamic insurance. The tribal tradition of pooling money among male relatives was known as *'āqila*.

Ibn al-Musayyib and Abū Salama b. ʻAbd al-Raḥmān related that Abū Hurayra (may Allah be pleased with him) said:

اِقْتَتَلَتِ امْرَأَتَانِ مِنْ هُذَيْلٍ، فَرَمَتْ إِحْدَاهُمَا الْأُخْرَى بِحَجَرٍ فَقَتَلَتْهَا وَمَا فِي بَطْنِهَا،
فَاخْتَصَمُوْا إِلَى النَّبِيِّ a، فَقَضَى أَنَّ دِيَةَ جَنِيْنِهَا غُرَّةٌ عَبْدٌ أَوْ وَلِيدَةٌ، وَقَضَى أَنَّ دِيَةَ الْمَرْأَةِ
عَلَى عَاقِلَتِهَا.

> Two women of Huhdayl fought and one of them threw a stone at the other and killed her and what was in her womb. They took the dispute to the Prophet (Allah bless him and give him peace), and he judged that the blood money owed for her fetus was a good slave, male or female, and judged that the blood money for the woman be paid by the *ʻāqila*.[11]

The theme of extending help to fellow beings occurs in many Prophetic Traditions.

According to al-Nu'mān b. Bashīr (may Allah be pleased with him), the Prophet (Allah bless him and give him peace) said:

مَثَلُ الْمُؤْمِنِيْنَ فِيْ تَوَادِّهِمْ وَتَرَاحُمِهِمْ وَتَعَاطُفِهِمْ مَثَلُ الْجَسَدِ. إِذَا اشْتَكَى مِنْهُ عُضْوٌ، تَدَاعَى
لَهُ سَائِرُ الْجَسَدِ بِالسَّهَرِ وَالْحُمَّى.

> In their mutual love (and affection), their mutual mercy (and sympathy) and their mutual compassion, the true believers are like the physical body. If one of its organs is afflicted with pain, the rest of the body rallies to it with sleeplessness and fever.[12]

According to Abū Hurayra (may Allah be pleased with him), the Prophet (Allah bless him and give him peace) said:

مَنْ نَفَّسَ عَنْ مُؤْمِنٍ كُرْبَةً مِنْ كُرَبِ الدُّنْيَا، نَفَّسَ اللهُ عَنْهُ كُرْبَةً مِنْ كُرَبِ يَوْمِ الْقِيَامَةِ.
وَمَنْ يَسَّرَ عَلَى مُعْسِرٍ، يَسَّرَ اللهُ عَلَيْهِ فِي الدُّنْيَا وَالْآخِرَةِ. وَمَنْ سَتَرَ مُسْلِمًا، سَتَرَهُ اللهُ فِي
الدُّنْيَا وَالْآخِرَةِ. وَاللهُ فِي عَوْنِ الْعَبْدِ مَا كَانَ الْعَبْدُ فِيْ عَوْنِ أَخِيْهِ.

> If someone relieves a believer of the agony of this world, Allah will relieve him of one of the agonies of the Day of Resurrection. If someone makes life easy for a person in distress, Allah will make life easy for him in this world and the Hereafter. If someone covers the faults of a Muslim in this world, Allah will cover his faults in this world and in the Hereafter. Allah does not cease helping His servant as long as His servant continues helping his brother.[13]

On the authority of Abū Mūsā al-Ash'arī (may Allah be pleased with him), Allah's Messenger (Allah bless him and give him peace) said:

اَلْمُؤْمِنُ لِلْمُؤْمِنِ كَالْبُنْيَانِ؛ يَشُدُّ بَعضُهُ بَعْضًا، وَشَبَّكَ بَيْنَ أَصَابِعِهِ.

> "The believer is related to the believer like a (fortified) wall; its one portion supports and strengthens the other," and he interlaced his fingers (to illustrate the point).[14]

If an individual is murdered and the identity of the murderer cannot be established, the heirs of the victim go to inspect the scene of the crime and adjure fifty residents of the locality to swear that they are not aware of the culprit nor have they sheltered him. Under the circumstances, either the people of the area or the swearers pay *dīya* (blood money). Imām al-Sarakhsī has stated this principle of Sharia in the following words:

> When a man comes across the dead body of someone in an area where people reside, fifty of them must swear on oath, "By Allah, we have not murdered the man and we do not know the identity of the killer either," and then they will make a compensatory payment.[15]

7.3.3 The structure of the takaful *company*

The structure of a *takaful* company is as follows: when a *takaful* company is formed, policyholders make contributions for their common good which the company maintains in individual accounts. Thus pooled funds are invested in sound financial products.

As part of the *takaful* contract, all policyholders are in agreement that if any one of them is hurt or suffers a loss, they will make a proportionate gift from their accounts to cover that loss. Moreover, profits are shared by the *takaful* holders.

7.3.4 Islamic insurance vs. conventional insurance

Conventional insurance is not Sharia-compliant as it involves elements of deception, gambling, excessive uncertainty and interest. But, as elaborated earlier, *takaful* is Sharia-compliant and it is approved.

Although it is in its early stages of development and growth, *takaful* is a financially sound alternative to conventional insurance. This is substantiated by the fact that *takaful* is gaining currency currently across Muslim and non-Muslim countries, including Iran, Turkey, Malaysia, Sudan, the Middle East, the United States and the United Kingdom.

7.4 Charging a fee on signing a deal between the seller and the buyer

Entering into commercial transactions by means of arbitration is appropriate and legal. Since agents offer their services and devote their time, their act of receiving fees from both the parties is allowable. Should a wholesaler offer a certain amount in return for selling his or her commodities, this arrangement is allowed in Muslim law.[16]

7.5 Offering a gift by way of intercession

Making a gift to someone in a position of strength to assuage evil conduct, to ward his maltreatment, to secure one's legal rights, to get a job for which one is qualified or to stay away from a prohibited activity is not impermissible when further options are not open. But, in such a situation, accepting a gift is disallowed; the hands of the solicitor of bribes contribute to that person's own destruction and Allah Almighty orders people not to let their own hands throw them into destruction.

وَأَنفِقُواْ فِي سَبِيلِ اللهِ وَلَا تُلْقُواْ بِأَيْدِيكُمْ إِلَى التَّهْلُكَةِ وَأَحْسِنُوَاْ إِنَّ اللهَ يُحِبُّ الْمُحْسِنِينَ

> And spend in the cause of Allah; and do not cast yourselves into destruction with your own hands; and adopt righteousness. Verily, Allah loves the righteous.[17]

The official who is offered a bribe should, realising his evil conduct, desist, repent of his crime and mend his behaviour so that he might escape torment in the Hereafter.[18] The tenderers of bribes are considered within their rights since they are seeking to obtain what is lawfully theirs, whereas the solicitor of bribes is culpable because they take what they do not deserve.

Notes

1 Islahi, Abdul Azim (November 1, 2013), "Book Review: Shariah Maxims Modern Applications in Islamic Finance," *Islamic Economic Studies*, Vol. 21, No. 2. Available at SSRN: https://ssrn.com/abstract=3169096

2 For details, see Zāhid Laṭīf and Muḥammad Mas'ūd Aḥmad 'Uthmānī's *Aṣr-iḥāḍir kay jadīdmasā'ilawr Dr MuḥammadṬāhir-ul-Qādrī*, pp. 39–46.

3 An Introduction to Takaful – An Alternative to Insurance, http://www.sbp.org.pk/departments/ibd/Takaful.pdf

4 Brian Kettell, *Introduction to Islamic Banking and Finance*, p. 129.

5 Muhammad Ayub, *Understanding Islamic Finance*, p. 495.

6 Qur'ān 13:11.

7 Narrated by al-Tirmidhī in *al-Sunan*: *Ṣifat al-Qiyāmawa al-Raqā'iqwa al-Wara'* [The Attributes of Resurrection, the Softening of Hearts and God wariness], Ch.: The Tradition, "Tie it and rely (upon Allah),"4:668 §2517.

8 Qur'ān 12:47–49.

9 Ibid., 5:2.

10 Ibid., 9:71.
11 Narrated by al-Bukhārī in *al-Ṣaḥīḥ*: *ad-Diyāt* [Blood money], Ch.: A woman's fetus and the blood money is owed by the father [of the killer] and the *'aṣaba* of the father, not his children, 6:2532 §6512; and Ibn 'Abd al-Barr in *al-Tamhīd*, 6:480–481.
12 Narrated by al-Bukhārī in *al-Ṣaḥīḥ: al-Adab* [Proper conduct], Ch.: Compassion for people and their livestock, 5:2238 §5665; Muslim in al-Ṣaḥīḥ: Piety, affinity and proper conduct, Ch.: The mutual compassion of the Muslims, their mutual affection and their mutual support, 4:1999 §2586.
13 Narrated by Imam Muslim in *al-Ṣaḥīḥ*: *Dhikr, du'ā'*, *tawba wa istighfār*: Remembrance [*dhikr*], supplication [*du'ā'*], repentance [*tawba*] and seeking forgiveness [*istighfār*], Ch.: The excellent merit of assembling at the recitation of the Qur'ān, 4:2074 §2699; and al-Tirmidhī in *al-Sunan*: *al-Ḥudūd* [The penalties] according to Allah's Messenger (Allah bless him and give him peace), Ch.: What has come to us concerning the pardoning of the Muslim, 4:34 §1425, 1930, 2945.
14 Narrated by al-Bukhārī in *al-Ṣaḥīḥ*: *al-Maẓālim* [Excesses], Ch.: Assisting the oppressed, 2:863 §2314; Muslim in *al-Ṣaḥīḥ*: Al-bir, wa al-*Ṣilat wa al-ādāb*:Piety, affinity and proper conduct, Ch.: The mutual compassion of the Muslims, their mutual affection and their mutual support, 4:1999 §2585.
15 Cited by al-Sarakhsī in *al-Mabsūṭ*, 26:109.
16 Commission, https://islamqa.info/en/21980
17 Qur'ān 2:195.
18 The Difference Between Rashwah (Bribery) and Wasaatah (Intervention), https://islamqa.info/en/87688

Bibliography

The Holy Qur'ān

Bukhārī, Abū 'Abd Allāh Muhammad b. Ismā'īl b. Ibrahīm b. Mughīra al-. (194–256/810–870). *Al-Adab al-Mufrad*. Beirut, Lebanon: Dār al-Bashā'ir al-Islāmiyya, 1409/1989.

Ibn 'Abd al-Barr, Yūsuf b. 'Abd Allāh(368–463/979–1071). *Al-Tamhīd li māfī al-muwaṭṭamin al-ma'ānīwa al-asānīd*. Marrakech: Ministry of Religious Affairs, 1387AH.

Islamic Question & Answer, https://islamqa.info/en/21980

Kettell, Brian. *Introduction to Islamic Banking and Finance*. Chichester, Great Britain: John Wiley & Sons, Ltd, 2011.

Muhammad Ayub. *Understanding Islamic Finance*. Chichester, Great Britain: John Wiley & Sons, Ltd., 2007.

Muslim, Ibn al-Ḥajjāj Abū al-Ḥasan al-Qushayrī al-Naysābūrī (206–261/821–875). *Al-Ṣaḥīḥ*. Beirut, Lebanon: Dār al-Iḥyā' al-Turāth al-'Arabī, 1997.

Sarakhsī, Shams al-Dīn al-. *Shams al-Din al-Mabsut*. Beirut, Lebanon: Dār al-Ma'rifa, 1978.

Tirmidhī, Abū 'Īsā Muhammad b. 'Īsā al-. *Isa al-Sunan*. Beirut, Lebanon: Dār Iḥyā' al-Turāth al-'Arabī, n.d.

8 The Islamic way of business and trade

In order to reinforce good behaviour in his followers, Allah's Messenger (Allah bless him and give him peace) taught higher ethics and manners as the quintessence of the Muslim religion. They are the spirit of the Islamic way of business and trade. That is why the Messenger (Allah bless him and give him peace) said:

إِنَّمَا بُعِثْتُ لِأُتَمِّمَ مَكَارِمَ الْأَخْلَاقِ.

I have been sent to perfect good character.[1]

According to 'Ā'isha (may Allah be well pleased with her):

قَالَ رَسُوْلُ اللهِ: إِنَّ مِنْ أَكْمَلِ الْمُؤْمِنِيْنَ إِيْمَاناً، أَحْسَنُهُمْ خُلُقًا وَأَلْطَفُهُمْ بِأَهْلِهِ.

Allah's Messenger (Allah bless him and give him peace) said: "The most perfect of the believers, where faith is concerned, is the finest of them in moral character and the kindest of them towards his family."[2]

Allah's Messenger (Allah bless him and give him peace) was the best model as regards pious conduct and good manners. He enjoined his followers to adopt the highly developed qualities of good character: aiding people in need, a benevolent attitude, generous dealing when selling, truthful speech, keeping promises and treating people gently.

The Prophet (Allah bless him and give him peace) himself, as the following Tradition narrated by Khadīja (may Allah be well pleased with her) attests, lived all these virtues:

إِنَّكَ لَتَصِلُ الرَّحِمَ، وَتَحْمِلُ الْكَلَّ، وَتَكْسِبُ الْمَعْدُومَ، وَتَقْرِي الضَّيْفَ، وَتُعِيْنُ عَلَى نَوَائِبِ الْحَقِّ.

You maintain ties of kinship, bear people's burdens, help the destitute, give hospitality to your guests and help those who have been afflicted by calamities.[3]

The Holy Qur'ān commands the believers to take Holy Prophet (Allah bless him and give him peace) as his or her ultimate role model in the following way:

لَقَدْ كَانَ لَكُمْ فِي رَسُولِ اللَّهِ أُسْوَةٌ حَسَنَةٌ لِّمَن كَانَ يَرْجُو اللَّهَ وَالْيَوْمَ الْآخِرَ وَذَكَرَ اللَّهَ كَثِيرًا

> *In truth, in (the sacred person of) Allah's Messenger there is for you a most perfect and beautiful model (of life) for every such person that expects and aspires to (meeting) Allah and the Last Day and remembers Allah abundantly.*[4]

The Prophet (Allah bless him and give him peace) described the character of a true believer, whether he or she is an employee, a business person, a student, a teacher or a preacher.

اَلْمُؤْمِنُ غِرٌّ كَرِيْمٌ وَالْفَاجِرُ خِبٌّ لَئِيْمٌ.

> The believer is straightforward and noble, and the evildoer is deceitful and ignoble.[5]

We must emulate Allah's Messenger (Allah bless him and give him peace) since he is the most excellent example of moral character. His personality alone is perfect in every regard and serves as a beacon of guidance for the whole humanity.

The Muslim religion has laid down a set of regulations so that the faithful might conduct their economic activities and their financial and commercial transactions accordingly. The directives are meant to govern the rights and obligations of parties to sale and purchase.

From among the scores of Qur'ānic verses and hundreds of Traditions on business transactions can be observed a strong culture of ethical values regarding sale and purchase. Complying with moral principles in the domain of commerce and trade is a precondition for stimulating robust economic growth.

Moreover, there must be no deceiving while selling a commodity or service to the customer. Running a business fairly is a form of service to the society and hence an act of worship in the eyes of the Lord of the Worlds.

Some of the business ethics and norms we can learn from Islam are fairness, integrity, mutual cooperation, free consent, avoidance of deception and exploitation, and refraining from hiding defects in a saleable product. The details of some business ethics are given next.

8.1 Truthfulness

The seller must inform the buyer about any defects in the item he or she offers for sale. 'Uqba b. 'Āmir (may Allah be pleased with him) said:

لَا يَحِلُّ لِامْرِئٍ يَبِيْعُ سِلْعَةً يَعْلَمُ أَنَّ بِهَا دَاءً إِلاَّ أَخْبَرَهُ.

It is not lawful for a Muslim to sell goods knowing that there is a defect in them without mentioning it.[6]

8.2 Honesty in dealings

Islam has attached fundamental importance to veracity as a moral value as it is an integral element in the establishment of social relations. The Almighty charges believers to speak the truth in any circumstances.

يَا أَيُّهَا الَّذِينَ آمَنُوا اتَّقُوا اللَّهَ وَقُولُوا قَوْلاً سَدِيدًا

O believers! Always fear Allah and say what is correct and straight.[7]

So blessed are truthful people that Allah Almighty commands believers to join their company.

يَا أَيُّهَا الَّذِينَ آمَنُواْ اتَّقُواْ اللّهَ وَكُونُواْ مَعَ الصَّادِقِينَ

O believers! Fear Allah persistently, and remain in the (company) of those who uphold the truth.[8]

The faithful must adhere to truth not only in religious but also in material affairs of life, not only in their words but also in their deeds.

وَإِن كُنتُمْ عَلَى سَفَرٍ وَلَمْ تَجِدُواْ كَاتِبًا فَرِهَانٌ مَّقْبُوضَةٌ فَإِنْ أَمِنَ بَعْضُكُم بَعْضًا فَلْيُؤَدِّ الَّذِي اؤْتُمِنَ
أَمَانَتَهُ وَلْيَتَّقِ اللّهَ رَبَّهُ وَلاَ تَكْتُمُواْ الشَّهَادَةَ وَمَن يَكْتُمْهَا فَإِنَّهُ آثِمٌ قَلْبُهُ وَاللّهُ بِمَا تَعْمَلُونَ عَلِيمٌ

And if you are on a journey and do not find a scribe, then take possession of a pledge in mortgage. Then, if one of you trusts the other, so he whose honesty has been trusted should deliver his trust and fear Allah, Who provides him subsistence. And do not conceal evidence. And the one who conceals it, his heart is certainly sinful. And Allah knows well whatever you do.[9]

Truth is the foundation of the Muslim religion, so dishonesty and faith cannot coexist in the same way as the fear of the Almighty cannot coexist with pride.

An essential part of growth in the business world is being straightforward. The element of truthfulness must be taken very seriously. It has an intrinsic value in trade and dishonest traders cannot win the confidence of customers.

Allah's Messenger (Allah bless him and give him peace) said:

اَلتَّاجِرُ الصَّدُوْقُ الأَمِيْنُ مَعَ النَّبِيِّيْنَ وَالصِّدِّيْقِيْنَ وَالشُّهَدَاءِ.

The truthful, trustworthy merchant will be with the Prophets, the truthful and the martyrs.[10]

Also, the Prophet (Allah bless him and give him peace) said:

إِنَّ التُّجَّارَ يُبْعَثُونَ يَوْمَ الْقِيَامَةِ فُجَّارًا إِلاَّ مَنِ اتَّقَى اللهَ وَبَرَّ وَصَدَقَ

"Indeed, the merchants will be resurrected on the Day of Resurrection as wicked, except the one who has fear of Allah, behaves charitably and is truthful."[11]

While persuading a customer to purchase saleable items, the seller's conversation must be truthful.

Ḥakīm b. Ḥizām (may Allah be pleased with him) reported that the Prophet (Allah bless him and give him peace) said:

اَلْبَيِّعَانِ بِالْخِيَارِ مَا لَمْ يَتَفَرَّقَا، أَوْ قَالَ: حَتَّى يَتَفَرَّقَا، فَإِنْ صَدَقَا وَبَيَّنَا بُورِكَ لَهُمَا فِيْ بَيْعِهِمَا، وَإِنْ كَتَمَا وَكَذَبَا مُحِقَتْ بَرَكَةُ بَيْعِهِمَا.

The seller and the buyer have the option (to revoke the sale) as long as they have not separated (or he said: "until they separate"). If they speak the truth and make things clear, they will be blessed in their sale. If they conceal and lie, the blessing of their transaction will be obliterated.[12]

Being truthful in promises and covenants is one of the characteristics by which the faithful are known. They are people of integrity as when they give word to anyone they keep it. Their conduct is especially true with regard to their duties towards Allah. Such people are sure to triumph, as Allah says in the Qur'ān:

وَالْمُوفُونَ بِعَهْدِهِمْ إِذَا عَاهَدُواْ وَالصَّابِرِينَ فِي الْبَأْسَاءِ وَالضَّرَّاءِ وَحِينَ الْبَأْسِ أُوْلَئِكَ الَّذِينَ صَدَقُوا وَأُولَئِكَ هُمُ الْمُتَّقُونَ

And when they make a promise, they fulfil it and are steadfast in hardship (i.e., poverty) and suffering (i.e., ailment) and at the time of fierce fighting (i.e., jihad). It is these who are truthful and it is these who are righteous.[13]

Elsewhere Allah Almighty defines their character.

وَالَّذِينَ هُمْ لِأَمَانَاتِهِمْ وَعَهْدِهِمْ رَاعُونَ

And those who are watchful of their trusts and their pledges.[14]

The Prophet (Allah bless him and give him peace) praised the noble trait of openness, straightforwardness and directness. Ardent believers, being value driven, practise honesty, truthfulness and trueness in all affairs including business transactions.

'Abd Allāh b. 'Amr (may Allah be pleased with him) narrated that Holy Prophet (Allah bless him and give him peace) said:

أَرْبَعٌ إِذَا كُنَّ فِيكَ، فَلَا عَلَيْكَ مَا فَاتَكَ مِنَ الدُّنْيَا: حِفْظُ أَمَانَةٍ، وَصِدْقُ حَدِيثٍ، وَحُسْنُ خَلِيقَةٍ، وَعِفَّةٌ فِي طُعْمَةٍ.

There are four things, if you internalise them, then whatever you miss in this world will not matter: preserving trust, speaking the truth, being of good character and moderation in eating.[15]

The truly righteous are mentally spiritual, so they do not pay in the same coin when they are swindled. They do not fail to meet the expectations of the individuals who trust them.

عَنْ أَبِي هُرَيْرَةَ قَالَ: قَالَ النَّبِيُّ e: أَدِّ الْأَمَانَةَ إِلَى مَنِ ائْتَمَنَكَ، وَلَا تَخُنْ مَنْ خَانَكَ.

According to Abū Hurayra (may Allah be pleased with him) that the Prophet (Allah bless him and give him peace) said: "Fulfil the trust for the one who entrusted you, and do not cheat the one who cheated you."[16]

Believers are trustworthy when they are consulted by their fellows and friends. On this score the Holy Prophet (Allah bless him and give him peace) said:

اَلْمُسْتَشَارُ مُؤْتَمَنٌ.

The person who is consulted is trustworthy.[17]

The Messenger (Allah bless him and give him peace) said at another place:

وَمَنْ أَشَارَ عَلَى أَخِيهِ بِأَمْرٍ يَعْلَمُ أَنَّ الرُّشْدَ فِي غَيْرِهِ فَقَدْ خَانَهُ.

The one who gives advice to his brother, knowing that what is better for him lies elsewhere, has betrayed him.[18]

The Messenger (Allah bless him and give him peace) prophesied that a time would come when things in society would become uneasy:

عَنْ أَبِي هُرَيْرَةَ قَالَ: قَالَ رَسُوْلُ اللهِ a: سَيَأْتِيْ عَلَى النَّاسِ سَنَوَاتٌ خَدَّاعَاتٌ، يُصَدَّقُ فِيْهَا الْكَاذِبُ، وَيُكَذَّبُ فِيْهَا الصَّادِقُ، وَيُؤْتَمَنُ فِيْهَا الْخَائِنُ، وَيُخَوَّنُ فِيْهَا الْأَمِيْنُ، وَيَنْطِقُ فِيْهَا الرُّوَيْبِضَةُ، قِيْلَ: وَمَا الرُّوَيْبِضَةُ؟ قَالَ: الرَّجُلُ التَّافِهُ فِيْ أَمْرِ الْعَامَّةِ.

> According to Abū Hurayra (may Allah be pleased with him) that Allah's Messenger (Allah bless him and give him peace) said: "There will come to the people years of treachery, when the liar will be regarded as honest, and the honest man will be regarded as a liar; the traitor will be regarded as faithful, and the faithful man will be regarded as a traitor; and the *ruwaybiḍa* will decide matters." It was said: "Who are the *ruwaybiḍa*?" He said: "Vile and base men who control the affairs of the people."[19]

Lying should be discouraged and virtues should be promoted in society in order to maintain peace and harmony.

When an increase in the attitude of breaching trust is witnessed, consider the Last Day is near. As the Prophet (Allah bless him and give him peace) said:

فَإِذَا ضُيِّعَتِ الْأَمَانَةُ فَانْتَظِرِ السَّاعَةَ.

> So when trustworthiness has been lost, expect the Last Hour.[20]

Scrupulous traders will benefit from their forthrightness on the Day of Reckoning. Allah's Messenger (Allah bless him and give him peace) said: "The truthful, trustworthy merchant will be with the Prophets, the truthful and the martyrs."[21]

The faithful ought to tread the path of truthfulness – a virtue that may lead one to the Garden of Paradise.

'Abd Allāh b. Mas'ūd (may Allah be well pleased with him) narrated that Allah's Messenger (Allah bless him and give him peace) said:

عَلَيْكُمْ بِالصِّدْقِ، فَإِنَّ الصِّدْقَ يَهْدِيْ إِلَى الْبِرِّ، وَإِنَّ الْبِرَّ يَهْدِيْ إِلَى الْجَنَّةِ، وَمَا يَزَالُ الرَّجُلُ يَصْدُقُ وَيَتَحَرَّى الصِّدْقَ حَتَّى يُكْتَبَ عِنْدَ اللهِ صِدِّيقًا. وَإِيَّاكُمْ وَالْكَذِبَ، فَإِنَّ الْكَذِبَ يَهْدِيْ إِلَى الْفُجُوْرِ، وَإِنَّ الْفُجُوْرَ يَهْدِيْ إِلَى النَّارِ، وَمَا يَزَالُ الرَّجُلُ يَكْذِبُ وَيَتَحَرَّى الْكَذِبَ حَتَّى يُكْتَبَ عِنْدَ اللهِ كَذَّاباً.

> Abide by truthfulness, for indeed truthfulness leads to righteousness and indeed righteousness leads to Paradise. A man continues telling the truth and trying hard to tell the truth until he is recorded with Allah as a truthful person. Refrain from falsehood, for indeed falsehood leads to wickedness, and wickedness leads to the Fire. A slave (of Allah) continues lying and trying hard to lie, until he is recorded with Allah as a liar.[22]

8.3 Disclosing defects

Integrity in financial affairs is an ethical requirement. Reliable persons fulfil promises, contracts and commitments they make in their profession. Allah describes the character of the faithful:

وَالَّذِينَ هُمْ لِأَمَانَاتِهِمْ وَعَهْدِهِمْ رَاعُونَ

And those who are watchful of their trusts and their pledges.[23]

On practising the policy of uprightness, the Messenger (Allah bless him and give him peace) said:

مَنِ اسْتَعْمَلْنَاهُ عَلَى عَمَلٍ، فَرَزَقْنَاهُ رِزْقًا، فَمَا أَخَذَ بَعْدَ ذَلِكَ فَهُوَ غُلُولٌ.

If we appoint somebody to do some work and grant him a provision, anything he takes beyond that is embezzlement.[24]

8.4   Giving full weight and measure

Islam provides complete guidance on how to interact with others in society. It preaches the lofty concepts of balance and accurate measure. A hallmark of business is weighing and measuring justly.

For the concept of justice, the Arabic word is *'adl*. This is one of the attributes of Allah. He never causes loss to anyone in anything. The Creator acts justly and fairly, and enjoins people to act accordingly. Taking our colour from this Divine attribute, we should practise fairness, integrity and uprightness. Allah says in the Qur'ān:

وَأَوْفُوا الْكَيْلَ إِذَا كِلْتُمْ وَزِنُواْ بِالْقِسْطَاسِ الْمُسْتَقِيمِ ذَلِكَ خَيْرٌ وَأَحْسَنُ تَأْوِيلًا

And measure in full whenever you measure out (anything), and (when you weigh anything) weigh with a straight balance. This (honesty) is better, and much better with regard to its consequence (as well).[25]

Cheating in any form is exploitation and corruption, which are expressly prohibited.

وَيْلٌ لِّلْمُطَفِّفِينَ○الَّذِينَ إِذَا اكْتَالُواْ عَلَى النَّاسِ يَسْتَوْفُونَ○وَإِذَا كَالُوهُمْ أَو وَّزَنُوهُمْ يُخْسِرُونَ○

Woe to those who give less in measure or weight! When (they) take by measure from others, they take (from them) full. And when they (themselves) give by measure or weigh to others, they give them less.[26]

Manufacturers, traders and sellers who deal in fraud should ponder well that the day of judgement is near when they will be punished for cheating Allah's creatures. In Qur'ān, Allah Almighty directs manufacturers, traders and sellers to give full measure:

وَأَوْفُواْ الْكَيْلَ وَالْمِيزَانَ بِالْقِسْطِ

And always give full measure and weight with justice.[27]

The injunction to sell equitably is very comprehensive. If an individual at work disappears from the place of work, shows up late, habitually procrastinates or does not put his or her soul into working, he or she is an unproductive employee. The pay of these people, in the light of the Qur'ān, is tainted.

The Holy Qur'ān related a story of a commercial people that exceeded limits regarding the matter of purchase and sale, deviated from justice pertaining to measure and weight, and engaged in the business of adulteration. Allah sent His Messenger Shuyab (peace be upon him) to call them to the right path. The Messenger (peace be upon him) said to his nation:

أَوْفُوا الْكَيْلَ وَلَا تَكُونُوا مِنَ الْمُخْسِرِينَ○ وَزِنُوا بِالْقِسْطَاسِ الْمُسْتَقِيمِ○وَلَا تَبْخَسُوا النَّاسَ
أَشْيَاءَهُمْ وَلَا تَعْثَوْا فِي الْأَرْضِ مُفْسِدِينَ○

Always fill up full measure and do not become injurious (to the rights of the people). And weigh with a straight balance. And do not give to the people their things (weighing) less than what is due, nor provoke strife in the land (by such moral, economic and social corruption and fraud).[28]

Governments the world over have laid down penalties for making or selling false or defective weights and measures of products. But a believer should act with fairness and shun fraudulent behaviour because Allah Almighty is watching, not out of fear of social consequences. Moral and religious sanctions should be enough for one to behave rightly.

Pragmatically speaking, individuals and nations given to fraud and injustice do not thrive. Prosperity is the lot of fair, upright and diligent characters.

وَالسَّمَاءَ رَفَعَهَا وَوَضَعَ الْمِيزَانَ○ أَلَّا تَطْغَوْا فِي الْمِيزَانِ○وَأَقِيمُوا الْوَزْنَ بِالْقِسْطِ وَلَا
تُخْسِرُوا الْمِيزَانَ○

And He is the One Who has maintained the sky raised high and (He is the One) Who has set up the balance (for justice), so that you violate not the balance whilst weighing. And keep weighing justly and do not make the balance fall short.[29]

Cheats will be penalised in the Afterlife for breaching the Sharia regarding weighing or measuring. If cheaters usurp the rights of others, they will face the consequences of their iniquity here and now. Allah Almighty will inflict punishment on them: tyrants will oppress them, excessive toiling will be their lot and rainwater will be withheld from them.

'Abd Allah b. 'Umar (may Allah be well pleased with him and his father) narrated:

أَقْبَلَ عَلَيْنَا رَسُوْلُ اللّٰه a فَقَالَ: يَا مَعْشَرَ الْمُهَاجِرِيْنَ، خَمْسٌ إِذَا ابْتُلِيتُمْ بِهِنَّ وَأَعُوْذُ بِاللّٰهِ أَنْ
تُدْرِكُوْهُنَّ، لَمْ تَظْهَرِ الْفَاحِشَةُ فِيْ قَوْمٍ قَطُّ حَتَّى يُعْلِنُوْا بِهَا إِلَّا فَشَا فِيْهِمُ الطَّاعُوْنُ وَالْأَوْجَاعُ

الَّتِيْ لَمْ تَكُنْ مَضَتْ فِيْ أَسْلَافِهِمُ الَّذِيْنَ مَضَوْا، وَلَمْ يَنْقُصُوا الْمِكْيَالَ وَالْمِيزَانَ إِلَّا أُخِذُوا
بِالسِّنِيْنَ وَشِدَّةِ الْمَئُونَةِ، وَجَوْرِ السُّلْطَانِ عَلَيْهِمْ، وَلَمْ يَمْنَعُوْا زَكَاةَ أَمْوَالِهِمْ إِلَّا مُنِعُوا الْقَطْرَ مِنَ
السَّمَاءِ، وَلَوْلَا الْبَهَائِمُ لَمْ يُمْطَرُوا، وَلَمْ يَنْقُضُوْا عَهْدَ اللهِ وَعَهْدَ رَسُوْلِهِ إِلَّا سَلَّطَ اللهُ عَلَيْهِمْ
عَدُوًّا مِنْ غَيْرِهِمْ، فَأَخَذُوا بَعْضَ مَا فِيْ أَيْدِيْهِمْ، وَمَا لَمْ تَحْكُمْ أَئِمَّتُهُمْ بِكِتَابِ اللهِ وَيَتَخَيَّرُوْا
مِمَّا أَنْزَلَ اللهُ إِلاَّ جَعَلَ اللهُ بْأَسَهُمْ بَيْنَهُمْ.

Allah's Messenger (Allah bless him and give him peace) turned to us and said: "Emigrants, there are five things with which you will be tested, and I seek refuge with Allah lest you live to see them: Immorality never appears among a people to such an extent that they commit it openly, but plagues and diseases that were never known among the predecessors will spread among them. They do not cheat in weights and measures but they will be stricken with famine, severe calamity and the oppression of their rulers. They do not withhold the obligatory charity of their wealth, but rain will be withheld from the sky, and were it not for the animals, no rain would fall on them. They do not break their covenant with Allah and His Messenger, but Allah will enable their enemies to overpower them and take some of what is in their hands. Unless their leaders rule according to the Book of Allah and seek all good from that which Allah has revealed, Allah will cause them to fight one another."[30]

8.5 Practising leniency

The Prophet (Allah bless him and give him peace) said that Allah Almighty is gentle and that He loves gentleness. He bestows for the sake of gentleness and kindness what He does not bestow due to harshness.[31] According to this Tradition, treating your customers with leniency and making allowances for those who are desperate is dear to Allah, the Exalted. Businesspeople with mild temperaments might merit Divine bounties.

Abū Hurayra (may Allah be pleased with him) reported that Allah's Messenger (Allah bless him and give him peace) said:

إِنَّ اللهَ يُحِبُّ سَمْحَ الْبَيْعِ، سَمْحَ الشِّرَاءِ، سَمْحَ الْقَضَاءِ.

Indeed Allah loves tolerance in selling, buying and repaying.[32]

Providing an exegesis of the Prophetic Tradition, al-'Aynī writes that it commends the policy of indulgence, excellent treatment of customers, assuming noble traits of character and abandoning disputes. In addition, the Messenger (Allah bless him and give him peace) bid those of his nation not to wear a stern expression while making demands (if the debtor happens to be economically distressed). The reason why the Messenger (Allah bless him and give him peace) urged his community to adopt these virtues is the fact that they attract Divine blessings. Allah's

Prophet (Allah bless him and give him peace) always directed his followers to do only what might benefit them from the religious as well as the material perspective. One will reap rewards by living by these principles of good behaviour; the Messenger (Allah bless him and give him peace) invoked mercy on such souls and entreated the Almighty to excuse out their iniquities. People who desire blessings and forgiveness from the Most Merciful Lord must follow the Prophet's directive on treating customers gently.[33]

The Prophet (Allah bless him and give him peace) said that a believer earns Divine forgiveness on account of his leniency.

غَفَرَ اللّٰهُ لِرَجُلٍ كَانَ قَبْلَكُمْ، كَانَ سَهْلاً إِذَا بَاعَ، سَهْلاً إِذَا اشْتَرَى، سَهْلاً إِذَا اقْتَضَى.

> Allah forgave a man who was before you. He was tolerant when selling and tolerant when making a demand.[34]

According to Abū Sa'īd al-Khudrī (may Allah be pleased with him), the Prophet (Allah bless him and give him peace) said:

أَفْضَلُ الْمُؤْمِنِيْنَ رَجُلٌ سَمْحُ الْبَيْعِ، سَمْحُ الشِّرَاءِ، سَمْحُ الْقَضَاءِ، سَمْحُ الِاقْتِضَاءِ.

> The best of the believers is the man who is generous while selling and purchasing, seeking the return of debt and making a demand.[35]

If two parties to a business agree to change the purchased item or straightaway annul the deal, then the purchaser may exercise the right. When there is no agreement and the customer wants to revoke the deal, and the shopkeeper agrees, it a deed of great merit. Such a considerate seller will receive forgiveness on the day people are raised from the dead.

According to Abū Hurayra (may Allah be pleased with him) that Allah's Messenger (Allah bless him and give him peace) said:

مَنْ أَقَالَ مُسْلِمًا، أَقَالَهُ اللّٰهُ عَثْرَتَهُ يَوْمَ الْقِيَامَةِ.

> Whoever agrees with a Muslim to cancel a transaction, Allah will forgive his sins on the Day of Resurrection.[36]

8.6 Prohibition of exploiting the ignorant

Depriving people of their rights or cheating them while doing business with them is expressly forbidden.

وَلَا تَبْخَسُوا النَّاسَ أَشْيَاءَهُمْ

> *Nor withhold from the people the things that are their due.*[37]

On this score a Hadith is related from Ibn 'Umar. A man came to the Prophet (Allah bless him and give him peace) and said that he was frequently deceived in business. So the Prophet (Allah bless him and give him peace) directed him:

إِذَا بَايَعْتَ، فَقُلْ لَا خِلَابَةَ.

When you buy, say: "No cheating."[38]

According to 'Alī (may Allah be pleased with him), the Blessed Prophet (Allah bless him and give him peace) said:

Deceiving an *al-mustarsal* (an ignorant entrant into the market) is usury.[39]

8.7 Restriction of the centralisation of wealth

The act of amassing wealth and property and depriving other needy fellow beings is a sin. Allah prohibits hoarding:

وَالَّذِينَ يَكْنِزُونَ الذَّهَبَ وَالْفِضَّةَ وَلَا يُنفِقُونَهَا فِي سَبِيلِ اللهِ فَبَشِّرْهُم بِعَذَابٍ أَلِيمٍ۝يَوْمَ يُحْمَى عَلَيْهَا فِي نَارِ جَهَنَّمَ فَتُكْوَى بِهَا جِبَاهُهُمْ وَجُنوبُهُمْ وَظُهُورُهُمْ هَذَا مَا كَنَزْتُمْ لِأَنفُسِكُمْ فَذُوقُوا مَا كُنتُمْ تَكْنِزُونَ

And those who hoard silver and gold and do not spend it in the cause of Allah, warn them of a grievous torment. The Day when this (gold, silver and wealth) will be heated in the Fire of Hell, their foreheads, sides and backs will be branded with this (heated material, and it will be said to them:) "This is the same (wealth) that you treasured for (the benefit of) your souls. So taste (this wealth) which you had been amassing."[40]

لَا يَكُونَ دُولَةً بَيْنَ الْأَغْنِيَاءِ مِنكُمْ

(This distribution system is to ensure) that (the whole wealth) may not circulate (only) amongst the rich of you (but should circulate amongst all the classes of society).[41]

8.8 Squandering resources

The faithful may not argue that they are at liberty to spend their wealth the way they like, seeing that they own resources. Allah Almighty does not approve the squandering of material resources:

وَكُلُوا وَاشْرَبُوا وَلَا تُسْرِفُوا إِنَّهُ لَا يُحِبُّ الْمُسْرِفِينَ

Eat and drink, but do not spend extravagantly because certainly He does not like the extravagant.[42]

وَآتِ ذَا الْقُرْبَى حَقَّهُ وَالْمِسْكِينَ وَابْنَ السَّبِيلِ وَلَا تُبَذِّرْ تَبْذِيرًا

And give to the kindred their rightful due, and also (give) to the needy and the wayfarer, and do not exhaust (your wealth) by expending wastefully.[43]

In the estimation of the Almighty, people who spend extravagantly are the brothers of the Devil.

إِنَّ الْمُبَذِّرِينَ كَانُواْ إِخْوَانَ الشَّيَاطِينِ وَكَانَ الشَّيْطَانُ لِرَبِّهِ كَفُورًا

Surely, the spendthrifts are the brothers of Satan.[44]

8.9 Proscription of money laundering

Money laundering means to move money that has been acquired dishonestly into foreign bank accounts or local legitimate businesses so that it is difficult for people to know the source of money. Acquiring money illegally is prohibited, as Allah says in the Holy Qur'ān:

يَا أَيُّهَا الَّذِينَ آمَنُواْ لاَ تَأْكُلُواْ أَمْوَالَكُمْ بَيْنَكُمْ بِالْبَاطِلِ إِلاَّ أَن تَكُونَ تِجَارَةً عَن تَرَاضٍ مِّنكُمْ
وَلاَ تَقْتُلُواْ أَنفُسَكُمْ

O believers! Do not devour one another's wealth unlawfully amongst yourselves unless it is a trade by your mutual agreement and do not kill yourselves.[45]

Also, the Almighty charged His Messengers (peace be upon them) and their fellows in faith to eat nothing but what is pure and wholesome.

يَا أَيُّهَا الرُّسُلُ كُلُوا مِنَ الطَّيِّبَاتِ وَاعْمَلُوا صَالِحًا إِنِّي بِمَا تَعْمَلُونَ عَلِيمٌ

O (My Esteemed) Messengers! Eat of the pure things (as your practice is) and do good deeds with persistence. Surely, I am Well Aware of whatever (deed) you do.[46]

Making unlawfully acquired money appear to be legal is immoral. Monetary wrongdoings and illegal tax avoidance, which fatten one's wallet, are crimes against the Creator and His creatures.

People's property and wealth are inviolable. In order to pre-empt corruption and theft, the Qur'ān charges the faithful how to act if someone steals.

وَالسَّارِقُ وَالسَّارِقَةُ فَاقْطَعُوا أَيْدِيَهُمَا جَزَاءً بِمَا كَسَبَا نَكَالًا مِّنَ اللهِ

(After proper judicial trial as per law,) cut off the hands of both the man as well as the woman who steal, in retribution of (the offence) which they have committed, a deterring punishment from Allah.[47]

An oft-quoted Hadith directs the people in government on adopting honesty, justness and fairness and warns against dishonesty, exploitation, bribery and fraud. The Messenger (Allah bless him and give him peace) revealed the secret of running the business of a state and how to handle criminals.

> 'Ā'isha (may Allah be well pleased with her) narrated that the Quraysh were worried about the case of the Makhzūmī woman who had stolen, and they said: "Who will speak concerning her?" Meaning, to Allah's Messenger (Allah bless him and give him peace). They said: "Who would dare, except Usāma b. Zayd, the beloved of the Prophet (Allah bless him and give him peace)?" So Usāma (may Allah be well pleased with him) spoke to him, and Allah's Messenger (Allah bless him and give him peace) said: "Usāma, are you interceding concerning one of the punishments of Allah?" Then he stood up and delivered a speech and said: "Those who came before you were only destroyed because when a noble man among them stole they would leave him alone, but if a peasant among them stole they would carry out the punishment on him. By Allah, if Fāṭima, the daughter of Muhammad, were to steal, I would cut off her hand."[48]

All workers must do their best while working. Any kind of corruption will incur penalty in the Hereafter. On this score, 'Adiyy b. 'Umayra al-Kindī narrated that Allah's Messenger (Allah bless him and give him peace) said:

يَا أَيُّهَا النَّاسُ مَنْ عَمِلَ مِنْكُمْ لَنَا عَلَى عَمَلٍ فَكَتَمَنَا مِنْهُ مِخْيَطًا فَمَا فَوْقَهُ فَهُوَ غُلٌّ يَأْتِي بِهِ يَوْمَ الْقِيَامَةِ " . فَقَامَ رَجُلٌ مِنَ الأَنْصَارِ أَسْوَدُ كَأَنِّي أَنْظُرُ إِلَيْهِ فَقَالَ يَا رَسُولَ اللهِ اقْبَلْ عَنِّي عَمَلَكَ . قَالَ " وَمَا ذَاكَ " . قَالَ سَمِعْتُكَ تَقُولُ كَذَا وَكَذَا . قَالَ " وَأَنَا أَقُولُ ذَلِكَ مَنِ اسْتَعْمَلْنَاهُ عَلَى عَمَلٍ فَلْيَأْتِ بِقَلِيلِهِ وَكَثِيرِهِ فَمَا أُوتِيَ مِنْهُ أَخَذَهُ وَمَا نُهِيَ عَنْهُ انْتَهَى

> "People, whoever among you is appointed by us to do some work, and he conceals a needle or less from us, it will be a yoke of iron on his neck that he will bring on the Day of Rising." An Anṣārī man who was black – it is as if I can see him now – stood up and said: "Allah's Messenger, dismiss me from working for you." He said: "Why is that?" He said: "I heard you say such and such." He said: "I do say that. Whoever we appoint

to do some work, let him bring everything, whether it is a little or a lot. Whatever he is given, he may take, and whatever he is forbidden, let him refrain from it."[49]

When the Messenger (Allah bless him and give him peace) was delivering his Last Sermon on the eve of his pilgrimage, he made clear the unlawfulness of taking possession of someone's wealth:

إِنَّ دِمَاءَكُمْ وَأَمْوَالَكُمْ وَأَعْرَاضَكُمْ عَلَيْكُمْ حَرَامٌ، كَحُرْمَةِ يَوْمِكُمْ هَذَا، فِيْ شَهْرِكُمْ هَذَا، فِيْ بَلَدِكُمْ هَذَا، إِلَى يَوْمِ تَلْقَوْنَ رَبَّكُمْ. أَلَا، هَلْ بَلَّغْتُ؟ قَالُوا: نَعَمْ. قَالَ: اَللَّهُمَّ اشْهَدْ، فَلْيُبَلِّغِ الشَّاهِدُ الْغَائِبَ، فَرُبَّ مُبَلَّغٍ أَوْعَى مِنْ سَامِعٍ.

"Indeed your blood, your property and your honour are inviolable, like the inviolability of this day of yours and this month of yours and this land of yours, until the day you meet your Lord. Listen, have I conveyed the message?" The Companions replied, "Yes." He said, "Allah! Bear witness. Let the one present inform those who are absent, for perhaps the one to whom it is conveyed will retain it better than he who hears it [directly]."[50]

According to The words of the Holy Prophet (Allah bless him and give him peace), "Hell is more fitting for him whose flesh is nourished by what is unlawful," should warn people against gaining unearned material goods.[51]

8.10 Receiving gifts in official capacity is bribery

If you are an employee at an institute or a manager in a firm, you draw your salary from your head. But if you receive gifts as bribery from others, they are illegal, since they are offered to you due to your position for favours in return. In this context a Hadith is cited next. The Prophet (Allah bless him and give him peace) said:

مَنِ اسْتَعْمَلْنَاهُ عَلَى عَمَلٍ، فَرَزَقْنَاهُ رِزْقًا، فَمَا أَخَذَ بَعْدَ ذَلِكَ فَهُوَ غُلُوْلٌ.

If we appoint somebody to do any (administrative) work and grant him a provision, anything he takes beyond that is a dishonestly acquired gain.[52]

The same concept is illustrated through a Hadith narrative. Abūḥumayd al-Sā'idī related:

اِسْتَعْمَلَ النَّبِيُّ e رَجُلًا مِنْ بَنِيْ أَسَدٍ، يُقَالُ لَهُ: ابْنُ الْأُتْبِيَّةِ عَلَى صَدَقَةٍ. فَلَمَّا قَدِمَ قَالَ: هَذَا لَكُمْ وَهَذَا أُهْدِيَ لِيْ. فَقَامَ النَّبِيُّ e عَلَى الْمِنْبَرِ . . . ثُمَّ قَالَ: مَا بَالُ الْعَامِلِ نَبْعَثُهُ فَيَأْتِيْ فَيَقُوْلُ: هَذَا لَكَ وَهَذَا لِيْ، فَهَلَّا جَلَسَ فِيْ بَيْتِ أَبِيْهِ وَأُمِّهِ فَيَنْظُرُ أَيُهْدَى لَهُ أَمْ لَا؟

وَالَّذِي نَفْسِي بِيَدِهِ، لَا يَأْتِي بِشَيْءٍ إِلَّا جَاءَ بِهِ يَوْمَ الْقِيَامَةِ يَحْمِلُهُ عَلَى رَقَبَتِهِ إِنْ كَانَ بَعِيرًا لَهُ رُغَاءٌ أَوْ بَقَرَةً لَهَا خُوَارٌ أَوْ شَاةً تَيْعَرُ.

The Prophet (Allah bless him and give him peace) appointed a man of the Banū Asad called Ibn al-'Utabiyya to collect the mandatory charity. When he came (to Medina), he said, "This is for you and this was given to me as a gift." The Prophet (Allah bless him and give him peace) stood on the pulpit . . . and said, "What is wrong with the agent we sent out? He comes and says, 'This is for you and this is for me.' Why did he not sit in the house of his father or mother to see whether a gift would come to him or not? By the One who has my soul in my hand, none of you will take anything (without right), but that he will carry it on his back on the Day of Resurrection. If it is a camel, it is will be grumbling; if a cow, it will be mooing; if it is a sheep, it will be bleating."[53]

8.11 The right to return purchased items

The business policy "sold items will be neither returned nor replaced" can be found on the windows of some shops. However, policy is contrary to the Islamic ethic of business, in which the defective goods should be taken back by the seller. From the Islamic perspective, buyers have every right to return substandard, flawed and malfunctioning items and get back their money. But if sellers do not return the money for a flawed product or do not exchange the article sold, they defy Allah's ordinance and cheats the buyer:

وَلَا تَأْكُلُوٓاْ أَمْوَالَكُم بَيْنَكُم بِالْبَاطِلِ

And do not eat up one another's wealth amongst yourselves through injustice.[54]

8.12 Pricing theory

The market is to be free and to respond to the natural laws of supply and demand; that is to say, prices are controlled by factors beyond human control. As a general principle, humans are not to interfere in the free market by fixing prices and setting profit margins. If sellers try to exploit the buyer with artificially inflated prices, the state is justified to interfere and normalize the prices.

If prices skyrocket in the market due to the shortage of certain commodities, then this is in accordance with the law of supply and demand. In such a circumstance, forcing a shopkeeper to sell articles at a low fixed price would be injustice. The conduct of the Messenger (Allah bless him and give him peace) in the following Tradition reinforces this point.

According to Anas b. Mālik (may Allah be pleased with him):

قَالَ غَلاَ السِّعْرُ عَلَى عَهْدِ رَسُولِ اللَّهِ . صلى الله عليه وسلم . فَقَالُوا يَا رَسُولَ اللَّهِ قَدْ غَلاَ
السِّعْرُ فَسَعِّرْ لَنَا . فَقَالَ " إِنَّ اللَّهَ هُوَ الْمُسَعِّرُ الْقَابِضُ الْبَاسِطُ الرَّازِقُ إِنِّي لأَرْجُو أَنْ أَلْقَى
رَبِّي وَلَيْسَ أَحَدٌ يَطْلُبُنِي بِمَظْلَمَةٍ فِي دَمٍ وَلَا مَالٍ

> When prices rose during the time of Allah's Messenger (Allah bless him and give him peace), the people said: "Messenger of Allah, prices have risen, so fix the prices for us." He said: "Indeed, Allah is the One who fixes prices, who withholds, gives lavishly and provides, and I hope that when I meet my Lord none will have any claim on me for an injustice regarding blood or property."[55]

However, if anyone prevents the free supply of merchandise with the intent to increase prices, that becomes a religious and legal issue. If such a person is caught, he or she will be dealt with by law enforcers in accordance with the enormity of the offence. However, such evil characters will be punished severely in the Hereafter.

According to Ma'qal b. Yasār (may Allah be pleased with him), he heard Allah's Messenger (Allah bless him and give him peace) say:

> If anyone interferes in the market rates of the Muslims so as to hike up prices, then it is Allah's obligation to throw him into the blazing fire of Hell.[56]

8.13 Trust

The concept of trust incorporates truthfulness and reliability. Trust is central to Islam and inherent in human nature. Being a trustworthy individual denotes honesty, fairness, impartiality and justness. A trader climbs the ladder of prosperity with a booming business when the clientele has confidence in and reliance on his or her person.

Those who faithfully observe their trusts, pledges and covenants are ethical in the sight of Allah and worthy of good comments. Allah describes people of integrity:

وَالَّذِينَ هُمْ لِأَمَانَاتِهِمْ وَعَهْدِهِمْ رَاعُونَ

> *Those who are watchful of their trusts and their pledges.*[57]

He then describes the colossal recompense they will merit on the Judgment Day.

أُوْلَئِكَ هُمُ الْوَارِثُونَ○الَّذِينَ يَرِثُونَ الْفِرْدَوْسَ هُمْ فِيهَا خَالِدُونَ○

> *It is they who will be the inheritors (of Paradise). They will (also) inherit the most superior Gardens of Paradise (where all the bounties, comforts*

and pleasures of nearness to Allah will abound). They will live there forever.[58]

In the following verse, Allah Almighty commands the followers of Islam to restore deposits to their owners.

إِنَّ اللّٰهَ يَأْمُرُكُمْ أَن تُؤَدُّواْ الْأَمَانَاتِ إِلَىٰ أَهْلِهَا

Surely, Allah commands you to entrust the belongings to those who are worthy of them.[59]

Requiring believers to give people what is due to them includes giving full measure and weight, and not cheating them out of their rights. Unfair and corrupt business practices are disapproved.

وَيَا قَوْمِ أَوْفُواْ الْمِكْيَالَ وَالْمِيزَانَ بِالْقِسْطِ وَلاَ تَبْخَسُواْ النَّاسَ أَشْيَاءَهُمْ وَلاَ تَعْثَوْاْ فِي الْأَرْضِ
مُفْسِدِينَ○ بَقِيَّةُ اللّٰهِ خَيْرٌ لَّكُمْ إِن كُنتُم مُّؤْمِنِينَ وَمَا أَنَاْ عَلَيْكُم بِحَفِيظٍ○

And, O my people, give full measure and full weight with justice, and do not give people their things less than their due. And do not spread destruction in the land by becoming mischief-mongers. That which is left over from Allah's provision (only that) is better for you if you have faith. And I am not a guardian over you.[60]

8.14 Fulfilment of promises

It goes without saying that no society can function smoothly and flourish without a culture that values promises and their fulfilment. It is essential to respect promise because this creates a stable society and supports a strong social fabric. Allah Almighty charges the faithful to honour their commitments:

وَأَوْفُواْ بِالْعَهْدِ إِنَّ الْعَهْدَ كَانَ مَسْؤُولًا

And always fulfil the promise. No doubt, the promise will be questioned about.[61]

Elsewhere Allah Almighty says:

وَأَوْفُواْ بِعَهْدِ اللّٰهِ إِذَا عَاهَدتُّمْ وَلاَ تَنقُضُواْ الْأَيْمَانَ بَعْدَ تَوْكِيدِهَا وَقَدْ جَعَلْتُمُ اللّٰهَ عَلَيْكُمْ كَفِيلاً
إِنَّ اللّٰهَ يَعْلَمُ مَا تَفْعَلُونَ

And always fulfil the promise of Allah when you promise, and do not break oaths after making them firm, whilst you have already made Allah a surety over you. Surely, Allah knows well whatever you do.[62]

In the following verse, the Qur'ān mentions one key noble trait of the Almighty Allah's ardent servants:

الَّذِينَ يُوفُونَ بِعَهْدِ اللهِ وَلَا يَنقُضُونَ الْمِيثَاقَ

Those who fulfil their pledge to Allah and do not breach their covenant.[63]

Hadith, the exegesis of the Qur'ānic messages, enjoins the faithful to back their words with action. If someone does not discharge contractual duties and obligations, he or she does not have faith.

Anas b. Mālik (may Allah be pleased with him) narrated that Holy Prophet (Allah bless him and give him peace) said in a discourse:

لاَ دِيْنَ لِمَنْ لاَ عَهْدَ لَهُ.

There is no religion for the one who does not keep his promises.[64]

According to a Prophetic Tradition, the one who pledges to someone to provide or do something and then betrays is not a complete believer (*mumin)*.

According to 'Abd Allāh b. 'Amr (may Allah be pleased with him), Allah's Messenger (Allah bless him and give him peace) said:

أَرْبَعٌ مَنْ كُنَّ فِيهِ كَانَ مُنَافِقًا خَالِصًا، وَمَنْ كَانَتْ فِيْهِ خَصْلَةٌ مِنْهُنَّ كَانَتْ فِيْهِ خَصْلَةٌ مِنَ النِّفَاقِ حَتىَّ يَدَعَهَا: إِذَا اؤْتُمِنَ خَانَ، وَإِذَا حَدَّثَ كَذَبَ، وَإِذَا عَاهَدَ غَدَرَ، وَإِذَا خَاصَمَ فَجَرَ.

There are four things which, if someone is cloaked in them, he is a sheer hypocrite, and if someone contains a trait of them, he contains a trait of hypocrisy until he gets rid of it: (1) if he is trusted, he betrays; (2) if he speaks, he lies; (3) if he makes a contract, he violates it; and (4) if he disputes, he acts immorally.[65]

The Messenger (Allah bless him and give him peace) invoked the curse of Allah Almighty on people who make promises with no intention of keeping them:

ذِمَّةُ الْمُسْلِمِيْنَ وَاحِدَةٌ، فَمَنْ أَخْفَرَ مُسْلِمًا فَعَلَيْهِ لَعْنَةُ اللهِ وَالْمَلاَئِكَةِ وَالنَّاسِ أَجْمَعِيْنَ لاَ يُقْبَلُ مِنْهُ صَرْفٌ وَلاَ عَدْلٌ.

The covenant of the Muslims is the same. Whoever breaks a Muslim's covenant, on him is the curse of Allah, the angels and all people. Neither repentance nor ransom will be accepted from him.[66]

When we study the biography of Allah's Messenger (Allah bless him and give him peace), we see that whenever he gave his word to anyone, whether a believer or a non-believer, he kept it without fail. That is why he was called the truthful (*Sadiq*) and trustworthy (*Amin*) even before the proclamation of his prophethood. He preached the Scriptural messages and translated his words into reality. Exemplifying the teachings of the Qur'ān, the Messenger (Allah bless him and give him peace) set an example for the human race in the fulfilment of promises, agreements and contracts with friends as well as with enemies.

عَنْ عَبْدِ اللَّه بْنِ أَبِي الْحَمْسَاءِ قَالَ: بَايَعْتُ النَّبِيَّ a بِبَيْعٍ قَبْلَ أَنْ يُبْعَثَ، وَبَقِيَتْ لَهُ بَقِيَّةٌ
فَوَعَدْتُهُ أَنْ آتِيَهُ بِهَا فِيْ مَكَانِهِ. فَنَسِيْتُ ثُمَّ ذَكَرْتُ بَعْدَ ثَلَاثٍ، فَجِئْتُ فَإِذَا هُوَ فِيْ مَكَانِهِ.
فَقَالَ: يَا فَتىً، لَقَدْ شَقَقْتَ عَلَيَّ، أَنَا هَاهُنَا مُنْذُ ثَلَاثٍ أَنْتَظِرُكَ.

> 'Abd Allah b. Abī al-Ḥamsā' (may Allah be well pleased with him) narrated: "I bought something from the Prophet (Allah bless him and give him peace) before his mission began, and there was something left for me to pay. I promised him that I would bring it to him at his place, then I forgot, and I remembered three (days) later. I came and found him in his place and he said: "Young man, you have vexed me. I have been here for three days waiting for you."[67]

Providing an exegesis on the preceding Tradition, al-'Aẓīmābādī writes that the Messenger (Allah bless him and give him peace) stayed there for a period of three days only to fulfil his promise to the man, not to get the amount of money that the man had promised to bring.[68]

Even when his enemies were planning to take his life, the Messenger (Allah bless him and give him peace) was worried about returning their deposits. So the night his enemies surrounded his house in order to kill him, before migrating to Medina, he left 'Alī (may Allah be pleased with him) in his bed to pay off their cash and jewellery.

Ibn Isḥāq, the Arab biographer of the Prophet (Allah bless him and give him peace), writes:

> The Messenger (Allah bless him and give him peace) told 'Alī (may Allah be well pleased with him) about his departure and ordered him to stay behind in Mecca in order to return goods which men had deposited with the Messenger (Allah bless him and give him peace), for anyone in Mecca who had property which he was anxious about left it with him because of his . . . honesty and trustworthiness.[69]

Undoubtedly, no one had been more truthful and honest than the final Messenger (Allah bless him and give him peace); he always delivered on his word. Even his most formidable antagonists admitted his trustworthiness, purity and virtue. The Caesar of Rome asked Abū Sufyān, before he converted to Islam, about the Messenger's general behaviour and conduct with the people. Abū Sufyān said to the effect they never suspected Muhammad (Allah bless him and give him peace) of being a liar nor did he ever act treacherously.[70]

Lastly, it should be noted that giving a pledge of support and keeping it on all occasions – whether it is made with the Almighty, the Messenger (Allah bless him and give him peace), with one another or even with non-believers – is a sacred responsibility. People who are casual about making explicit promises with colleagues, friends or relatives must realise that they are offenders. Instead of undertaking promises at the drop of a hat, one should think twice about this.

8.15 Contentment

Contentment signifies a happy and satisfied state of mind. It refers to an attitude towards life and a way of thinking that brings about gratification and gratefulness under all circumstances. A contented soul looks forward to the future with optimism. Good or bad, every experience of a satisfied fellow is beneficial and meaningful.

Acquiring the good things of this world in order to seek Divine approbation is necessary to a certain extent. But for seeking an increase in wealth day and night so that an earner is engrossed in them entirely is destructive for the soul.

Contentment is a state of mind and heart which does not leave one with the feeling of being deprived or destitute though one lacks money and material goods. In contrast, greedy people may be overwhelmed by the desire to accumulate more wealth until death approaches them. A warning is sounded here against mindlessly preoccupying oneself with stockpiling.

أَلْهَاكُمُ التَّكَاثُرُ ○ حَتَّىٰ زُرْتُمُ الْمَقَابِرَ ○

Your greed for massive wealth and the superiority complex has made you negligent (of the Hereafter), until you go down to the graves.[71]

One example of a worldly person who indulged in the splendour of worldly life is Qārūn. He was a person at the time of the Prophet Mūsā (peace be upon him), who had so much treasure that even a troop of strong men would find it hard to carry their keys.

إِنَّ قَارُونَ كَانَ مِن قَوْمِ مُوسَىٰ فَبَغَىٰ عَلَيْهِمْ وَآتَيْنَاهُ مِنَ الْكُنُوزِ مَا إِنَّ مَفَاتِحَهُ لَتَنُوءُ
بِالْعُصْبَةِ أُولِي الْقُوَّةِ إِذْ قَالَ لَهُ قَوْمُهُ لَا تَفْرَحْ إِنَّ اللَّهَ لَا يُحِبُّ الْفَرِحِينَ

No doubt Qārūn (Korah) was of the people of Mūsā (Moses) but he oppressed them. And We gave him so much of treasures that it was hard for a powerful party of strong men to (carry) his keys while his people said to him: "Do not be arrogant and conceited (out of rejoicing). Verily Allah does not like those who gloat."[72]

That man of untold wealth was arrogant, oppressed his people and was proud of his knowledge and skill. Due to his own arrogance, he received a severe penalty.

فَخَسَفْنَا بِهِ وَبِدَارِهِ الْأَرْضَ فَمَا كَانَ لَهُ مِن فِئَةٍ يَنصُرُونَهُ مِن دُونِ اللَّهِ وَمَا كَانَ مِنَ الْمُنتَصِرِينَ

Then We sank him (Qārūn [Korah]) and his house into the earth. So except Allah, there was no (such) party that could help him (in saving from the torment). Nor could he stop the torment himself.[73]

Even when one is not in easy and comfortable conditions, but is pleased with Allah Almighty and one's allotted share in the world, one will not be sad and depressed. Real wealth lies in a positive mental attitude.

On this score, according to Abū Hurayra (may Allah be pleased with him), the Prophet (Allah bless him and give him peace) said:

لَيْسَ الْغِنَى عَنْ كَثْرَةِ الْعَرَضِ، وَلَكِنَّ الْغِنَى غِنَى النَّفْسِ.

Affluence does not consist of plenty of money, but true affluence is the contended self![74]

On the one hand, a great many people live in luxury yet they are persistently heard whining because they desire more resources. They suffer ceaselessly, little realising that their psychological pain and distress is mainly self-inflicted. On the other hand, the truly well off are happy with their lot, even if they have just enough money and food to stay alive. These people are mentioned in the following Tradition.

According to 'Abd Allāh b. 'Umar (may Allah be well pleased with him and his father), Allah's Messenger (Allah bless him and give him peace) said:

قَدْ أَفْلَحَ مَنْ أَسْلَمَ، وَرُزِقَ كَفَافًا، وَقَنَّعَهُ اللهُ بِمَا آتَاهُ.

He is successful who has embraced Islam, has been provided with sufficient sustenance and made contended by Allah with what He bestows upon him.[75]

If an excess of wealth breeds pride and arrogance, then it has a detrimental effect on one's spiritual state. Should Allah Almighty endow one with the wealth of contentment and patience which inculcate humility, and the virtue of often turning to the Lord of Mercy, then one is truly lucky.

The Holy Prophet (Allah bless him and give him peace) instilled the attribute of contentment in his followers, saying that the most affluent of all people is the one who is satisfied with Allah Almighty over the distribution of His sustenance.

Al-Ḥasan narrated, from Abū Hurayra (may Allah be pleased with him), that Allah's Messenger (Allah bless him and give him peace) said:

مَنْ يَأْخُذُ عَنِّيْ هَؤُلَاءِ الْكَلِمَاتِ؛ فَيَعْمَلُ بِهِنَّ، أَوْ يُعَلِّمُ مَنْ يَعْمَلُ بِهِنَّ؟ فَقَالَ أَبُو هُرَيْرَةَ : فَقُلْتُ : أَنَا يَا رَسُوْلَ اللهِ، فَأَخَذَ بِيَدِي، فَعَدَّ خَمْسًا، وَقَالَ: اتَّقِ الْمَحَارِمَ، تَكُنْ أَعْبَدَ النَّاسِ، وَارْضَ بِمَا قَسَّمَ اللهُ لَكَ، تَكُنْ أَغْنَى النَّاسِ، وَأَحْسِنْ إِلَى جَارِكَ، تَكُنْ مُؤْمِنًا، وَأَحِبَّ لِلنَّاسِ مَا تُحِبُّ لِنَفْسِكَ، تَكُنْ مُسْلِمًا، وَلَا تُكْثِرِ الضَّحِكَ؛ فَإِنَّ كَثْرَةَ الضَّحِكِ يُمِيْتُ الْقَلْبَ.

"Who will take these statements from me, so that he may act upon them, or teach one who will act upon them?" So Abū Hurayra (may Allah be pleased with him) said: "I said: 'I shall, Messenger of Allah!' So he took my hand and, enumerating five (things), said: "Be on guard against the unlawful and you shall be the most worshipping among the people, be satisfied with what Allah has allotted for you and you shall be the richest of the people, be kind to your neighbour and you shall be a believer, love for the people what you love for yourself and you shall be a Muslim. And do not laugh too much, for indeed excessive laughter kills the heart."[76]

We should beseech Allah, the Exalted, to grant us contentment of the heart, an exceptional commodity.

'Aṭā' b. al-Sā'ib narrated, on the authority of Sa'īd:

كَانَ ابْنُ عَبَّاسٍ يَقُوْلُ: اَللَّهُمَّ، قَنِّعْنِي بِمَا رَزَقْتَنِي، وَبَارِكْ لِي فِيْهِ، وَاخْلُفْ عَلَى كُلِّ غَائِبَةٍ لِي بِخَيْرٍ.

Ibn 'Abbās (may Allah be pleased with him) used to pray: "Allah, make me content with the provision You have given me and bless me in it and appoint good for me in everything which I do not have."[77]

Another Tradition instructs the faithful to seek satisfaction with their allotted portion in the world. The following supplication in the estimation of the Messenger (Allah bless him and give him peace) did not carry less value than a chapter of the Qur'ān.

Jābir b. 'Abd Allāh (may Allah be well pleased with him and his father) narrated that Allah's Messenger (Allah bless him and give him peace) used to teach his Companions the *istikhāra* (a prayer of guidance recited during times of indecision), asking for the good in all matters, as he would teach them a chapter of the Qur'ān. He said that when one of the believers is intending to do something, he or she should pray two cycles of prayer outside the obligatory prayer and then say:

اَللَّهُمَّ إِنِّيْ أَسْتَخِيرُكَ بِعِلْمِكَ، وَأَسْتَقْدِرُكَ بِقُدْرَتِكَ، وَأَسْأَلُكَ مِنْ فَضْلِكَ الْعَظِيْمِ. فَإِنَّكَ تَقْدِرُ وَلَا أَقْدِرُ، وَتَعْلَمُ وَلَا أَعْلَمُ، وَأَنْتَ عَلَّامُ الْغُيُوبِ. اَللَّهُمَّ إِنْ كُنْتَ تَعْلَمُ أَنَّ هَذَا الْأَمْرَ

خَيرٌ لِيْ فِيْ دِيْنِيْ، وَمَعَاشِيْ، وَعَاقِبَةِ أَمْرِيْ، فَاقْدُرْهُ لِيْ وَيَسِّرْهُ لِيْ، ثُمَّ بَارِكْ لِيْ فِيْهِ. وَإِنْ
كُنْتَ تَعْلَمُ أَنَّ هَذَا الْأَمْرَ شَرٌّ فِيْ دِيْنِيْ، وَمَعَاشِيْ، وَعَاقِبَةِ أَمْرِيْ، فَاصْرِفْهُ عَنِّيْ وَاصْرِفْنِيْ
عَنْهُ، وَاقْدُرْ لِيَ الْخَيْرَ حَيْثُ كَانَ، ثُمَّ ارْضِنِيْ بِهِ.

Allah, I ask You for the best by Your knowledge and I ask You for strength by Your power and I ask You for some of Your immense bounty. You have power and I do not. You know and I do not. You are the Knower of the unseen worlds. Allah, if You know that this matter is good for me in my religion and my livelihood and the end of my affair (or he said: "my affair sooner and later"), then ordain it for me and make it easy for me and then bless me in it. If You know that this matter is bad for me in my religion and my livelihood and the end of my affair (or he said: "my affair sooner and later"), then avert it from me and avert me from it and ordain something better for me wherever it may lie and make me content with it. He added: "Then he should name the thing he wants to do."[78]

Cultivating contentment in a trading lifestyle is important in many aspects. Islamic tradition and thinking approve – rather, urge – to be satisfied and happy with what he or she granted is this world, whilst laziness is disapproved habits. With a fast-paced world, 100% success in business is never guaranteed. If some loss in business transpires, this may result in feelings of anxiety, depression and regret. However, by practising contentment, traders can live in a state of mind that can see value and worth in every transaction, no matter what the outcome.

The case for contentment and satisfaction must not mislead anyone: it does not imply complacency and indolence. The Qur'ānic ruling that "*And that man (according to justice) will get only that for which he will have strived.*"

وَأَن لَّيْسَ لِلْإِنسَانِ إِلَّا مَا سَعَىٰ ○

And that man (according to justice) will get only that for which he will have strived. (As for Bounty, no one has any right to it. That is merely Allah's bestowal and pleasure, granting as much as He wills to whom He may please.)[79]

The following statements of the Caliph 'Umar b. al-Khaṭṭāb (may Allah be pleased with him) tell the faithful that there is no excuse for laziness in work.

None of you must lag behind in the matter of seeking livelihood and (just) pray: "Allah, grant me with provisions," and he should know that the sky rains neither gold nor silver.[80]

O poor people! Raise your heads, for there is a clear path before you. Race to do good deeds and do not become a burden on people.[81]

8.16 Altruism

Most people assert their rights and privileges. However, Islam directs its followers to discharge their obligations towards their juniors, peers and seniors; thus an altruistic social society is developed. Its members take pleasure in serving others, instead of amassing wealth and comforts of life for themselves and for their family. They let go of their own rights so as to bring happiness to the hearts of their fellow beings. They do not perform good acts so that they might be reciprocated; through their virtues, they seek the approbation of the Lord. The Qur'ān depicts their character in these words:

وَيُطْعِمُونَ الطَّعَامَ عَلَى حُبِّهِ مِسْكِينًا وَيَتِيمًا وَأَسِيرًا○إِنَّمَا نُطْعِمُكُمْ لِوَجْهِ اللهِ لَا نُرِيدُ مِنكُمْ جَزَاءً وَلَا شُكُورًا○

> *And they give (their own) food, in deep love of Allah, to the needy, the orphan and prisoner (out of sacrifice, despite their own desire and need for it), (and say:) "We are feeding you only to please Allah. We do not seek any recompense from you nor (wish for) any thanks."*[82]

The Islamic morals of self-sacrifice can bring success in business and provide inner satisfaction to the businessmen to follow the teachings of Qur'ān and Prophet in true letter and spirit. Altruistic souls are sure to reap the rewards of their generosity in the future abode with the Lord.

A Prophetic Tradition reports that once a man died and entered the Garden of Paradise. When asked what caused him to enter it, he said that he had conducted transactions with people and directed his servants to deal mildly with the debtors. Allah reciprocated his kindness with forgiveness.

Abū Hurayra (may Allah be pleased with him) narrated that Allah's Messenger (Allah bless him and give him peace) said:

كَانَ تَاجِرٌ يُدَايِنُ النَّاسَ، فَإِذَا رَأَى مُعْسِرًا، قَالَ لِفِتْيَانِهِ: تَجَاوَزُوْا عَنْهُ، لَعَلَّ اللهَ أَنْ يَتَجَاوَزَ عَنَّا، فَتَجَاوَزَ اللهُ عَنْهُ.

> There was a merchant who used to lend money to people. When he saw someone in difficulty, he would say to his employees: "Make allowances for him so that perhaps Allah will make allowances for us." So as a result, Allah made allowances for him.[83]

The following Tradition also preaches the value of generosity to both buyers and sellers.

Allah's Messenger (Allah bless him and give him peace) said on another occasion:

أَدْخَلَ اللهُ عَزَّ وَجَلَّ الْجَنَّةَ رَجُلاً كَانَ سَهْلاً مُشْتَرِياً، وَبَائِعًا، وَقَاضِيًا، وَمُقْتَضِيًا.

Into Paradise Allah admits the person who buys and sells any commodity with ease, and makes a demand without any difficulty.[84]

8.17 Forgiving and overlooking

If someone hurts our feelings, usurps our rights or ill-treats us, we may experience a flash of anger and feel like reciprocating in a like manner. However, the Prophet (Allah bless him and give him peace) taught the faithful that harbouring a grudge against someone who has wronged them is not a becoming attitude for them. The words of the All-Glorious Lord and the Blessed Prophet (Allah bless him and give him peace) instruct us on how to handle our uncomfortable, uneasy and negative feelings when others affect us negatively.

Generally, people feel affronted when they are disregarded or mistreated; they are reluctant to be indulgent towards offenders and try to fight back in a similar manner. Under such circumstances, Allah, the Exalted, tells the faithful that it is better to let it pass and put it out of their minds. This Divine intention is obvious in the following verse:

وَلَا يَأْتَلِ أُوْلُوا الْفَضْلِ مِنكُمْ وَالسَّعَةِ أَن يُؤْتُوا أُوْلِي الْقُرْبَى وَالْمَسَاكِينَ وَالْمُهَاجِرِينَ فِي سَبِيلِ
اللَّهِ وَلْيَعْفُوا وَلْيَصْفَحُوا أَلَا تُحِبُّونَ أَن يَغْفِرَ اللَّهُ لَكُمْ وَاللَّهُ غَفُورٌ رَّحِيمٌ

And (now) those of you who are exalted (by way of the Dīn *[Religion]) and are affluent (world wise) must not swear that they will not provide (financial help) to the relatives, the needy and the Emigrants (who were involved in this offence of false accusation). They should forgive (their misconduct) and overlook (their mistake). Do you not like that Allah should forgive you? And Allah is Most Forgiving, Ever-Merciful.*[85]

All believers are motivated by Quran to follow the path of mercifulness and forgivingness. By reminding them of this heartfelt desire, Allah Almighty reveals to them how they should handle others when they are treated badly. Through this ordinance He fosters compassion, mercy, forgiveness and reconciliation amongst the practitioners of Islam.

Since human beings are not angels – i.e. they are infallible creatures – the faithful know that their fellow beings have been created with a tendency to make mistakes. So believers deal with others gently and are generous with forgiveness.

الَّذِينَ يُنفِقُونَ فِي السَّرَّاءِ وَالضَّرَّاءِ وَالْكَاظِمِينَ الْغَيْظَ وَالْعَافِينَ عَنِ النَّاسِ وَاللَّهُ يُحِبُّ
الْمُحْسِنِينَ

They are the ones who spend in the cause of Allah whether they are affluent or indigent (in both the conditions), sublimate their anger and tolerate (the faults of the) people; and Allah loves those who are benevolent.[86]

Allah's Messenger (Allah bless him and give him peace) prayed for those who are lenient while demanding what is due to them.

Jābir b. 'Abd Allāh (may Allah be well pleased with him and his father) reported that the Holy Prophet (Allah bless him and give him peace) said:

رَحِمَ اللّٰهُ رَجُلاً سَمْحًا إِذَا بَاعَ، وَإِذَا اشْتَرَى، وَإِذَا اقْتَضَى.

> May Allah show mercy to a man who is generous when he sells, and when he makes a demand![87]

The devotees of Allah take their colour from Allah – the Pardoner, Effacer, Forgiver – and overlook the unintended mistakes of others.[88] The people who choose to pardon, exonerate and excuse others will find Allah reciprocating.[89] The Divine attributes of clemency, mercy, compassion, tolerance and grace are set out explicitly in the following verse:

وَلَوْ يُؤَاخِذُ اللّٰهُ النَّاسَ بِظُلْمِهِم مَّا تَرَكَ عَلَيْهَا مِن دَآبَّةٍ

> *And had Allah seized people (instantly) for their injustice, He would not have left any living being (on the surface of the earth).*[90]

Allah loves those who pardon others but penalises scandal-mongerers and people who strive to humiliate others. To slur the faithful, to slight them or to pry into their faults is not appropriate for a believer. The following Hadith illustrates this point.

عَنِ بْنِ عُمَرَ قَالَ: صَعِدَ رَسُوْلُ اللهِ e الْمِنبَرَ فَنَادَى بِصَوْتٍ رَفِيْعٍ، فَقَالَ: يَا مَعْشَرَ مَنْ قَدْ أَسْلَمَ بِلِسَانِهِ، وَلَمْ يَفْضِ الْإِيْمَانُ إِلَى قَلْبِهِ، لَا تُؤْذُوا الْمُسْلِمِيْنَ وَلَا تُعَيِّرُوْهُمْ، وَلَا تَتَّبِعُوْا عَوْرَاتِهِمْ، فَإِنَّهُ مَنْ يَتَّبِعْ عَوْرَةَ أَخِيْهِ الْمُسْلِمِ؛ يَتَّبِعِ اللهُ عَوْرَتَهُ؛ وَمَنْ يَتَّبِعِ اللهُ عَوْرَتَهُ يَفْضَحْهُ، وَلَوْ فِيْ جَوْفِ رَحْلِهِ.

> Ibn 'Umar (may Allah be well pleased with him and his father) reported that Allah's Messenger (Allah bless him and give him peace) ascended the pulpit and called out in a raised voice: "You who accepted Islam with his tongue, while faith has not reached his heart! Do not harm the Muslims, nor revile them, nor spy on them to expose their secrets, for indeed whoever tries to expose his Muslim brother's secrets, Allah exposes his secrets wide open, even if he were in the depth of his house."[91]

The following Tradition sheds a greater amount of light on the same subject matter.

According to Abū Hurayra (may Allah be pleased with him), Allah's Messenger (Allah bless him and give him peace) said:

لَا تَحَاسَدُوْا، وَلَا تَنَاجَشُوْا، وَلَا تَبَاغَضُوْا، وَلَا تَدَابَرُوْا، وَلَا يَبِعْ بَعْضُكُمْ عَلَى بَيْعِ بَعْضٍ.
وَكُوْنُوْا عِبَادَ اللهِ إِخْوَانًا. الْمُسْلِمُ أَخُو الْمُسْلِمِ؛ لَا يَظْلِمُهُ، وَلَا يَخْذُلُهُ، وَلَا يَحْقِرُهُ. اَلتَّقْوَى
هَاهُنَا (وَيُشِيرٌ إِلَى صَدْرِهِ ثَلَاثَ مَرَّاتٍ). بِحَسْبِ امْرِيءٍ مِنَ الشَّرِّ أَنْ يَحْقِرَ أَخَاهُ الْمُسْلِمَ.
كُلُّ الْمُسْلِمِ عَلَى الْمُسْلِمِ حَرَامٌ دَمُهُ وَمَالُهُ وَعِرْضُهُ.

You must not be jealous of one another, you must not outbid one another, you must not have spite against one another, you must not turn your backs on one another, and one of you must not buy in opposition to another's purchase. Servants of Allah! Become brothers to one another. The Muslim is the brother of the Muslim; he does not wrong him, he does not forsake him, and he does not scorn him. God wariness and piety is here (and Allah's Messenger pointed to his sacred breast three times). It is evil enough for a Muslim to scorn his Muslim brother. The Muslim's blood, his property and his honour are forbidden (and inviolable) for the other Muslim.[92]

8.18 Unburdening the burdened

Primarily, Sharia is based on the principle of relieving hardship (*raf' al-ḥaraj*) from the people and facilitating them in their matters.

مَا يُرِيدُ اللهُ لِيَجْعَلَ عَلَيْكُم مِّنْ حَرَجٍ وَلَكِن يُرِيدُ لِيُطَهِّرَكُمْ وَلِيُتِمَّ نِعْمَتَهُ عَلَيْكُمْ لَعَلَّكُمْ
تَشْكُرُونَ

Allah does not want to make things hard for you, but He wants to purify you, and complete the bestowal of His favour upon you so that you may become grateful.[93]

In another verse, the Almighty says:

هُوَ اجْتَبَاكُمْ وَمَا جَعَلَ عَلَيْكُمْ فِي الدِّينِ مِنْ حَرَجٍ

He has chosen you, and has not laid upon you any hardship or constriction (in the matter of) Dīn (Religion).[94]

The Prophet Muhammad (Allah bless him and give him peace) was the most ardent worshipper of Allah, the Exalted, and there was nothing he would not do to please Allah. However, whenever he was given an option between the performance of two good actions, he always went for the easier, for his conduct would become a normative practice for his followers.

On this score, 'Urwa (may Allah be pleased with him) related that 'Ā'isha (may Allah be well pleased with her) said:

مَا خُيِّرَ رَسُوْلُ اللهِ a بَيْنَ أَمْرَيْنِ قَطُّ إِلَّا أَخَذَ أَيْسَرَهُمَا مَا لَمْ يَكُنْ إِثْمًا، فَإِنْ كَانَ إِثْمًا، كَانَ أَبْعَدَ النَّاسِ مِنْهُ.

Allah's Messenger (Allah bless him and give him peace) was not given a choice between two matters but that he took the easier of the two as long as it was not a wrong action. If it was a wrong action, he was the furthest of people from it.[95]

The Messenger (Allah bless him and give him peace) liked to make things light and easy for people. He commanded his deputies to cheer people up by making things easy and not to overburden them in difficult situations.

عَنْ سَعِيْدِ بْنِ أَبِي بُرْدَةَ عَنْ أَبِيْهِ عَنْ جَدِّهِ، قَالَ: لَمَّا بَعَثَهُ رَسُوْلُ اللهِ a وَمُعَاذَ بْنَ جَبَلٍ قَالَ لَهُمَا: يَسِّرَا وَلاَ تُعَسِّرَا، وَبَشِّرَا وَلاَ تُنَفِّرَا وَتَطَاوَعَا.

Sa'īd b. Abī Burda related from his father that his grandfather said: "When Allah's Messenger (Allah bless him and give him peace) sent him and Mu'ādh b. Jabal, he said to them: "Make things easy and do not make them difficult. Give them good news and do not make them feel aversion. Obey one another."[96]

Reducing the burden from the people in their difficult situation is also the practice of Allah Almighty. As it is evident from the following Shariah Law in relation to worship: during illness, the faithful may pray sitting or even lying; on journeys, they must shorten prayer and may skip fasts; without water, they may perform dry ablutions.

Granting relief to a debtor in straitened circumstances or even foregoing the entire amount of debt, if one can afford it, is a desirable act. Allah Almighty says:

وَإِن كَانَ ذُو عُسْرَةٍ فَنَظِرَةٌ إِلَىٰ مَيْسَرَةٍ وَأَن تَصَدَّقُواْ خَيْرٌ لَّكُمْ إِن كُنتُمْ تَعْلَمُونَ

And if a debtor is under financial stress, he should be given respite till he feels at ease to pay. And your forgoing (the loan) is better for you if you know (what significance it has in the sight of Allah to console the poor).[97]

When we realise that the pleasure and forgiveness of Allah, the Exalted, are our success, we can lift people out of worries of life and grant them respite. The following Hadith illustrates the concept of granting relief to one who is insolvent together with the motive for this virtuous action.

'Ubāda b. al-Walīd b. 'Ubāda al-Ṣāmit reported:

خَرَجْتُ أَنَا وَأَبِيْ نَطْلُبُ الْعِلْمَ فِيْ هَذَا الْحَيِّ مِنَ الْأَنْصَارِ قبْلَ أَنْ يَهْلِكُوْا. فَكَانَ أَوَّلُ مَنْ
لَقِيْنَا أَبَا الْيَسَرِ صَاحِبَ رَسُوْلِ اللَّهِ وَمَعَهُ غُلَامٌ لَهُ، مَعَهُ ضِمَامَةٌ مِنْ صُحُفٍ، وَعَلَى أَبِي
الْيَسَرِ بُرْدَةٌ وَمَعَافِرِيٌّ، وَعَلَى غُلَامِهِ بُرْدَةٌ وَمَعَافِرِيٌّ، فَقَالَ لَهُ أَبِيْ: يَا عَمِّ، إِنِّيْ أَرَى فِيْ
وَجْهِكَ سَفْعَةً مِنْ غَضَبٍ، قَالَ: أَجَلْ، كَانَ لِيْ عَلَى فُلَانِ ابْنِ فُلَانٍ الْحَرَامِيِّ مَالٌ، فَأَتَيْتُ
أَهْلَهُ فَسَلَّمْتُ، فَقُلْتُ: ثَمَّ هُوَ؟ قَالُوا: لَا، فَخَرَجَ عَلَيَّ ابْنٌ لَهُ جَفْرٌ، فَقُلْتُ لَهُ: أَيْنَ أَبُوْكَ؟
قَالَ: سَمِعَ صَوْتَكَ فَدَخَلَ أَرِيكَةَ أُمِّيْ، فَقُلْتُ: اخْرُجْ إِلَيَّ، فَقَدْ عَلِمْتُ أَيْنَ أَنْتَ. فَخَرَجَ
فَقُلْتُ: مَا حَمَلَكَ عَلَى أَنِ اخْتَبَأْتَ مِنِّيْ؟ قَالَ: أَنَا وَاللَّهِ أُحَدِّثُكَ ثُمَّ لَا أَكْذِبُكَ، خَشِيْتُ
وَاللَّه أَنْ أُحَدِّثَكَ فَأَكْذِبَكَ، وَأَنْ أَعِدَكَ فَأُخْلِفَكَ، وَكُنْتَ صَاحِبَ رَسُولَ اللَّه a وَكُنْتُ
وَاللَّهِ مُعْسِرًا. قَالَ: قُلْتُ: آللَّهِ؟ قَالَ: آللَّهِ، قُلْتُ: آللَّهِ؟ قَالَ: آللَّهِ، قُلْتُ: آللَّهِ؟ قَالَ: آللَّهِ،
قَالَ: فَأَتَى بِصَحِيفَتِهِ فَمَحَاهَا بِيَدِهِ، فَقَالَ: إِنْ وَجَدْتَ قَضَاءً فَاقْضِنِيْ وَإِلَّا أَنْتَ فِيْ حِلٍّ،
فَأَشْهَدَ بَصَرُ عَيْنَيَّ هَاتَيْنِ – وَوَضَعَ إِصْبَعَيْهِ عَلَى عَيْنَيْهِ – وَسَمِعَ أُذُنَيَّ هَاتَيْنِ وَوَعَاهُ قَلْبِيْ
هَذَا – وَأَشَارَ إِلَى مَنَاطِ قَلْبِهِ – رَسُولَ اللَّه a وَهُوَ يَقُولُ: مَنْ أَنْظَرَ مُعْسِرًا أَوْ وَضَعَ
عَنْهُ، أَظَلَّهُ اللَّه فِيْ ظِلِّهِ.

"My father and I went out seeking knowledge among this group of the Helpers before they died. The first one whom we met was Abū al-Yasar (may Allah be pleased with him), the Companion of Allah's Messenger (Allah bless him and give him peace). A slave of his was with him, and he had a binding of (paper) sheets with him. Abū al-Yasar was wearing a *burda* and a *ma'āfirī* garment, and his slave was wearing a *burda* and a *ma'āfirī* garment. My father said to him: 'Uncle, I see signs of anger on your face.' He said: Yes, I was owed money by so-and-so, the son of so-and-so al-Harāmī (from the tribe of Banū Harām). I went to his family and greeted them with salām and said: 'Is he there?' They said: 'No.' Then a young son of his came out to me, and I said to him: 'Where is your father?' He said: 'He heard your voice and he hid behind my mother's bed.' I said: 'Come out to me, for I know where you are.' He came out, and I said: 'What made you hide from me?' He said: 'By Allah, I will tell you, and I will not lie to you. By Allah, I was afraid that if I spoke to you I would lie to you, and if I made a promise to you I would break it. You were a Companion of Allah's Messenger (Allah bless him and give him peace), and, by Allah, I was in (financial) difficulty.' I said: 'Do you swear by Allah?' He said: 'I swear by Allah.' I said: 'Do you swear by Allah?' He said: 'I swear by Allah.' I said: 'Do you swear by Allah?' He said: 'I swear by Allah.' He brought me his promissory note and erased it with his own hand.' He said: 'When you can afford it, pay it off, otherwise you are let off. I bear witness that these two eyes of mine saw' – and he put his fingers on his eyes – 'and these two ears of mine heard, and my heart understood' – and he pointed to his heart – 'Allah's Messenger (Allah bless him and give him peace) when he said: "Whoever waits for one who is in (financial) difficulty (to pay a debt) or waives it for him, Allah will shade him in His shade.''''[98]

8.19 Conditions of a valid sale transaction

A business transaction is a contract which must be fulfilled, as per Allah's command to the faithful.[99] Besides, the faithful keep treaties and contracts when they make them.[100] Muslims are required to comply with the contracts and the treaties they enter into, providing that they are sound and do not breach any Sharia rulings. Contracts that are religiously invalid must not be ratified.

'Amr b. 'Awf al-Muzanī narrated from his father and from his grandfather that Allah's Messenger (Allah bless him and give him peace) said:

اَلصُّلْحُ جَائِزٌ بَيْنَ الْمُسْلِمِيْنَ إِلَّا صُلْحًا حَرَّمَ حَلَالًا أَوْ أَحَلَّ حَرَامًا، وَالْمُسْلِمُوْنَ عَلَى شُرُوْطِهِمْ إِلاَّ شَرْطًا حَرَّمَ حَلَالًا أَوْ أَحَلَّ حَرَامًا.

> Reconciliation is allowed among the Muslims, except for reconciliation that makes the lawful unlawful or the unlawful lawful. And the Muslims will be held to their conditions, except the conditions that make the lawful unlawful or the unlawful lawful.[101]

If a contract is voidable due to an illegal stipulation which may be adjusted, then the necessary amendment is made and the contract is adhered to. A Hadith illustrates this point:

عَنْ عَائِشَةَ، قَالَتْ أَتَتْهَا بَرِيرَةُ تَسْأَلُهَا فِي كِتَابَتِهَا فَقَالَتْ إِنْ شِئْتِ أَعْطَيْتُ أَهْلَكِ وَيَكُونُ الْوَلَاءُ لِي. وَقَالَ أَهْلُهَا إِنْ شِئْتِ أَعْطَيْتِهَا مَا بَقِيَ . وَقَالَ سُفْيَانُ مَرَّةً إِنْ شِئْتِ أَعْتَقْتِهَا وَيَكُونُ الْوَلَاءُ لَنَا . فَلَمَّا جَاءَ رَسُولُ اللَّهِ صلى الله عليه وسلم ذَكَّرَتْهُ ذَلِكَ فَقَالَ " ابْتَاعِيهَا فَأَعْتِقِيهَا، فَإِنَّ الْوَلَاءَ لِمَنْ أَعْتَقَ ". ثُمَّ قَامَ رَسُولُ اللَّهِ صلى الله عليه وسلم عَلَى الْمِنْبَرِ . وَقَالَ سُفْيَانُ مَرَّةً فَصَعِدَ رَسُولُ اللَّهِ صلى الله عليه وسلم عَلَى الْمِنْبَرِ . فَقَالَ " مَا بَالُ أَقْوَامٍ يَشْتَرِطُونَ شُرُوطًا لَيْسَتْ فِي كِتَابِ اللهِ، مَنِ اشْتَرَطَ شَرْطًا لَيْسَ فِي كِتَابِ اللهِ فَلَيْسَ لَهُ، وَإِنِ اشْتَرَطَ مِائَةَ مَرَّةٍ

> According to 'Ā'isha (may Allah be well pleased with her), the Mother of the Faithful, that Barīra (may Allah be well pleased with her), a slave, came to her to ask her help in buying her freedom by paying her master instalments every year. 'Ā'isha (may Allah be well pleased with her) told her: "If you like, I will pay off your people but your inheritance will go to me." Her owners demurred and said: "If you like, you can give her what

remains but her inheritance will remain with us." When Allah's Messenger (Allah bless him and give him peace) came, 'Ā'isha mentioned the whole incident to him. The Messenger (Allah bless him and give him peace) said: "Buy her and set her free. Inheritance goes to the one who sets her free." Then he ascended the pulpit and said: "Why is it that some people make conditions which are not in the Book of Allāh? Any condition which is not in the Book of Allah is invalid even if it is stipulated a hundred times."[102]

Transacting a commodity for something else or engaging in a sale has the following six elements: the seller, the buyer, the price, the commodity purchased, the verbal offer and the verbal acceptance.

The rest of this section provides details regarding the validity of a sale.

8.19.1 Consent

The seller must not be unjustly forced or blackmailed to sell anything: the agreement of someone unjustly forced to sell his or her property is not valid. The following Qur'ānic verse stipulates consent in trading.

يَا أَيُّهَا الَّذِينَ آمَنُواْ لاَ تَأْكُلُواْ أَمْوَالَكُمْ بَيْنَكُمْ بِالْبَاطِلِ إِلاَّ أَن تَكُونَ تِجَارَةً عَن تَرَاضٍ مِّنكُمْ
وَلاَ تَقْتُلُواْ أَنفُسَكُمْ

O believers! Do not devour one another's wealth unlawfully amongst yourselves unless it is a trade by your mutual agreement and do not kill yourselves.[103]

On trading with mutual consent, Abū Sa'īd al-Khudrī (may Allah be pleased with him) reported that Allah's Messenger (Allah bless him and give him peace) said:

إِنَّمَا الْبَيْعُ عَنْ تَرَاضٍ.

Transactions may only be done by mutual consent.[104]

Islam does not permit one to force a buyer into selling a commodity against his or her will. Hushaym narrated:

سَيَأْتِيْ عَلَى النَّاسِ زَمَانٌ عَضُوْضٌ؛ يَعَضُّ الْمُوْسِرُ عَلَى مَا فِيْ يَدَيْهِ وَلَمْ يُؤْمَرْ بِذَلِكَ. قَالَ
اللّٰه تَعَالَى: ﴿وَلاَ تَنسَوُاْ الْفَضْلَ بَيْنَكُمْ﴾ وَيُبَايِعُ الْمُضْطَرُّوْنَ وَقَدْ نَهَى النَّبِيُّ عَنْ بَيْعِ
الْمُضْطَرِّ، وَبَيْعِ الْغَرَرِ، وَبَيْعِ الثَّمَرَةِ قَبْلَ أَنْ تُدْرِكَ.

There will come a difficult time when the rich man will hold fast to that which is in his hand although he was not enjoined to do that. Allah says (in the Qur'ān 2:237): "*And never forget extending generosity (and behaving excellently) towards each other (even in moments of stress and strain).*" And those who are under compulsion (of force or necessity) will be bought from. The Prophet (Allah bless him and give him peace) forbade forced sales, transactions of ambiguity, and selling crops before they have ripened.[105]

8.19.2 Rationality

The condition of adulthood and maturity must exist for one's ability to sell things. However, savants exclude, from the stipulation of rationality. If a child sells minor items at his or her father's shop without reaching the age of discrimination, the sale is valid. However, if the child sells the shop itself, this sale is be invalid.

8.19.3 What is sold should be lawful property

The ownership of lawful property is permissible in Islam. What is impure in itself according to Islam may not be regarded as property, and thus it may not be contracted. Human organs may not be traded as they are not property but bestowed by the Creator. It is unlawful for faithful to trade their corpses.

8.19.4 The seller should own the item to be sold

One may sell something that is in one's possession. Therefore, if one sells mobile phones that one does not own, for example, the sale is void. This requirement emerges from the following Hadith reports.

لاَ تَبِعْ مَا لَيْسَ عِنْدَكَ.

Do not sell what you do not possess.[106]

According to Ibn 'Umar (may Allah be well pleased with him and his father), the Prophet (Allah bless him and give him peace) said:

مَنِ ابْتَاعَ طَعَامًا فَلاَ يَبِعْهُ حَتَّىٰ يَقْبِضَهُ.

When someone buys food, he should not sell it until he has taken delivery of it.[107]

According to Ibn 'Abbās (may Allah be pleased with him), Allah's Messenger (Allah bless him and give him peace) said:

مَنِ ابْتَاعَ طَعَامًا فَلَا يَبِعْهُ حَتَّى يَكْتَالَهُ.

Whoever buys food should not sell it until he has measured it.

8.19.5 The seller should be able to deliver the commodity

That the commodity must be deliverable is a fundamental requirement for a valid sale. Therefore, if the commodity that was sold cannot be delivered, the transaction is incomplete and hence null and void. You may not sell anything you have yet to receive. The sale of a fish in a pond, fruit on a tree or an animal that has run away has no legal force. In like fashion, the trade of an article that has been stolen from one is illicit.

8.19.6 The price should be clear

The value of the article must be determined beforehand, so that no dispute may arise when it is delivered.

8.19.7 The commodity should be known

The commodity should be determined – how much it is, what make it is, what kind it is – and known to both contracting parties. All the relevant information must be furnished. For instance, it is not lawful to sell property not precisely identified, such as "I sell you one of these two bags" or "I sell you one of these pots." These measures are taken in order to protect the purchaser from risk, as the Messenger (Allah bless him and give him peace) prohibited transactions where risk is involved.[108]

A commodity may be purchased on seeing it or inspecting through visual means, such as with a picture or a video. However, the buyer is entitled to cancel the deal if he or she finds that the particular commodity does not fit the description.

Notes

1 Narrated by al-Bayhaqī in *al-Sunan al-kubrā*, 10:191 §20571.
2 Narrated by al-Tirmidhī in *al-Sunan*: *Al-Īmān*: Faith according to Allah's Messenger (Allah bless him and give him peace), Ch.: What has come to us concerning the perfecting of faith, its increase and its diminution, 5:9 §2612; and Ibn Abī Shayba in *al-Muṣannaf*, 5:210 §25319.
3 Narrated by al-Bukhārī in *al-Ṣaḥīḥ*: *Bad'al-Waḥy* [The beginning of inspiration], Ch.: How inspiration began, 1:3 §3.
4 Qur'ān 33:21.
5 Narrated by Abū Dāwūd in *al-Sunan*: *al-Adab* [Proper conduct], Ch.: Regarding good interaction with people 4:251 §4790.
6 Narrated by al-Bukhārī in *al-Ṣaḥīḥ*: *al-Buyū'* [Sales], Ch.: A buyer and seller making things clear and not concealing anything and showing good faith, 2:731 §1972.
7 Qur'ān 33:70.

8 Ibid., 9:119.
9 Ibid., 2:283.
10 Narrated by al-Tirmidhī in *al-Sunan*: *al-Buyū'* [Sales], Ch.: What has been related about those who deal in trade and what the Prophet (Allah bless him and give him peace) called them, 3:515 §1209; 'Abd b. Ḥumayd in *al-Musnad*, 1:299 §966; and al-Mundhirī in *al-Targhībwa al-Tarhīb*, 2:365 §2745.
11 Narrated by al-Tirmidhī in *al-Sunan*: *al-Buyū'* [Sales], Ch.: What has been related about those who deal in trade and what the Prophet (Allah bless him and give him peace) called them, 3:515 §1210; al-Dārimī in *al-Sunan*, 2:322 §2538; al-Ṭabarānī in *al-Mu'jam al-kabīr*, 5:44 §4540; and al-Bayhaqī in *Shu'ab al-Īmān*, 4:219 §4848.
12 Narrated by al-Bukhārī in *al-Ṣaḥīḥ*: *al-Buyū'* [Sales], Ch.: A buyer and seller making things clear and not concealing anything and showing good faith, 2:732 §1973.
13 Qur'ān 2:177.
14 Ibid., 23:8.
15 Narrated by Aḥmad b. Ḥanbal in *al-Musnad*, 2:177 §6652.
16 Narrated by al-Tirmidhī in *al-Sunan*: *al-Buyū'* [Sales], Ch.: (38), 3: 564 §1264.
17 Narrated by Aḥmad b. Ḥanbal in *al-Musnad*, 5:274 §22414.
18 Narrated by Abū Dāwūd in *al-Sunan*: *al-'Ilm* [Knowledge], Ch.: Caution in issuing a decree, 3:321 §3657.
19 Narrated by Ibn Mājah in *al-Sunan*: *al-Fitan* [Troubles], Ch.: Hard times, 2:1339 §4036.
20 Narrated by al-Bukhārī in *al-Ṣaḥīḥ*: *al-'Ilm* [Knowledge], Ch.: On the one who is asked for knowledge while he is engaged in a conversation and then finishes his conversation before answering the question, 1:33 §59.
21 Narrated by al-Tirmidhī in *al-Sunan*: *al-Buyū'* [Sales], Ch.: What has been related about those who deal in trade and what the Prophet (Allah bless him and give him peace) called them, 3:515 §1209; 'Abd b. Ḥumayd in *al-Musnad*, 1:299 §966; and al-Mundhirī in *al-Targhībwa al-Tarhīb*, 2:365 §2745.
22 Narrated by al-Tirmidhī in *al-Sunan*: *al-Birr wa al-Ṣila* [Piety and affinity], Ch.: What has been related about truthfulness and falsehood, 4:347 §1971.
23 Qur'ān 23:8.
24 Narrated byAbū Dāwūd in *al-Sunan*: *al-Kharājwa al-imārawa al-fay'* [Land tax, leadership and spoils acquired without fighting], Ch.: Regarding granting provision to employees, 3:134 §2943; al-Ḥākim in *al-Mustadrak*, 1:563 §1472; and al-Bayhaqī in *al-Sunan al-kubrā*, 6:355 §12799.
25 Qur'ān 17:35.
26 Ibid., 83:1–3.
27 Ibid., 6:152.
28 Ibid., 26:181–183.
29 Ibid., 55:7–9.
30 Narrated by Ibn Mājah in *al-Sunan*, *al-Fitan* [The troubles], Ch.: Punishments, 2:1332 §4019.
31 Narrated by Imam Muslim in *al-Ṣaḥīḥ*: *al-Birr wa al-ṣilawa al-ādāb* [Piety, filial duty and good manners], Ch.: The virtue of gentleness, 4:2003 §2593; and Aḥmad b. Ḥanbal in *al-Musnad*, 1:112 §902.
32 Narrated by al-Tirmidhī in *al-Sunan*: *al-Buyū'* [Sales], Ch.: What has been related about tolerance in selling, buying and repaying, 3:609 § 1319.
33 Al-'Aynī, *'Umat al-Qārī*, 11:189.
34 Narrated by al-Tirmidhī in *al-Sunan*: *al-Buyū'* [Sales], Ch.: What has been related about taking a camel or other animals on loan, 3:610 §1320; and Aḥmad b. Ḥanbal in *al-Musnad*, 3:340 §14699.
35 Narrated by al-Ṭabarānī in *al-Mu'jam al-awsaṭ*, 7:297 §7544; al-Haythamī in *Majma' al-Zawā'id*, 4:75; and *al-Targhībwa al-Tarhīb*, 2:354 §2701.

36 Narrated by Ibn Mājah in *al-Sunan*: *al-Tijāra* [Trade], Ch.: Letting someone off, 2:741 §2199.
37 Qur'ān 7:85.
38 Narrated by al-Bukhārī in *al-Ṣaḥīḥ*: *al-Buyū'* [Sales], Ch.: The kind of deception disliked in transactions, 2:745 §2011.
39 Narrated by al-Bayhaqī in *al-Sunan al-Kubrā*, 5:348 §10707.
40 Qur'ān 9:34–35.
41 Ibid., 59:7.
42 Ibid., 7:31.
43 Ibid., 17:26.
44 Ibid., 17:27.
45 Ibid., 4:29.
46 Ibid., 23:51.
47 Ibid., 5:38.
48 Narrated by Abū Dāwūd in *al-Sunan*: *al-Ḥudūd* [The prescribed punishments], Ch.: Regarding interceding about a legal punishment, 4:132 §4373.
49 Narrated by Abū Dāwūd in *al-Sunan*: *al-Qaḍā'* [Judgements], Ch.: Regarding gifts for workers, 3:300 §3581.
50 Narrated by al-Bukhārī in *al-Ṣaḥīḥ*: *Bk al-ḥajj*, 2:620 §1654,ḍ and Muslim in *al-Ṣaḥīḥ*, 3:1305–1306 §1679.
51 Narrated by al-Ḥākim in *al-Mustadrak*, 4:141 §7164.
52 Narrated by Abū Dāwūd in *al-Sunan*: *al-Kharājwa al-Imārawa al-Fay'* [The land tax, imperial authority and the bestowal of booty], Ch: Regarding granting provision to (government) employees, 3:134 §2943.
53 Narrated by al-Bukhārī in *al-Ṣaḥīḥ*: *al-Aḥkām* [The rules of law], Ch.: Gifts to public officials, 6:2624 §6753.
54 Qur'ān 2:188.
55 Narrated by Ibn Mājah in *al-Sunan*: *al-Tijārāt* [Trade], Ch.: Whoever does not like to fix prices, 2:741 §2200.
56 Narrated by al-Ḥākim in *al-Mustadrak*, 2:15 §2168; and al-Bayhaqī in *Shu'ab al-Īmān*, 7:525 §11214.
57 Qur'ān 23:8.
58 Ibid., 23:10–11.
59 Ibid., 4:58.
60 Ibid., 11:85–86.
61 Ibid., 17:34.
62 Ibid., 16:91.
63 Ibid., 13:20.
64 Narrated by Aḥmad b. Ḥanbal in *al-Musnad*, 3:135 §12406.
65 Narrated by al-Bukhārī in *al-Ṣaḥīḥ*: *al-Īmān* [Faith], Ch.: The sign of the hypocrite, 1:21 §34; and al-Bayhaqī in *al-Sunan al-Kubrā*, 9:230.
66 Narrated by al-Bukhārī in *al-Ṣaḥīḥ*: *Faḍā'il al-Madīna* [The excellent qualities of Medina], Ch.: The inviolability of Medina, 2:661 §1771.
67 Narrated by Abū Dāwūd in *al-Sunan*: *al-Adab* [Proper conduct], Ch.: Regarding promises, 4:299 §4996.
68 Cited by al-'Aẓīm Ābādī in *'Awn al-Ma'būd*, 13:232.
69 Narrated by Ibn Isḥāq in *al-Sīra*, p. 224 (English translation).
70 Narrated by al-Bukhārī in *al-Ṣaḥīḥ*: *Bad' al-Waḥy* [The beginning of inspiration], Ch.: How inspiration began, 1:3 §7.
71 Qur'ān 102:1–2.
72 Ibid., 28:76.
73 Ibid., 28:81.
74 Narrated by al Bukhārī in *al Ṣaḥīḥ*: *al Riqāq* [The softening of hearts], Ch.: Wealth is the wealth of the soul, 5:2368 §6081; and Abū Ya'lā in *al-Musnad*, 11:132 §6259.

75 Narrated by Imam Muslim in *al-Ṣaḥīḥ*: *al-Zakāt* [The Alms-due], Ch.: Sufficiency and contentment, 2:730 §1054; Ibn Dirham in *Kitāb al-Zuhd wa Ṣifat al-Zāhidīn*, 1:56 §93; and Ibn Abī'Āṣim in *Kitāb al-Zuhd*, 1:8.
76 Narrated by al-Tirmidhī in *al-Sunan*: *al-Zuhd* [Abstinence], Ch.: Whoever guards most against the unlawful is the most worshipping among the people, 4:551 §2305.
77 Narrated by al-Bukhārī in *al-Adab al-Mufrad*, p. 237 §681.
78 Narrated by al-Bukhārī in *al-Ṣaḥīḥ*: *al-Tahajjud* [Night-time ritual prayer], Ch.: What has come down about doing voluntary prayers in groups of two cycles of prayer, 1:391 §1109.
79 Qur'ān 53:39.
80 Narrated by al-Kittānī in *al-Tartīb al-idāriyya*, 2:23.
81 Narrated by al-Bayhaqī in *Shu'ab al-Īmān*, 2:81 §1216; Ibn Ja'd in *al-Musnad*, 1:285 §1921; and al-Kittānī in *al-Tartīb al-idāriyya*, 2:23.
82 Qur'ān 76:8–9.
83 Narrated by al-Bukhārī in *al-Ṣaḥīḥ*: *al-Buyū'* [Sales], Ch.: On someone giving a person in difficulties time to pay, 2:731 §1972; and Muslim in *al-Ṣaḥīḥ*: *al-Musāqāt* [Share-cropping], Ch.: The virtue of giving a person in difficulties time to pay, 3:1196 §1562.
84 Narrated by Aḥmad b. Ḥanbal in *al-Musnad*, 1:58 §410.
85 Qur'ān 24:22.
86 Ibid., 3:134.
87 Narrated by al-Bukhārī in *al-Ṣaḥīḥ*: *al-Buyū'* [Sales], Ch.: Making things easy and showing generosity when buying and selling, 2:730 §1970; Ibn Mājah in *al-Sunan*: *al-Tijārāt* [Trade], Ch.: being lenient during transactions, 2:742 §2203; and al-Bayhaqī in *al-Sunan al-Kubrā*, 5:357 §10760.
88 Qur'ān 64:14.
89 Ibid.
90 Ibid., 16:61.
91 Narrated by al-Tirmidhī in *al-Sunan*: *Al-bir, wa al-Ṣilat*: On righteousness and maintaining good relations with relatives, Ch.: What has been related about honouring the believer, 4:378 §2032.
92 Narrated by Imam Muslim in *al-Ṣaḥīḥ*: *Al-bir, wa al-Ṣilat wa al-ādāb*, Piety, affinity and good manners, Ch.: The prohibition of wronging the Muslim, deserting him, and despising him, his goods, his blood and his wealth, 4:1986 §2564; and Ibn Ḥajar al-'Asqalānī in *Fatḥ al-Bārī*, 10:483.
93 Qur'ān 5:6.
94 Ibid., 22:78.
95 Narrated by al-Bukhārī in *al-Ṣaḥīḥ*: *al-Adab* [Proper conduct], Ch.: The words of the Prophet (Allah bless him and give him peace): "Make things easy and do not make them difficult," 5:2269 §5775.
96 Ibid., 5:2269 §5773.
97 Qur'ān 2:280.
98 Narrated by Imam Muslim in *al-Ṣaḥīḥ*: *al-Zuhdwa al-Raqā'iq* [Abstinence and the softening of hearts], Ch.: The lengthy Hadith of Jābir (may Allah be well pleased with him) and the story of Abū al-Yasar, 4:2301–2302 §3006.
99 Qur'ān 5:1.
100 Ibid., 2:177.
101 Narrated by al-Tirmidhī in *al-Sunan*: *al-Aḥkām* [The rules of law], Ch.: What has been related from Allah's Messenger (Allah bless him and give him peace) about reconciliation, 3:634 §1352; al-Suyūṭī in *al-Durr al-Manthūr fī al-Tafsīr bi al-Ma'thūr*, 2:712; and ShāhWalīAllāh, *ḥujjatAllāh al-Bāligha*, 1:663.
102 Narrated by al-Bukhārī in *al-Ṣaḥīḥ*: Bā.: *al-Masājid* [The mosques], Ch.: Mentioning buying and selling on the pulpit in the mosque, 1:174 §444.
103 Qur'ān 4:29.
104 Narrated by Ibn Mājah in *al-Sunan*: *al-Tijārāt* [Trade], Ch.: A transaction with the option to cancel, 2:737 §2185.

105 Narrated by Abū Dāwūd in *al-Sunan*: *al-Buyū'* [Sales], Ch.: Regarding forced sales, 3:255 §3382.
106 Narrated by Abū Dāwūd in *al-Sunan*: *al-Ijāra* [Employment], Ch.: Regarding a man selling what he does not possess, 3:283 §3503.
107 Narrated by al-Bukhārī in *al-Ṣaḥīḥ*: *al-Buyū'* [Sales], Ch.: What is mentioned about selling food and hoarding, 2:750 §2024.
108 Narrated by al-Tirmidhī in *al-Sunan*: *al-Buyū'* [Sales], Ch.: What has been related about sales of *al-gharar* (a sale involving uncertainty or deceit) are disliked, 3:532 §1230.

Bibliography

The Holy Qur'ān

Abū Dāwūd, Sulaymān b. Ash'ath b. Isḥāq b. Bashīr al-Sijistānī (202–275/817–889). *Al-Sunan*. Beirut, Lebanon: Dār al-Fikr, 1414/1994.

Abū Ya'lā, Aḥmad b. 'Alī b. Mathnā b. Yaḥyā b. 'Īsā b. al-Hilāl al-Mūṣilī al-Tamīmī (210–307/825–919). *Al-Musnad*. Damascus, Syria: Dār al-Ma'mūn li al-Turāth, 1404/1984.

'Asqalānī, Ibn Ḥajar Aḥmad b. 'Alī al-. *Fatḥ al-Bārīsharḥ Ṣaḥīḥ al-Bukhārī*. Beirut, Lebanon: Dār al-Ma'rifa, 1379AH.

'Aynī, Badr al-Dīn al-. *'Umdat al-qārīsharḥ Ṣaḥīḥ al-Bukhārī*. Beirut, Lebanon: Dār Iḥyā' al-Turāth al-'Arabī, n.d.

'Aẓīmābādī, Abū al-Ṭayyab Muhammad Shams al-Ḥaqq al-. *'Awn al-Ma'būd Sharḥ Sunan Abī Dāwūd*. Beirut, Lebanon: Dār al-Kutub al-'Ilmiyya, 1415AH.

Bayhaqī, Aḥmad b. al-Ḥusayn al-. *Al-Sunan al-kubrā*. Mecca, Saudi Arabia: Maktaba Dār al-Bāz, 1994.

———. *Shu'ab al-Īmān*. Beirut, Lebanon: Dar al-Kotob al-Ilmiyah, 1990.

Bukhārī, Abū 'Abd Allāh Muhammad b. Ismā'īl b. Ibrahīm b. Mughīra al-. (194–256/810–870). *Al-Adab al-Mufrad*. Beirut, Lebanon: Dār al-Bashā'ir al-Islāmiyya, 1409/1989.

Dārimī, 'Abd Allāh al-. *Al-Sunan*. Beirut, Lebanon: Dār al-Kitāb al-'Arabī, 1407.

Guillaume, Andrea M. *The Life of Muhammad* (a translation of Ibn Isḥāq's *Sīrat Rasūl Allāh*). Oxford: Oxford University Press, 1965.

ḥākim, Muhammad b. 'Abd Allāh al-. *Al-Mustadrak'alā al-ṣaḥīḥayn*. Beirut, Lebanon: Dar al-Kotob al-Ilmiyah, 1990.

Ḥanbal, Aḥmad b. *Al-Musnad*. Beirut, Lebanon: Dar al-Kotob al-Ilmiyah, 1986.

Haythamī, Nūr al-Dīn Abū al-Ḥasan'Alī al-. *Majma' al-zawā'idwamanba' al-fawā'id*. Cairo: Dār al-Rayān li al-Turāth, 1987.

Ibn Abī'āṣim, 'Amr. *Al-Sunna*. Beirut, Lebanon: Al-Maktab al-Islāmī, 1400AH.

Ibn Abī Shayba, 'Abd Allāh b. Muhammad. *Al-Muṣannaf*. Riyadh: Maktaba al-Rushd, 1409AH.

Ibn al-Ja'd, Abū al-Ḥasan'Alī b. Ja'd b. 'Ubayd Hāshimī (133–230/750–845). *Al-Musnad*. Beirut, Lebanon: Mu'assisa Nādir, 1410/1990.

Ibn Dirham, Abū Sa'īd Aḥmad b. Muhammad b. Ziyād b. Bishr b. Dirham. *Al-Zuhd wa Ṣıfat al-Zahıdın*. Ṭanṭa: Dar al-Ṣaḥaba li-Tutrāth, 1408AH.

Ibn Mājah, Abū 'Abd Allāh Muhammad b. Yazīd al-Qazwīnī (209–273/824–887). *Al-Sunan*. Beirut, Lebanon: Dār al-Kutub al-'Ilmiyya, 1419/1998.

Kittānī, Muhammad 'Abd al-Ḥayy b. 'Abd al-Kabīr b. Muhammad al-Ḥasanī al-Idrīsī al- (1305–1382/1888–1962). *Al-Tartīb al-idāriyya*. Beirut, Lebanon: Dar al-Kotob al-Ilmiyah, 1422/2001.

Mundhirī, 'Abd al-'Aẓīm al-. *Al-Targhībwa al-tarhīb*. Beirut, Lebanon: Dar al-Kotob al-Ilmiyah, 1417AH.
Muslim, Ibn al-*Ḥajj*āj Abū al-Ḥasan al-Qushayrī al-Naysābūrī (206–261/821–875). *Al-Ṣaḥīḥ*. Beirut, Lebanon: Dār al-Iḥyā' al-Turāth al-'Arabī, 1997.
Shāh Walī Allāh. *Ḥujjat Allāh al-Bāligha*. Beirut, Lebanon: Dār al-Jīl, 1426 ah/2005 ad.
Suyūṭī, Jalāl al-Dīn Abū al-Faḍl 'Abd al-Raḥmān b. Abī Bakr b. Muhammad b. Abī Bakr b. 'Uthmān al- (849–911/1445–1505). *Al-Durr al-Manthūrfi al-Tafsīr bi al-Ma'thūr*. Beirut, Lebanon: Dār al-Ma'rifa, 1993.
Ṭabarānī, Sulaymān b. Aḥmad al-. *Al-Mu'jam al-awsaṭ*. Cairo: Dār al-Ḥaramayn, 1415AH.
———. *Al-Mu'jam al-kabīr*. Mosul: Maktaba al-'Ulūmwa al-Ḥikam, 1983.
Tirmidhī, Abū 'Īsā Muhammad b. 'Īsā al-. *Al-Sunan*. Beirut, Lebanon: Dār Iḥyā' al-Turāth al-'Arabī, n.d.

9 Sharia rules on giving and receiving loans

9.1 Documentation and witnesses for loan agreement

Whenever we give or take credit, it is preferable to set it down in writing so that no confusion may arise and disagreements may not spoil friendly relations. Allah Almighty says:

يَا أَيُّهَا الَّذِينَ آمَنُواْ إِذَا تَدَايَنتُم بِدَيْنٍ إِلَى أَجَلٍ مُّسَمًّى فَاكْتُبُوهُ وَلْيَكْتُب بَّيْنَكُمْ كَاتِبٌ
بِالْعَدْلِ وَلاَ يَأْبَ كَاتِبٌ أَنْ يَكْتُبَ كَمَا عَلَّمَهُ اللّهُ فَلْيَكْتُبْ وَلْيُمْلِلِ الَّذِي عَلَيْهِ الْحَقُّ وَلْيَتَّقِ
اللّهَ رَبَّهُ وَلاَ يَبْخَسْ مِنْهُ شَيْئًا فَإن كَانَ الَّذِي عَلَيْهِ الْحَقُّ سَفِيهًا أَوْ ضَعِيفًا أَوْ لاَ يَسْتَطِيعُ أَن
يُمِلَّ هُوَ فَلْيُمْلِلْ وَلِيُّهُ بِالْعَدْلِ وَاسْتَشْهِدُواْ شَهِيدَيْنِ من رِّجَالِكُمْ فَإِن لَّمْ يَكُونَا رَجُلَيْنِ فَرَجُلٌ
وَامْرَأَتَانِ مِمَّن تَرْضَوْنَ مِنَ الشُّهَدَاء أَن تَضِلَّ إْحْدَاهُمَا فَتُذَكِّرَ إِحْدَاهُمَا الأُخْرَى وَلاَ يَأْبَ
الشُّهَدَاء إِذَا مَا دُعُواْ وَلاَ تَسْأَمُوْاْ أَن تَكْتُبُوْهُ صَغِيرًا أَو كَبِيرًا إِلَى أَجَلِهِ ذَلِكُمْ أَقْسَطُ عِندَ اللّهِ
وَأَقْومُ لِلشَّهَادَةِ وَأَدْنَى أَلاَّ تَرْتَابُواْ إِلاَّ أَن تَكُونَ تِجَارَةً حَاضِرَةً تُدِيرُونَهَا بَيْنَكُمْ فَلَيْسَ عَلَيْكُمْ
جُنَاحٌ أَلاَّ تَكْتُبُوهَا وَأَشْهِدُوْاْ إِذَا تَبَايَعْتُمْ وَلاَ يُضَآرَّ كَاتِبٌ وَلاَ شَهِيدٌ وَإِن تَفْعَلُواْ فَإِنَّهُ فُسُوقٌ
بِكُمْ وَاتَّقُواْ اللّهَ وَيُعَلِّمُكُمُ اللّهُ وَاللّهُ بِكُلِّ شَيْءٍ عَلِيمٌ

O believers! Whenever you strike deals with one another for a fixed period, reduce the transaction to writing. And the scribe amongst you should write it with justice, and should not refuse to write as Allah has taught him to write. So he should write (i.e., meet the requirements of documentation with utmost honesty, in accordance with Islamic law). And he on whom the liability (i.e., debt) falls should dictate the contents of the contract. And he should fear Allah, Who is his Sustainer, and (whilst writing) he should not diminish anything (from the indebted sum). Then if he who has undertaken the liability is mentally deficient or physically weak or lacks the ability to dictate the contents, his guardian should dictate with fairness. And get two witnesses out of your own men. But if two men are not available, then a man and two women: (they) should be from amongst those whom you like as witnesses (i.e., consider trustworthy), so that if either of the two women forgets, the other may remind her. And the witnesses should not refuse whenever they are called (for evidence). And do not be weary of writing it down for its term, whether the transaction is small or large. This documentation by you is more just in the sight of Allah, and makes evidence more solid and nearer to keeping you from doubt, except that if transactions are hand-to-hand which you carry out amongst yourselves, then there is no sin on you if you do not write it down. And take witnesses whenever you bargain amongst yourselves. And let no harm be done to either the scribe or the witness, but if you do so, it will be sheer disobedience on your part. And keep fearing Allah. And Allah grants you knowledge (of the principles of mutual dealing) and Allah knows everything well.[1]

This is the longest verse in the Qur'ān. It teaches commercial morality in the most practical manner, in order that we might avoid misgivings when making loans.

9.2 The excellent merit of granting loans

Extending interest-free loans to cash-strapped individuals is a matter of great charity since this relieves them of their immediate pressing needs.

Anas b. Mālik (may Allah be pleased with him) reported that Allah's Messenger (Allah bless him and give him peace) said:

عَنْ أَنَسِ بْنِ مَالِكٍ قَالَ: قَالَ رَسُوْلُ اللهِ: رَأَيْتُ لَيْلَةَ أُسْرِيَ بِيْ عَلَى بَابِ الْجَنَّةِ مَكْتُوْبًا: الصَّدَقَةُ بِعَشْرِ أَمْثَالِهَا، وَالْقَرْضُ بِثَمَانِيَةَ عَشَرَ، فَقُلْتُ: يَا جِبْرِيْلُ، مَا بَالُ الْقَرْضِ أَفْضَلُ مِنَ الصَّدَقَةِ؟ قَالَ: لِأَنَّ السَّائِلَ يَسْأَلُ وَعِنْدَهُ، وَالْمُسْتَقْرِضُ لَا يَسْتَقْرِضُ إِلاَّ مِنْ حَاجَةٍ.

"On the night on which I was taken on the Night Journey, I saw written at the gate of Paradise: 'Charity brings a tenfold reward and a loan brings an eighteenfold reward.' I said, 'Jibrīl! Why is a loan better than charity?' He said, 'Because the beggar asks when he has something, but the one who asks for a loan does so only because he is in need.'"[2]

9.3 The etiquette of recovering a loan

Keeping in view the fact that generally the debtor is financially distressed, one should gently make demands for getting back the debt.

Ibn 'Umar and 'Ā'isha (may Allah be well pleased with them) narrated that Allah's Messenger (Allah bless him and give him peace) said:

مَنْ طَالَبَ حَقًّا فَلْيَطْلُبْهُ فِيْ عَفَافٍ وَافٍ أَوْ غَيْرِ وَافٍ.

Whoever demands his rights let him do so in a decent manner as much as he can.[3]

9.4 Repayment of loans

On the one hand, people of faith with abundance of wealth and resources are enjoined to give respite to debtors and to waive loan repayment if they can afford to. But on the other hand, debtors are under obligation to discharge their loans, whether they are large or small, as early as possible. If borrowers had not cleared their debts during their lifetime, the Messenger (Allah bless him and give him peace) was not ready to pray the funeral rites.

In the following narration, the Prophet (Allah bless him and give him peace) did pray over a debtor, when Abū Qatāda (may Allah be pleased with him) had guaranteed the payment of his debt.

عَنْ سَلَمَةَ بْنِ الْأَكْوَعِ g قَالَ: كُنَّا جُلُوْسًا عِنْدَ النَّبِيِّ a إِذْ أُتِيَ بِجَنَازَةٍ، فَقَالُوْا: صَلِّ عَلَيْهَا، فَقَالَ: هَلْ عَلَيْهِ دَيْنٌ؟ قَالُوْا: لَا، قَالَ: فَهَلْ تَرَكَ شَيْئًا؟ قَالُوْا: لَا فَصَلَّى عَلَيْهِ. ثُمَّ أُتِيَ بِجَنَازَةٍ أُخْرَى، فَقَالُوْا: يَا رَسُوْلَ اللّٰهِ، صَلِّ عَلَيْهَا، قَالَ: هَلْ عَلَيْهِ دَيْنٌ؟ قِيلَ: نَعَمْ، قَالَ: فَهَلْ تَرَكَ شَيْئًا؟ قَالُوْا: ثَلَاثَةَ دَنَانِيرَ، فَصَلَّى عَلَيْهَا. ثُمَّ أُتِيَ بِالثَّالِثَةِ، فَقَالُوْا: صَلِّ عَلَيْهَا، قَالَ: هَلْ تَرَكَ شَيْئًا؟ قَالُوْا: لَا، قَالَ: فَهَلْ عَلَيْهِ دَيْنٌ؟ قَالُوْا: ثَلَاثَةُ دَنَانِيرَ، قَالَ: صَلُّوْا عَلَى صَاحِبِكُمْ، قَالَ: أَبُو قَتَادَةَ صَلِّ عَلَيْهِ يَا رَسُوْلَ اللّٰهِ، وَعَلَيَّ دَيْنُهُ، فَصَلَّى عَلَيْهِ.

> Salama b. al-Akwa' reported: "One day we were sitting with the Prophet (Allah bless him and give him peace) when a dead man was brought for burial. They said: 'Pray over him.' He said: 'Has he any debts?' They answered: 'No.' He asked: 'Has he left anything?' They said: 'No,' so he prayed over him. Then another dead man was brought for burial and they said: 'Messenger of Allah, pray over him.' He asked: 'Has he any debts?' It was said: 'Yes.' He said: 'Has he left anything?' They replied: 'Three dinars.' He prayed over him. Then a third was brought and they said: 'Pray over him.' He asked: 'Has he left anything?' They answered: 'No.' He asked: 'Has he any debts?' They said: 'Three dinars.' He said: 'Pray over your companion.' Abū Qatāda (may Allah be pleased with him) said: 'Messenger of Allah, pray over him and I will pay his debt.' So he prayed over him."[4]

The Tradition exhorts the faithful to help in the payment of loans of the deceased who were unable to clear their debts during life.

If anyone defaults in paying their loans, their virtues will be reduced and they will face hardships in the Afterlife unless the Lord shows mercy.

Ibn 'Umar (may Allah be well pleased with him and his father) related Allah's Messenger (Allah bless him and give him pcacc) said:

مَنْ مَاتَ وَعَلَيْهِ دِينَارٌ أَوْ دِرْهَمٌ قُضِيَ مِنْ حَسَنَاتِهِ لَيْسَ ثَمَّ دِينَارٌ وَلَا دِرْهَمٌ.

> Whoever dies owing a *dinar* or a *dirham,* it will be paid back from his good deeds, because then there will be no *dinar* or *dirham.*[5]

Thawbān (may Allah be pleased with him) narrated that Allah's Messenger (Allah bless him and give him peace) said:

مَنْ فَارَقَ الرُّوحُ الْجَسَدَ وَهُوَ بَرِيءٌ مِنْ ثَلَاثٍ: الْكَنْزِ، وَالْغُلُولِ، وَالدَّيْنِ، دَخَلَ الْجَنَّةَ.

If anyone's soul departs from his body while he is free of three – buried treasure, goods stolen from the gains of war and debt – he will enter Paradise.[6]

A severe warning is addressed to debtors who delay the clearance of debts until their dying moment.

Abū Hurayra (may Allah be pleased with him) reported that the Prophet (Allah bless him and give him peace) said:

نَفْسُ الْمُؤْمِنِ مُعَلَّقَةٌ بِدَيْنِهِ حَتَّى يُقْضَى عَنْهُ.

The believer's soul is suspended by his debt until it is settled for him.[7]

9.5 Allowing delay to a penniless person

After borrowing money, debtors may go through hard times and may be unable to discharge the debt. Such people should be granted a delay until a time of ease. On helping out the debtor, the Qur'ān goes one step further: if the creditor remits the debt entirely by way of charity, this will be a benevolent and much commendable deed.

وَإِن كَانَ ذُو عُسْرَةٍ فَنَظِرَةٌ إِلَىٰ مَيْسَرَةٍ وَأَن تَصَدَّقُواْ خَيْرٌ لَّكُمْ إِن كُنتُمْ تَعْلَمُونَ

And if a debtor is under financial stress, he should be given respite till he feels at ease to pay. And your forgoing (the loan) is better for you if you know (what significance it has in the sight of Allah to console the poor).[8]

The faithful are urged to help out their fellow beings with interest-free loans. If a debtor has fallen on hard times and is not in a position to return the loan, it is a great virtue to grant respite to him or her. The Divine Essence will be bountiful towards such generous people, as per the words of the Messenger (Allah bless him and give him peace):

عَنْ بُرَيْدَةَ الْأَسْلَمِيِّ عَنِ النَّبِيِّ a قَالَ: مَنْ أَنْظَرَ مُعْسِرًا كَانَ لَهُ بِكُلِّ يَوْمٍ صَدَقَةٌ، وَمَنْ أَنْظَرَهُ بَعْدَ حِلِّهِ كَانَ لَهُ مِثْلُهُ فِي كُلِّ يَوْمٍ صَدَقَةٌ.

Burayda al-Aslamī reported that the Prophet (Allah bless him and give him peace) said: "Whoever gives respite to one in difficulty will have (the reward of) an act of charity for each day. Whoever gives him respite after payment becomes due will have (the reward of) an act of charity equal to (the amount of the loan) for each day."[9]

Those who make allowances for poor debtors will find Allah generous in the Hereafter. They will be under the shade of Allah's Throne on the Day of Resurrection when others will be exposed to the scorching heat of the sun.

Abū al-Yasar (may Allah be pleased with him), the Companion of the Prophet, reported that Allah's Messenger (Allah bless him and give him peace) said:

مَنْ أَحبَّ أَنْ يُظِلَّهُ اللهُ فِي ظِلِّهِ، فَلْيُنْظِرْ مُعْسِرًا أَوْ لِيَضَعْ لَهُ.

Whoever would like Allah to shade him with His shade, let him give respite to one in difficulty, or waive repayment of the loan.[10]

On this theme, the following is a faith-inspiring narrative which demonstrates Allah's generosity towards people who are kind to the downtrodden. Abū Hurayra (may Allah be pleased with him) reported that Allah's Messenger (Allah bless him and give him peace) said:

إِنَّ رَجُلًا لَمْ يَعْمَلْ خَيْرًا قَطُّ وَكَانَ يُدَايِنُ النَّاسَ. فَيَقُولُ لِرَسُولِهِ: خُذْ مَا تَيَسَّرَ وَاتْرُكْ مَا عَسُرَ، وَتَجَاوَزْ، لَعَلَّ اللهَ تَعَالَى أَنْ يَتَجَاوَزَ عَنَّا. فَلَمَّا هَلَكَ، قَالَ اللهُ لَهُ: هَلْ عَمِلْتَ خَيْرًا قَطُّ؟ قَالَ: لَا، إِلَّا أَنَّهُ كَانَ لِيْ غُلَامٌ، وَكُنْتُ أُدَايِنُ النَّاسَ، فَإِذَا بَعَثْتُهُ لِيَتَقَاضَى، قُلْتُ لَهُ: خُذْ مَا تَيَسَّرَ وَاتْرُكْ مَا عَسُرَ، وَتَجَاوَزْ، لَعَلَّ اللهَ يَتَجَاوَزُ عَنَّا. قَالَ اللهُ تَعَالَى: قَدْ تَجَاوَزْتُ عَنْكَ.

There was a man who was extremely lax in performing good deeds and he loaned money to people. (When he loaned money out) he would instruct his secretary, "Take (in repayment of a loan) what is easy and leave what is difficult and overlook it, for perhaps Allah Most High will overlook us (our offences)." When the man perished, Allah said to him, "Did you ever do any good actions?" The man replied, "No, but I did have a young servant and I used to loan money to people, so when I sent him to collect the money owed, I would say to him, "Take what is easy and leave what is difficult and overlook it, for perhaps Allah Most High will overlook us." Allah then said to him, "I have overlooked your faults."[11]

People of means who visit the House of Allah regularly in order to perform pilgrimage, both major and minor, while exploiting people, must meditate on the morals of this Tradition and the Divine arrangement of forgiving humans. Those of us who peevishly complain of being beset by hardships and trouble, day in and day out, ought to take into consideration the Divine style of relieving pain and suffering: unremitting feelings of discomfort depart from the people who devote themselves to the service of others.

According to Abū Hurayra (may Allah be pleased with him), the Prophet (Allah bless him and give him peace) said:

مَنْ نَفَّسَ عَنْ مُؤْمِنٍ كُرْبَةً مِنْ كُرَبِ الدُّنْيَا، نَفَّسَ اللهُ عَنْهُ كُرْبَةً مِنْ كُرَبِ يَوْمِ الْقِيَامَةِ. وَمَنْ يَسَّرَ عَلَى مُعْسِرٍ، يَسَّرَ اللهُ عَلَيْهِ فِي الدُّنْيَا وَالْآخِرَةِ. وَمَنْ سَتَرَ مُسْلِمًا سَتَرَهُ اللهُ فِي الدُّنْيَا وَالْآخِرَةِ. وَاللهُ فِي عَوْنِ الْعَبْدِ مَا كَانَ الْعَبْدُ فِي عَوْنِ أَخِيهِ.

> If someone relieves a believer of the agony of this world, Allah will relieve him of one of the agonies of the Day of Resurrection. If someone makes life easy for a person in distress, Allah will make life easy for him in this world and the Hereafter. If someone covers the faults of a Muslim in this world, Allah will cover his faults in this world and in the Hereafter. Allah does not cease helping His servant as long as His servant continues helping his brother.[12]

This Prophetic Tradition holds out inducements for such virtuous actions as helping the faithful in their hour of distress, concealing their shortcomings and failures, and doing one's best to lift them out of their distress. This Tradition is meant to cement relations among believing Muslims on the basis of mutual love, harmony and approval of the Almighty.

9.6 Return of the loan in a better way

The Messenger (Allah bless him and give him peace) used to pay back his debts to lenders generously by timely return of the money and by paying extra amount to what was actually lended to him.

It is narrated that Abū Hurayra (may Allah be pleased with him) said:

اِسْتَقْرَضَ رَسُوْلُ اللهِ a سِنًّا فَأَعْطَى سِنًّا فَوْقَهُ وَقَالَ خِيَارُكُمْ مَحَاسِنُكُمْ قَضَاءً.

> Allah's Messenger (Allah bless him and give him peace) borrowed a camel, and gave back a camel that was better than it, and he said: "The best of you are those who are the best in paying off debts."[13]

Returning a better animal or an article than the one taken is permissible, if it is not a condition of the loan and if the borrower makes the gift of his or her own accord. Imam Yaḥyā b. Sharaf al-Nawawī writes, providing an explanation on the preceding Hadith, that returning what was borrowed in a better form is a praiseworthy act and was the normative practice of Allah's Messenger (Allah bless him and give him peace).[14]

The theme of repaying a loan in a better manner to the creditor occurs in the following Tradition.

عَنْ أَبِيْ هُرَيْرَةَ أَنَّ رَجُلًا تَقَاضَى رَسُوْلَ اللهِ فَأَغْلَظَ لَهُ، فَهَمَّ بِهِ أَصْحَابُهُ، فَقَالَ رَسُوْلُ
اللهِ a: دَعُوْهُ فَإِنَّ لِصَاحِبِ الْحَقِّ مَقَالًا، ثُمَّ قَالَ: اشْتَرُوْا لَهُ بَعِيرًا فَأَعْطُوْهُ إِيَّاهُ، فَطَلَبُوهُ فَلَمْ
يَجِدُوا إِلاَّ سِنًّا أَفْضَلَ مِنْ سِنِّهِ، فَقَالَ: اشْتَرُوْهُ فَأَعْطُوْهُ إِيَّاهُ فَإِنَّ خَيْرَكُمْ أَحْسَنُكُمْ قَضَاءً.

Abū Hurayra (may Allah be pleased with him) narrated that a man behaved in a rude manner while trying to collect a debt from Allah's Messenger (Allah bless him and give him peace). So his Companions were about to harm him. Allah's Messenger (Allah bless him and give him peace) said: "Leave him, for indeed the owner of the right has the right to speak." Then the Messenger (Allah bless him and give him peace) directed (them): "Purchase a camel for him and give it to him." So they searched but they did not find a camel but of a better age than his camel. So the Messenger (Allah bless him and give him peace) said: "Buy it and give it to him, for indeed the best of you is the best in repaying."[15]

Once al-Sā'ib (may Allah be pleased with him) said to the Prophet (Allah bless him and give him peace):

كُنْتَ شَرِيْكِيْ فِيْ الْجَاهِلِيَّةِ فَكُنْتَ خَيْرَ شَرِيْكٍ لاَ تُدَارِيْنِي وَلاَ تُمَارِيْنِي.

You were my partner in the pre-Islamic period and you were the best of partners. You did not contend or dispute with me.[16]

The secret of salvation in the Afterlife lies in adopting and demonstrating good manners and becoming behaviour.

Ibn Mas'ūd (may Allah be pleased with him) reported that Allah's Messenger (Allah bless him and give him peace) said:

حُرِّمَ عَلَى النَّارِ كُلُّ هَيِّنٍ لَيِّنٍ سَهْلٍ قَرِيْبٍ مِنَ النَّاسِ.

Everyone who is gentle and kindly, of an easy disposition and approachable is kept away from the Hellfire.[17]

9.7 Juristic conditions for contracting a loan

Qarḍ – allowing somebody to borrow something on condition that its equal is returned afterwards – is recommended in Islam. The Qur'ānic instructions on contracting loans are as follows:

وَلْيُمْلِلِ الَّذِي عَلَيْهِ الْحَقُّ

And he on whom the liability (i.e., debt) falls should dictate the contents of the contract.[18]

مِن بَعْدِ وَصِيَّةٍ يُوصِينَ بِهَا أَوْ دَيْنٍ

(This division shall also be accomplished) after the will which is made without any prejudice towards the heirs or after the (payment of) debt.[19]

It is established that that the faithful may engage in lending and borrowing money or tangible articles, seeing that even the Prophet (Allah bless him and give him peace) himself borrowed money.

In business transactions, at times, traders get loans from one another. They should know the legal rulings on getting and advancing loans. Some important conditions for the validity of a loan are stated here:

- The contracting parties must be qualified: they must be sane and of Islamic legal age; they must not be coerced.
- The item must be specific, or an unspecific item of a definite type of asset, for example, lending this pound, or one pound from these several pounds.
- The asset must be worthy of ownership from the religious perspective, so it is not lawful to lend something that is unlawful to possess, such as intoxicants or swine.
- One's disposal over one's assets must not be suspended.
- The borrower must receive the item. If the contract is made and the borrower does not receive the item, he or she is not regarded as the owner. In such a case, the lender may not demand the payment of the asset he or she had "advanced."
- In the matter of debts, either party may insert any reasonable condition. However, the lending party may not derive a material benefit from it. If any lender does so, his or her benefit will be considered usurious.

The borrower is under obligation to take good care of the borrowed asset so that he or she may return it in a good condition: the Word of Allah charges the faithful to render back the trusts to those whom they are due.

إِنَّ اللَّهَ يَأْمُرُكُمْ أَن تُؤَدُّوا الْأَمَانَاتِ إِلَىٰ أَهْلِهَا

Allah commands you that you restore deposits to their owners.[20]

- If the borrower uses the loaned assets for something other than the purpose for which he or she borrowed them, and they are damaged, he or she is responsible for making good the damage.
- If an item is damaged whilst being used carefully, the borrower is not required to pay a penalty.
- At the time of receiving money or an asset as a loan, the borrower must intend to to abide by the loan agreement and return the borrowed money or asset within due time.

Notes

1 Qur'ān 2:282.
2 Narrated by Ibn Mājah in *al-Sunan*: *al-Ṣadaqāt* [Charitable donations], Ch.: Lending, 2:812 §2431; and al-Ḥalabī in *al-Sīrat al-ḥalabiyya*, 2:135.
3 Narrated by Ibn Mājah in *al-Sunan*: *al-Ṣadaqāt* [Charitable donations], Ch.: Asking in a polite manner and taking one's rights without behaving in an indecent manner, 2:809 §2421; and al-Kinānī in *Miṣbāḥ al-Zujāja*, 3:66 §1395.
4 Qur'ān 4:100.
Narrated by al-Bukhārī in *al-Ṣaḥīḥ*: *ḥawāla* [Debt transfer], Ch.: It is permitted for the debts of a dead person to be transferred to someone else, 2:800 §2168.
5 Narrated by Ibn Mājah in *al-Sunan*: *al-Ṣadaqāt* [Charitable donations], Ch.: Stern warning concerning debt, 2:807 §2414.
6 Narrated by Ibn Mājah in *al-Sunan*: 4:138 §1573.
7 Narrated by al-Tirmidhī in *al-Sunan*: *al-Janā'iz* [Funeral Ceremonies], Ch.: What has been related that the believer's soul is suspended by his debt until it is settled for him, 3:389–390 §1079.
8 Qur'ān 2:280.
9 Narrated by Ibn Mājah in *al-Sunan*: *al-Ṣadaqāt* [Charitable donations], Ch.: Giving respite to one who is in difficulty, 2:808 §2418.
10 Ibid., 2:808 §2419.
11 Narrated by al-Nasā'ī in *al-Sunan: al-Buyū'* [Sales], Ch.: On dealing with others well and being kind in seeking repayment of loans, 7:381 §3696; and al-Ḥākim in *al-Mustadrak*, 2:33§2223.
12 Narrated by Imam Muslim in *al-Ṣaḥīḥ*: *Dhikr, du'ā', tawba wa istighfār*: Remembrance [*dhikr*], supplication [*du'ā'*], repentance [*tawba*] and seeking forgiveness [*istighfār*], Ch.: The excellent merit of assembling at the recitation of the Qur'ān, 4:2074 §2699; al-Tirmidhī in *al-Sunan*: *al-Ḥudūd [The penalties]* Ch.: What has come to us concerning the pardoning of the Muslim, 4:34.
13 Narrated by Imam Muslim in *al-Ṣaḥīḥ*: *al-Musāqāt* [Sharecropping], Ch.: It is permissible to lend animals and it is recommended to pay in full, giving something better than that which is owed 3:1225 §1601.
14 Yaḥyā al-Nawawī, *Sharḥ Ṣaḥīḥ Muslim*, 12:7.
15 Narrated by al-Tirmidhī in *al-Sunan*: *al-Buyū'* [Sales], Ch.: What has been related about taking a camel or other animal on loan, 3:608 §1317.
16 Narrated by Ibn Mājah in *al-Sunan*, *al-Tijārāt* [Trade], Ch.: Partnership and profit sharing, 2:768 §2287.
17 Narrated by Aḥmad b. Ḥanbal in *al-Musnad*, 1:415 §3938; and Ibn Ḥibbān in *al-Ṣaḥīḥ*, 2:215 §469.
18 Qur'ān 2:282.
19 Ibid., 4:12.
20 Ibid., 4:58.

Bibliography

The Holy Qur'ān

Bukhārī, Abū'Abd Allāh Muhammad b. Ismā'īl b. Ibrahīm b. Mughīra al-. (194–256/810–870). *Al-Adab al-Mufrad*. Beirut, Lebanon: Dār al-Bashā'ir al-Islāmiyya, 1409/1989.

Ḥākim, Muhammad b. 'Abd Allāh al-. *Al-Mustadrak'alā al-ṣaḥīḥayn*. Beirut, Lebanon: Dar al-Kotob al-Ilmiyah, 1990.

Ḥalabī, 'Alī b. Burhān al-Dīn al- (d. 1404AH). *Al-Sīra al-ḥalabiyya*. Beirut, Lebanon: Dār al-Ma'rifa, 1400AH.

Ḥanbal, Aḥmad b. *Al-Musnad*. Beirut, Lebanon: Dar al-Kotob al-Ilmiyah, 1986.

Ibn Mājah, Abū 'Abd Allāh Muhammad b. Yazīd al-Qazwīnī (209–273/824–887). *Al-Sunan*. Beirut, Lebanon: Dār al-Kutub al-'Ilmiyya, 1419/1998.

Kinānī, Aḥmad b. Abī Bakr b. Ismā'īl al- (762–840AH). *Miṣbāḥ al-Zujāja fī Zawa'īd b. Mājah*. Beirut, Lebanon: Dār al-'Arabiyya, 1403AH.

Muslim, Ibn al-*Ḥajj*āj Abū al-Ḥasan al-Qushayrī al-Naysābūrī (206–261/821–875). *Al-Ṣaḥīḥ*. Beirut, Lebanon: Dār al-Iḥyā' al-Turāth al-'Arabī, 1997.

Nasā'ī, Aḥmad b. Shu'ayb Abū 'Abd al-Raḥmān al- (215–303/830–915). *al-Sunan*. Beirut, Lebanon: Dār al-Kutub al-'Ilmiyya, 1416/1995.

Nawawī, Abū Zakariyyā Yaḥyā b. Sharaf b. Murrī b. al-Ḥasan b. al-Ḥusayn b. Muhammad b. Jumu'a b. Ḥizām al- (631–677/1233–1278). *Riyāḍ al-Ṣāliḥīn min Kalām Sayyid al-Mursalīn*. Beirut, Lebanon: Dār al-Khayr, 1412/1991.

Tirmidhī, Abū 'Īsā Muhammad b. 'Īsā al-. *Al-Sunan*. Beirut, Lebanon: Dār Iḥyā' al-Turāth al-'Arabī, n.d.

10 *Zakāt*

Wealth and personal effects are, from the Islamic perspective, the blessings of Allah, the Cherisher and Sustainer of the worlds. The Almighty intends for people of means to spend their material resources on the needy, in order to maintain the circulation of wealth in society. One way to keep cash circulating is through *zakāt*, the system of Islamic obligatory charitable donations.

The Arabic word *zakāt* literally means "increase and growth." The implication of almsgiving is that one's wealth will grow as it is expended on the needs of the downtrodden; Allah rewards people's munificence in the world without diminishing their recompense in the next. Almsgiving was declared an obligatory duty in the second year of Hijra in the month of Shawwāl.

For the faithful, *zakāt* is not a general tax, as some non-Muslims mischaracterize it. Instead, it is a religious obligation to demonstrate one's love for the Almighty through deeds of charity and concern for the downtrodden sections of society: the poor, orphans and widows.

10.1 Importance of *zakāt*

With its innumerable facets, *zakāt* is a bond between those that have surplus wealth and the needy within society. An effective way to redistribute wealth is through payment of prescribed alms. Almsgiving is a means of stimulating the continuous flow of cash.

لَا يَكُونَ دُولَةً بَيْنَ الْأَغْنِيَاءِ مِنكُمْ

(This distribution system is to ensure) that (the whole wealth) may not circulate (only) amongst the wealthy among you (but should circulate amongst all the classes of society).[1]

The payers of compulsory almsgiving must not act as though they are doing a favour to the needy, since it is the affluent individuals' obligation to help the poor.

وَفِي أَمْوَالِهِمْ حَقٌّ لِّلسَّائِلِ وَالْمَحْرُومِ○

And in their wealth was appointed a due share for the beggars and the destitute (i.e., all the needy).[2]

The preceding verse implies that the Islamic law discourages the exchange of wealth among the affluent alone, as well as a lavish lifestyle, and charges believers to raise the living standards of the poor as the destitute have a Divinely decreed right over their personal possessions.

Allah Almighty enjoins the faithful to pay the prescribed charity on their wealth if they possess the *niṣāb* (the minimum amount a Muslim must have to be obligated to pay *zakāt*). Mandatory charitable donations are a great help for those of our fellows who fall on hard times.

وَأَقِيمُوا الصَّلَاةَ وَآتُوا الزَّكَاةَ وَأَطِيعُوا الرَّسُولَ لَعَلَّكُمْ تُرْحَمُونَ

And establish (the system of) prayers and (ensure) the payment of zakāt *(the Alms-due) and accomplish (absolute) obedience to the Messenger (Allah bless him and give him peace) so that you may be granted mercy.*[3]

Elsewhere, Allah Almighty says in this regard:

وَأَقِيمُوا الصَّلَاةَ وَآتُوا الزَّكَاةَ وَأَقْرِضُوا اللَّهَ قَرْضًا حَسَنًا وَمَا تُقَدِّمُوا لِأَنفُسِكُم مِّنْ خَيْرٍ تَجِدُوهُ
عِندَ اللَّهِ هُوَ خَيْرًا وَأَعْظَمَ أَجْرًا

And establish Prayer and pay zakāt *(the Alms-due) and lend Allah a goodly loan. And whatever good you will send forward for yourselves, you will find it in the presence of Allah much better and in reward still greater.*[4]

Zakāt (compulsory alms-giving) is the third pillar of Islam, as noted in the following Tradition. On the obligatory nature of the prescribed charity, Ibn 'Umar (may Allah be pleased with him and his father) narrated that Allah's Messenger (Allah bless him and give him peace) said:

بُنِيَ الْإِسْلَامُ عَلَى خَمْسٍ: شَهَادَةِ أَنْ لَا إِلَهَ إِلَّا اللهُ وَأَنَّ مُحَمَّدًا رَسُوْلُ اللهِ، وَإِقَامِ الصَّلَاةِ،
وَإِيْتَاءِ الزَّكَاةِ، وَالْحَجِّ، وَصَوْمِ رَمَضَانَ.

Islam has been founded on five things: (1) the testimony that there is no God but Allah and that Muhammad is Allah's Messenger (Allah bless him and give him peace), (2) performance of the ritual Prayer, (3) payment of *zakāt* (the Alms-due), (4) the Pilgrimage, and (5) the fast of Ramaḍān.[5]

Those who are faithful pay *zakāt* and will enter the Garden of Paradise.

According to Abū al-Dardā' (may Allah be pleased with him), Allah's Messenger (Allah bless him and give him peace) said:

خَمْسٌ مَنْ جَاءَ بِهِنَّ مَعَ إِيْمَانٍ دَخَلَ الْجَنَّةَ. مَنْ حَافَظَ عَلَى الصَّلَوَاتِ الْخَمْسِ عَلَى وُضُوْئِهِنَّ، وَرُكُوْعِهِنَّ، وَسُجُوْدِهِنَّ، وَمَوَاقِيْتِهِنَّ، وَصَامَ رَمَضَانَ، وَحَجَّ الْبَيْتَ إِنِ اسْتَطَاعَ إِلَيْهِ سَبِيْلاً، وَأَعْطَى الزَّكَاةَ طَيِّبَةً بِهَا نَفْسُهُ وَأَدَّى الْأَمَانَةَ.

Someone who performs five things will enter the Garden of Paradise. That is someone who (1) observes the five ritual Prayers (punctually and thoroughly) taking care of minor ritual ablution *[wuḍū']*, bowing *[rukū']* and prostration *[sujūd)*, and the set times; (2) keeps the fast of Ramaḍān; (3) performs the Pilgrimage to the Sacred House, if he is capable of making a journey to it; (4) pays *zakāt* (the Alms-due) to purify himself (his lower self); and (5) fulfils the trust.[6]

Discharging the obligation of *zakāt* purifies one of the faults of stinginess and greed. Also, generous givers to charity protect their wealth by attracting Divine blessings and driving evil away from it.

According to al-Ḥasan (may Allah be pleased with him), Allah's Messenger (Allah bless him and give him peace) said:

حَصِّنُوْا أَمْوَالَكُمْ بِالزَّكَاةِ، وَدَاوُوْا أَمْرَاضَكُمْ بِالصَّدَقَةِ، وَاسْتَقْبِلُوْا أَمْوَاجَ الْبَلَاءِ بِالدُّعَاءِ وَالتَّضَرُّعِ.

Fortify your properties with the obligatory Alms-due, cure your illnesses with charitable donation, and confront the waves of tribulation with supplication and tearful entreaty![7]

10.2 Insufficiency of paying *zakāt*

Apart from *zakāt*, a compulsory duty, there are other rights due from one's personal effects such as helping the deprived and the destitute in their difficult situations. The following Scriptural verse establishes the rights of the needy over the wealth of the affluent, even after they have paid 2.5% of their total savings after a year has passed, as *zakat*.

وَفِي أَمْوَالِهِمْ حَقٌّ لِّلسَّائِلِ وَالْمَحْرُومِ ○

And in their wealth was appointed a due share for the beggars and the destitute (i.e., all the needy).[8]

Elsewhere Allah Almighty said:

لَن تَنَالُواْ الْبِرَّ حَتَّىٰ تُنفِقُواْ مِمَّا تُحِبُّونَ

You can never attain piety unless you spend (in the cause of Allah) out of that which you like the most.[9]

Helping the needy by providing them with necessities of life is an act of a believer, which is much appreciated by Allah Almighty and Prophet (Allah bless him and give him peace) as it is evident by the following tradition of the Messenger (Allah bless him and give him peace):

أَنَّ فِي الْمَالِ حَقًّا سِوَى الزَّكَاةِ.

Indeed there is a duty on wealth apart from *zakāt* (the Alms-due).[10]

10.3 Two kinds of *zakāt*

There are two kinds of *zakāt*: on wealth (*zakāt al-māl)* and on the self (*zakāt al-fiṭr)*. Both are incumbent upon people of resources. Regarding almsgiving on wealth, there are scores of verses in the Qur'ān.

Two of them are cited here:

وَأَقِيمُواْ الصَّلَاةَ وَآتُواْ الزَّكَاةَ وَارْكَعُواْ مَعَ الرَّاكِعِينَ

And establish Prayer and pay zakāt *(the Alms-due) regularly and kneel down (together) with those who kneel down.*[11]

وَأَقِيمُواْ الصَّلَاةَ وَآتُواْ الزَّكَاةَ وَمَا تُقَدِّمُواْ لِأَنفُسِكُم مِّنْ خَيْرٍ تَجِدُوهُ عِندَ اللهِ إِنَّ اللهَ بِمَا تَعْمَلُونَ بَصِيرٌ

And (always) establish Prayer and pay zakāt *(the Alms-due) regularly. And whatever virtue you will send ahead, you shall find it with Allah. Surely, Allah is watching all that you are doing.*[12]

Almsgiving on the self is an amount of food or money which is given in charity at the end of Ramaḍān before the 'Īd prayers. A Tradition reads in this regard:

عَنِ ابْنِ عُمَرَ k، قَالَ: فَرَضَ رَسُوْلُ اللهِ a زَكَاةَ الْفِطْرِ صَاعًا مِنْ تَمْرٍ، أَوْ صَاعًا مِنْ شَعِيْرٍ، عَلَى الْعَبْدِ وَالْحُرِّ، وَالذَّكَرِ وَالْأُنْثَى، وَالصَّغِيْرِ وَالْكَبِيْرِ مِنَ الْمُسْلِمِيْنَ، وَأَمَرَ بِهَا أَنْ تُؤَدَّى قَبْلَ خُرُوْجِ النَّاسِ إِلَى الصَّلَاةِ.

> According to Ibn 'Umar (may Allah be pleased with him and his father), Allah's Messenger (Allah bless him and give him peace) made *zakāt al-fiṭr* incumbent on the Muslims – slave and free, male and female, young and old – being a *ṣā'* (approximately 3 kilograms) of dates or a *ṣā'* of barley. He commanded that it be paid before people went out to the prayer.[13]

One must pay *zakāt al-fiṭr* prior to offering the 'Īd prayer, otherwise, it will be just a voluntary donation.

Ibn 'Abbās (may Allah be pleased with him) narrated:

فَرَضَ رَسُوْلُ اللّٰه a زَكَاةَ الْفِطْرِ طُهْرَةً لِلصَّائِمِ مِنَ اللَّغْوِ وَالرَّفَثِ، وَطُعْمَةً لِلْمَسَاكِيْنِ. مَنْ أَدَّاهَا قَبْلَ الصَّلاَةِ فَهِيَ زَكَاةٌ مَقْبُوْلَةٌ وَمَنْ أَدَّاهَا بَعْدَ الصَّلاَةِ فَهِيَ صَدَقَةٌ مِنَ الصَّدَقَاتِ.

> Allah's Messenger (Allah bless him and give him peace) enjoined *zakāt al-fiṭr* to purify the fasting person from idle talk and obscenities, and to feed the poor. Whoever pays it before the *Īd* prayer, it is an accepted *zakāt*, and whoever pays it after the prayer, it is (ordinary) charity.[14]

10.4 Benefits of *zakāt*

If people faithfully give *zakāt*, they may redeem their souls, merit rewards and contribute greatly towards building society by lifting people out of poverty. Some advantages of donating to charity are listed here.

10.4.1 Self-purification

Zakāt purifies the individual who sincerely gives the obligatory alms. The fulfilment of this religious duty preserves the giver from self-absorption and narcissism.

وَسَيُجَنَّبُهَا الْأَتْقَى○الَّذِي يُؤْتِي مَالَهُ يَتَزَكَّى○

> *But the most pious one shall be saved from this (Fire), who gives his wealth away (in the cause of Allah) to attain purity (of his soul and assets).*[15]

The Messenger (Allah bless him and give him peace) cleansed and purified the believers among associates by taking alms out of their property. In this regard Allah instructed the Prophet as follows:

خُذْ مِنْ أَمْوَالِهِمْ صَدَقَةً تُطَهِّرُهُمْ وَتُزَكِّيهِم بِهَا وَصَلِّ عَلَيْهِمْ

> *Collect alms (zakāt – the Alms-due) from their wealth so that by these (alms) you may purify them (of their sins) and (by this purification of faith and riches) bestow upon them blessing and pray for them.*[16]

10.4.2 Generosity

Since humans are naturally greedy, their quest for more material gains knows no bounds if they do not cleanse themselves. Believers who part with their money by way of fulfilling the Divine command of giving to charity are preserved from the niggardliness of their souls. How the payment of the prescribed alms helps one overcome his or natural stinginess is described in the Qur'ān:

وَمَن يُوقَ شُحَّ نَفْسِهِ فَأُوْلَئِكَ هُمُ الْمُفْلِحُونَ

And he who is saved from the miserliness of his (ill-commanding) self, it is they who are successful and victorious.[17]

10.4.3 Examining the degree of love for Allah, the Exalted

The believers' love for Allah is tested when they separate themselves from the worldly goods they apprise. Putting them to the test, the Beloved asks them to give up their most prized possessions:

إِنَّ اللهَ اشْتَرَى مِنَ الْمُؤْمِنِينَ أَنفُسَهُمْ وَأَمْوَالَهُم بِأَنَّ لَهُمُ الْجَنَّةَ

Surely, Allah has bought from the believers their souls and wealth in return for (the promise of) Paradise for them.[18]

The truth of one's claim to love the Divine requires one to forgo the desires of the self, for the path of Allah.

لَن تَنَالُواْ الْبِرَّ حَتَّىٰ تُنفِقُواْ مِمَّا تُحِبُّونَ

You can never attain piety unless you spend (in the cause of Allah) out of that which you like the most.[19]

10.4.4 Restoration of social and religious values

The payment of the prescribed alms to the destitute restores social and religious values with the result that they manage to live with dignity and sense of worth. By alleviating conditions of extreme poverty, altruism unites people's hearts. If financially crushed people languish in impoverishment, they might even lose their faith. Allah's Messenger (Allah bless him and give him peace) said:

كَادَ الْفَقْرُ أَنْ يَكُوْنَ كُفْرًا.

Poverty may result in infidelity.[20]

10.4.5 Unburdening troubled souls

Through the act of financial support, a believer seeking Divine approbation relieves the anxiety and stress of families in a state of extreme poverty. Allah Almighty, in turn, will assuage their fears and hardships on the Day of Rising. The Prophet (Allah bless him and give him peace) said:

مَنْ نَفَّسَ عَنْ مُؤْمِنٍ كُرْبَةً مِنْ كُرَبِ الدُّنْيَا، نَفَّسَ اللّٰهُ عَنْهُ كُرْبَةً مِنْ كُرَبِ الْآخِرَةِ، . . .
وَاللّٰهُ فِيْ عَوْنِ الْعَبْدِ مَا كَانَ الْعَبْدُ فِيْ عَوْنِ أَخِيْهِ.

> Whoever relieves a Muslim of a burden from the burdens of the world, Allah will relieve him of a burden from the burdens of the Hereafter. . . . And Allah is engaged in helping the servant as long as the servant is engaged in helping his brother.[21]

10.4.6 Circulation of wealth

As *zakāt* is a means of redistributing resources, this virtue bridges the divide between rich and poor. The Qur'ān says in this regard:

لَا يَكُونَ دُولَةً بَيْنَ الْأَغْنِيَاءِ مِنكُمْ

> *(This distribution system is to ensure) that (the whole wealth) may not circulate (only) amongst the rich of you (but should circulate amongst all the classes of society).*[22]

10.4.7 Brotherhood

The act of helping poor fellow beings brings about brotherhood in the true sense of the word.

فَإِن تَابُواْ وَأَقَامُواْ الصَّلَاةَ وَآتَوُاْ الزَّكَاةَ فَإِخْوَانُكُمْ فِي الدِّينِ

> *(Even) then if they repent and establish Prayer and pay zakāt (the Alms-due), they are your brothers in* Dīn *(Religion).*[23]

10.5 Who shall give *zakāt*?

With the aim of distinguishing the downtrodden from the well-off, the Messenger (Allah bless him and give him peace) established a limit known as *niṣāb*. When one's net worth surpasses the minimum exemption limit, any excess is subject to the alms prescribed. The payment of *zakāt* (an obligatory charity) is mandatory for the faithful who:

1 Possess the prescribed *niṣāb* amount for a year; the Prophet (Allah bless him and give him peace) said in this regard:

مَنِ اسْتَفَادَ مَالًا فَلَا زَكَاةَ فِيهِ حَتَّىٰ يَحُولَ عَلَيْهِ الْحَوْلُ عِنْدَ رَبِّهِ

Whoever acquires wealth, there is no mandatory *zakat* on it until a year has passed (in one's possession).[24]

2 Are mature, that is, they have reached puberty;
3 Are sane;
4 Are free, so captives are excepted.

Niṣāb refers to a threshold of resources above which any surplus is subject to obligatory charity. It is the least amount of wealth which makes one legally responsible to pay legal alms.

The threshold for gold is 20 *mithqāl* (about 94 grams), the threshold for silver is 200 *dirhams* (about 640 grams), the threshold of food grains and fruit is 5 *awsuq* (673.5 kilograms), the threshold of camels is 5 camels, the threshold of cows is 5 cows, and the threshold of sheep is 40 sheep.

10.6 Recipients of *zakāt*

Zakāt, or the stipulated amount of alms, should be distributed among the following categories of people:

1 Those who are poor;
2 Those who are indigent;
3 Those who are employed to collect charities;
4 Those whose hearts are being reconciled;
5 Those taken captive;
6 Those in debt;
7 Those who toil in the cause of Allah;
8 Those who are on a journey.

The proceeds of the prescribed charity must be spent on the categories of people that the Qur'ān has described.[25] In the Ḥanafī school of law, one may distribute the required amount of prescribed charity to all of the categories of the needy, some of them or confine oneself to just one class.

The prescribed charity should be collected and distributed locally. The Prophet (Allah bless him and give him peace) appointed Mu'ādh as a governor of Yemen in the tenth year of Hijra before the Farewell Pilgrimage. On that occasion, the Messenger (Allah bless him and give him peace) gave him a set of instructions. One instruction of the Prophet (Allah bless him and give him peace) to Mu'ādh is cited here:

فَأَعْلِمْهُمْ أَنَّ اللَّهَ افْتَرَضَ عَلَيْهِمْ صَدَقَةً فِي أَمْوَالِهِمْ، تُؤْخَذُ مِنْ أَغْنِيَائِهِمْ وَتُرَدُّ عَلَى فُقَرَائِهِمْ.

Tell them that Allah has enjoined upon them charity (*zakāt*) from their wealth, to be taken from their rich and given to their poor.[26]

However, surplus cash from a posh area should be deposited in the public treasury so that the state may allocate resources to the needy in the far-flung areas.

The valid recipients of the obligatory charity are outlined in the following verse:

إِنَّمَا الصَّدَقَاتُ لِلْفُقَرَاءِ وَالْمَسَاكِينِ وَالْعَامِلِينَ عَلَيْهَا وَالْمُؤَلَّفَةِ قُلُوبُهُمْ وَفِي الرِّقَابِ وَالْغَارِمِينَ
وَفِي سَبِيلِ اللهِ وَابْنِ السَّبِيلِ فَرِيضَةً مِّنَ اللهِ وَاللهُ عَلِيمٌ حَكِيمٌ

Indeed, the zakāt *donations are meant for the poor and the indigent, and those who are deployed to collect charities and those in whose hearts the inculcation of love for Islam is aimed at. And, (moreover, spending* zakāt *for the) freeing of human lives (from the yoke of slavery) and removing the burden of those who are to pay debt and (those who toil hard) in the cause of Allah and the wayfarers (is true). This (all) has been prescribed by Allah, and Allah is All-Knowing, Most Wise.*[27]

However, many Muslims tend to feel that they are not permitted to give the obligatory alms to their poor relatives and to members of their family. This is their personal bias, and not a Sharia edict. The relatives who are not in one's line – that is, parents, children, siblings and spouse – are eligible for to receive *zakāt*. Islam espouses the notion of giving the prescribed alms to relatives other than those to whom one is legally bound to be provide for. Allah Almighty will grant the giver his or her reward twice over for discharging this responsibility and for doing good to their relatives. A Prophetic Tradition reads:

عَنْ سَلْمَانَ بْنِ عَامِرٍ الضَّبِّيِّ قَالَ: قَالَ رَسُوْلُ اللهِ a: الصَّدَقَةُ عَلَى الْمِسْكِيْنِ صَدَقَةٌ، وَعَلَى
ذِي الْقَرَابَةِ اثْنَتَانِ، صَدَقَةٌ وَصِلَةٌ.

Salmān b. al-Ḍabbī narrated that Allah's Messenger (Allah bless him and give him peace) said: "Charity given to the poor is charity, and that given to a relative is two things: charity and upholding the ties of kinship."[28]

The givers of obligatory charity should first take close relatives and neighbours into consideration as they have a greater right to receiving their *zakāt* funds.

10.7 *Zakāt* on unlawfully acquired resources

One might hear some people making queries regarding giving to charity out of illegally acquired wealth. They make the case that if one gives ill-gotten gains to charity, even one's dirty personal effects become sanitised in this fashion. Instead of treating their desires as religious principles, people should take direction and guidance from Allah Almighty and His Messenger (Allah bless him and give him peace). Allah, the Exalted, will have nothing to do with material help that has been tainted. The economic code of Islam stipulates that every gain and handout should be wholesome, honest and honourable. Words and deeds of purity and piety mount up to Him, while unrighteousness fails to ascend to Him.

إِلَيْهِ يَصْعَدُ الْكَلِمُ الطَّيِّبُ وَالْعَمَلُ الصَّالِحُ يَرْفَعُهُ

The pure words ascend to Him alone, and He is the One Who elevates (the grades of) a pious deed.[29]

On this score Abū Hurayra (may Allah be pleased with him) reported that Allah's Messenger (Allah bless him and give him peace) said:

إِذَا أَدَّيْتَ الزَّكَاةَ، فَقَدْ قَضَيْتَ مَا عَلَيْكَ. وَمَنْ جَمَعَ مَالًا حَرَامًا، ثُمَّ تَصَدَّقَ بِهِ، لَمْ يَكُنْ لَهُ فِيْهِ أَجْرٌ، وَكَانَ أَجْرُهُ عَلَيْهِ.

If you pay your *zakāt* (Alms-due), you have done your duty. If someone amasses unlawful wealth, then donates it as charity, he is not credited with any reward for that, and its reward is entered in his debit account.[30]

The Almighty receives only pious deeds and virtuous acts of charity; He does not bless unlawfully acquired offerings.

عَنْ أَبِيْ هُرَيْرَةَ g قَالَ: قَالَ رَسُوْلُ اللَّه a: مَنْ تَصَدَّقَ بِعَدْلِ تَمْرَةٍ مِنْ كَسْبٍ طَيِّبٍ، وَلَا يَقْبَلُ اللّٰهُ إِلَّا الطَّيِّبَ، وَإِنَّ اللّٰهَ يَتَقَبَّلُهَا بِيَمِيْنِهِ ثُمَّ يُرَبِّيْهَا لِصَاحِبِهِ، كَمَا يُرَبِّيْ أَحَدُكُمْ فَلُوَّهُ حَتَّى تَكُوْنَ مِثْلَ الْجَبَلِ.

According to Abū Hurayra (may Allah be pleased with him) that Allah's Messenger (Allah bless him and give him peace) said: "Whoever gives in charity as much as a date from honest earnings – and Allah only accepts what is good – Allah will accept it in His right hand and will then increase it in size for the giver, just like one of you might rear a foal, until it is the size of a mountain."[31]

10.8 Rates of *zakāt*

Muslims who are in possession of a certain amount of resources are under obligation to pay 2.5% of their means after one lunar year (354 days). Following the Gregorian year (365 days), one may pay 2.577%. Ten per cent is paid on the produce of the land fed by rain and springs, while 20 per cent is paid on the lands watered by tube wells and other artificial means.

10.9 Conditions for obligating *zakāt*

The payment of the prescribed charity is due when a believer meets the following requirements:

1 The wealth has been in the believer's possession for more than one lunar year (354 days).
2 The resources reach *niṣāb* (over and above an exemption limit sanctioned by the Sharia).
3 The believer possesses the material goods and have been at his or her disposal for a year.
4 Assets have been increasing or may increase.
5 The wealth exceeds the normal needs of the owner and reaches *niṣāb* (the legal threshold for *zakāt*).

There are people who believe that obligatory charity is to be paid only in Ramaḍān, the ninth month of the Islamic calendar. However, *zakāt* can be paid in advance, throughout the entire year or after passing a whole year with wealth in their possession.

If someone has reached the legal threshold for paying the prescribed alms but is in debt, he or she should first settle the sum of owed money. When the Muslim month of fasting drew near, 'Uthmān b. '(Affān) directed people to pay mandatory charity due on their personal effects after clearing their loans:

هَذَا شَهْرُ زَكَاتِكُمْ، فَمَنْ كَانَ عَلَيْهِ دَيْنٌ فَلْيُؤَدِّ دَيْنَهُ حَتَّى تَحْصُلَ أَمْوَالُكُمْ فَتُؤَدُّوْنَ مِنْهُ الزَّكَاةَ.

> This is the month for you to pay your *zakāt* (Alms-due). If you have any debts, then pay them off so that you can sort out your wealth and take the *zakāt* (Alms-due) from it.[32]

10.10 Types of wealth subject to the prescribed alms

10.10.1 Cash assets

The details of cash assets are as follows.

10.10.1.1 Gold and silver

The *niṣāb* (the minimum threshold) for gold is about 94 grams and the *niṣāb* for silver is 640 grams.

10.10.1.2 Money

The prescribed alms are mandatory on all monetary wealth when they reach the minimum amount of *zakāt* allowable. The minimum limit of wealth for reaching the threshold is the equivalent market value of either gold or silver.

10.10.2 Financial investment assets

Regarding *zakāt* on financial investment assets, details are supplied next.

10.10.2.1 Investment accounts

The rate of the prescribed alms mandatory on the balance of the investment accounts (principal plus profit) is 2.5%, following the lunar calendar.

10.10.2.2 Zakāt *on investment funds*

Investment funds are trade goods as they are bought and sold. After calculating the value of the investment funds, the investor should give mandatory Islamic almsgiving. The rate of the prescribed alms on investment funds varies. Details are given next.

10.10.2.2.1 *MURĀBAḤA*-BASED FUNDS

Murābaḥa means a sale on a mutually approved profit. Technically, it is a contract of sale in which the object of sale is delivered at the time of entering into the contract, whereas the price becomes due as debt. Islamic banks have adopted *murābaḥa* as a mode of financing.

In *murābaḥa*-based funds, the rate of *zakāt* is 2.5%, which is mandatory on the balance (principal plus profit), which is to treat them as assets of trade.

10.10.2.2.2 *IJĀRA* (LEASE FUNDS)

Literally, *ijāra* (which is synonymous with the English term "leasing" and "rental") means to rent something to another person. In Islamic jurisprudence, the term *ijāra* means the sale of a usufruct of a particular property in exchange for rent. It refers to a contract under which an Islamic bank purchases a commodity, a building or another facility, and leases it to a client against an agreed rental payment.

Zakāt is obligatory on lease fund returns only after they complete one year in one's ownership. However, prescribed charity is not obligatory on the assets of funds invested in leased property and equipment.

10.10.2.2.3 *ṢUKUK* (ISLAMIC BONDS)

The Arabic word *ṣukūk* means "certificates" and the term refers to Islamic bonds. They are similar to asset-backed bonds. The Islamic Financial Services Board (IFSB) defines *ṣukūk* this way:

> *Ṣukūk* . . . are certificates with each *ṣakk* representing a proportional undivided ownership right in tangible assets, or a pool of predominantly tangible assets, or a business venture. These assets may be in a specific project or investment activity in accordance with Sharia rules and principles.[33]

Zakāt is due on all kinds of *ṣukūk* certificates of assets.

10.10.2.2.4 *ZAKĀT* ON SHARES, BONDS AND TREASURY BILLS

The rate of the stipulated amount of alms on shares, bonds, and treasury bills is 2.5% of the market value for a lunar year.

10.10.3 Valuable metals and gems

The rate of the stipulated amount of alms on the market value of precious metals and gems is 2.5% for a lunar year.

10.10.4 **Zakāt** *on debts*

Before computing how much *zakāt* you are obliged to pay on your possessions, some loans must be included in the calculation of your alms, while others do not need to be. Details are given next.

1 If a believer possesses the amount which makes *zakāt* obligatory but also has outstanding debts, then he or she should deduct his or her amount of debt from the wealth at the end of the year; if there is still a minimum amount that is subject to *zakāt*, then it is subject to 2.5% *zakāt*. Otherwise *zakāt* is not payable on assets.
2 *Zakāt* is due on debts that are owed to a believer who is confident that the debt will be paid.
3 A believer is under obligation to give alms on money owed to him or her, whether it is a loan or a business debt.

10.10.5 **Zakāt** *on the produce of cultivated land*

Like compulsory charity, *'ushr* (one-tenth of the produce of land) is levied on the produce of land. Legally, it is absolutely binding on agricultural produce. Ten per cent is paid on the produce of the land fed by rain and springs, while 20 per cent is paid on the lands watered by tube wells and other artificial means.

If the tithe land is watered naturally by rain or springs, then it is subject to a tenth part of the produce, and if the tithe land is irrigated by artificial means – for example, wells, tube wells or canals – then it is subject to a twentieth part of the yield. On the basis of the following Qur'ānic quotation, *'ushr* is levied on crops obtained through farming:

وَآتُواْ حَقَّهُ يَوْمَ حَصَادِهِ وَلَا تُسْرِفُواْ إِنَّهُ لَا يُحِبُّ الْمُسْرِفِينَ

And (also) give away its due (as appointed by Allah) on the day of harvest (of the crop and the fruit), and do not spend wastefully.[34]

The following Qur'ānic quotation is the source for the injunction to spend in the cause of Allah, the Exalted when one gathers the harvest:

يَا أَيُّهَا الَّذِينَ آمَنُواْ أَنفِقُواْ مِن طَيِّبَاتِ مَا كَسَبْتُمْ وَمِمَّا أَخْرَجْنَا لَكُم مِّنَ الأَرْضِ

O believers! Spend (in the way of Allah) of your lawful and clean earnings and of that which We bring forth for you from the earth.[35]

In another report, Jābir b. 'Abd Allāh (may Allah be well pleased with him and his father) said that he heard the Prophet (Allah bless him and give him peace) say:

فِيْمَا سَقَتِ الْأَنْهَارُ وَالْغَيْمُ الْعُشُوْرُ، وَفِيْمَا سُقِيَ بِالسَّانِيَةِ نِصْفُ الْعُشْرِ.

On that which is irrigated by rivers and rain, one-tenth is due, and on that which is artificially irrigated, half of one-tenth.[36]

Land irrigated without much exertion and resources is subject to a high rate of tax. However, when is watered by artificial methods, less amount is to be paid to the needy in the way of Allah Almighty.

10.10.6 Animals and livestock

The prescribed threshold for *zakāt* on camels, cows and sheep[37] is listed in Tables 10.1–10.3.

10.10.7 The issue of zakāt *on merchandise and stock*

Muslim jurists hold divergent views on the payment of the obligatory charity on merchandise and stock which remains in the possession of their owners for a year.

Table 10.1 Threshold and *zakāt* on camels

Number of camels	Zakāt *due*
1–4 camels	No *zakāt* due
5–9 camels	One sheep
10–14 camels	Two sheep
15–19 camels	Three sheep
20–24 camels	Four sheep
25–35 camels	One she-camel (above one year of age)
36–45 camels	One she-camel (above two years of age)
46–60 camels	One she-camel (above three years of age)
61–75 camels	One she-camel (above four years of age)
76–90 camels	Two she-camels (above two years of age)
91–120 camels	Two she-camels (above three years of age)
Above 120 camels	For every 40: a she-camel (above two years), and for every 50: a she-camel (above three years)

Table 10.2 Threshold and *zakāt* on cows/buffalos

Numbers of cows/bulls	Zakāt *due*
1–29 cows/buffalos	No *zakāt* due
30–39 cows/buffalos	One cow/bull aged one year
40–59 cows/buffalos	One cows/bulls aged two years
60–69 cows/buffalos	Two cows/bulls aged one year
70–79 cows/buffalos	One cow/bull aged two years and one cow/bull aged one year
80–89 cows/buffalos	Two cows/bulls aged two years
90–99 cows/buffalos	Three cows/bulls aged two years

Table 10.3 Threshold and *zakāt* on sheep/goats

Numbers of sheep/goats	Zakāt *due*
1–39 sheep/goats	No *zakāt* due
40–120 sheep/goats	One sheep/goat
121–200 sheep/goats	Two sheep/goats
201–300 sheep/goats	Three sheep/goats

The following Sharia regulations are valuable and beneficial:

1 Commodities that are acquired with the intention of reselling are considered as stock. When one purchases property with the aim of selling it at a profit,

it will be subject to *zakāt*. But if the property was bought for personal use and not for selling, it will not be subject to *zakāt*.

2 *Zakāt* is binding on the present market value of pieces of the merchandise.
3 Furniture which one has at home or at the shop for personal use is not subject to *zakāt*. Mechanical devices which are utilised for manufacturing goods are not classed as merchandise, hence no *zakāt* is due on them.
4 *Zakāt* is obligatory on goods that are manufactured in factories. In addition, *zakāt* is mandatory on crude materials which are used for making products.
5 In the event an individual has gold, silver and merchandise, but individually they are not equal to the value of *niṣāb*, their value will be judged jointly. If the aggregate value measures up to the estimation of *niṣāb*, then the prescribed alms are due.

10.11 When must *zakāt* be paid on a commodity?

A Muslim must give *zakāt* on a commodity that has been in one's possession for a year at the least when the following conditions are met:

1 The commodity is purchased with the intention of selling.
2 The proprietor buys it with a view to making a profit on it when selling it.

When one buys vehicles for personal use, they are not commodities, hence they are not subject to *zakāt*. So no mandatory charity is due on one's residence, clothing, edibles, vehicles, books (not meant for trade) and instruments for earning livelihood such as saws, agricultural tools and industrial machinery. If, however, one trades in vehicles and purchases them with the aim of reselling them at a profit, they, being articles of trade, would be subject to *zakāt*.

10.11.1 **Zakāt** *on merchandise per se or its profit: the first position*

One group of jurists holds that proprietors must give *zakāt* on the total value of their tradeable commodities after a period of one year.

10.11.2 **Zakāt** *on merchandise per se or its profit: the second position*

Ancient jurists and some modern jurists maintain that *zakāt* is due on the profits of commodities that have been sold after the passage of one year, but no *zakāt* is mandatory on one's merchandise and stocks. Details on both positions are supplied by Wahbah al-Zuhayl. Below as such:

To create wealth, nowadays people invest their capital in sources of earning other than land and trade. For example, they erect buildings and lease them out, set up manufacturing plants, and build planes for fast travel and vessels for transporting goods by sea. Some more sources of earning include keeping poultry and livestock. *Zakāt* is not due on these sources of income. Rather *zakāt* is obligatory on the income and the profit which they generate.

Since the afore-mentioned methods of earning did not exist in the days of old, ancient jurists did not lay down rules regarding paying prescribed alms on them. However, jurists hold that *zakāt* is not liable to residential accommodations, household goods, tools of trade, industrial or agricultural machinery as well as animals for riding.

The second conference of Muslim scholars and the second conference of Islamic researchers in 1385 AH/1965 AD held the view that if no Sharia injunction or juristic opinion exists on the assets which are capable of growth they should be treated like factories, boats and aircraft – no *zakāt* is due on them but obligatory charity is due on their income, provided that the assets are eligible for *zakāt* and one possesses them for a year.

2.5% *zakāt* is payable on the share of every shareholder, no matter what the profit of the company is.

Four Sunni schools of religious law concur that *zakāt* is due when one reaches the threshold and the wealth remain sin one's possession for a year. Except for Imam al-Shafi'ī, other jurists hold that *zakāt* is due if one reaches the threshold at a certain time and then again reaches the threshold even a little before completing a year.

According to another opinion, obligatory charity is due on just possessing wealth that is subject to *zakāt* and the passage of a year is not a stipulation. This position is attributed to Ibn 'Abbās, Ibn Mas'ūd, Mu'āwiya and some Followers such as Zuhrī, Ḥasan Baṣrī, Makhūl, 'Umar b. 'Abd al-Azīz, Imam Bāqir, Imam Ṣādiq, Nāṣir and Dāwūd, the Externalist.[38]

Notes

1 Qur'ān 59:7.
2 Ibid., 51:19.
3 Ibid., 24:56.
4 Ibid., 73:20.
5 Narrated by al-Bukhārī in *al-Ṣaḥīḥ*: *al-Īmān* [Faith], Ch.: The Prophet's (Allah bless him and give him peace) saying: "Islam is [Faith]based on five things," 1:21 §8; and Muslim in *al-Ṣaḥīḥ*: *al-Īmān* [Faith], Ch.: Explanation of the pillars of Islam and its powerful supports, 1:45 §16.
6 Narrated by Abū Dāwūd in *al-Sunan*; *al-Ṣalāt* [The ritual prayer], Ch.: Observance of the timing of the ritual prayers, 1:116 §439; al-Ṭabarānī in *al-Mu'jam al-Ṣaghīr*, 2:56 §772; al-Mundhirī in *al-Targhīb wa al-Tarhīb*, 1:148; 300 §544; 1105; al-Haythamī in *Majma' al-Zawā'id*, 1:47; and Ibn Rajab in *Jāmi' al-'Ulūmwa al-ḥikam*, 1:215.
7 Narrated by Abū Dāwūd in *al-Sunan*: *al-Marāsīl* [Traditions traced back no further than the second generation after the Prophet (Allah bless him and give him peace)], p. 133; and al-Ṭabarānī in *al-Mu'jam al-Awsaṭ*, 2:279 §1923.
8 Qur'ān 51:19.
9 Ibid., 3:92.
10 Narrated by al-Tirmidhī in *al-Sunan*: *al-Zakāt* [The Alms-due], Ch.: What has come to us about there is a duty on wealth besides the Alms-due, 3:48 §659; and Sā'īd b. Manṣūr in *al-Sunan*, 5:100 §926.

11 Qur'ān 2:43.
12 Ibid., 2:110.
13 Narrated by al-Bukhārī in *al-Ṣaḥīḥ*: *al-Zakāt* [The Alms-due], Ch.: The obligation of *sadaqat al-fiṭr* (an obligatory charity for every believer who possesses a minimum amount of wealth), 2:547 §1432; and Muslim in *al-Ṣaḥīḥ*: *al-Zakāt* [The Alms-due], Ch.: *Zakāt al-fiṭr* is due from the Muslims, 2:677 §984.
14 Narrated by Ibn Mājah in *al-Sunan*: *Abwābal-Zakāt* [The chapters regarding *zakāt*], Ch.: *Ṣadaqa al-fiṭr* [Charity donations given to the needy at the end of Ramaḍān], 1:585 §1827.
15 Qur'ān 92:17–18.
16 Ibid., 9:103.
17 Ibid., 59:9.
18 Ibid., 9:111.
19 Ibid., 3:92.
20 Narrated by al-Bayhaqī in *Shu'ab al-Īmān*, 5:267 §6612; and al-Khaṭīb al-Tabrīzī in *Mishkāt al-Maṣābīḥ*, 3:82 §5050.
21 Narrated by al-Tirmidhī in *al-Sunan*, *al-Ḥudūd* [The penalties], Ch.: What has been related about covering (the faults of) the Muslim, 4:34 §1426.
22 Qur'ān 59:7.
23 Ibid., 9:11.
24 Narrated by al-Tirmidhī in *al-Sunan*: *Abwābal-Zakāt* [The chapters regarding *zakāt*], Ch.: What has been related about there is no obligatory almsgiving on acquired wealth until a year has passed, 3:25 §631.
25 Qur'ān 9:60.
26 Narrated by Ibn Mājah in *al-Sunan*: *Abwābal-Zakāt* [The chapters regarding *zakāt*], Ch.: The obligation of *zakāt*, 1:568 §1783.
27 Qur'ān 9:60.
28 Narrated by Ibn Mājah in *al-Sunan*: *Abwābal-Zakāt* [The chapters regarding *zakāt*], Ch.: The virtue of charity, 1:591 §1844.
29 Qur'ān 35:10.
30 Narrated by Ibn Khuzayma in *al-Ṣaḥīḥ*, 4:110 §2471; Ibn Ḥibbān in *al-Ṣaḥīḥ*, 5:11 §3216; and al-Ḥākim in *al-Mustadrak*, 1:547 §1440.
31 Narrated by al-Bukhārī in *al-Ṣaḥīḥ*: *al-Zakāt* [The Alms-due], Ch.: Allah does not accept charity from dishonestly acquired property, only accepting it from honest earnings, 2:511 §1344.
32 Narrated by Mālik in *al-Muwaṭṭa'*: *Zakāt* [The Alms-due], Ch.: *Zakāt* (Alms-due) on debts, 1:253 §593; and al-Bayhaqī in *al-Sunan al-kubrā*, 4:148 §7395.
33 Capital adequacy requirements for sukūk, securitisations and real estate investment, https://www.ifsb.org/standard/eng/Sukuk.pdf.
34 Qur'ān 6:141.
35 Ibid., 2:267.
36 Narrated by Imam Muslim in *al-Ṣaḥīḥ*: *al-Zakāt* [The Alms-due], Ch.: On what one-tenth or half of one-tenth is due, 2:675 §981.
37 Sheikh-Dr. Nabil, Islamic Heritage Center, www.ihcproject.com/sheikhdr-nabil/
38 Wahbah al-Zuhaylī, *al-Fiqh al-Islāmīwaadillatu-hu*, 2:864–865.

Bibliography

The Holy Qur'ān

Abū Dāwūd, Sulaymān b. Ash'ath b. Isḥāq b. Bashīr al-Sijistānī (202–275/817–889). *Al-Sunan*. Beirut, Lebanon: Dār al-Fikr, 1414/1994.

Bayhaqī, Aḥmad b. al-Ḥusayn al-. *Al-Sunan al-kubrā*. Mecca, Saudi Arabia: Maktaba Dār al-Bāz, 1994.

———. *Shu'ab al-Īmān*. Beirut, Lebanon: Dar al-Kotob al-Ilmiyah, 1990.
Bukhārī, Abū 'Abd Allāh Muhammad b. Ismā'īl b. Ibrahīm b. Mughīra al-. (194–256/810–870). *Al-Adab al-Mufrad*. Beirut, Lebanon: Dār al-Bashā'ir al-Islāmiyya, 1409/1989.
Ḥākim, Muhammad b. 'Abd Allāh al-. *Al-Mustadrak'alā al-ṣaḥīḥayn*. Beirut, Lebanon: Dar al-Kotob al-Ilmiyah, 1990.
Haythamī, Nūr al-Dīn Abū al-Ḥasan'Alī al-. *Majma' al-zawā'idwamanba' al-fawā'id*. Cairo: Dār al-Rayān li al-Turāth, 1987.
Ibn Ḥibbān, Abūḥātim Muhammad. *Al-Ṣaḥīḥ*. Beirut, Lebanon: Mu'assasa al-Risāla, 1993.
Ibn Khuzayma, Muhammad b. Isḥāq. *Al-Ṣaḥīḥ*. Beirut, Lebanon: al-Maktab al-Islāmī, 1970.
Ibn Mājah, Abū 'Abd Allāh Muhammad b. Yazīd al-Qazwīnī (209–273/824–887). *Al-Sunan*. Beirut, Lebanon: Dār al-Kutub al-'Ilmiyya, 1419/1998.
Ibn Rajab al-Ḥanbalī, Abū al-Faraj 'Abd al-Raḥmān b. Aḥmad (736–795AH). *Jāmi' al-'Ulūm wa al-ḥikamfī SharḤ Khamsīn ḥadīth min Jawāmi' al-Kalim*. Beirut, Lebanon: Dār al-Ma'rifa, 1408AH.
Khaṭīb al-Tabrīzī, Walī al-Dīn Abū 'Abd Allāh Muhammad b. 'Abd Allāh al-(d. 741AH). *Mishkāt al-MaṣābīḤ*. Beirut, Lebanon: Dār al-Kutub al-'Ilmiyya, 1424/2003.
Mālik, Ibn Anas b. Mālik b. Abī'āmir b. 'Amr b. Ḥārith al-AṣbaḤī (93–179/712–795). *Al-Muwaṭṭā'*. Beirut, Lebanon: Dār Iḥyā' al-Turāth al-'Arabī, 1990.
Mundhirī, 'Abd al-'Aẓīm al-. *Al-Targhībwa al-tarhīb*. Beirut, Lebanon: Dar al-Kotob al-Ilmiyah, 1417AH.
Muslim, Ibn al-*Ḥajj*āj Abū al-Ḥasan al-Qushayrī al-Naysābūrī (206–261/821–875). Al-Ṣaḥīḥ. Beirut, Lebanon: Dār al-Iḥyā' al-Turāth al-'Arabī, 1997.
Sa'īd b. Manṣūr, Abū'Uthmān al-Khurāsānī (d. 227 AH). *Al-Sunan*. Riyadh, Saudi Arabia: Dār al-Aṣma'ī, 1414AH.
Sheikh-Dr. Nabil, Islamic Heritage Center, www.ihcproject.com/sheikhdr-nabil/
Ṭabarānī, Sulaymān b. Aḥmad al-. *Al-Mu'jam al-awsaṭ*. Cairo: Dār al-Ḥaramayn, 1415AH.
———. *Al-Mu'jam al-ṣaghīr*. Beirut, Lebanon: al-Maktab al-Islāmī, 1985.
Tirmidhī, Abū 'Īsā Muhammad b. 'Īsā al-. *Al-Sunan*. Beirut, Lebanon: Dār Iḥyā' al-Turāth al-'Arabī, n.d.
Wahbah al-Zuhaylī. *al-Fiqh al-Islāmīwaadillatu-hu*, 2:864–865. Beirut, Lebanon: Dār al-Qlm, 2002.

11 Contemporary issues in Islamic business and trade

11.1 Strategic planning: an Islamic perspective

To attain a particular goal or gain an advantage, people need to develop a plan of action and then execute it. The same is true of running a business as well. Encarta defines strategic planning as "the planning of all the activities of a business to ensure competitive advantage and profitability." Every corporation employs strategic planning in order to realise its targets. When it sets priorities, its employees focus on working towards achieving them. Islam urges humans to lead a well-disciplined life so as to make it productive. A great many examples from the sacred sources of Islam encourage the faithful to plan and to making suitable arrangements for carrying out activities in the future. Planning is the practice of the Almighty as well. The Qur'ān explains how Allah Almighty, the Best of Planners, works out a course of action and then carries it out. The following verse exemplifies this Divine practice:

أَلَمْ تَرَ أَنَّ اللَّهَ أَنزَلَ مِنَ السَّمَاءِ مَاءً فَأَخْرَجْنَا بِهِ ثَمَرَاتٍ مُّخْتَلِفًا أَلْوَانُهَا وَمِنَ الْجِبَالِ جُدَدٌ بِيضٌ
وَحُمْرٌ مُّخْتَلِفٌ أَلْوَانُهَا وَغَرَابِيبُ سُودٌ

Have you not seen that Allah sent down water from the sky? Then We brought forth with that the fruits which have different colours. And, similarly, in the mountains there are white and red streaks with a variety of shades and there are deep black (streaks) as well.[1]

The Almighty has been running the celestial bodies according to a system from which they do not deviate.

خَلَقَ السَّمَاوَاتِ وَالْأَرْضَ بِالْحَقِّ يُكَوِّرُ اللَّيْلَ عَلَى النَّهَارِ وَيُكَوِّرُ النَّهَارَ عَلَى اللَّيْلِ وَسَخَّرَ
الشَّمْسَ وَالْقَمَرَ كُلٌّ يَجْرِي لِأَجَلٍ مُّسَمًّى أَلَا هُوَ الْعَزِيزُ الْغَفَّارُ

He created the heavens and the earth with a decreed celestial order and planning. He causes the night to overlap the day and the day to overlap the night. And He is the One Who has subjected the sun and the moon (to a system). Each (star and planet) rotates in its orbit till an appointed time. Beware! He is the One Who is All-Dominant (over the entire system), the Most Forgiving.[2]

If an orphan owns material resources, but he or she is unable to think for him- or herself and work out how to organise the resources, then the guardian should wait until he or she has learned to manage their life and wealth.

وَابْتَلُواْ الْيَتَامَى حَتَّىَ إِذَا بَلَغُواْ النِّكَاحَ فَإِنْ آنَسْتُم مِّنْهُمْ رُشْدًا فَادْفَعُواْ إِلَيْهِمْ أَمْوَالَهُمْ

And evaluate and test the orphans (for the sake of their training) till they attain to (the age of) marriage. Then if you discern in them ingenuity (and the knack of planning), hand over their assets to them.[3]

The heavens, arranged in layers one above another, are an excellent creation of Allah, the Exalted. He directs our attention to the marvellous celestial bodies that adhere to the Divine laws of motion. A close look at them demonstrates that His is the perfect plan and arrangement.

الَّذِي خَلَقَ سَبْعَ سَمَاوَاتٍ طِبَاقًا مَّا تَرَى فِي خَلْقِ الرَّحْمَنِ مِن تَفَاوُتٍ فَارْجِعِ الْبَصَرَ هَلْ تَرَى
مِن فُطُورٍ ○ ثُمَّ ارْجِعِ الْبَصَرَ كَرَّتَيْنِ يَنقَلِبْ إِلَيْكَ الْبَصَرُ خَاسِأً وَهُوَ حَسِيرٌ○ وَلَقَدْ زَيَّنَّا
السَّمَاءَ الدُّنْيَا بِمَصَابِيحَ وَجَعَلْنَاهَا رُجُومًا لِّلشَّيَاطِينِ وَأَعْتَدْنَا لَهُمْ عَذَابَ السَّعِيرِ ○

He Who has created seven (or numerous) heavenly spheres corresponding to one another (layer upon layer). You will not find any irregularity and disproportion in the system of the creation of the Most Kind (Lord). So have a (meditative and thoughtful) look around: do you find in this (creation) any incongruity or disharmony (i.e., degeneration or falling apart)? Look around time and again with (an inquisitive) vision (from different angles and with scientific methods. Every time) your sight will return to you fatigued and frustrated (in finding any shortcoming or imperfection). And surely, We have adorned the lowest heaven of the universe with lights (in the form of stars, planets, other asteroids and meteoroids).[4]

Scores of examples from the conduct of the Prophet (Allah bless him and give him peace) also show that his life was disciplined, and, before setting himself a special assignment, he worked out its particulars. Before the battle of Uḥud, the Messenger (Allah bless him and give him peace) posted some Companions at their stations for battle. The Qur'ān gives an account of his strategic planning.

وَإِذْ غَدَوْتَ مِنْ أَهْلِكَ تُبَوِّئُ الْمُؤْمِنِينَ مَقَاعِدَ لِلْقِتَالِ

And (recall the time) when, early morning, you left your blessed abode (on the eve of the battle of Uḥud), and were positioning the Muslims at their posts for the battle (in defence against the aggression by Meccan invaders).[5]

If the Messenger entered into a treaty of peace with non-Muslims, he worked out the minutiae of the contract.[6]

In response to would-be warfare against the fledgling state of Medina, the Prophet (Allah bless him and give him peace) worked out a sagacious defence mechanism. He carefully devised a plan of action to safeguard the state against aggression. When the Companions migrated to Medina, the Meccan establishment made a great effort to wipe out Islam in the War of the Trench. The Quraysh and their allies rode against Medina. At the suggestion of Salmān the Persian (may Allah be pleased with him), the Messenger (Allah bless him and give him peace) commissioned a deep trench to be dug around the unprotected quarters of the city. Since the trench was impassable, the army of the clans encamped outside the city for a few days but then retreated.[7]

11.2 Importance of strategic planning in businesses

To achieve their targets, organisations and corporations must create plans and then execute them. The rationale for gathering empirical knowledge in matters pertaining to this world is addressed fully by Scriptural verses. In the following excerpt of the Qur'ān, Allah Almighty invites us to study His creation and then reflect on it, for many signs of Allah's power are in the natural phenomena scattered throughout the world:

إِنَّ فِي خَلْقِ السَّمَاوَاتِ وَالْأَرْضِ وَاخْتِلَافِ اللَّيْلِ وَالنَّهَارِ وَالْفُلْكِ الَّتِي تَجْرِي فِي الْبَحْرِ بِمَا
يَنفَعُ النَّاسَ وَمَا أَنزَلَ اللهُ مِنَ السَّمَاءِ مِن مَّاءٍ فَأَحْيَا بِهِ الْأَرْضَ بَعْدَ مَوْتِهَا وَبَثَّ فِيهَا مِن
كُلِّ دَآبَّةٍ وَتَصْرِيفِ الرِّيَاحِ وَالسَّحَابِ الْمُسَخَّرِ بَيْنَ السَّمَاءِ وَالْأَرْضِ لَآيَاتٍ لِّقَوْمٍ يَعْقِلُونَ

Verily, in the creation of the heavens and the earth, and in the alternation of the night and the day, and in the ships (and vessels) which sail through the ocean carrying cargo profitable for the people, and in the (rain)water which Allah pours down from the sky, reviving therewith the earth to life after its death, and (the earth) in which He has scattered animals of all kinds, and in the changing wind directions, and in the clouds (that trail) between the sky and the earth, duty-bound (under Allah's command) – certainly (in these) are (many) signs (of Allah's Power) for those who put their reason to work.[8]

Trees and vegetation are irrigated by the same water, yet their yield – where colour, size, taste is concerned – is different. The following Scriptural message closes with the Divine invitation "*there are (great) signs in it for the people who apply reason*," the foundation for undertaking strategic planning.

وَفِي الْأَرْضِ قِطَعٌ مُتَجَاوِرَاتٌ وَجَنَّاتٌ مِنْ أَعْنَابٍ وَزَرْعٌ وَنَخِيلٌ صِنْوَانٌ وَغَيْرُ صِنْوَانٍ يُسْقَى
بِمَاءٍ وَاحِدٍ وَنُفَضِّلُ بَعْضَهَا عَلَى بَعْضٍ فِي الْأُكُلِ إِنَّ فِي ذَٰلِكَ لَآيَاتٍ لِقَوْمٍ يَعْقِلُونَ

And there are, in the earth, tracts (of different kinds) that are adjacent to each other and the gardens of grapes and crops and palm trees, clustered and non-clustered. All these are irrigated with the same water. And (despite that) We make some of them superior to others in taste. Verily, there are (great) signs in it for the people who apply reason.[9]

In addition,

وَاللَّهُ خَيْرُ الْمَاكِرِينَ

"*And Allah is the Best of secret planners.*"[10]

The preceding verses demonstrate how the Almighty has been running the universe systematically, we too should draw a road map – a road map to run our businesses smoothly. The companies that are well organized and managed, they reap the rewards in this world. They may achieve the objective of sustainable economic growth. Their employees feel assimilated into the company. The whole staff, from top to bottom, has a sense of direction, so they focus on it. A vision of the future thus enables the organisation to undertake and realise its long-term development.

11.3 The principles of marketing in Islam

Since Islam is a *Dīn*, not just a religion, it gave humanity all regulations necessary to lead a productive life. So it follows that the Sharia cannot be separated from socio-economic activities. Islam regards commerce as a vital factor in sustaining human life. To make one's business a success, one needs to advertise so as to attract customers. However, the code of conduct of marketing should be guided by the Qur'ān and the Traditions, the primary sources of the Muslim religion, which the faithful are required to adhere to, not by lewd and immoral ideas of publicity and marketing campaigns.

Oxford Advanced Learner's Dictionary defines advertising as "the activity of presenting, advertising and selling a company's products in the best possible way." From the religious perspective, "Islamic marketing is the study of marketing phenomena in relation to Islamic principles and practices or within the context of Muslim societies."[11] So Islamic marketing is founded on the idea of advertising, promoting and selling products without violating any Divine injunctions. Some rules and regulations on marketing, from the Islamic perspective, are given next.

11.3.1 Adherence to the truth

While advertising, businesspeople must stick to the truth. They should draw attention to the advantages of the saleable items and provide information to the target audience. What they promote via print or electronic media must show the real nature of the product or service. By lying one might make a profit on the spot, yet the earner will receive no blessing. The Messenger (Allah bless him and give him peace) said:

اَلْبَيِّعَانِ بِالْخِيَارِ مَا لَمْ يَتَفَرَّقَا، أَوْ قَالَ: حَتَّى يَتَفَرَّقَا، فَإِنْ صَدَقَا وَبَيَّنَا بُوْرِكَ لَهُمَا فِيْ بَيْعِهِمَا،
وَإِنْ كَتَمَا وَكَذَبَا مُحِقَتْ بَرَكَةُ بَيْعِهِمَا.

> The seller and the buyer have the option (to revoke the sale) as long as they have not separated (or he said: "until they separate"). If they speak the truth and make things clear, they will be blessed in their sale. If they conceal and lie, the blessing of their transaction will be obliterated.[12]

Some shopkeepers "technically" deceive prospective purchasers because they refrain from telling the truth. Well acquainted with the defect of the items on sale, they leave it to customers to identify the faults. Sly traders tell customers plainly that they must check whether the commodity on sale is reliable, unreliable or malfunctioning. These technical methods of deception, which involve withholding the truth, are abhorrent to the Divine.

11.3.2 Prohibition of music and singing

As advertisement and marketing are legal matters, they should contain nothing that disregards any Divine injunction. Music and singing, the key features of immoral styles of advertisement, should have nothing to do with the publicity campaigns of the faithful.

The Qur'ān tells Muslims that Allah

وَيَنْهَى عَنِ الْفَحْشَاءِ وَالْمُنكَرِ وَالْبَغْيِ

> *forbids indecency, evil deeds, defiance and disobedience.*[13]

This Divine prohibition must be observed while publicizing and broadcasting.

11.3.3 Honesty

If you are morally upright in advertising, then your integrity, openness and authenticity will earn you a place in the market. Thus, you will be blessed in doing your business. A Prophetic Tradition warns us against losing trustworthiness.

Once a Bedouin came into the presence of the Messenger (Allah bless him and give him peace) and asked: "When is the Last Hour?" After a while Allah's Messenger (Allah bless him and give him peace) said:

فَإِذَا ضُيِّعَتِ الْأَمَانَةُ فَانْتَظِرِ السَّاعَةَ.

When trustworthiness has been lost, expect the Last Hour.[14]

11.3.4 The element of seduction

Treading in the footsteps of the immoral forms of media which build glamour, many Muslim marketing managers give women prominent roles advertisement even if a product is neither specific to women nor even remotely related to them. Such advertisers, instead of selling services or commodities, market women themselves. Employing women in marketing to perform in this manner contravenes the following Divine directive.

وَقُل لِّلْمُؤْمِنَاتِ يَغْضُضْنَ مِنْ أَبْصَارِهِنَّ وَيَحْفَظْنَ فُرُوجَهُنَّ وَلَا يُبْدِينَ زِينَتَهُنَّ إِلَّا مَا ظَهَرَ
مِنْهَا وَلْيَضْرِبْنَ بِخُمُرِهِنَّ عَلَى جُيُوبِهِنَّ وَلَا يُبْدِينَ زِينَتَهُنَّ إِلَّا لِبُعُولَتِهِنَّ أَوْ آبَائِهِنَّ أَوْ آبَاءِ
بُعُولَتِهِنَّ أَوْ أَبْنَائِهِنَّ أَوْ أَبْنَاءِ بُعُولَتِهِنَّ أَوْ إِخْوَانِهِنَّ أَوْ بَنِي إِخْوَانِهِنَّ أَوْ بَنِي أَخَوَاتِهِنَّ أَوْ
نِسَائِهِنَّ أَوْ مَا مَلَكَتْ أَيْمَانُهُنَّ أَوِ التَّابِعِينَ غَيْرِ أُوْلِي الْإِرْبَةِ مِنَ الرِّجَالِ أَوِ الطِّفْلِ الَّذِينَ لَمْ
يَظْهَرُوا عَلَى عَوْرَاتِ النِّسَاءِ وَلَا يَضْرِبْنَ بِأَرْجُلِهِنَّ لِيُعْلَمَ مَا يُخْفِينَ مِن زِينَتِهِنَّ

Direct the believing men to keep their eyes always lowered and guard their private parts. That is purer for them. Surely, Allah is Well Aware of (the works) which they are busy doing. And direct the believing women that they (too) must keep their eyes lowered and guard their chastity, and must not show off their adornments and beautification except that (part of it) which becomes visible itself. And they must keep their veils (and head-coverings) drawn over their chests (too), and must not display their adornments (to anyone) except their husbands, or their fathers or the fathers of their husbands, or their sons or the sons of their husbands, or their brothers or the sons of their brothers or the sons of their sisters, or (the women of) their (own faith, the Muslim) women or their female slaves or such male servants as are free from any lust and sexual urge, or the children who (being minor) have (yet) no sense of women's private parts. (They too are exceptions.) Nor must they (whilst walking) strike their feet (on the ground in such a manner that ornaments jingle and) thus get revealed and known what they are keeping hidden (under the command of Sharia).[15]

11.3.5 The prohibition of nudity

Nudity and sexist images should have nothing to do with advertising. Vulgar ads are offensive in the eyes of the Sustainer and Cherisher of the universe. One may promote a business without the display of scantily dressed models. Modesty must be observed by both genders under all circumstances. Allah's Messenger (Allah bless him and give him peace) said:

اَلْإِيْمَانُ بِضْعٌ وَسَبْعُوْنَ شُعْبَةً، فَأَفْضَلُهَا: قَوْلُ لَا إِلَهَ إِلَّا اللهُ، وَأَدْنَاهَا إِمَاطَةُ الْأَذَى عَنِ
الطَّرِيْقِ. وَالْحَيَاءُ شُعْبَةٌ مِنَ الْإِيْمَانِ.

> Faith consists of seventy-odd branches, the finest of which is (affirming the Oneness of Allah by) saying: "There is no God but Allah," and the least of which is clearing trouble from the road. Modesty is also a (significant) branch of faith.[16]

Here is another rule related to clothes the dressing of male and female models advertising commodity for sale. They should consider well whether they abide by the Tradition of the Prophet (Allah bless him and give him peace) – the Prophet whose mercy and intercession they and everyone will crave on the Day of Judgment.

Narrated by 'Alī (may Allah be well pleased with him), the Prophet (Allah bless him and give him peace) said to him:

لَا تُبْرِزْ فَخِذَكَ، وَلَا تَنْظُرْ إِلَى فَخِذِ حَيٍّ وَلَا مَيِّتٍ.

> Do not show your thigh, and do not look at the thigh of anyone, living or dead."[17]

Notes

1 Qur'ān 35:27.
2 Ibid., 39:5.
3 Ibid., 4:6.
4 Ibid., 67:3–5.
5 Ibid., 3:121.
6 Narrated by al-Bukhārī in *al-Ṣaḥīḥ*: *al-Ṣulḥ* [Concord], Ch.: How it is recorded: "This is the reconciliation between so-and-so the son of so-and-so and so-and-so the son of so-and-so" when one is not ascribed to his tribe or lineage, 2:959 §2551.
7 Narrated by Ibn Ḥajar al-'Asqalānī in *Fatḥ al-Bārī*, 7:393.
8 Qur'ān 2:164.
9 Ibid., 13:4.
10 Ibid., 3:54.
11 D. Kadirov (2014), "Islamic Marketing as Macromarketing", *Journal of Islamic Marketing*, Vol. 5, No. 1, pp. 2–19. https://doi.org/10.1108/JIMA-09-2012-0054
12 Narrated by al-Bukhārī in *al-Ṣaḥīḥ*: *al-Buyū'* [Sales], Ch.: A buyer and seller making things clear and not concealing anything and showing good faith, 2:732 §1973.
13 Qur'ān 16:90.
14 Narrated by al-Bukhārī in *al-Ṣaḥīḥ*: *al-'Ilm* [Knowledge], Ch.: On the one who is asked for knowledge while he is engaged in a conversation and then finishes his conversation before answering the question, 1:33 §59.
15 Qur'ān 24:31–32.

16 Narrated by al-Bukhārī in *al-Ṣaḥīḥ: al-Īmān* [Faith], Ch.: The matters of faith, 1:12 §9.
17 Narrated by Ibn Mājah in *al-Sunan*: *Kitab al Jnā'z*: The chapters on what has been narrated regarding funerals, Ch.: What was narrated concerning washing the deceased, 1:469 §1460.

Bibliography

The Holy Qur'ān

'Asqalānī, Ibn Ḥajar Aḥmad b. 'Alī al-. *Fatḥ al-Bārī sharḥ Ṣaḥīḥ al-Bukhārī*. Beirut, Lebanon: Dār al-Ma'rifa, 1379AH.
Bukhārī, Abū 'Abd Allāh Muhammad b. Ismā'īl b. Ibrahīm b. Mughīra al-. (194–256/810–870). *Al-Ṣaḥīḥ*. Beirut, Lebanon, Damascus, Syria: Dār al-Qalam, 1401/1981.
Ibn Mājah, Abū 'Abd Allāh Muhammad b. Yazīd al-Qazwīnī (209–273/824–887). *Al-Sunan*. Beirut, Lebanon: Dār al-Kutub al-'Ilmiyya, 1419/1998.

12 Islamic system of banking and finance

Islamic banking is a financial management system which runs in accordance with Islamic law. They do not charge interest on their transactions. Provision of Islamic financial services system helps achieve the objectives of an Islamic economic system. Operations of an Islamic bank are based on Islamic principles of transactions of which profit and loss sharing (PLS) is a key feature, which is why Islamic banks are generally designated as PLS banks.

According to the General Secretariat of the OIC, "An Islamic bank is a financial institution whose status, rules and procedures expressly state commitment to the principle of Islamic Sharia and to the banning of the receipt and payment of interest on any of its operations."[1] Dr Ziaul Ahmed has offered the following definition, "Islamic banking is essentially a normative concept and could be define conduct of banking in consonance [with] the ethos of the value system of Islam."[2]

Islamic banks take different forms: full-fledged financial institutions, Islamic "windows" (separate, Sharia-compliant units) in conventional banks, and Islamic subsidiaries of conventional financial institutions.

12.1 The objectives of Islamic banks

Islamic banks have been set up so that people might better themselves through them. Material resources should be employed with a view to doing good to owners and the rest of society. That is why banks which comply with Sharia ordinances shun interest – the foundation of a great many social, moral, religious vices. They are run on the principles of profit and loss sharing modes. Furthermore, Islamic banks offer believers and Muslim corporations an Islamic alternative of investing wealth rather than dealing in interest.

12.2 Role of Islamic banks in economic development

Islamic banks finance various sectors, for example, manufacturing, agriculture, education, and health. They fight poverty and mitigate unemployment by lending money for productive projects and extending interest-free loans to individuals. Sharia-compliant financial instruments encourage investment, a fundamental goal of all financial institutions. Lastly, Sharia-compliant banks, like their conventional counterparts, do business and earn profit but without resorting to the evil of charging interest. So Islamic banks are a door to development of humanity; they meet Muslims' material needs and guard their religion.

12.3 Features of Islamic banking

Given that Muslim customers are partial to the financial instruments that Islamic banks employ, conventional banks are less appealing to them. Islamic banks earn the confidence of cautious clients. They compete with conventional commercial banks in that they provide many Sharia-complaint conventional banking services – such as ATM machines, loans, leasing and credit cards – to their clientele. Although Islamic banking is in its infancy in many Muslim lands, its growth has seen tremendous progress in the last few decades.

The principles on which Islamic banks are run have wide moral and ethical appeal. An Islamic bank has several distinctive features derived from Islamic law. The following points define the nature and scope of the Sharia-compliant bank.

12.3.1 Elimination of interest (ribā)

Ribā is unequivocally prohibited in the Noble Qur'ān and the Prophetic Traditions. Muslim states, therefore, are duty bound to abolish interest, "nominal or excessive, simple or compound, fixed or floating"[3] as early as possible. Therefore, the first feature of a Sharia-compliant bank must be that it does not charge interest. An interest-ridden Muslim economy may never flourish, as Allah Almighty deprives economies of prosperous growth if they are interest based, whereas He increases blessings on interest-free economies manifold.[4] In Islamic banks, the institution of interest is replaced by customers' participation in profit and loss.

12.3.2 Public service–driven

Islamic commercial banks serve the public interest rather than individual or group interests, to realise the socio-economic goals of Islam. They pledge depositors the repayment of their funds.

12.3.3 Investment of funds

The capital in the possession of Islamic banks is invested in lawful ventures alone, which are calculated to achieve socio-economic development. Their funds are invested in projects on a partnership basis between the bank or the entrepreneur and the provider of investment. No investment may be made in prohibited businesses such as selling intoxicants or swine.

12.3.4 Multi-purpose financial institutions

Sharia-compliant banks are multi-purpose in nature, not purely commercial banks. These banks offer a variety of services to its clientele. They play a vital role in partnering with new businesses. A considerable part of their financing is dedicated to specific projects or ventures.

12.3.5 Careful evaluation of investment demand

Conventional banks generally assess applications and take applicants' collateral into consideration in order to avoid risks as much as possible. They are concerned with ensuring the security of their principle sum plus interest. On the contrary, Islamic banks operate under an in-built mechanism of risk sharing, so they are more careful before approving a loan amount. They closely observe the development of the project and evaluate it deeply, with an emphasis on its viability. Sharia-compliant banks are extra vigilant about ensuring that the amount of money on loan is dedicated to the purchase of machinery or equipment desired by a customer. So clients must establish they would run socially beneficial businesses which create real wealth.

12.4 Prospects of Islamic banking

Global financial institutes rekindled an interest in the performance of Islamic banks almost a decade ago, when the world was in economic meltdown. In 2008, conventional financial systems the world over were in crisis, yet "the Islamic financial services industry expanded 78 per cent."[5] On account of its intrinsic goodness, Islamic banks were better off in the global financial crisis. Even during the global economic downturn no Islamic financial institute was bailed out; this speaks volumes about what may be in store for Islamic banks.

Further, Islamic banking is as yet a rather young and growing industry. Still the emergence of Sharia-compliant banks in recent decades has been a noteworthy trend in the financial world. Because it is an inclusive paradigm, it appeals to non-Muslim customers as well, who believe that Islamic doctrines lead to ethical financial solutions.

12.5 A blueprint for an interest-free economic system

Muslims may never prosper, socially and religiously, if they choose to neglect the commandments of the Almighty regarding all affairs of their life. Their welfare is utterly dependant on putting the Divine commandments into practice. The same is true about business activities. The solution to a great many of their economic ills lies in freeing their economy from usurious practices. Here are some practical guidelines on freeing our businesses from the shackles of interest, offered by Shaykh-ul-Islam Dr Muhammad Tahir-ul-Qadri.

1 Minimising the budget deficit: first, government expenditures have to be axed; next, financial corruption within the economy should brought under control and monitored closely.
2 Maximizing the sources of revenue: The income tax system must be overhauled completely.

   a. Revenue and government sources cannot increase under this income tax system; neither can the people take the righteous path, nor can interest-free economy be promoted.
   b. The current income tax system is totally unjust and unrealistic. It is meant only for building up bank balances of the ruling mafia who do not care in helping the government to increase treasury. A healthy system of taxation has to be put in place that will encourage even small industrialists, businessmen and traders to voluntarily declare their assets and tax returns. They should not be compelled to [indulge in] corruption. After paying taxes honestly, they should not fear hiding or declaring their lawful means of earning nor should they pursue illegal wealth. They should also be provided with a constitutional system for the future.

3. Eliminating the misappropriation of government resources/budgets.
4. Eliminating interest from loans to provincial governments and other government agencies. Loans/grants should be reduced to the equivalent to the amount of interest, which will not cause any major differences.
5. Elimination of interest payment to the State Bank of Pakistan. Interest is paid to the State Bank on different treasury bills, which is just a book entry. For example, in 1990, the State Bank received interest from the government. It was just 33% of the total receiving. After the interest is eliminated, the government budget deficit will considerably decrease.[6]

12.6 Conclusion

In the following verse, Allah Almighty states the purpose of the prophethood of the final Messenger (Allah bless him and give him peace).

﴿هُوَ الَّذِي أَرْسَلَ رَسُولَهُ بِالْهُدَىٰ وَدِينِ الْحَقِّ لِيُظْهِرَهُ عَلَى الدِّينِ كُلِّهِ وَلَوْ كَرِهَ الْمُشْرِكُونَ﴾

> *Allah is He Who sent His Messenger (Allah bless him and give him peace) with guidance and the* Dīn *(Religion) of truth to make him (the Messenger) dominant over every (other exponent of)* Dīn, *though much to the dislike of the polytheists.*[7]

A misunderstanding lies here regarding making Islam dominant over other religions. It is generally understood that Islam should prevail over other religions. However, this meaning is not logical: other world religions are not adyān; they are just madhāhib. The word madhāhib or religion refers to devotional acts and rituals. Whereas the word Dīn refers to a complete code of life dealing with all aspects of human life, they may be economic, political, social or judicial. The meaning here is that in this verse followers of Islam are not asked to dominate other religions of the world theologically or ritual wise, rather they are asked to work on their systems; they may be political system, economic system, banking and commerce, judicial system, educational system, etc., and make these systems comparable and competitive to the conventional systems of the world such as capitalism, socialism or any other system. A true follower of Islam can only achieve this by following Quran and tradition of the Prophet (Allah bless him and give him peace) in true letter and spirit.

Notes

1 The Lawyer and Jurists, www.lawyersnjurists.com/article/overall-banking-system-of-al-arafah-islami-bank-ltd/
2 Ibid.
3 Dr Muhammad Tahir-ul-Qadri, *Interest Free Banking in Islamic Perspective*, pp. 15.
4 Qur'ān 2:276.
5 Dr Hussain Mohi-ud-Din Qadri, *Islamic Banking in Pakistan: Theoretical, practical and legal development*, pp. 30.
6 Dr Muhammad Tahir-ul-Qadri, *Interest-Free Banking in Islamic Perspective*, pp. 59–60.
7 Qur'ān 9:33.

Bibliography

The Holy Qur'ān

Dr Muhammad Tahir-ul-Qadri. *Interest-Free Banking in Islamic Perspective*. Lahore, Pakistan: Minhaj-ul-Quran Publications, 2017.

The Lawyer and Jurists, www.lawyersnjurists.com/article/overall-banking-system-of-al-arafah-islami-bank-ltd/

Glossary

***'adl*:** justice, equilibrium. The principle of economic justice is central to Islamic economic thought.

***'āqila*:** the foundation of *takaful,* or Islamic insurance. The relatives or the tribe of a criminal are obliged to pay blood money.

***awqiya*:** a unit of currency equal to five *dirhams*.

***bay' al-ḥasāt*:** determining the object of sale as the one on which a pebble thrown will fall, or selling goods with unspecified quality, size and design. It is prohibited due to its uncertainty, hazard, risk or chance.

***bay' al-'īna*:** also called *bay' al-muḥtaj,* this is a sale of the financially distressed. This contract involves the sale and the buy-back transaction of assets by a seller. A seller will sell the asset to a buyer on a cash basis. The seller will later buy back the same asset on a deferred-payment basis where the price is higher than the cash price. *Bay' al-'īna* can also be applied when a seller sells an asset to a buyer on a deferred basis. The seller will later buy back the same asset on a cash basis at a price which is lower than the deferred price. The net result is a loan with interest, hence its illegality.[1]

***bay' al-gharar*:** sale surrounded by ambiguity as a result of lack of information. A future contract, when the quantity is not determined, is an example. *Bay' al-gharar* is condemned by the Prophet (Allah bless him and give him peace).[2]

***bay' al-muḥāqala*:** A type of sale in which grains in ears are traded for dry grains. This may also refer to a business transaction in which a landlord leases a piece of land to an individual who pays rent in the form of its produce of grains. It is prohibited due to ignorance of the subject matter of sale.

***bay' al-mulāmasa*:** sale by touching the item beign sold without examining it closely. It is prohibited due to ignorance of the subject matter of sale.

***bay' al-munābadha*:** a business deal closed by throwing a garment from one party to another without making any inspection by either party. It is prohibited because of its resemblance to gambling.

***bay' al-sinīn*:** a sale in which the object is agricultural produce – for example, fruits, dates – which is sold for years in advance. A seller and a purchaser make a deal whereby the latter purchases from the former the produce of the land for years ahead. It is prohibited due to excessive uncertainty; in this deal a purchaser may get nothing.

***Bitcoin*:** a type of digital currency. Its use is illegal as it does not fall under the definition of *māl* (tangible things) in Islam.

***ḍabīḥa*:** the prescribed method of ritual slaughter of all lawful animals for food. It is a humane method of killing an animal.

***Dīn*:** a code of life that embraces all aspects of human life. Note that the word *madhab* (religion or creed) is used for a set of beliefs and rituals of worship. Islam is a *Dīn* – a far more comprehensive, all-encompassing concept than the English word "religion" carries.

***dinar*:** currency in the form of gold coins (prevalent in the past).

***dirham*:** currency in the form of silver coins (prevalent in the past).

***dīya*:** financial compensation for the shedding of blood that is paid to the heirs of a victim. In Islam, the compensation required for taking a life is 100 camels.

***al-fajr*:** the early morning prayer which is observed before sunrise.

***al-Falaq*:** literally, "explosion." This is the title of the second to the last chapter of the Qur'ān.

***al-gharar*:** deception as a result of withholding known information from the buyer. *Gharar* is deception either through ignorance of the goods, the price, or a faulty description of the goods, in which one or both parties stand to be deceived through ignorance of an essential element of exchange. *Gharar* is divided into three types: *gharar fāḥish* (excessive), which vitiates the transaction; *gharar yasīr* (minor), which is tolerated; and *gharar mutawassiṭ* (moderate), which falls between the other two categories. Any transaction can be classified as forbidden because of excessive *gharar*.[3]

***ḥabal al-ḥabāla*:** the sale of unborn animals. In the Time of Ignorance it was a normal practice to sell the fetus of a camel still in the womb of the she-camel. This is prohibited in the Muslim religion as it is the sale of an unidentified, non-existent and non-deliverable entity.

***ḥajj*:** The religious journey to Mecca that all able-bodied and affluent Muslims are required to make at least once in their lives. It is the fifth pillar of Islam. The occasion of *ḥajj* stimulates economic growth.

***halal*:** permissible and lawful in Muslim law. Generally, the term *halal* is applied to permissible food and drinks, in particular meat from an animal that has been killed according to Muslim law.

***Ḥanafī*:** a follower of Ḥanafī school of thought. The founder of the school was Abūḥanīfa al-Nu'mān b. al-Thabit (699–767). The Ḥanafī school has the largest number of followers in the Muslim world.

Ḥanbalī: a follower of the Ḥanbalī school of thought. The founder of the school, Aḥmad b. Ḥanbal (784–855), strictly adhered to the normative practice of the Messenger (Allah bless him and give him peace), thereby narrowing the margin of the consensus of opinion and analogical deduction and rejecting reasoning. Although he was a student of the moderate al-Shāfi'ī, Aḥmad b. Ḥanbal preferred an uncompromising approach to Islamic jurisprudence.

***ḥarām*:** anything prohibited by Muslim law.

***iḥsān*:** doing what is beautiful. This concept means to give more than is due and to receive less than is one's right.

ijāra: giving on rent, leasing, hiring out. In this type of contract, a lessor (owner) leases out an asset or equipment at an agreed rental fee and pre-determined lease period. The ownership of the leased equipment remains in the hands of a lessor. In Islamic finance, an *ijarā* contract does lead to purchase and usually refers to giving on rent such things as land, car, plant and office.

ijtihād: independent reasoning. It constitutes one of the four sources of Islamic religious law and is employed where the primary sources, the Qur'ān and Sunna, are silent.

istikhāra: a prayer for seeking goodness. Performing *istikhāra* is a desirable practice. This highly recommended supplication to Allah should be recited prior to important tasks such as travelling, buying and selling, choosing a marriage partner or launching an enterprise.

al-jallāla: an animal that feeds on filth and impurities. It consistently eats the droppings of other animals, impurities, carrion or swine. An animal turns into a *jallāla* when the consumption of impurities changes its protein, structure, odour, colour and even taste. Consuming meat and drinking milk from animals that often feed on impurities is prohibited.

jihad: striving, struggle. This is often mistranslated as "holy war" by western scholars. *Jihad* is divided into greater *jihad* and lesser *jihad*. The former refers to making a spiritual struggle within oneself to stop oneself sinning, breaking religious or moral laws; the latter signifies a holy war fought by Muslims in order to defend Islam. Greater *jihad* is regarded as more difficult and leading to greater rewards.

Ka'ba: the square stone building in the centre of the Great Mosque in Mecca, towards which Muslims face when they are at ritual prayer. The site is most holy to believers. In its south-eastern corner a sacred Black Stone is set.

kabā'ir: a major sin or offence against Islamic law or norms laid down by Islam. There are two types of sins: major sins (*kabā'ir*) and minor sins (*ṣaghā'ir*). If the Holy Qur'ān and the Prophetic Traditions prescribe a penalty for a crime, issue a severe warning of chastisement in the eternal world or invoke a curse on its perpetrator, then this defiance falls into the category of *kabā'ir*.

kharāj: land tax. This was introduced by the caliph Umar in order to replace the system of distributing conquered land among Muslim fighters. The tax was imposed on land, not individuals, with the tax base being the cultivable land and a proportional tax rate.[4]

khinzīr: pigs.

Mālikī: a follower of the Mālikī school of thought. The school was founded by Mālik b. Anas (715–795) in Medina. Known as the "Imam of the Medinites," Mālik paid a particular attention to the Sunna, the customs of Medina during the Messenger's time, and the consensus of opinions during the reign of the four rightly guided caliphs.

maysir: easy, left-handed. *Maysir* refers to gambling and any form of business activity where financial gains are acquired from mere chance, speculation or conjecture. It is proscribed.

mithqāl: a unit of weight equal to 4.5 grams.

***muṣḥaf*:** a collection of paper sheets. The word *muṣḥaf* also refers to a physical, written copy of the Holy Qur'ān.

***al-mukhābara*:** renting land in exchange for a portion of its produce.

***murābaḥa*:** trading with promise of a profit. This type of contract refers to a sale and purchase transaction for the financing of an asset whereby the cost and the profit margin are made known and agreed upon in advance by all parties involved. The settlement for the purchase can be either on a deferred lump sum basis or on an instalment basis, and is specified in the agreement. Islamic banks have adopted *murābaḥa* as a mode of financing.[5]

***al-mustarsal*:** a purchaser who is not aware of the price of an item in the market and is exploited by a seller on account of this lack of knowledge. Deceiving such a person is a form of usury.

***muzābana*:** selling an estimated amount of fresh dates on the tree for dried dates that are measured. This is prohibited on account of ignorance and uncertainty in the delivery of subject matter.

***niṣāb*:** the minimum amount that a Muslim must have to be obliged to pay *zakāt*. Believers who possess wealth, gold or silver below the *niṣāb* are exempted from paying the obligatory charity.

***qarḍ*:** literally, "cutting off." *Qarḍ* means allowing somebody to borrow something on condition that the same or its equal is returned afterwards. This is recommended in Islam.

***Qur'ān*:** the Recitation. Qur'ān is the holy book of Islam, written in the Arabic language, containing the word of Allah as revealed to Muhammad, Allah's Prophet (Allah bless him and give him peace).

***raf' al-ḥaraj*:** relieving hardship. The Sharia injunctions are based on the principle of easing and removing hardship from people: for example, the faithful are allowed to combine two prayers in certain conditions.

Ramaḍān: the ninth month of the Islamic year, when Muslims do not eat or drink between sunrise and sunset.

***ribā*:** an increase, expansion, growth, addition in a particular item. This refers to an addition to the principal amount that is paid by the borrower to the lender, which is stipulated in a loan transaction.

***ribā al-buyū'*:** a sale transaction in which a commodity is exchanged for an unequal amount of the same commodity and supply is postponed.

***ribā al-duyūn*:** debt usury. *Ribā al-duyūn* is interest earned on lending money to another party.

***ribā al-faḍl*:** the selling of one commodity for another of the same kind on the spot in excess which is taken in exchange of specific homogenous commodities and encountered in their hand-to-hand purchase and sale.

***ribā al-nasī'a*:** the time that is allowed to the borrower to pay off a loan in return for the "addition" or the "premium." Hence it is equal to the interest charged on loans. (The word *nasī'a* means to "delay," "postpone" or "defer.")

***rukū'*:** a component of ritual prayer. It refers to bowing down, while placing hands on knees, before prostrating oneself.

***ruwaybiḍa*:** a lowly, contemptible person who speaks out about public affairs.

ṣā': a measurement of volume equal to 3 litres.

ṣaghā'ir: a minor sin. There is no prescribed punishment in this world, and no warning of Hellfire, Divine wrath or curse, for a minor sin. If believers stay away from major sins, they will be forgiven their minor sins. Persisting in a minor sin, however, may make it a cardinal sin.

Shāfi'ī: a follower of Shāfi'ī school of thought. A scion of the Qurashī line, Muhammad b. Idrīs al-Shāfi'ī (d. 204 AH), was the founder of the Shāfi'ī school of jurisprudence. Al-Shāfi'ī was a disciple of Mālik. The Shāfi'ī school flourishes in Egypt, Syria, Yemen, East Africa and the Malay Archipelago.

Sharia: the system of religious laws based on the Holy Qur'ān and the narrative practice of the Messenger (Allah bless him and give him peace) that Muslims follow.

Shawwāl: the tenth month of the lunar Islamic calendar.

shukr: gratitude, thankfulness, or acknowledgment. It is a highly esteemed virtue in the Muslim religion.

siḥr: magic. *Siḥr* refers to every effect with a cause is mysterious, subtle or supernatural.

sujūd: prostration to Allah in the direction of the Ka'ba. Prostrating oneself in ritual prayer is one of the integrals of prayer.

ṣukūk: certificates. The term *ṣukūk* signifies Islamic bonds. They are similar to asset-backed bonds. *Ṣukūk* serve as an alternative to conventional bonds which are not considered unlawful by most practising Muslims.

tadlīs: deception, cheating. *Tadlīs* refers to hiding a fault in the contract's object such as an asset, commodity, or property so as to deceive a buyer.

taqwā: being conscious and cognizant of Allah. This is generally translated as "piety" or "fear of Allah."

takaful: Islamic insurance.

Uḥud: a mountain north of Medina, Saudi Arabia. It was the site of the second battle between the Muslims of Medina and the Meccan forces.

'ushr: one-tenth of the produce of irrigated land.

wuḍū': ablutions. A ritual purification, it signifies the Islamic procedure for washing parts of the body before observing ritual prayer.

zakāt: an obligatory charity prescribed in the Holy Qur'ān. The Qur'ān determined the recipients of *zakāt*.

zakāt al-fiṭr: an amount of food or money which is given in charity at the end of Ramaḍān before the 'Īd prayers.

zakāt al-māl: an obligatory charity which is paid on the savings which reach the prescribed threshold.

Notes

1 Ahmed El Ashker, and Rodney Wilson, *Islamic Economics: A Short History*, pp. 409–410.
2 Ibid., 409.
3 Ibid., 411.
4 Ibid., 413.
5 Ibid., 414.

Bibliography

The Holy Qur'ān

'Abd al-Razzāq, Abū Bakr b. Hammām b. Nāfi' al-Ṣan'ānī (126–211/744–826). *Al-Muṣannaf.* Beirut, Lebanon: al-Maktab al-Islāmī, 1403AH.

'Abd b. Ḥumayd, Abū Muhammad b. Naṣr al-Kasī (d. 249/863). *Al-Musnad.* Cairo, Egypt: Maktaba al-Sunna, 1408/1988.

Abū al-Mahāsin, Yūsuf b. Mūsā al-Ḥanafī. *al-Mu'taṣar min al-Mukhtasarmin Mashkal al-āthār.* Beirut, Lebanon: 'Ālim al-Kutub, 1418/1998.

Abū Dāwūd, Sulaymān b. Ash'ath b. Isḥāq b. Bashīr al-Sijistānī (202–275/817–889). *Al-Sunan.* Beirut, Lebanon: Dār al-Fikr, 1414/1994.

Abū Nu'aym, Aḥmad b. 'Abd Allāh b. Aḥmad b. Isḥāq b. Mūsā b. Mihrān al-Aṣbahānī (336–430/948–1038). *al-Musnad al-Mustakhraj 'alāṢaḥīḥ al-Imām Muslim.* Beirut, Lebanon: Dār al-Kutub al-'Ilmiyya, 1996.

———. *ḥilya al-Awliyā' wa Ṭabaqāt al-Aṣfiyā'.* Beirut, Lebanon: Dār al-Kitāb al-'Arabī, 1400/1980.

Abū Ya'lā, Aḥmad b. 'Alī b. Mathnā b. Yaḥyā b. 'Īsā b. al-Hilāl al-Mūṣilī al-Tamīmī (210–307/825–919). *Al-Musnad.* Damascus, Syria: Dār al-Ma'mūn li al-Turāth, 1404/1984.

'Ajlūnī, Ismā'īl b. 'Umar al-. *Kashf al-khafā' wa muzīl al-ilbās 'amma ashtahara min al-aḥādīth 'alā alsinat al-nās.* Beirut, Lebanon: Mu'assasa al-Risāla, 1985.

'Asqalānī, Ibn Ḥajar Aḥmad b. 'Alī al-. *Al-Dirāya fī takhrīj aḥādīth al-Hidāya.* Beirut, Lebanon: Dār al-Ma'rifa, n.d.

———. *Al-Iṣāba fī tamyīz al-Ṣaḥāba.* Beirut, Lebanon: Dār al-Jīl, 1412AH.

———. *Fatḥ al-Bārī sharḥ Ṣaḥīḥ al-Bukhārī.* Beirut, Lebanon: Dār al-Ma'rifa, 1379AH.

'Aynī, Badr al-Dīn al-. *'Umdat al-qārī sharḥ Ṣaḥīḥ al-Bukhārī.* Beirut, Lebanon: Dār Iḥyā' al-Turāth al-'Arabī, n.d.

'Aẓīm Ābādī, Abū al-Ṭayyab Muhammad Shams al-Ḥaqq al-. *'Awn al-Ma'būd Sharḥ Sunan Abī Dāwūd.* Beirut, Lebanon: Dār al-Kutub al-'Ilmiyya, 1415AH.

Baghdādī, Khaṭīb al-. *Tārīkh Baghdād.* Beirut, Lebanon: Dar al-Kotob al-Ilmiyah, n.d.

Bayhaqī, Aḥmad b. al-Ḥusayn al-. *Al-Sunan al-kubrā.* Mecca, Saudi Arabia: Maktaba Dār al-Bāz, 1994.

———. *al-Sunan al-Ṣughrā.* Medina, Saudi Arabia: Maktabaal-Dār, 1410/1989.

———. *Shu'ab al-Īmān.* Beirut, Lebanon: Dar al-Kotob al-Ilmiyah, 1990.

Bazzār, Aḥmad b. 'Amr al-. *Al-Musnad (al-Baḥr al-zakhār).* Beirut, Lebanon: Mu'assasa 'Ulūm al-Qur'ān, 1409AH.

Bukhārī, Abū 'Abd Allāh Muhammad b. Ismā'īl b. Ibrahīm b. Mughīra al-. (194–256/810–870). *Al-Adab al-Mufrad.* Beirut, Lebanon: Dār al-Bashā'ir al-Islāmiyya, 1409/1989.

———. *Al-Ṣaḥīḥ*. Beirut, Lebanon, Damascus, Syria: Dār al-Qalam, 1401/1981.

Dāraquṭnī, 'Alī b. 'Umar al-. *Al-Sunan*. Beirut, Lebanon: Dār al-Ma'rifa, 1966.

Dārimī, 'Abd Allāh al-. *Al-Sunan*. Beirut, Lebanon: Dār al-Kitāb al-'Arabī, 1407.

Daylamī, Abū Shujā' Shīrawayh al-. *Al-Firdaws bi ma'thūr al-khiṭāb*. Mecca, Saudi Arabia: Dar al-Kotob al-Ilmiyah, 1986.

Dhahabī, Shams al-Dīn Muhammad b. Aḥmad al-. *Al-Kabā'ir*. Beirut, Lebanon: Dār al-Nadwa al-Jadīda, n.d.

Ghazālī, Abūḥāmid Muhammad b. Muhammad al-Ghazālī al- (450–505AH). *Iḥyā' al-'Ulūm*. Beirut, Lebanon: Dār al-Ma'rifa, 2001.

Ḥakīm al-Tirmidhī, Abū 'Abd Allāh Muhammad b. 'Alī b al-Ḥasan b. Bashir al-. *Nawādir al-UṣūlfīAḥadīth al-Rasūl*. Beirut, Lebanon: Dār al-Jīl, 1992.

Ḥākim, Muhammad b. 'Abd Allāh al-. *Al-Mustadrak 'alā al-ṣaḥīḥayn*. Beirut, Lebanon: Dar al-Kotob al-Ilmiyah, 1990.

Ḥalabī, 'Alī b. Burhān al-Dīn al- (d. 1404AH). *Al-Sīra al-ḥalabiyya*. Beirut, Lebanon: Dār al-Ma'rifa, 1400AH.

Ḥanbal, Aḥmad b. *Al-Musnad*. Beirut, Lebanon: Dar al-Kotob al-Ilmiyah, 1986.

Haythamī, Nūr al-Dīn Abū al-Ḥasan'Alī al-. *Majma' al-zawā'id wa manba' al-fawā'id*. Cairo: Dār al-Rayān li al-Turāth, 1987.

Hindī, ḥusām al-Dīn 'Alā' al-Dīn 'Alī al-Muttaqī al-. *Kanz al-'ummāl*. Beirut, Lebanon: Mu'assasa al-Risāla, 1979.

Ḥusaynī, Ibrahīm b. Muhammad al- (1054–1120AH). *Al-Bayān wa al-Ta'rīf*. Beirut, Lebanon: Dār al-Kitāb al-'Arabī 1401AH.

Ibn 'Abd al-Barr, Yūsuf b. 'Abd Allāh (368–463/979–1071). *Al-Tamhīd li mā fī al-muwaṭṭa min al-ma'ānī wa al-asānīd*. Marrakech: Ministry of Religious Affairs, 1387AH.

Ibn Abī al-Dunyā, Abū Bakr'Abd Allāh b. Muhammad b. al-Qurashī (208–281AH). *al-Ahwāl*. Egypt: Maktaba āl Yāsir, 1413AH.

Ibn Abī'āṣim, 'Amr. *Al-Sunna*. Beirut, Lebanon: Al-Maktab al-Islāmī, 1400AH.

Ibn Abī Shayba, 'Abd Allāh b. Muhammad. *Al-Muṣannaf*. Riyadh: Maktaba al-Rushd, 1409AH.

Ibn al-Ja'd, Abū al-Ḥasan'Alī b. Ja'd b. 'Ubayd Hāshimī (133–230/750–845). *Al-Musnad*. Beirut, Lebanon: Mu'assisa Nādir, 1410/1990.

Ibn al-Jārūd, Abū Muhammad 'Abd Allāh b. 'Alī (d. 307/919). *Al-Muntaqā min al-Sunan al-Musnadā*. Beirut, Lebanon: Mu'assisa al-Kitāb al-Thaqāfiyya, 1418/1988.

Ibn al-Mubārak, Abū 'Abd al-Raḥmān 'Abd Allāh b. Wāḍiḥ al-Marwazī (118–181/736–798). *Kitābal-Zuhd*. Beirut, Lebanon: Dār al-Kutub al-'Ilmiyya, 1411/1991.

Ibn al-Qaysarānī, Abū al-Faḍl Muhammad b. Ṭāhir b. 'Alī b. Aḥmad al-Maqdasī (448–507/1056–1113). *Tadhkira al-ḥuffāẓ*. Riyadh, Saudi Arabia: Dār al-Sami'ī, 1415AH.

Ibn al-Sunnī, Aḥmad b. Muhammad al-Daynūrī (284–364AH). *'Amal al-Yawm wa al-Layla*. Beirut, Lebanon: Dār Ibn ḥazm, 1425/2004.

Ibn Dirham, Abū Sa'īd Aḥmad b. Muhammad b. Ziyād b. Bishr b. Dirham. *Al-Zuhd wa Ṣifat al-Zāhidīn*. Ṭanṭā: Dār al-Ṣaḥāba li-Tutrāth, 1408AH.

Ibn ḥazm, 'Alī Aḥmad b. Sa'īd. *Al-Muḥallā*. Beirut, Lebanon: Dār al-āfāq al-Jadīda, n.d.

Ibn ḥibbān, Abūḥātim Muhammad. *Al-Ṣaḥīḥ*. Beirut, Lebanon: Mu'assasa al-Risāla, 1993.

Ibn Kathīr, Abū al-Fidā' Ismā'īl b. 'Umar. *Tafsīr al-Qur'ān al-'Aẓīm*. Beirut, Lebanon: Dar al-Fikr, 1401AH.

Ibn Khuzayma, Muhammad b. Isḥāq. *Al-Ṣaḥīḥ*. Beirut, Lebanon: al-Maktab al-Islāmī, 1970.

Ibn Mājah, Abū 'Abd Allāh Muhammad b. Yazīd al-Qazwīnī (209–273/824 887). *Al-Sunan*. Beirut, Lebanon: Dār al-Kutub al-'Ilmiyya, 1419/1998.

Ibn Qudāma al-Maqdisī. *Al-Mughnī fī fiqh al-Imām Aḥmad b. Ḥanbal al-Shaybānī*. Beirut, Lebanon: Dar al-Fikr, 1405ah.

Ibn Rajab al-Ḥanbalī, Abū al-Faraj 'Abd al-Raḥmān b. Aḥmad (736–795AH). *Jāmi' al-'Ulūm wa al-ḥikamfī Sharḥ Khamsīn ḥadīth min Jawāmi' al-Kalim*. Beirut, Lebanon: Dār al-Ma'rifa, 1408AH.

Ibn Rushd, Muhammad b. Aḥmad. *Bidāyat al-mujtahid*. Beirut, Lebanon: Dar al-Fikr, n.d.

Jurjānī, 'Alī b. Muhammad b. 'Alī Sayyid Sharīf al- (740–816 AH). *Al-Ta'rifāt*. Beirut, Lebanon: 'ālim al-Kutub, 1416/1996.

Kāsānī, 'Alā' al-Dīn al-. *Badā'i' al-sanā'i'*. Beirut, Lebanon: Dār al-Kitāb al-'Arabī, 1982.

Khaṭīb al-Tabrīzī, Walī al-Dīn Abū 'Abd Allāh Muhammad b. 'Abd Allāh al-(d. 741AH). *Mishkāt al-Maṣābīḥ*. Beirut, Lebanon: Dār al-Kutub al-'Ilmiyya, 1424/2003.

Kinānī, Aḥmad b. Abī Bakr b. Ismā'īl al- (762–840AH). *Miṣbāḥ al-Zujāja fī Zawa'īd b.* Mājah. Beirut, Lebanon: Dār al-'Arabiyya, 1403AH.

Kittānī, Muhammad 'Abd al-Ḥayy b. 'Abd al-Kabīr b. Muhammad al-Ḥasanī al-Idrīsī al- (1305–1382/1888–1962). *Al-Tartīb al-idāriyya*. Beirut, Lebanon: Dar al-Kotob al-Ilmiyah, 1422/2001.

Mālik, Ibn Anas b. Mālik b. Abī'āmir b. 'Amr b. Ḥārith al-Aṣbaḥī (93–179/712–795). *Al-Muwaṭṭā'*. Beirut, Lebanon: Dār Iḥyā' al-Turāth al-'Arabī, 1990.

Munāwī, 'Abd al-Ra'ūf b. Tāj al-Dīn al-. *al-Taysīr bi-sharḥ al-Jāmi' al-ṣaghīr*. Saudi Arabia, Riyadh: Maktaba al-Imām al-Shāfi'ī, 1408/1988AD.

———. *Fayḍ al-Qadīr sharḥ al-Jāmi' al-ṣaghīr*. Egypt: Maktaba Tijāriyya al-Kubrā, 1356AH.

Mundhirī, 'Abd al-'Aẓīm al-. *Al-Targhīb wa al-tarhīb*. Beirut, Lebanon: Dar al-Kotob al-Ilmiyah, 1417AH.

Muslim, Ibn al-*Ḥajj*āj Abū al-Ḥasan al-Qushayrī al-Naysābūrī (206–261/821–875). *Al-Ṣaḥīḥ*. Beirut, Lebanon: Dār al-Iḥyā' al-Turāth al-'Arabī, 1997.

Nasā'ī, Aḥmad b. Shu'ayb Abū 'Abd al-Raḥmān al- (215–303/830–915). *al-Sunan*. Beirut, Lebanon: Dār al-Kutub al-'Ilmiyya, 1416/1995.

———. *al-Sunan al-Kubrā*. Beirut, Lebanon: Dār al-Kutub al-'Ilmiyya, 1411/1991.

———. *'Amal al-Yawm wa al-Layla*. Beirut, Lebanon: Mu'assisa al-Risāla, 1407/1987.

Nawawī, Abū Zakariyyā Yaḥyā b. Sharaf b. Murrī b. al-Ḥasan b. al-Ḥusayn b. Muhammad b. Jumu'a b. Ḥizām al- (631–677/1233–1278). *Riyāḍ al-Ṣāliḥīn min Kalām Sayyid al-Mursalīn*. Beirut, Lebanon: Dār al-Khayr, 1412/1991.

———. *SharḥṢaḥīḥ Muslim*. Karachi, Pakistan: Qādīmī Kutub Khānah, 1375/1956.

Qazwīnī, 'Abd al-Karīm b. Muhammad Rāfi'ī al-. *Al-Tadwīn fī Akhbār Qazwīn*. Beirut, Lebanon: Dār al-Kutub al-'Ilmiyya, 1987.

Qudā'ī, Abū 'Abd Allāh Muhammad b. Salama b. Ja'far b. 'Alī al- (d. 454/1062). *Musnad al-Shihāb*. Beirut, Lebanon: Mu'assisa al-Risāla, 1407AH.

Qurṭubī, Abū 'Abd Allāh Muhammad b. Aḥmad al-. *Al-Jāmi' li aḥkām al-Qur'ān*. Cairo: Dār al-Sha'b, 1372AH.

Rāzī, Fakhr al-Dīn Muhammad b. 'Umar al-. *Al-Tafsīr al-kabīr*. Beirut, Lebanon: Dar al-Kotob al-Ilmiyah, 1421AH.

Sa'īd b. Manṣūr, Abū'Uthmān al-Khurāsānī (d. 227 AH). *Al-Sunan*. Riyadh, Saudi Arabia: Dār al-Aṣma'ī, 1414AH.

Sarakhsī, Shams al-Dīn al-. *Al-Mabsūṭ*. Beirut, Lebanon: Dār al-Ma'rifa, 1978.

Shāh Walī Allāh. *Ḥujjat Allāh al-Bāligha*. Beirut, Lebanon: Dār al-Jīl, 1426AH/2005AD.

Sha'rānī al-. *Kashf al-gumma 'an jamī' al-umma*. Egypt: Dār al-'Ilm, 2002.

Shawkānī, Muhammad b. 'Alī al-. *Nayl al-awṭār sharḥ Muntaqā al-akhbār*. Beirut, Lebanon: Dār al-Jīl, 1973.

Shaybānī, Abū Bakr Aнmad b. 'Amr b. al-ḍaḥḥāk b. Makhlad al- (206–287/822–900). *Al-āḥād wa al-Mathānī*. Riyadh, Saudi Arabia: Dār al-Rāya, 1411/1991.
Suyūṭī, Jalāl al-Dīn Abū al-Faḍl 'Abd al-Raнmān b. Abī Bakr b. Muhammad b. Abī Bakr b. 'Uthmān al- (849–911/1445–1505). *Al-Durr al-Manthūrfi al-Tafsīr bi al-Ma'thūr*. Beirut, Lebanon: Dār al-Ma'rifa, 1993.
———. *Tanwīr al-ḥawālik Sharḥ Muwaṭṭa' Mālik*. Egypt: Maktaba al-Tajjāriyya al-Kubrā, 1389/1969.
Ṭabarānī, Sulaymān b. Aḥmad al-. *Al-Mu'jam al-awsaṭ*. Cairo: Dār al-Ḥaramayn, 1415AH.
———. *Al-Mu'jam al-kabīr*. Mosul: Maktaba al-'Ulūm wa al-ḥikam, 1983.
———. *Al-Mu'jam al-ṣaghīr*. Beirut, Lebanon: al-Maktab al-Islāmī, 1985.
———. *Musnad al-Shāmiyyīn*. Beirut, Lebanon: Mu'assasa al-Risāla, 1985.
Ṭabarī, Abū Ja'far Muhammad b. Jarīr al-. *Ṭārīkh al-umam wa al-mulūk*. Beirut, Lebanon: Dar al-Kotob al-Ilmiyah, 1407AH.
Tirmidhī, Abū 'Īsā Muhammad b. 'Īsā al-. *Al-Sunan*. Beirut, Lebanon: Dār Iḥyā' al-Turāth al-'Arabī, n.d.
Wahbah al-Zuhaylī. *Al-Fiqh al-Islāmī wa Adillatu-hū*. Beirut, Lebanon: Dār al-Qlm, 2002.
Zayla'ī, Abū Muhammad 'Abd Allāh b. Yūsuf al-Ḥanafī al- (d. 762/1360). *Naṣb al-Rāya li-Aḥadīth al-Hidāya*. Egypt: Dār al-Ḥadīth, 1357/1938.

English books

Ahmed, A.F. El-Ashker, and Rodney Wilson. *Islamic Economics: A Short History*. Leiden, Boston: Brill, 2006.
Ayub, Muhammad *Understanding Islamic Finance*. Chichester, Great Britain: John Wiley & Sons, Ltd, 2007.
Guillaume, Andrea M. *The Life of Muhammad* (a translation of Ibn Isḥāq's *Sīrat Rasūl Allāh*). Oxford: Oxford University Press, 1965.
Kettell, Brian. *Introduction to Islamic Banking and Finance*. Chichester, Great Britain: John Wiley & Sons, Ltd, 2011.
Tahir-ul-Qadri, Muhammad. *Interest-Free Banking in Islamic Perspective*. Lahore, Pakistan: Minhaj-ul-Quran Publications, 2017.

Websites

Basic Principles of Halal and Haram, https://mjchalaaltrust.co.za/halal-standards-basic-principles/
Compilation Guide on Prudential and Structural Islamic Finance Indicators, www.ifsb.org/PSIFI_08/download/compilation_guide%202007.pdf
Islamic Question & Answer, https://islamqa.info/en/21980
Islamic Question & Answer, https://islamqa.info/en/87688
Sheikh-Dr. Nabil, Islamic Heritage Center, www.ihcproject.com/sheikhdr-nabil/
The Lawful and Prohibited in Islam, www.islamicstudies.info/literature/halal-ḥarām.htm
The Lawyer and Jurists, www.lawyersnjurists.com/article/overall-banking-system-of-al-arafah-islami-bank-ltd/
What is Halal: A Guide for Non-Muslims, www.icv.org.au/about/about-islam-overview/what-is-halal-a-guide-for-non-muslims/

Index

Printed in Great Britain
by Amazon

39336074R00156